Harry W. Richardson
Chang-Hee C. Bae
Editors

Globalization and Urban Development

With 31 Figures
and 75 Tables

Springer

Professor Harry W. Richardson
The James Irvine Chair of Urban and Regional Planning
and Professor of Economics
University of Southern California
LOS Angeles
CA 90089-0626
USA
E-mail: hrichard@usc.edu

Dr. Chang-Hee Christine Bae
Associate Professor
Department of Urban Design and Planning
University of Washington
Box 355740
Seattle, WA 98195
USA
E-mail: cbae@u.washington.edu

Library of Congress Control Number: 2005928540

ISBN-10 3-540-22362-2 Springer Berlin Heidelberg New York
ISBN-13 978-3-540-22362-7 Springer Berlin Heidelberg New York

Springer is a part of Springer Science+Business Media
springeronline.com

Printed in Germany

Cover design: Erich Kirchner
Production: Helmut Petri
Printing: Strauss Offsetdruck

SPIN 11019114 Printed on acid-free paper – 88/3153 – 5 4 3 2 1 0

To the Memory of Gill-Chin Lim

As this book was in its final stages of production, Gill died tragically in an auto accident on the Michigan State University campus in East Lansing. Some of the contributors to the book were old friends, some were new, but we all wish to join in its dedication to his memory. Of course, we are only a handful of the hundreds, perhaps thousands, who were shocked and grieved by his premature passing. The scale of the outpouring of condolences, sympathies and remembrances by his friends, colleagues and students was truly amazing until we remember that Gill was not only a first-class scholar but a wonderful human being. He had an infinite pool of close friends and admirers and not a single enemy.

Born in Korea, Gill received B.S. and M.S. degrees in Architectural Engineering at Seoul National University before coming to the United States to take his Master's in Planning at Harvard and his Ph.D. in Planning at Princeton. He started his teaching career at Princeton, later moving to Northwestern, then to Illinois, before on to Michigan State University where he established a new program in international planning. Along the way, he founded an international program in Public Policy and Management at the Korea Development Institute (Korea's premier think tank) where he served as the Dean for some years and continued to be a Distinguished Professor there at the time of his death. He published (at our last count) 32 books, 45 refereed journal articles and 79 book chapters.

Gill was a global citizen, but close enough to his cultural roots to wear Hanbok (Korean national costume) at social functions. He gave his time as generously to his students as to famous academics; the fable is that he knew each student in classes of 200 by name, but in Gill's case it was probably true. He was a published poet, artist and an activist for world peace. No one played a larger role in promoting global planning in the profession (he was a leading figure in the Global Planning Educators Interest Group), and he was generous with his own resources in financing student travel grants and prizes, not to mention raising the tradition of Asian gift giving to a new level. Gill, we miss you, but we are proud that one of your last publications will be in our book.

Harry W. Richardson
Chang-Hee Christine Bae

Preface

The papers in this book were first presented at a conference at the Villa Serbelloni in Bellagio, Italy, better known as the Rockefeller Foundation Bellagio Center, in August 2002. The conference was a wonderful experience from both a professional and a hedonistic perspective. It was supported by travel funds and payments in-kind (food and accommodation) from the Rockefeller Foundation, and the editors are very grateful for this support which made the conference, a special issue of the *Annals of Regional Science*, and this book possible. The idea was to focus on the specific urban impacts of globalization and to give substantial but not 100% attention to the major regions in the developing world; scholars from 12 countries participated in the book. This is not the first research project on this very important topic, and it will not be the last. We hope that it contributes to this interesting debate.

Harry W. Richardson
Chang-Hee Christine Bae

Contents

Introduction

Harry W. Richardson[1], **Chang-Hee Christine Bae**[2]

[1] School of Policy, Planning and Development, University of Southern California, Los Angeles, CA 90089-0626, USA (e-mail: hrichard@usc.edu)
[2] Department of Urban Design and Planning, University of Washington, Seattle, WA 98195, USA (e-mail: cbae@u.washington.edu)

Globalization continues to be a major issue for academic and professional analysis by social scientists, planners and others. However, one aspect of globalization that has received somewhat less attention is how it has affected urbanization. The purpose of this book is to examine the urban impacts of globalization in a selection of cities and urban systems in different parts of the world, primarily but not solely in developing countries.[1] It brings together scholars from 12 countries, so obviously the scope is more representative than encyclopedic.

The book is divided into four sections. Two chapters deal with the general context of globalization. The next part of the book consists of five chapters about how globalization affects cities and regional systems in five countries: India, South Korea, the Philippines, Indonesia and South Africa. The third and longest part of the book focuses on individual cities scattered throughout the world: Rio-Sao Paulo, Mexico City, Bogota, Tijuana-San Diego, Los Angeles, St. Petersburg, Tokyo, Shanghai, and Karachi. The examples illustrate that cities are impacted by globalization at all levels of development. The final section of the book identifies three specific issues, although they also focus on individual cities: Chicago and Seoul on information technology, New York and Tokyo on the environmental transition, and Bangkok on how globalization may or may not influence urban form.

The book provides detail about 14 cities and 15 countries. Yet it would need at least 30 chapters to present the so-called "megacities" individually. Also, some important regions are omitted: Europe apart from St. Petersburg, Sub-Saharan Africa except for the special case of South Africa, and the Middle East. These regions have been covered elsewhere in the literature and will surely be analyzed again and again. So, the point is not to be comprehensive because it is impossible but rather to make enough of a contribution to advance the state of knowledge.

---

[1] The Editors are grateful to the Rockefeller Foundation for help with travel funds for chapter authors from developing countries and with in-kind support for a meeting at the Bellagio Center in Bellagio, Italy.

The chapters share many elements in common. They are all, with one or two partial exceptions, highly empirical. This contrasts with much of the research on globalization that tends to be theoretical, conceptual and very normative. The main feature of the book is its focus on the *urban* impacts of globalization rather than on a more general analysis (the first half of Lim's chapter deals with the latter, and there is no reason to expand on this in the Introduction). The contribution of Lim's chapter is its attempt to develop a conceptual framework that integrates the spatial and non-spatial aspects of globalization. The major idea is that globalization trends lead to resource allocation consequences and that these in turn result in urban impacts. He suggests that the framework lends itself to either positive or normative analysis, and hence is easily adaptable to public policy prescriptions.

The book looks at urban areas in both developed and developing countries, and focuses on several overriding themes. First, the alternative concepts of globalization are outlined and evaluated in several of the chapters with the aim of arriving at a workable definition relevant for urban impact analysis.

Second, several of the chapters deal with some of the more macro issues e.g. debt crises, foreign direct investment (FDI), international interventions, trade liberalization, the geographical redistribution of manufacturing,[2] the "New Economy", and income distribution effects. However, these topics are not explored from the perspective of economy-wide consequences but only in terms of their urban impacts.

Third, four of these chapters are comparative, analyzing city pairs (Sohn, Kim and Hewings; Bae; and Tolosa) or multiple cities (Cai and Zit). Urban comparative analysis is often problematic, even when the cities are in close proximity. For example, although Tolosa treats Rio de Janeiro-Sao Paulo as an Extended Metropolitan Region, their economic structures and pace of development are very different. Similarly, Bae shows that the concept of a cross-border metropolis when applied to San Diego-Tijuana is debatable because of differences in economic specialization and socioeconomic status; at best, the two metropolises are complementary rather than unitary, and they have reacted to globalization in different ways.

Fourth, this introduction offers, on the basis of the results of these chapters, a rough cost-benefit assessment of globalization's urban impacts. The experiences offer little satisfaction to the anti-globalization forces, despite some periodic negative impacts on poverty, potentially unfavorable effects on the city size distribution, and neglected regions such as most of Sub-Saharan Africa. All dynamic economic change results in winners and losers (a point emphasized most in Chakravorty's chapter), and globalization is no exception. Similarly, Gilbert quotes the World Bank's statement (2002: 40) that "there will be room for some new entrants to the market for global manufactures and services, and some well-located cities in countries that reform their policies, institutions, and infrastructure will surely develop successful clusters. Equally, it seems plausible that if all countries reformed, there would be more well-located sites than new clusters, so some would have missed the boat." The apparently irreversible trend towards globalization has created

---

[2] Despite the long history of international involvement, globalization has intensified in the past two decades (the so-called "third wave"), as measured for example by the rise in developing country manufacturing exports share from 25 to 80%.

many opportunities, especially in the developing world (of which the most striking beneficiary has been China).

Globalization issues are now receiving considerable attention in both the academic and public policy realms. This book addresses some aspects of these issues that have been somewhat researched, but are so severely under-researched that many important questions remain. The most relevant precursors to this research are probably the edited books by Lo and Yeung (1998) and Lo and Marcutillio (2001). The Lo and Yeung book is very useful but it has three major limitations: the concept of globalization remains ill-defined; there are only four city-specific case studies; and the research predates the post-1997 financial crisis. This last problem is the most serious because East Asia and South-East Asia had been held up as exemplars of the unbridled success of globalization as a process for raising national living standards. The Lo and Marcutillio book is complementary to this volume; it contains several case studies, some of which overlap with the cities covered here. Its main limitations are its restriction to Asian countries and its more limited focus on topics related to environmental sustainability.

Another strand of research that has attracted many researchers emphasizes a more conceptual, even a theoretical, approach (pioneering examples include Friedmann 1986; Castells 1989; King 1990; Sassen 1991, 1998; and Taylor 1999). This perspective has mushroomed in recent years, and there is now several listserves where globalization theorists exchange ideas and organize sessions at planning, geography and related academic conferences. This research field has raised some interesting questions, but this book focuses much more on detailed empirical analysis rather than on the "stylized facts" often used to buttress the more theoretical propositions.

With respect to the urban hierarchy chapters, Mathur discusses how globalization and the related India's liberalization after 1991 impacted the national urban system. This was primarily the result of a growth in FDI (although small by Asian standards, only 8 percent of the level of China and only a quarter of that in South Korea, a country with less than 5% of India's population). Its manifestations are well known: peripheral growth in both office space and housing; selective migration to cities transforming their economies in favor of IT sectors; private sector participation in infrastructure provision; and permitting cities to access capital markets. The impacts were geographically concentrated in six large cities (Mumbai, Delhi, Chennai, Bangalore, Hyderabad, and Ahmedabad). The macroeconomic effects of globalization have been dominant; local structural change has been negatively impacted by State policies (e.g., with respect to land and water uses) that have not kept up with the pace of market reform. High rates of economic growth have not, in general, resulted in accelerated urban growth or more urban jobs; sectoral growth has been very selective; there have been some real estate impacts (e.g., new shopping plazas and residential-commercial conversions, typically suburban); and efforts to improve city institutions and management.

Korea was impacted by early trends in globalization only because of its export-oriented industrialization. More recently, trade liberalization, market opening and foreign direct investment have had impacts on the domestic economy, although the shift towards high-order services has been slow, and the urban manufacturing base is slowly being hollowed-out. The urban hierarchy consequences, especially the strengthening of the larger cities including the Seoul metropolitan area, have been dramatic. Incheon is positioning itself to take advantage of globalization in general, and what is happening in China and Japan in particular, with the goal of establishing itself as a dominant Northeast Asian hub in transportation and communications. The attention given to attracting global events in sport and culture reflects the aim for world city status. There is also a major conflict between the long-held desire to achieve balanced regional development and accepting the implicit spatial implications of globalization.

Given the vast size of Indonesia with its scattered islands, there are probably few countries in the world where the issue of decentralization is more important. As suggested by Chakravorty, decentralization is one of the main themes of ideological globalization. Silver describes the implementation of decentralization from 1999, but the reform pressures from international donors since the 1970s antedate the current globalization movement. In principle (an assessment of practice needs more time), the reforms follow the globalized desiderata: an expansion of the role for local governments, new funding mechanisms with discretionary authority, local legislative assemblies, and increases in power for the district head and city mayors. The effects have differed from place to place, depending on whether the localities had the natural resources to generate new revenues, and the impact of globalization on natural resource exports has probably widened rather than narrowed regional disparities. International agencies and bilateral donors have played a significant role by making loans and grants to build up human resource and institutional capacities at the local level. The central government's influence on major capital projects has been reduced, but intergovernmental transfers will continue to be important as an instrument for reducing interregional disparities.

Pernia and Quising analyze how the economic openness associated with globalization has affected regional development in the Philippines. Although Metro Manila continues to dominate among the 14 regions, there has been some acceleration of development in a few regions, namely Southern Tagalog and Central Luzon (both adjacent to Metro Manila), the Cordillera Autonomous Region (CAR), and Central Visayas. Using five-year panel data, they find that exports and FDI promote both regional growth and poverty reduction, but with little impact in promoting regionally balanced development. They suggest that a major reason is that globalization trends tend to follow domestic patterns as determined by market forces and public policies (to locations favored by good infrastructure, human resource capacities, agglomeration economies, and supportive policies, including the Export Processing Zones). The policy implication is to promote (with private sector participation) both physical and social infrastructure at target locations.

A further difference between the earlier research and ours is that much of the earlier work focused on the "global city," especially New York, London, Tokyo and Paris. These cities have widespread impacts on other cities and other countries via their role as multinational corporate headquarters and financial centers, and play a determining role in the form that globalization takes. The chapters in this book look at the problem from a different perspective. How do the forces of globalization impact the urban-spatial systems and individual cities of particular countries? In a sense, we are studying the issues as a reactive rather than a proactive process. This explains the attention paid to cities not yet, if ever, in the global city category, such as Johannesburg

(Geyer), Karachi (Qutub), Mexico City (Graizbord, Rowland and Aguilar), Bogota (Gilbert) and St. Petersburg (Trumbull).

Johannesburg is probably the only viable global city candidate in Sub-Saharan Africa, but still lags far behind those in other parts of the world. Also, the effects of globalization on the spatial structure of the metropolitan region have been significant, driving the international and financial corporations out of the central city into the northern suburbs and peripheral corridors. Migration from both the rural areas and outside South Africa has fueled the growth of the metropolis, and this has made conditions in Johannesburg's central city more difficult because of decaying infrastructure. Geyer doubts that Johannesburg is near world city status, and suggests that its relative competitive position may be deteriorating.

Karachi's prospects remain plagued by ethnic and political tensions and a less than ideal competitive framework. Qutub's survey of entrepreneurs suggested that government policies interfered with the investment climate by unnecessary restrictions, the failure to develop institutions that facilitated market expansion and inappropriate education policies. He argues that this helps to explain Karachi's inability to develop a significant international services sector.

Mexico City is a first class cosmopolitan city, but its economic power is being undermined by cost-ineffective uses of public investment funds, high crime rates, political dissension and the growing economic strength of selected provincial cities. However, as a global city it is, at best, second tier. Its changes in economic structure follow the classic pattern of a shift towards services and the geographical decentralization of economic activity. The long-established high income and social disparities have been aggravated by deterioration in conditions for the working poor and improvement in the wealth of the new elite, especially those associated with the "new economy."

Bogota is far from the global urban hierarchy's upper rungs, although there are signs of improved city management: a succession of competent mayors has made major strides in improving the transport system, reducing its notorious crime, and generally raising its image. However, it is poorly located within both the region and the local economy, its economic structure is weak in terms of high-technology sectors, its educational system is deficient and the level of computer literacy is low. There are also some problems in infrastructure provision and the city suffers from recurrent financial crises, relieved somewhat by loans from the international agencies.

St. Petersburg has not even achieved secondary world city status, partly because of the continuing shackles from its Soviet past. It continues to have low external connectivity, inadequate infrastructure (especially in transportation), a degraded environment, undefined property rights, widespread corruption, and limited access to information technology. On the other hand, its cultural heritage and associated tourist potential is an asset. There has been economic progress, especially the expansion of seaborne trade (St. Petersburg's port handles a third of Russia's imports, and has undergone major expansion). Much depends on what happens in the Russian economy at large, and on the extent of reverse migration, especially of entrepreneurs currently living elsewhere.

Seoul (Choe), Rio de Janeiro-Sao Paulo (Tolosa) and Shanghai (Cai and Zit) are closer to global city status. Seoul has experienced the most significant changes among this group as a result of significant market opening, and the

Seoul Metropolitan Area still accounts for 46 percent of the national population.

The structural changes in the economy of the Rio de Janeiro and Sao Paulo metropolitan areas as an extended metropolitan region towards high technology sectors have been significant and Sao Paulo has made major strides in IT services. Yet, structural deficiencies (such as a spatially concentrated pattern of large establishments and the lack of regional economic interdependencies) remain, and are exacerbated by obstructive Federal and State policies. Also, the large size and long-term domestic rather than international orientation of the Brazilian economy have limited the global influence of Sao Paulo and extensive decentralization within Brazil has somewhat weakened its economic power.

Shanghai's already formidable influence has been propeled forward by the rapid expansion and transformation of the Chinese economy, but the centralization of political power in Beijing and the long-term historical global status of Hong Kong make them formidable competitors; it is possible, however, that their complementaries may be more important. Cai and Zit assess Shanghai in a broader perspective by developing a World City Index to compare it with 32 existing and potential world cities. Their index measures not only economic variables but also less tangible indicators such as the politico-economic system, environmental quality and image. Shanghai's index score is about 30–40 percent of those of Hong Kong and Singapore and only 10–15 percent of the level of the scores for New York, London and Tokyo. However, if economic dynamism and infrastructure endowment are critical for world city formation, and with the entry of China into WTO, Shanghai is a promising candidate for world city status.

Sorensen details the long history of Tokyo's (probably successful) efforts to become a world city. More recently, policymakers in Japan have been concerned about the rise of Hong Kong and Shanghai. In this environment, developers have been successful in arguing for the redevelopment of neighborhoods, sometimes with single-family homes, to build new internationally competitive office space, often to the chagrin of local residents and environmental groups. In the struggle for urban space, the Government has consistently favored economic growth over environmental conservation, and globalization trends have strengthened the developers' hand.

Los Angeles is a paradox. In some respects (e.g. cultural hegemony, a multiethnic cosmopolitan population, the world's third largest port complex), it is the most global city in the world. Yet not one Fortune 500 company is headquartered there and it is not a major financial center, and it fails on almost all of the "world city" criteria. It has been much less impacted by globalization-related "deindustrialization" than other major U.S. cities, and the manufacturing sector (a mix of very low-tech and high-tech industries consisting mainly of small and medium-sized firms) remains quite strong. Its income distribution is somewhat unequal, but this is largely explained by the large recent immigration population, many of them poorly educated with limited skills from Central America. Perhaps the most important globalization-Los Angeles link is the contribution of the region's very large and increasingly high-tech entertainment sector to cultural globalization, certainly much more important than corporate influences.

Turning further south in California, the Tijuana-San Diego metropolitan region functions as a transborder metropolis, unique because of the wide income differentials. Despite immigration controls, the border is porous, especially for work and shopping. In addition, the two metropolitan economies are much more complementary than competitive, with San Diego specializing in the "new economy" (e.g., high-order services) while Tijuana remains predominantly a manufacturing center, supplemented by day-trip tourism. The twin metropolis concept may be more figment than reality because there is not much cooperation in several areas such as trade and social infrastructure, facilitating border crossings, expanding educational opportunities, dealing with the severe environmental problems, and attending to fiscal and income distribution issues. There are formal connections (e.g. Joint Committees), but progress is hampered by the disconnect between the centralized political system in Mexico and the more decentralized structure in the United States. However, in terms of social and cultural interactions, the linkages between the cities in southern San Diego County and Tijuana are very strong (one-half of Tijuana's population can legally cross the border). Globalization offers prospects for developing the "binational" metropolis, but it is unclear whether the required institutional capacity and the political will can be generated.

There is a disciplinary bias in the contributions; most of the authors are economists, planners or geographers. The result is that the book deals primarily with the economic and urban planning implications of globalization. Social and cultural issues are not given much attention with the exception of the discussion of the "parallel worlds" in Bangkok (Jenks) and the emphasis on "ideological globalization" (Chakravorty).

Jenks argues that the attempt to alleviate Bangkok's transportation problems by constructing "Skytrain" (the elevated railway) has benefited international institutions and individuals much more than the local population as a result of the choice of an elevated system, the location of stations and high fares. The Skytrain is treated as a metaphor to examine the relationship between globalization and urban form. The rail network was built 3–4 stories above ground level, creating parallel vertical worlds, with links to international-oriented establishments (hotels, shopping malls, and office buildings) above the traditional street chaos with its cheap buses and motorcycles. Globalization has impacted real estate development in Bangkok but so far has not influenced urban form. Globalization does have urban impacts, but the end result is not cultural imperialism because street life goes on, despite the homogenization of products and the franchising of global establishments.

Chakravorty suggests that the spread of ideas (that free markets, decentralization and good governance are all beneficial) is a parallel aspect of globalization to economic trends and may be more important in the developing world because its global reach has been wider. Also, he argues that whereas the urban impacts of economic globalization are clear (some cities benefit while others are left out), those of ideological globalization are more pernicious, and may be detrimental to cities in the global periphery, resulting in a further relative decline in cities that are already lagging. He pleads for mitigation of the tension between market orientation and interregional/urban divergences.

Globalization is interconnected with many other influences (e.g. structural adjustment programs [SAPs] and trade liberalization) that blur the definition of globalization and make it difficult to isolate its precise effects. It is more or less an insoluble problem that we have to live with. As a generalization, these forces have had an adverse impact on the welfare of the poor. For example, SAPS resulted in a decline in formal sector employment with the result that incomes were squeezed in the informal sector. Similarly, other reform policies (e.g. public sector employment cuts, reductions in urban subsidies to water, transport, food and energy, and tariff reductions for protected industries) probably impact the poor more than other groups. With respect to trade liberalization, it is easy to demonstrate in a two-country theoretical model that pursuing the principle of comparative advantage can result in a win-win situation, but in a dynamic multilateral world the results are much more complicated. A country may neglect comparative advantage for non-economic, perhaps political, reasons. Currency fluctuations may undermine the potential benefits from freer trade. Some countries may lack the institutional, organizational and entrepreneurial capacity to exploit the trade-opening opportunities. Thus, there are gainers and losers, and the losers are more likely to be the poorest countries and the poorest segments of society in those countries. In the long run, the number of beneficiaries will increase, but the "transition costs" for the lower-income groups will be higher and stretched out over a longer period.

The protests at the WTO meetings in Seattle, The Hague, Cancun and Savannah and at high-level World Bank meetings in Washington, D.C. might either be interpreted as misguided or as reflective of serious concerns. Regardless, despite the rhetoric about how globalization adversely affects the urban poor, there has been little empirical analysis to test such a hypothesis. A few papers in this book, e.g. those on the Philippines (Pernia and Quishing) and Los Angeles (Richardson and Gordon), pay some attention to this issue but fall short of a test. The evidence on the Philippines suggests that globalization contributes to poverty reduction but at the expense of interregional inequities. This is because the primate city is usually the main beneficiary from globalization.

Some of the urban impacts associated with globalization are environmental. These might be direct such as the entry of multinational polluting industries or the recent growth in automobile ownership. More likely, they will be indirect, such as the environmental costs of rapid urban development in large cities that have been transformed by the forces of globalization. Bass et al. (2005) and Satterthwaite (2001) argue that global agents, such as the international donors, have focused on politically correct but low priority environmental problems in developing country cities rather than on the key issues of water supply and sanitation and communicable diseases (in Satterthwaite's pithy if inelegant phrase, the problems are "bugs and shit.") Only one chapter in this book focuses exclusively on environmental problems (that by Marcotullio, Rothenberg and Nakahara), and this is primarily a historical comparison of the environmental transition in New York and Tokyo. It shows that the urban environmental transition began much earlier in New York and was much slower than in Tokyo. Both cities shared a similar transition, but Tokyo's experience was much more compressed in time. More generally, under the influence of globalization forces, the environmental experiences of developing country cities will be different and they will have to deal with the full range of environmental problems simultaneously rather than sequentially. There are briefer discussions about environmental problems in the papers on San Diego-Tijuana (Bae) and St. Petersburg (Trumbull) that are consistent with this argument, with St. Petersburg and Tijuana facing multiple environmental problems that have to be dealt with at the same time.

Another important issue is whether the information technology (IT) revolution that has been accelerated by globalization will widen the "digital divide" between the developed and the developing world. This is a complex research question not addressed in the book. There is a chapter about IT (Sohn, Kim and Hewings), but it is much narrower in scope, focusing on how information technology has affected the urban spatial structure in Chicago and Seoul. The chapter develops formal models of urban spatial structure combined with IT-related variables and derives a spatial econometric version of these models, based on two types of impact: concentration, an attraction effect measured by the level of activity in a zone; and dispersion, a spillover effect into surrounding zones, representing distributional impacts. A key finding in both Chicago and Seoul was that, despite the dispersion potential of IT, the limited availability of and accessibility to information infrastructure in many areas have resulted in more concentration than might have been expected. Also, the spillover effect differed between Chicago and Seoul with large activity clusters in Chicago located closer to areas with IT infrastructure while in Seoul smaller clusters were more dispersed. However, because of its more advanced IT network, Chicago may nevertheless be faster in attaining an even spatial distribution of economic activity. If the expansion of IT is an offshoot of globalization, its ultimate impact on urban spatial structure in different cities in different regions of the world remains unclear.

The literature on globalization appears to be sharply bifurcated into pro-globalization and con-globalization camps. This division is not limited to advocacy group circles but also permeates academic discussions. While it is true that globalization presents cities with challenges as well as opportunities (and not all cities rise to these challenges), the balance of the findings in this book is that globalization has benefited cities, especially the larger cities and the countries where they are located, in terms of economic development. It is a balance, however, rather than the rose-tinted view of globalization painted by the World Bank, among others. The income distribution impacts are problematic, at least in the short run. In many countries, the large cities have gained at the expense of smaller cities and peripheral locations, so that spatial inequities have widened. Also, the experiences have varied from one part of the world to another. For example, China has gained substantially from globalization with a strong balance of payments and rising incomes, to the benefit of some Chinese cities, especially Shanghai and Beijing (Cai and Sit). Yet even in China, there are vast differences in the response to globalization between the cities of Western China (i.e. minimal favorable impacts) and those in the rest of the country. Urban India has also performed well in an era of globalization, certainly in contrast with its pre-1991 highly regulated closed economy. Some other parts of the world have done poorly. For example, there is no city in sub-Saharan Africa (with the possible exception of the large cities in the Republic of South Africa) that has benefited from globalization to any significant extent (a minor qualification is the global distribution of pharmaceuticals, but only a tiny proportion of AIDS victims have received free or highly subsidized anti-AIDS drugs).

This book is partial in its geographical scope. The chapters on the United States, in particular, are very specific and outside the mainstream of globalization research. For example, there is no chapter about the links between globalization and deindustrialization in the developed world, especially the United States. Similarly, as pointed out above, there is no discussion about the impacts of globalization on urban Europe, with the notable exception of the St. Petersburg chapter. On the other hand, the different regions of the developing world are reasonably well covered. It is impossible to cover all the issues and all the potential locations in a book of modest size. This is a research beginning, not the last word.

References

Bass S, Reid H, Satterthwaite D, Steele P (2005) Reducing Poverty and Sustaining the Environment: The Politics of Local Engagement. Earthscan, London

Castells M (1989) The Informational City. Basil Blackwell, Oxford

Friedmann J (1986) The world city hypothesis. Development and Change 17(1): 69–83

King AD (1990) Global Cities: Post-Imperialism and the Internationalization of London. Routledge, London

Lo F-C, Marcutillio P, eds. (2001) Globalization and the Sustainability of Cities in the Asia Pacific Region. United Nations University Press, Tokyo

Lo F-C, Yeung Y-M, eds. (1998) Globalization and the World of Large Cities. United Nations University Press, Tokyo

Sassen S (1991) The Global City: New York, London, Tokyo. Princeton University Press, Princeton NJ

Sassen S (1998) New technologies and the globalization of cities 391–409, In Lo and Yeung op.cit., pp. 391–409

Satterthwaite D (2001) Environmental Problems in an Urbanizing World: Finding Solutions in Africa, Asia and Latin America. Stylus Publications, London

Taylor PJ (1999) World cities and territorial states under conditions of contemporary globalization. Globalization and World Cities Research Bulletin, 9

World Bank (2002) Globalization, Growth and Poverty: Building an Inclusive World Economy. Oxford University Press, New York

I. Globalization in General

Globalization, spatial allocation of resources and spatial impacts: A conceptual framework

Gill-Chin Lim

Michigan State University, 201 UPLA Blg., East Lansing, MI, USA (e-mail: Limg@msu.edu) and KDI School of International Policy and Management, Seoul, Korea

Abstract. The main objective of this paper is to develop an integrated conceptual framework in which relationships among globalization, spatial allocation of resources and spatial impacts are constructed. The paper begins with debates on globalization and summarizes persistent problems of the world and new trends of globalization. Then it observes the historical transformation of industrial cities and investigates the factors affecting the spatial allocation of resources which create spatial impacts. The overall framework can be used as a basis to create and define research tasks about globalization and urban spatial development.

1. Introduction

Globalization has become one of the most frequently talked about subjects in academia, the mass media and the public policy arena in recent years. And yet, what it means is not clear. Proponents of globalization argue that it brings positive benefits to people, while critics claim that it damages the well-being of the poor.

Globalization brings about benefits and costs, and there are winners and losers in the globalization process. Globalization hurts societies not able to compete with larger forces originating in the global scene. Societies which lack political cohesion, social justice, knowledge and ethical norms can easily fall prey to global forces. Some countries in Asia and Latin America have proven this thesis. Societies which possess these positive qualities are able to respond to global challenges and capture new opportunities for further social progress. Proponents of globalization are knowledgeable professionals, large businesses, advanced nations and international organizations such as the World Bank, the International Monetary Fund (IMF) and the World Trade Organization (WTO). Opposition comes from those individuals and entities that suffer monetarily or mentally from the globalization processes. Businesses and organizations under protective policies are likely to oppose globalization.

These observations imply that in order to make reliable observations about the impact of globalization, in general or on a specific aspect of a society, it is necessary to have a broad conceptual understanding about the nature of globalization and its impacts.

This paper examines the relationship between globalization and urban spatial development. In Sect. 2, I first discuss the arguments for and against globalization. Section 3 presents persistent global problems and new trends that may directly or indirectly affect the spatial allocation of human activities. Section 4 makes an historical observation on urban development, describing the transformation of industrial cities. In Sect. 5, I list factors that may affect the spatial allocation of resources and variables with which spatial impacts can be measured. In Sect. 6, I present an integrated conceptual framework to analyze the relationship between globalization and spatial impacts. This framework can be used to develop research tasks for geographers, planners, regional scientists and policy analysts interested in spatial aspects of human activities.

2. Globalization: Proponents and opponents

The debate on globalization usually surrounds economic globalization. In this line of thinking, it refers to an integration of the world economy, removing trade barriers and allowing freedom of interaction. International organizations such as the World Bank, the IMF and the WTO are leading proponents of globalization. Multinational corporations also are in favor of global integration of economic affairs, because they gain from freer transactions in international markets.

However, trade liberalization in general hurts employees in traditionally protected sectors. Under economic globalization, new factories are set up abroad, and cheaper imported goods and services threaten domestic producers. Proponents of economic globalization argue that, in the long run, free trade will increase the overall output of the world and that of the poor nations, eventually making all nations and people better off.

Nonetheless, liberalization has negatively affected certain sectors of the population in rich as well as poor nations. This explains why massive and violent protests break out against major international agencies and their meetings. In recent years, we have seen people rallying against the World Bank, the IMF, the WTO and the World Economic Forum in Washington, D.C., Seattle, Davos, Prague, Cancun and Savannah, Georgia.

2.1. Proponents: The case of the World Bank

The World Bank is one the most influential proponents of globalization. A recent study by the World Bank (Dollar and Collier 2002) makes the following observations on globalization:

- Globalization reduces poverty.
- Globalization generally reduces inequality between nations.
- 3 billion people live in 24 "new globalizing" developing countries. They recorded an average 5% growth rate in the 1990s. Growth reduces poverty.
- Populations living on less than $1 per day have decreased from 1.4 to 1.2 billion since 1980.

- There has been 2% growth in rich countries; there is a convergence in per capita income.
- There has been negative growth in the less globalized countries. They include 2 billion people in sub-Saharan Africa, the Middle East and the former USSR.

Based on these observations, the World Bank offers the following policy recommendations.

- Development of a round of trade negotiations.
- Improving the investment climate in developing countries.
- Better delivery of education and health services.
- Social protections tailored to the more dynamic labor market in an open economy.
- Greater volume of foreign aid, better managed.
- Debt relief.
- Tackling global environmental problems: greenhouse gases and global warming.

2.2. Opponents: Scholars and civic leaders

Protesters and critics of globalization originate from various countries, and their backgrounds vary. Notable critics of international organizations include Chossudovsky (1998), and Nader and Wallch (1996).

Michael Chossudovsky, a Canadian professor, has long been a harsh critic of globalization. In his book, *The Globalization of Poverty: Impact of IMF and World Bank Reforms*, Chossudovsky argues that since the beginning of the 1980s, real salaried earnings in the modern sector declined by more than 60 % in many debtor nations in the Third World. Using World Bank data for 1993, he shows that:

- Low-income Third World countries have 56 % of the world population, but only 4.9 percent of the world income.
- Middle-income Third World countries have 22.2 % of the world population, and 12.2 percent of the world income.
- Third World countries as a whole have 78.2 % of the world population, but only 17.1 percent of the world income.
- Poor countries as a whole have 85.2 % of the world population, but just 21.5 % of the world income.
- OECD countries have only 14.7 % of the world population, but 77.9 % of the world income.
- Rich countries as a whole have only 14.8 % of the world population, and 78.5 % of the world income.

Chossudovsky's view is that global changes in economic structure have changed fundamentally since the early 1980s. The activities of the World Bank and the IMF, according to Chossudovsky, increased poverty, damaged the environment and generated other social ills in Third World and Eastern European countries. The "Thirdworldization" of the former eastern bloc took place, and structural adjustments brought about results opposite to their stated objectives. He cites the IMF and the World Bank's tacit acknowledgement of its failure.

"Although there have been a number of studies on the subject over the past decade, one cannot say with certainty whether programs have "worked" or not.... On the basis of existing studies, one certainly cannot say whether the adoption of programs supported by the Fund led to an improvement in inflation and growth performance. In fact it is often found that programs are associated with a rise in inflation and a fall in the growth rate." (p. 69)

Ralph Nader and Lori Wallch, who specifically examined the case of the United States, contend that globalization hurts people, and that the GATT and the NAFTA are subversive to the democratic process. In the autumn of 1994, just before the vote by the Congress on the Uruguay Round of GATT, which would establish the World Trade Organization, Nader and Wallch offered a $10,000 donation to the charity of choice of any member of the Congress who would (1) sign an affidavit stating that he or she had read the five hundred page agreement, and (2) successfully answer ten simple questions about its content. No one accepted. After the vote was postponed until December 1994, Hank Brown, the Colorado Republican Senator, took the challenge and answered all questions correctly. On December 1, 1994, Congress passed the GATT 235 to 200 in the House and 68 to 32 in the Senate, according to Nader and Wallach, without having an understanding of its substance.

2.3. Stiglitz–Rogoff debate

Perhaps the most interesting debate about economic globalization broke out between Joseph Stiglitz, former Chief Economist and Senior Vice President of the World Bank, and Kenneth Rogoff, Economic Counselor and Director of the Research Department of the IMF.

In mid-2002, Stiglitz wrote a book titled *Globalization and Its Discontent.* (Stiglitz 2002) Stiglitz 's argument is well summarized in his preface, *"The IMF policies, in part based on the outworn presumptions that markets, by themselves, lead to efficient outcomes, failed to allow for desirable government interventions in the markets, measures which can guide economic growth and make everyone better off."* (p. xii)

Drawing upon his observations on the IMF's work in Ethiopia, East Asia, Russia, Eastern Europe and other nations, he asserts that the policy makers at the IMF use outdated economic models, and adhere to the "Washington Consensus" that protects the interests of rich countries rather than poor ones. The policies at the IMF are made without transparency, and the true interests of the people are not represented in the decision-making process. Finance ministers and central bank governors are defenders of the interests of the financial community. The privatization and market approaches damage the well-being of poor nations rather than helping them grow and stabilize.

However, Stiglitz is not opposed to globalization. He believes that globalization generates positive benefits, and is therefore here to stay. But, it is necessary to pursue globalization in a different way than the IMF has done. Stiglitz suggests new global public institutions to help set rules and changes in the governance system at the IMF, the World Bank and the WTO, in order to ensure transparency. He proposes reform of the IMF and the world financial system, reform of the World Bank and development assistance, reform of the

WTO and balancing the trade agenda. He is ultimately interested in helping *"make globalization fairer, and more effective."* (p. 247) He wants to see globalization with a more human face. To this end, Stiglitz calls for the responsibility of developing countries and the developed world's involvement in international institutions.

No sooner had Stiglitz's book appeared than Rogoff sent an open letter in the *IMF Survey* under the heading of "Rogoff's discontent with Stiglitz." He makes three substantive points. First, Stiglitz's ideas in the book are agreeable to the IMF people, but are basically old hat. Second, Stiglitz's blueprints to improve the IMF's macroeconomic policies are, at best, highly controversial, and at worst, snake oil. Third, Stiglitz was a heroic whistle-blower at the World Bank, speaking against the macroeconomic policies adopted during the Asian crisis in the 1990s, and undermining confidence.

Rogoff contends that Stiglitz's policy prescriptions to help emerging market debtors in crisis – by raising the profile of fiscal deficits – will not work. According to Rogoff, Stiglitz's prescriptions, which rely on issuing more debt and printing more money, will result in higher inflation, lower growth and a damaging impact on all people, especially the indigent. Against Stiglitz's claim that he shares the ideas of John Maynard Keynes, Rogoff brands Stiglitz's theories as Laffer's supply side economics. He disputes that the IMF is tone-deaf and insensitive to criticisms. While Stiglitz does not consider markets the best mechanism to implement economic policies, and thinks the government can do better, Rogoff believes the government fails more than the market.

Both Stiglitz and Rogoff are proponents of globalization, but they differ from each other about how public institutions – in this case the World Bank and the IMF – design policies to benefit from globalization. Stiglitz's criticism of the IMF uses similar logic and evidence to that used by Chossudovsky and Nader and Wallch, who are unforgiving opponents of globalization.

2.4. Critical observations on the debates

There are some critical observations to be made on the arguments for and against globalization and the debate between Stiglitz and Rogoff.

First, currently, globalization is taken mainly as economic processes involving trade relations and market processes. Second, globalization is a complex process, the nature of which is not completely understood. Third, globalization means different things, delivering different outcomes to different countries and different groups of people. Fourth, the proponents, in their arguments for globalization, usually leave out some of the most important issues concerning the well-being of people, such as human rights, the burden of military spending, corruption and cultural identity, which fall in the political and cultural arenas. Fifth, opponents are concerned about negative, unexpected impacts of economic globalization, and feel it should be stopped or considerably changed.

There are non-economic aspects of globalization, such as political and cultural globalization, which affect lives of many people in a far-reaching way. However, due to the narrow understanding of globalization, there exists a high degree of confusion. To reduce this confusion, globalization needs a better definition. It should be defined in terms of specific items, and cover not only economic, but also political and cultural aspects. First of all, for policy makers of governments, international agencies and businesses, it is crucial to understand the persistent global problems which beset people and which they must endeavor to solve. Second, they have to have a firm grasp on global trends, which proffer both risks and opportunities, for which they seek solutions.

3. Persistent global problems and new trends

3.1. Persistent global problems

Several persistent problems beset our world. First of all, there is a large number of people living in abject poverty and live a short span of life. In 1998, 1.2 billion people were living on less than US $1 per day (World Bank 2003). Under these circumstances, people in poor nations live much shorter lives than those in rich nations. In 2001, the average life expectancy at birth, which is a critical representative indicator measuring overall well-being, was 59.1 years in low-income countries compared to 78.1 years in high-income countries. The differences in life expectancy between the rich and poor nations are dismally striking: 78.7 in Norway, 76.9 in the United States and 81.3 in Japan in contrast to 51.8 in Nigeria, 45.7 in Ethiopia and 34.5 in Sierra Leone. (UNDP 2003).

Second, there exists a variety of global and local environmental problems. We are frequently warned about imbalance in our ecological system. Damage to the environment has continued both in developed and developing countries. At the local and national levels, we are experiencing an increase in air and water pollution, solid waste and unsafe disposal of hazardous material. We also see environmental problems of a global scale:acid rain, ocean dumping, greenhouse effects, a loss of biodiversity and ozone depletion. Brown (2003) recently gave a highly critical assessment of the current status of the environment.

Third, amid persistent poverty and environmental damage, regional wars among nations and conflicts within nations are occurring in many parts of the world. Intense frictions still persist and emerge among people with different ethnic, religious and political beliefs. Under these circumstances, the majority of nations maintain formidable military forces under the name of national security. In 2001, the world spent about 3.5 % of all gross national products for military purposes. NATO's military spending was 2.2%, Non- NATO Europe 2.3%, Russia 4.3%, Middle East and North Africa 7.2%, Central and South Asia 3.8%, East Asia and Australasia 3.3%, Caribbean, Central and Latin America 1.7%, and Sub-Saharan Africa 3.4%. The total amount of military expenditure for the world was US $ 835.242 billion. (International Institute for Strategic Studies 2002) The most dramatic incident of violence took place on September 11, 2001, claiming three thousand lives and heavy property damage in New York and other areas in the US. In the domain of public decision-making in most nations, "military security," manifesting in the form of weapons and troops, took a higher priority over what might be called "civil security," security concerning food, housing, medical care, education and other necessities for decent human life.

Fourth, human rights are being violated in many parts of the world. Torture, threats and incarceration without proper trials are frequently heard of, and women and children are being abused and deprived of their rights. In some nations, people are killed without due process of law and disappear without a trace. (U.S. Department of State 1999-2002)

Fifth, corruption prevails in the public and private sectors of many, especially less developed nations, influencing their decision-making process. There are numerous incidents of corruption among politicians and bureaucrats. A study by Transparency International (2001) which ranked 91 countries in terms of the Corruption Perceptions Index (CPI) for 2001, exposed that almost two-thirds of the countries had an index score of less than 5 out of a score of 10 (the cleanest). Developed, rich countries such as Finland, Denmark, New Zealand, Iceland, Singapore and Sweden scored 9 or higher out of a clean score of 10. But 55 countries, which are among the world's poorest, received a CPI of less than 5, indicating high levels of perceived corruption in governments. (Transparency International 1998, 2001)

Sixth, there is a problem of education in less developed and even some developed countries. In less developed nations, many are illiterate. The adult literacy rate (% age 15 and above) in the least developed nations was 53.3 % in 2001. In Sierra Leone, it was 36.0; in Niger 16.5; in Ethiopia 43.3 (UNDP 2003). It also should be noted that the illiteracy rate is higher for women. In the meantime, in more developed countries where the literacy rate is almost 100%, there are problems of quality assurance, and of cultural and functional illiteracy (Hirsch 1987).

3.2. New trends: Risks and opportunities

The picture depicted above shows serious obstacles that prevent us from moving toward a just, free and peaceful society. Despite these severe and critical obstacles, there are new trends in the global scene that have significantly impacted our patterns of thinking and living in recent years. These trends provide us with both risks and opportunities.

First, the economic interconnectedness among nations will continue to increase. As international trade, multinational joint ventures, strategic alliances and international financial flows increase, a new international economic structure will be created, forcing old institutions to undertake reforms. The distinction between domestic and international markets is becoming less meaningful.

Second, there is an ideological shift toward democracy and market mechanisms. Earlier, the shifts took place in parts of the Pacific Rim. More recently, we have observed monumental changes in the Soviet Union and Eastern Europe. China amended its constitution to liberalize its economic system. Also noteworthy are recent reforms in Bolivia, Mexico and other Latin American nations. Popular demand for a more democratic government is likely to be sustained during the 21st century.

Third, there has been substantial transformation and restructuring of national and international organizations and systems of governments. At the national level, many countries – for example, Poland, China and Korea- are seeking ways to decentralize their political system. At the international level, examples of such transformation and restructuring trends include the integration of Europe into a single market, the emergence of the Newly Industrialized Countries (NICs), the Pacific Rim as an emerging and dynamic global economic force, the greater economic integration of the United States, Canada and Mexico through NAFTA, and the Southern African Development Community (SADC). In South America, there are economic integration efforts such as the Andean Group and MERCOSUR (Argentina, Brazil, Paraguay and Uruguay). A broader form of integration throughout South America is conceivable as other large trading blocs in the rest of the world develop. There is also a movement toward Islamic economic cooperation. The Black Sea Economic Cooperation Pact, another example of regional cooperation, was formed by the nations bordering the Black Sea, including a number of states of the Commonwealth of Independent States. A dramatic event in the restructuring of international systems took place on May14, 2002 in a meeting in Reykjavik, Iceland, where NATO and Russia agreed to have a cooperative relationship, truly putting an end to the Cold War.

Fourth, we will see rapid advances in science and technology that may radically transform our lives in unimagined ways. We will have to keep our eyes on progress in material science, information technology, communications and transportation systems, superconductors, genetic engineering and fusion technology. In particular, advances in information technology are rapidly altering the production, distribution and use of knowledge, material goods, and services, creating both positive and negative consequences.

Fifth, there is a rising awareness of important global ecological issues. People are more astute about worldwide ecological interdependencies. In many nations, a number of grassroots organizations have been formed to engage in a variety of environmental movements. The problems of transnational acid rain, deforestation, greenhouse effects, ozone depletion and other matters of global ecology have mandated new thinking and action in the public arena. These issues will remain an important agenda for research and public policy.

Finally, of critical importance, but often neglected in public discussion, is the global emergence of multicultural values and lifestyles. In major metropolitan areas of the world, people's lives link more closely to the globally-oriented centers of activities such as the financial, political and/or cultural centers of Paris, Tokyo, London, New York and Washington, D.C. than to each country's respective hinterland. These centers also act as dynamic agents of social transformation both in international and domestic affairs. In this context, the roles of various social fabrics are reexamined. Many nations are becoming increasingly more diverse in ethnic and racial composition. The increasing level of diversity and pluralism will pose a challenge to social integration, not just locally or nationally, but also globally.

It is important to point out that these trends have emerged simultaneously. We have experienced important changes on a global scale in the past; a prime example being the technological changes during the industrial revolution. Never before in human history, however, have such extensive changes occurred virtually simultaneously in so many different spheres of activities – economic, ecological, technological, ideological, organizational and cultural. This phenomenon makes the new century potentially pivotal in history.

3.3. Spatial implications of globalization

The problems, risks and opportunities described above directly and indirectly affect the spatial allocation of resources. For instance, the persistent poverty that sometimes concentrates in urban areas may further expand the area of decay. The widespread use of information technology around the world, which is believed to make human activities more footloose, may reduce the density of urban areas. The increasing economic interdependencies may lead to substantial international migration of capital, jobs and people creating a new pattern of cities and regions.

4. Historical observations on urban development: Transformation of industrial cities

Sorting out the important factors affecting the physical structure of cities and regions requires a review of the historical development of urban form.

4.1. From core dominants cities to megalopolis

The 19th century industrial cities were formed with business activities concentrated in the center. Needs for interregional transportation of raw materials and finished products, as well as marginal transportation cost structures within cities, were mainly responsible for the 19th century core dominant cities.

However, the core dominant cities of the 19th century have transformed to the spreading metropolises during the 20th century. Some of the notable urban transformations we have witnessed in the 20th century are:

- Massive expansion of metropolitan areas and the birth of new cities.
- Suburbanization of both population and employment.
- Relative decline of the central city.

These transformations are related to:

- Growth of national population.
- Rural-urban migration.
- Large-scale operation of industries (scale economies).
- Advances in production technology.
- Improvements in transportation.
- Rising real income.
- Government policies affecting housing market and land use.
- Ethnic, income and other discrimination.
- Income inequality.

Based on the observation of these long-term historical trends of the 20th century, it could be suggested that there would emerge the megalopolis, conurbation, or even the ecumenopolis, indicating that cities of super size would be born.

4.2. New trends and the future of urban development

However, since about the middle of the 1960s, we started observing rather different trends. These new trends were:

- Some large metropolitan areas in advanced industrialized countries stopped growing or began declining in population.
- Regional shifts of population were also apparent. In the USA, the Sun Belt areas grew rapidly while the Snow (or Rust) Belt, i.e. the older industrial areas of the Northeast and the Midwest, declined.
- Significant changes took place in employment growth patterns.
- Some evidence of a back-to-the-city movement, popularly termed "gentrification," occurred.

The factors behind these new phenomena are not quite clear; neither convincing theoretical, nor rigorous empirical work has been provided to explain these trends with consistency. However, it is worth considering the following factors:

- Diseconomies of scale/agglomeration.
- Changing comparative advantages of cities.
- Increases in energy costs.
- Changes in demographic composition.
- Development of communication technology.
- Changing preferences of people regarding location and life style.

A question is raised, "Are these phenomena a clean break from the past or a temporary short-term fluctuation?" In this context, two contrasting views about the future of urban form can be constructed. One is a view that cities will die; dispersal will continue and core dominant cities will disappear. Experts in information technology who emphasize the power of footloose cyber operation support this view. According to this view, urban economies will shrink and their populations will fall. On the other hand, a different view, "Urban Revival," can be proposed: the centers of the nation's large cities will regain their strength and enjoy a so-called gentrification process. This view would assert that urban economies will grow, and cities will have much larger populations.

5. Factors affecting spatial allocation of resources and their spatial impacts

5.1. Factors affecting the spatial allocation of resources

The foregoing review provides us with backgrounds to identify important factors that may affect the spatial allocation of resources. The following are key factors:

- Overall population growth and distribution.
- Population distribution among large and small cities.
- Energy costs.
- Communications and other technologies.
- Cultural factors.
- Scale economies and diseconomies of cities.

- Industrial composition.
- Changing comparative advantages of cities.
- Demographic and social factors.
- Income growth and distribution.
- Political landscape of urban areas.
- Environmental constraints.

i. Overall population growth and its distribution between rural and urban areas. Other things being equal, overall population growth will increase the size and density of urban areas. In countries where urbanization is at a lower level, there will be a substantial increase in the size of cities.

ii. Population distributions among large and small cities. A very critical issue is: Where will these people go? Large metropolitan areas such as New York, Chicago, medium sized cities, or small urban places? Studies on city size distribution strongly suggest that population distribution becomes more even as per capita GNP and total population increases. If we follow this line of logic, the growth of large metropolitan areas is likely to be relatively slower than that of small cities.

iii. Energy costs. Even the most optimistic plans for "fusion technology" do not foresee a widespread use of "unlimited fusion energy" as a possibility in the near future. If we assume that energy costs will increase in real terms in the future, the impact of increased energy costs would lead to more centralized and dense developments. This view is based on the assumptions of

a. Centralized employment centers.
b. The importance of work trips as a key element of residential location behavior.
c. People not resorting to other adjustment behaviors such as changes in driving habits, carpooling, multipurpose trips, public transit use, purchase of fuel-efficient cars, etc.
d. A smooth housing supply in central cities.

On the other hand, the degree of concentration of population in city centers will be at a lower level under the following conditions.

a. Decentralized employment centers.
b. The importance of non-work trips.
c. People make significant adjustments in travel behavior.
d. A limited housing supply.

iv. Communications and other technologies. Rapid developments in electronic communications technology reduce the need for face-to-face contacts in business transactions and other human relations. This will apparently lead to a tendency for decentralization and sprawl. In an extreme case of full on-line activities, one might argue that central cities will be vacant, because there will be no need to go to central urban institutions. However, even in the era of the most sophisticated electronic technology, certain face-to-face human contacts are valued (e.g. for consumption- rather than production-related activities). This indicates that dependency on the central core of the city may be reduced to a certain extent, but the unique role of the center as a major business sector as a center of human interaction is likely to be preserved.

v. Cultural factors. The central city is historical in many ways. It contains the most important elements of cultural activities, such as museums and the performing arts. As a society becomes more affluent, the demand for and awareness of the value of historical and cultural elements increases. Therefore, even with extremely efficient communications technology, people will travel to the center of urban areas to have first-hand experiences for certain activities, contributing to the tendency for centrality.

vi. Scale economies and diseconomies of cities. There is no clear theoretical or empirical analysis showing that cities are oversized in the sense that the negative benefits of large-scale cities exceed the positive benefits. But there have been many casual observations which show the cost side of urban life. People complain about urban ills, such as pollution, crime, traffic congestion and lack of housing. Probably it is safe to say that the growth of large cities is likely to be slower than in the past.

vii. Industrial Composition. One of the distinctive features of post-industrial society is a major shift in industrial composition, specifically, a rise in the proportion of the service sector. Service sector employments can be highly footloose (particularly with the development of communications technology), but historically they have been concentrated centrally because of the need for face-to-face contacts and linkages with other businesses. Decentralization of the service sector is quite likely with the advancement in information technology, but some kind of clustering is still possible due to the minimum level of face-to-face contacts required. A possible form of metropolis in this context is a clustered sprawl, or multi-modal development.

viii. Changing comparative advantages of cities. The growth of large metropolitan areas in older industrial areas has been associated with the comparative advantages they have enjoyed, including natural resources, labor force and location. With the diffusion of innovation, dispersal of population, improved communications and transportation systems, the importance of their comparative advantages has been substantially reduced. In addition, public policy is changing, further weakening their position. For example, policy measures such as subsidized migration or strict growth control measures alter the comparative advantages of cities and regions.

ix. Demographic and social factors. In advanced industrial nations, because of new values and cultural syndromes, demographic characteristics are undergoing radical change; there has been a substantial decrease in the proportion of typical nuclear families; the proportion of single member households is increasing; the older population is increasing; and the number of multi-work families also increases. The five-day work week is now the norm in many countries. It is also possible to have a four-day work week in the future. With these trends, dependency on the work trip will decrease and the non-work trip will be even more important. We observe the increasing importance of leisure that would decentralize population. However, the growth of single member households may create a force toward centralization, because of their housing preferences and other consumption patterns.

x. Income growth and distribution. The effects of rising real income will create a large aggregate demand for living space, environmental quality, cultural life, and outdoor activities. It could contribute to the tendency toward a dispersal of urban areas. Assuming that current policies and economic systems in the world continue, the pattern of income distribution in most countries will not change significantly in the near future. Even with persistent pursuit of the idea of equality, the current disparities in economic status among population groups are likely to continue. This suggests that the pattern of social economic segregation will be observed in most cities in the future. If income distribution becomes worse, the areas with poor segments of society will expand.

xi. Political landscape of urban areas. In the USA, the system of urban government is deeply rooted in the idea of decentralization and local autonomy, which has contributed to urban dispersal. Although there has been some movement towards centralization (metropolitan government, for instance), the tradition of political fragmentation in urban areas is likely to survive in the USA. This political landscape reinforces the tendency of decentralization and physical segregation by social and economic groups. In the meantime, many countries (e.g., Poland, China and Korea) have been governed by centralized systems, even in large urban regions. However, some of these nations are now pursuing the decentralization of urban governance. The political landscape of urban areas will play a role in shaping urban form.

xii. Environmental constraints. The rising environmental awareness of the public may create a call for the preservation of raw land and for high-density urban development. But with rising incomes, a major source of demand for environmental awareness, there is a conflict between the desire for more living space and more preservation. The U.S. is still a low-density country with abundant land. Unless the free market system of land is abolished and replaced by public land ownership, development of raw land will not be completely stopped. The size and density of urban areas will increase in countries where land is scarce and environmental awareness is increasing.

To summarize, on one hand, there are factors contributing to physical growth of urban areas and further decentralization tending toward lower-density development. On the other hand, there are forces creating incentives for limiting urban size and promoting concentration. It is important for urban scholars and professionals to distinguish between the forces that contribute to the overall pattern of urban form on the macro scale and the forces that are responsible for the sub-area level development on the micro scale.

5.2. Spatial impacts

These factors create an impact on space. Some of the important variables to measure spatial impacts are:

- Industrial activities.
- Population.
- Density.
- Housing.
- Transportation.
- Natural resources.
- Public facilities.
- Pattern of clustering.

6. An integrated conceptual framework

The foregoing discussion can be put together in an integrated framework to construct a conceptual framework. Figure 1 shows the relationships among

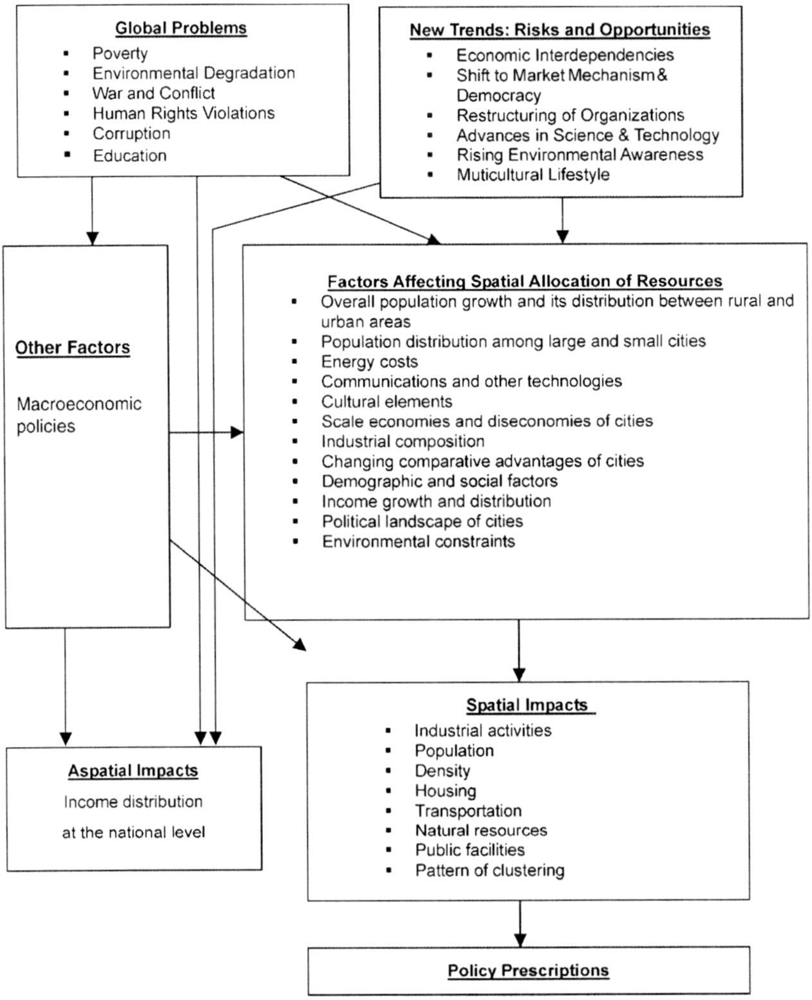

Fig 1. Conceptual framework

Global Problems, New Trends, Other Factors, Factors Affecting the Spatial Allocation of Resources, Aspatial Impacts and Spatial Impacts.

Global Problems, New Trends and Other Factors influence Factors Affecting Spatial Allocation of Resources, which in turn create Spatial Impacts. Global Problems, New Trends and Other Factors also produce Aspatial Impacts. This framework can be used to examine a particular aspect of the impacts generated by globalization. The examination could be descriptive or explanatory. Policy implications can be made from the study of aspatial and spatial impacts. The figure can serve as a framework to develop research tasks for geographers, planners, regional scientists, and policy analysts interested in the spatial allocation of human activities.

References

Brown LR (2003) Plan B: Rescuing a planet & a civilization in trouble. W. W. Norton & Company, New York

Chossudovsky M (1998) The globalisation of poverty: impacts of IMF and World Bank reforms. Atlantic Highlands, London, Zen Books, Penang, Malaysia

Dollar D, Collier P (2001) Globalization, growth, and poverty: Building an inclusive world economy. Oxford University Press, Oxford

Hirsch ED (1987) Cultural literacy. Houghton Mifflin, New York

International Institute for Strategic Studies (2002) The military balance 2002–2003. Oxford University Press, Oxford

International Monetary Fund (1998) World economic outlook October 1998. IMF, Washington DC

James H (1996) International monetary cooperation since Bretton Woods. IMF, Washington DC

Nader R, Wallch L (1996) GATT, NAFTA and the subversion of the democratic process. In: Mander J, Goldsmith E (eds) The case against the global economy and for a turn toward the local. Sierra Club Books, San Francisco

Rogoff K (2002) Rogoff's discontent with Stiglitz. IMF Survey 31(13) July: 209–211

Stiglitz J (2002) Globalization and its discontent. Norton & Company, New York

Transparency International (1998) Combating corruption: Are lasting solutions emerging? Pope J, Mohn C, Cote-Freeman S (eds) Transparency International, Berlin

Transparency International (2001) The corruption perception index 2001. Transparency International, Berlin

U.S. Department of State (1999–2002) Country reports on human rights practices. Released by the Bureau of Democracy, Human Rights, and Labor

United Nations Development Programme (2003) Human development report 2003. Millennium development goals: A compact among nations to end human poverty. Oxford University Press, Oxford

World Bank (2003) World development report 2003. Sustainable development in a dynamic world. Oxford University Press, Oxford

Urban development in the global periphery: The consequences of economic and ideological globalization

Sanjoy Chakravorty

Department of Geography and Urban Studies, Temple University, Philadelphia, Pa 19122, USA
(e-mail: sanjoy@temple.edu)

Abstract. Globalization has two elements: economic globalization refers to the integration of global markets, while ideological globalization refers to the political ideas that underlie the spread of markets, trade, and democracy. Economic globalization is limited in its reach in the developing world: some cities have done well; some, despite not being globalized, have regional importance; and large regions and numerous cities have been bypassed. Ideological globalization, on the other hand, is far more widespread from an intellectual and a policy perspective. The tenets of ideological globalization are likely to work further to the relative detriment of the cities/regions in the global periphery. This is a "cumulative causation" argument that raises questions about the development prospects of peripheral regions.

JEL Classification: F01, H7, Z1

1. Introduction

What are the consequences of globalization for urban development in cities in the global periphery? This is a question of some significance, not only in academic terms, but also to begin to understand the emerging global map of welfare distribution and the policies that may be devised to address these consequences. In order to move toward some answers it is necessary to unpack three of the key terms – globalization, urban development, and periphery – and then analyze how the former influences the latter. The key themes I develop in this paper relate to the unevenness of globalization in international and intra-national terms which has created a large number of peripheral cities and regions, the relatively wider spread of the ideologies of globalization, and their implications at the local level. I suggest that economic globalization is only part of the appropriate framework for understanding urban development issues in a broad theoretical sense. A fuller understanding needs to incorporate ideological globalization – or the ideas on markets, trade, democracy, and governance that underlie economic globalization – which may be of more consequence than economic globalization itself for cities and regions in the periphery. This is significant because while economic globalization has created groups of cities with varying degrees of integration in the global economy, ideological globalization reinforces these divergent trends, working to the detriment of peripheral cities and regions.

The paper is presented in four parts. First, I elaborate on the idea of the periphery and show the extent to which economic globalization is associated with increasing regional polarization. Next, I briefly discuss the diversity of intellectual approaches to globalization and argue that from a policy perspective there is significant congruence. Third, I show why urban development policies in the periphery must be growth-oriented. Finally, I discuss three important tenets of ideological globalization and show how these principles lead to further marginalization of cities that are already on the margins.

2. The periphery of the global economy

Geographers are well aware that "periphery" or margin is a relative term. In any given system of places it is possible to identify places that are most developed along some agreed upon dimension, say average income; this is the core. In such a system there are places that are much less advanced (the periphery or the margin), and places that are at intermediate levels of development (the transitional regions). This is a well-known framework that has been applied to several geographical scales: at the sub-national regional level such as States or provinces in large countries like the U.S., China, and India; at the inter-national regional level such as Europe or southeast Asia; and at the global level. That is, the periphery is constituted not in absolute space but in relative space. Hence, it is possible to construct global hierarchies of cities (global city-world city-national center-regional center-local center) or regions.

This is an old problem in regional studies and in development studies. The core-periphery problem was identified early by Myrdal (1957) and Hirschman (1958) at the intra-national scale. Myrdal was particularly pessimistic about the development prospects of lagging regions as a result of what he called "cumulative causation", a process in which advanced, industrial, metropolitan regions continue to attract capital and skilled labor away from lagging regions. This results in "backwash" or the scouring away of lagging regions while the advanced regions continue to grow more rapidly. The core-periphery problem has been identified at the international scale by dependency theorists such as Baran (1957) and Frank (1967) who argue that the international core (First World metropolitan regions, or the metropole) grows by keeping the peripheral regions (especially in Latin America) poor and dependent on unequal trade with the core. In other words, the periphery is not new.

It is possible to argue the global periphery is constructed in two steps. First is the marginalization of many countries from global flows of capital and technology. Second is the marginalization of regions within these and other countries where there is little new capital investment. Let us consider the international dimension first and ask: is globalization associated with increased peripheralization? That is, have the gaps between leading and lagging regions (at different geographical scales) grown wider in the last two decades, and are there more regions now that are peripheral?

2.1. The international scale

At the international scale the answer is a resounding yes. Let us look at the evidence. Lant Pritchett (1997, 3), looking at income growth in developed and developing countries from 1870 on, says that "(D)ivergence in relative productivity levels and living standards is the dominant feature of modern economic history". He and other economic historians such as Jeffrey Williamson (1997) point out that the world's economies can be divided into two clubs – high income and low income – and economic globalization leads to convergence within clubs and divergence between clubs. Milanovic's (2002) calculations of world inequality over the past two decades shows that inequality at a global level is increasing, and at a Gini coefficient of around 0.68 it is the highest it has ever been and higher than in any single nation.

Now consider some recent data on summary indicators of global integration. Two points are highlighted in data from the World Development Indicators (World Bank 2001, Table 6.1) on two crucial indicators – trade in goods, and gross FDI – measured at two points in time (1989 and 1999) covering the decade of economic globalization's full flowering.

First, economic globalization, whether measured by trade or capital flows, is primarily a First World phenomenon; and just as significant, this is increasingly true. In 1989 trade in goods accounted for over 28% of Purchasing Power Parity (PPP) GDP in the high-income economies; by 1999 it accounted for over 37%. The corresponding numbers for the low-income economies was 7.2 and 7.8%. In 1999 trade in goods and services were worth $10,589 billion in the high-income countries, $1,231 billion in East Asia and the Pacific, $772 billion in Latin America, and only $187 billion in Sub-Saharan Africa and $173 billion in South Asia (World Bank 2001). Similarly, FDI as a percentage of GDP is far more important in high-income economies than in low income ones. As with trade in goods this difference is increasing – from 15 fold to 25 fold in the ten-year period. "Fifteen emerging market economies, mainly in East Asia, Latin America, and Europe, accounted for 83% of all net long-term private capital flows to developing countries in 1997" (World Bank 2001, 317).

Second, there is great variation in the significance of trade among developing nations. In several countries, notably in Africa, trade in goods has actually declined, whereas the greatest gains have generally been seen in the Latin American economies. In China, India, and Brazil, vast countries with large economies, trade in goods accounts for small proportions of their economies (8% in China, 3.6% in India). In general, trade is seen to be most significant in the relatively small, open economies (South Korea, Malaysia, Thailand, and perhaps as a result of NAFTA, Mexico). Remember that these trade figures include exports *and* imports, which, of course, include oil. The FDI data are similar to the trade data: general decline in Africa (where in every country other than Nigeria and Zambia, gross FDI accounts for less than 1% of GDP), some increase in Asia (also where the vast majority of countries have FDI at less than 1% of GDP), and significant increases in Latin America. Except in Latin America, FDI generally accounts for a miniscule proportion of the GDP. As a result, in almost all developing nations the domestic economy continues to be overwhelmingly important, and capital and migration streams flow more in response to domestic economic compulsions and conditions rather than international ones.

2.2. The sub-national scale

At the sub-national interregional scale too there is mounting evidence that divergence in development levels is the norm (see Fedorov 2002 on Russia; Fan 1995, Gustafsson and Shi 2002, Kanbur and Zhang 2003 on China; Chakravorty 2000 and Ghosh et al. 1998 on India; Akita and Lukman 1995; Aswicahyono et al. 1996 and Sjoholm 2000 on Indonesia; Ahuja et al. 1997 and Daniere 1996 on Thailand, etc.). For instance, in Russia Fedorov (2002) finds that the Gini of regional income inequality rose from 0.106 in 1990 to 0.287 in 1999; the Wolfson index of polarization increased from 0.099 to 0.403 over the same period. Looking only at rural inequality between counties Gustafsson and Shi (2002, 179) found that "most of the income inequality in rural China in 1995 was found to be spatial and the uneven development of mean income across counties stood for most... of the rapid increase in income inequality". In Thailand, Ahuja et al. write (1997, 42): "The urban or rural location of residence explains 17–18% of the [income] inequality in 1975, and the region of residence explains 14–15% (and) the explanatory power of both variables increases substantially over time: in 1992 the location of residence explains 28–29% of the inequality and the region of residence explains between 25–27% ... this suggests that the spatial dimension of inequality is gaining importance in Thailand." Chakravorty's (2000) analysis of new industrial investment in India finds strong evidence of intra-regional convergence and interregional divergence.

There is general agreement in this literature that leading regions are the prime recipients of new productive investment; as a result growth is concentrated in a few places while stagnation, even regression, is widespread. One of the interesting findings is that society-wide inequality changes (in Russia, China, India, Thailand) are driven by regional income differences; that is, interregional inequality is the driving force behind income inequality changes. However, the pre-global urban hierarchies appear to be susceptible to change. Rapid growth can be seen all across the city class size spectrum, just as the absence of growth and even decline are present among all size classes – that is, urban size is not related to growth or decline. The cities most likely to be bypassed by globalization are in inland or land-locked regions. Coastal locations are as privileged now as during the colonization period, though simple coastal location is no guarantee of success.[1]

3. Globalization or globalizations?

It is clear that economic globalization has bypassed many countries and cities, perhaps the vast majority of the low income developing nations. Does this mean that there are large parts of the globe that are untouched by globalization? The answer to this question must begin with the recognition of a clear distinction between two contrasting overarching views of globalization. One

[1] It must be noted that there is also a significant literature on interregional convergence (see Sala-i-Martín, 1996). Much of the evidence comes from the developed world (the U.S., the European Union, Australia), with some scattered support from developing nations (see Cardenas and Ponton 1996 on Colombia).

school of thought sees globalization as a homogenizing process, an economic and cultural assault led by the American juggernauts of Cocacolonization and McDonaldization. Some academics (such as Behrman and Rondinelli 1992) have gone so far as to suggest that in order to succeed in the global economy there are certain universal "cultural imperatives" that cities must follow. The opposite view is that globalization promotes, more than anything else, difference and plurality – of culture and values, of taste, of political formations, of identity – and at the same time generates resistance that is empowering and liberating (see Robertson 1992; Hall and Hubbard 1998).[2] This dichotomous view of globalization is reflected in popular accounts such as *Jihad vs. McWorld* (Barber 1995) and *The Lexus and the Olive Tree* (Friedmann 1999), and in academic discourse in terms of the global and the local, and the ungainly term of choice, "glocalization" (see Grant and Short 2002).

I suggest that it is not necessary to resolve these contrasting views of globalization in order to agree that from a *policy* perspective there is significant convergence. Economic globalization is driven by an ideology that was perhaps best enunciated in the tenets of the Washington Consensus, or its kinder, gentler cousin: Universal Convergence (Williamson 1990, 2000). As far as urban development is concerned, this ideological apparatus includes support for markets and trade, democracy and decentralization, and "good governance" based on inclusion, transparency, and social justice. These ideological elements of globalization are far more pervasive than economic globalization, which, as shown before, has barely touched large parts of the developing world. However, as also shown before, this is not the only ideology that has coinage in the global south; the ideology of identity and identity politics may be more persuasive to more people in the developing world than is the ideology of markets, democracy, and good governance. The critical question before us is this: which matters more for urban development in the periphery, the ideology of markets or the ideology of identity and resistance? Given the overwhelming evidence on policy reform – more than one hundred countries have instituted market-oriented structural reforms (Chossudovsky 1997), bilateral and multilateral assistance is almost invariably tied to the opening of markets, decentralization, etc. – it is clear that urban development policy, at the national and local levels, is guided by the ideology of markets.

4. The significance of economic growth for urban development

Before we analyze the impacts of ideological globalization on cities in the periphery, let us establish that the primary goal of all cities is to generate economic growth. If we agree that there is a global hierarchy of cities (from global city to local center), and that the periphery is constituted at several geographical scales, it is necessary to identify the common characteristics of core regions that differ from peripheral regions at different geographical scales. Perhaps the simplest measure is population growth; in the core city regions they are high (3% and above per year) as a result of heavy net

[2] In fact, the anti-globalization protests are themselves seen to be part of globalization (Sen 2002), and can be interpreted to suggest that the U.S. is the most anti-global nation (Robertson 2002).

in-migration; the peripheral cities may also be experiencing population growth, but usually at rates less than national/regional urban growth rates, perhaps at rates even below the rate of natural increase (2% and below). It is clear that one of the primary tasks of urban development institutions in both classes of cities is *growth management*: to provide shelter, services, and work for the thousands of new people who permanently join the city every day. Simultaneously, urban development institutions must also focus on *investment attraction*: to bring work to the city, so that people come and bring dynamic.

It is not clear that these two objectives are different from a policy perspective. A city that manages to keep its traffic flowing smoothly, keeps crime down, collects garbage regularly, and is able to provide adequate housing (whether through public sector projects or by establishing institutions that facilitate real estate markets) is a successful city – one that manages growth well, and by doing so attracts new growth opportunities. It is important to remember that urban size is by itself not a hindrance to effective management or growth attraction. New York, Los Angeles, and London are giant metropolitan areas; yet few suggest that they have been too successful in attracting growth and henceforth should focus only on growth management. In other words, the separation of growth management from growth attraction is a false dichotomy. Virtually all cities in the developing world have growing populations that have to be managed and provided with urban services, whether or not they are growing economically, whether or not they are cities in core regions. All cities in the developing world need to attract investment and generate economic growth as by definition they have a "growth deficit" and the only way to move out of a low-income trap is through economic growth. The bottom line is that every developing nation city seeks economic growth; if this were possible without population growth many cities would choose that option. Indeed, if growth was well distributed, not only between cities in an urban system, but also between urban and rural areas, then growth management would be a minor issue.

5. Ideology and its negative consequences for the periphery

As shown earlier, urban economic growth during globalization is very uneven, in some cases as a result of global flows of capital, often as a result of local political economic conditions. It is these conditions of local political economy that the forces or tenets of ideological globalization seek to influence. Three of these tenets are most important: First, trade and markets are good: cities are natural locations of trade; therefore trade must be encouraged. Markets allocate resources efficiently; hence cities must become more market-oriented. Second, decentralization is also good, it encourages local decision-making and democratic processes; hence governments must decentralize money and power to local bodies (municipalities). Third, good governance (e.g., just, inclusive and transparent government) can cushion the shocks of openness and it can tackle the serious problems of poverty and inequality while making cities more attractive for investment. It follows that good governance should be the goal of local governing bodies. On the surface these are laudable principles indeed. But consider their implications for cities in the periphery.

First, consider the emphasis on trade and markets. In order to trade, a city must produce something that others (cities) want – whether it is plastics or metals or information or entertainment, i.e., there must be some exportable good or service that can be sold at some market (a global market if possible, at least a national or regional market). The problem of the peripheral cities is essentially this: they receive little new productive investment, therefore they cannot competitively produce for global markets, and often the regional markets are so impoverished that they cannot absorb new products with new built-in technologies. These cities are very far down in the value chains of manufacturing, i.e., the value added per unit of labor or capital is very low (Kaplinski 2001). Not only are these cities absent from global systems of production and exchange, but if by some unusual circumstance some of these cities were to become part of global trade in manufactures (say in footwear), the value added would be too low to move these cities out of the periphery.[3] This is at a time when the core cities continue to strengthen their global trading links and keep moving up the value chain. It seems inevitable that opening markets and relying on global trade will increase productivity and incomes in the core cities relative to peripheral cities.

Second, consider decentralization. Decentralization calls for devolution of revenue and authority to local government bodies, which then increasingly become responsible for local services and planning. In theory, this would have the advantage of increased democratization and public participation and curb the influence of large cities and other traditional centers of authority. In practice, however, decentralization creates a new set of problems, which work once again to the detriment of the peripheral cities and regions. In order for decentralization to be effective it is necessary to have supportive institutions and human capital at the local level. Such institutions and human capital are not readily available in even most of the largest cities of the developing world (where formal urban planning as opposed to urban public works or services began as late as the 1960s). Urban planners are not available, urban planning schools do not exist (and where they do exist they tend to be technocratic institutions), and infrastructure finance institutions are virtually unheard of. In such situations what kind of municipal planning and development can small and medium sized cities undertake? What happens and is likely to happen (see the case of Bolivia in Kohl 2002, or China in Kanbur and Zhang 2003) is that the larger cities, despite having to share resources, are better able to take advantage of decentralization and devolution as a result of a freer hand in local decision-making and revenue generation (see World Bank 2000, Tables D4 and D5, on large city advantages in terms of size of local government and revenues raised by it.) It is possible to identify a few exceptions to this statement (in Brazil, China, and India for instance), to identify specific medium-sized cities that have done well in terms of economic growth, but in most cases their successes have arisen from locational advantages and, in rare cases, inspired leadership. In the general case, decentralization leads to

[3] Consider a city like Kanpur in Uttar Pradesh or Bhopal in Madhya Pradesh (both in India). Even by India's limited globalization successes these cities are completely off the radar of investors. Other than their existing trading links (Kanpur, for example, is significant producer of finished leather goods) what new links can they forge and how?

further marginalization of the already disadvantaged, nowhere more so than in the small and medium -sized cities in inland regions.

Finally, consider the principle of good governance. According to the World Bank (2000, 10): "Good governance implies inclusion and representation of all groups in the urban society – and accountability, integrity, and transparency of government actions – in defining and pursuing shared goals." Nothing could be more desirable than these objectives; the question is, how can these objectives be achieved? Fundamentally, good governance hinges on the workings of urban politics. This is a big issue that has occupied political scientists and sociologists working in developed and developing nation contexts. I do not intend to offer any quick summary of that literature here, nor do I intend to fully explore the scope of urban politics in the developing world today. My intent is to raise a few questions on the globalization-urban politics relationship, focusing on two issues: inequality and identity.

It is commonplace now to assume that globalization has led to increases in urban income inequality. However, there is considerable confusion and misinformation on this issue. There is clear evidence of increasing regional inequality in many parts of the world (as suggested in an earlier section in this paper), just as there is some evidence of increasing social or national inequality. But there is practically no evidence on increasing urban inequality in the developing world,[4] not to mention the fact that inequality data for individual cities do not exist. Also consider two facts: First, income distribution patterns are more or less immune to change (in either direction) barring revolution or significant social transition, second, income inequality is notoriously susceptible to mis-measurement (because of poor survey designs and under-reporting by the rich and over-reporting by the poor) and heavily dependent on definitions (of income, income receiving unit, etc.); as a result, income distribution data are rarely comparable over time.

The mechanism via which the inequality increase is expected to have taken place is the technological shift and higher productivity (and resulting higher income) of those sections of the population that are directly involved in global production and/or trade (software and export sector workers). For the sake of argument let us assume that this is possible. In the global core cities the numbers of such workers are so large that even if urban inequality increases, the welfare gains may outweigh the costs of higher inequality. In regional core cities the numbers of such workers are likely to be small enough to make no difference in inequality (for example, in all of India, a well-known technology leader, the number of software sector workers is estimated to be less than 500,000). In the peripheral cities, by definition there are few such high productivity workers. Had there been large numbers of high productivity workers in these cities they may not have remained peripheral. Therefore, urban inequality levels in peripheral regions are unlikely to have changed significantly as a result of globalization. It is possible that some fluctuation may have taken place a result of recessions or poor crop outputs (i.e., related to some temporary phenomenon rather than a structural shift). Therefore, urban inequality is in general not a pressing issue in urban development. Poverty is, and urban welfare policy and urban governance should attempt to

---

[4] Even in China, a well known case of increasing regional and national inequality, urban inequality levels remain at very low levels – between 16 and 20.

address poverty directly rather than attempt to tinker with the distribution pattern. In particular, raising the bogey of inequality in the peripheral cities may do more harm than good.

The issue of identity-based politics is more urgent. In multi-ethnic societies the ethnic composition of cities tends to change quite rapidly as a result of growth. New migrants from different ethnic groups move there for work; this changes the composition of the population and may result in political struggles over control of state resources. In some scenarios these struggles sporadically flare up into ethnic violence (e.g., India, Pakistan, Indonesia, Nigeria, Kenya), and in worse scenarios they result in all-out civil war (in several nations of Africa).[5] Also, in the cities that are not growing, the perceived absence of opportunity and relative ethnic homogeneity leads to parochial regional politics – identity-based politics which morphs into ethnic nationalism, tribalism, separatism, and violence. It is necessary to recognize that one of the ideological counterpoints to economic globalization is identity politics. It is possible for corporate theorists to declare the end of the nation state, and to promote the birth of a neo-utopian "true global marketplace" (Ohmae 1995). But when the GNP of China was $317 while that of Shenzen in China was $5,695 (Ohmae's data; current numbers would be different, but the reliability of Chinese data is so notorious that it is perhaps better to leave the point in very general: vast interurban and interregional income disparities) is it irrational to expect parochialism and jingoism under the banner of that other global invention of the nineteenth century – nationalism?

I do not mean to suggest that the principles of "good governance" necessarily work against the prospects of the peripheral cities and regions. Indeed, urban violence is very much in evidence in many regional core cities too (Mumbai, Ahmadabad, Jakarta). What is worrisome is the possibility of rejection of good governance principles, along with a rejection of globalization in the peripheral cities. In these relatively static, growth-deprived places there are few internal challenges spurred by inter-ethnic competition. Instead we tend to see the continuation of power oligarchies and entrenched interests, which often coalesce into regional ethnic identity politics. Governance takes a backseat to regional mobilization, and in the eyes of investors, foreign and domestic alike, these cities appear to be anachronisms. It is not the nation-state *per se* that appears tired, old, and outdated (as many have suggested, see Rohlen 2002), but the state in the peripheral cities and regions that appears tired, old, and unable to keep up with the dynamic core cities.

6. Conclusions: Urban development in the global periphery

I have argued here that economic globalization has a clear regional dimension – entire regions are either incorporated within global flows or they are almost entirely left out. Hence, the appropriate scale of analysis of marginalization may not be the city but the sub-national region. I have also suggested that the true significance of globalization for urban/regional development may lie in

---

[5] The emerging scholarship on the links between high inequality levels and low growth rates (mediated through inefficient redistributive policies) is of particular relevance here (see Alesina and Rodrik 1994 for an overview).

the globalization of ideas rather than trade. Ideas about the value of markets and trade, the need for political reform through democracy and decentralization, and good governance based on social justice and inclusion, have far greater policy significance and social impact. These ideas, when translated into policies, have effects at urban, regional and national scales. It is possible that the implementation of these ideas creates some real development paradoxes for peripheral cities and regions. I have shown how these ideas can lead to further relative declines in already lagging places. The most pertinent issue in urban development then arises from these paradoxes: if markets, trade, democracy, decentralization, and good governance are all desirable entities, how can they be used to improve absolute and relative welfare conditions in peripheral and marginalized cities and regions? Albert Hirschman's words on the "tunnel effect" now have renewed urgency.

> One might conclude that the tunnel effect will always come into being as, within each social class, those who are not advancing empathize initially with those who are. But this need not happen if each class is composed of ethnic or religious groups that are differentially involved in the growth process... If, in segmented societies, economic advance becomes identified with one particular ethnic or language group or with members of one particular religion or region, then those who are left out or behind are unlikely to experience the tunnel effect: they will be convinced almost from the start of the process that the advancing group is achieving an unfair exploitative advantage over them. (Hirschman 1973, 49)

The challenge now is to find equitable regional solutions within a market framework. A return to the nationalist model of old appears to be out of the question for a number of reasons. But the tension between market orientation and regional divergence has to be mitigated to some degree, or else the benefits of efficient markets may be washed away in bloody conflict at worst, or debilitating distributional struggles at best. It is necessary to renew thinking about approaches that take into account the political economy of peripheral regions.

References

Ahuja V, Bidani B, Ferreira F, Walton M (1997) Everyone's miracle? Revisiting poverty and inequality in East Asia. World Bank, Washington DC

Akita T, Lukman RA (1995) Interregional inequalities in Indonesia: A sectoral decomposition analysis for 1975–92. Bulletin of Indonesian Economic Studies 31:61–81

Alesina A, Rodrik D (1994) Distributive politics and economic growth. Quarterly Journal of Economics 108:465–90

Aswicahyono HH, Bird K, Hill H (1996) What happens to industrial structure when countries liberalize? Indonesia since the mid-1980's. The Journal of Development Studies 32:340–63

Baran P (1957) The Political Economy of Growth. Monthly Review Press, New York

Barber B (1995) Jihad vs. McWorld: How Globalism and Tribalism are Reshaping the World. Ballantine Books, New York

Behrman J, Rondinelli D (1992) The cultural imperatives of globalization: urban economic growth in the twenty-first century. Economic Development Quarterly 6:115–26

Cardenas M, Ponton A (1995) Growth and convergence in Colombia: 1950–1990. Journal of Development Economics 47:5–37

Chakravorty S (2000) How does structural reform affect regional development: Resolving contradictory theory with evidence from India. Economic Geography 76:367–394

Chossudovsky M (1997) The Globalization of poverty: Impacts of IMF and World Bank reforms. Third World Network, Penang, Malaysia
Daniere A (1996) Growth, inequality and poverty in South-east Asia: The case of Thailand. Third World Planning Review 18:373–396
Fan CC (1995) Of belts and ladders: State policy and uneven regional development in post-Mao China. Annals of the Association of American Geographers 85:421–449
Fedorov L (2002) Regional inequality and regional polarization in Russia, 1990–99. World Development 30:443–456
Frank AG (1967) Capitalism and underdevelopment in Latin America. Monthly Review Press, New York
Friedmann TL (1999) The lexus and the olive tree: Understanding globalization. Farrar, Strauss and Giroux, New York
Ghosh B, Marjit S, Neogi C (1998) Economic growth and regional divergence in India: 1960 to 1995. Economic and Political Weekly 33:1623–1630
Gustafsson B, Shi L (2002) Income inequality within and across counties in rural China 1988 and 1995. Journal of Development Economics 69:179–204
Grant R, Short JR (eds) (2002) Globalization and the margins. Palgrave Macmillan, Basingstoke, UK, and New York
Hall T, Hubbard P (1998) The entrepreneurial city. Wiley, Chichester
Hirschman AO (1958) The strategy of economic development. Yale University Press, New Haven
Hirschman AO (1973) The changing tolerance for income inequality in the course of economic development. Quarterly Journal of Economics 87:544–565
Kanbur R, Zhang X (2003) Fifty years of regional inequality in China: A journey through central planning, reform and openness. Paper presented at UNU WIDER Conference on Spatial inequality in Asia, March 2003. Paper downloaded on April 5, 2003 from http://www.wider.unu.edu/conference/conference-2003-1/conference2003-1.htm
Kaplinsky R (2001) Globalisation and unequalisation: What can be learned from value chain analysis. Journal of Development Studies 37:117–146
Kohl B (2002) Stabilizing neoliberalism in Bolivia: Popular participation and privatization. Political Geography 21:449–472
Milanovic B (2002) True world income distribution, 1988 and 1993: First calculation based on household surveys alone. Economic Journal 112:51–92
Myrdal G (1957) Economic theory and underdeveloped regions. Duckworth, London
Ohmae K (1995) The end of the nation state: The rise of regional economies. The Free Press, New York
Pritchett L (1997) Divergence. Big time. Journal of Economic Perspectives 11:3–17
Robertson R (1992) Globalisation. Sage, London
Robertson R (2002) Opposition and resistance to globalization. In: Grant R, Short JR (eds) Globalization and the margins. Palgrave Macmillan, Basingstoke, UK and New York
Rohlen TP (2002) Cosmopolitan cities and nation states: Open economics, urban dynamics, and government in East Asia. Asia/Pacific Research Center, Stanford, Mimeo
Sala-i-Martín X (1996) Regional cohesion: Evidence and theories of regional growth and convergence. European Economic Review 40:1325–1352
Sen A (2002) Globalization, inequality, and global protest. Development 45:11–16
Sjoholm F (2000) Economic recovery in Indonesia: The challenge of combining FDI and regional development. Paper presented at the IRSA International Conference, Jakarta, Mimeo
Williamson J (1990) Latin American adjustment: How much has happened? Institute of International Economics, Washington DC
Williamson J (2000) What should the World Bank think about the Washington Consensus? World Bank Research Observer 15:251–264
Williamson JG (1997) Globalization and inequality, past and present. World Bank Research Observer 12:117–135
World Bank (2000) Cities in transition: World Bank urban and local government strategy. The World Bank, Washington DC
World Bank (2001) World development indicators 2001. The World Bank, Washington DC

II. The Urban Hierarchy

Impact of globalization on cities and city-related policies in India

Om Prakash Mathur

HDFC Chair in Housing and Urban Economics, National Institute of Public Finance and Policy, 18/2, Satsang Vihar Marg, Special Institutional Area, (Near JNU), New Delhi 110 067, India (e-mail: opm@nipfp.org.in)

Abstract. This chapter explores the implications of India's post-1991 liberalization and globalization on the national urban system. Globalization (and the macroeconomic policies associated with it) not only resulted in rapid economic growth but affected cities in different ways, primarily by the growth of foreign direct investment (FDI). The urban population distribution in India reflects the absence of primacy; in fact, the million-plus cities grew more slowly in the 1990s in an era of lower population growth. High-quality residential and office space has been developed on the urban outskirts, fostered by rapidly rising land prices. FDI has focused on a limited set of sectors (including knowledge-based industries), resulting in selective (not unskilled) migration and growth along urban corridors rather than within cities. The macroeconomic reforms and globalization have forced many policy changes at the city level: Private sector involvement in infrastructure development and management; allowing city access to capital markets; and setting up central government funding programs to promote urban structural change. The impacts of globalization on cities (as opposed to the macroeconomic reforms) can be exaggerated: The scale of FDI is low compared with other Asian countries, the direct impacts were geographically concentrated in six larger cities, globalization has not accelerated urban growth, only a few economic sectors have been impacted, and the most obvious changes have been in the built environment (e.g., new buildings) and spatial structure.

1. Introduction

The post-1991 period has seen notable changes in India's macroeconomic policies, with the result that the Indian economy today is far more open and far more integrated with the global system than at any time since the 1960s. External trade has been considerably liberalized. Import substitution which was the centerpiece of the country's development strategy has been substituted by export orientation. The industrial licensing system has been abolished. The erstwhile limitations on foreign investment and capital and technology flows have been eased.

Changes have taken place during the same period in the nature and pattern of urban growth. The economic and spatial structure of cities, particularly the large cities, has begun to reflect the changing composition of the global and regional markets. New townships with high quality infrastructure have sprung up on the periphery of large cities. Continuing relevance of public provision of city-level infrastructural services is being increasing questioned, and has led to, in several instances, a major restructuring of the institutional and financial systems.

Is there a link between the changes that have taken place in cities and city-related policies and the globalization of the Indian economy? To what extent are the changes at the level of cities attributable to, or influenced by, the post-1991 macroeconomic policies? To what extent have cities restructured themselves to global codes and regulations? This paper attempts to address these questions. The paper recognizes that causalities between macroeconomic policies and cities are often difficult to establish, more so in the case of India which has witnessed, during the same period, strong trends towards decentralization of power and re-emergence of local governments as decision-making entities for several of the city-level functions.[1] Recent changes in the functioning of cities are the cumulative result of the processes of globalization and decentralization.

The paper is divided into three sections. Section one gives a brief account of the process of globalization in India, referring to the key changes in its macroeconomic policies, and their impact on the overall economic growth. This section looks at how globalization has spread out to different states and major cities in the country. Section two of the paper analyses the nature and pattern of urban growth during the post-1991 period, and follows it up with an examination of the changes that have occurred in the country's urban economic structure and the functions and role of major cities. It dwells on how the opening up of the Indian economy has affected land prices in major cities and led to the development of new townships and urban corridors with high quality infrastructure. This section also provides examples of cities that have been able to redefine their roles in the emerging global scenario. It discusses the new institutional and financing arrangements that have emerged as an alternative to public provision and public financing of city-level infrastructure and services. Several observations relating to the scale and depth of globalization, and the potential of globalization in reshaping the economy of cities are made in the concluding section of the paper.

2. The emerging global context of the Indian economy

Globalization in India, expressed in terms of a freer flow of goods and services, capital, technology, and information, owes itself to a macroeconomic crisis that erupted in 1991. Until then, India's economy grew and developed within a highly closed and protected domestic market, relying to a large extent on domestic production of goods and services, domestic savings, and indigenous technology. Its links with the global markets were weak and

[1]See, Constitution (seventy-fourth) Amendment Act (1992) on Municipalities, Government of India, New Delhi.

Table 1. Economic components of globalization in India

Indicators	1990	2000
Merchandize exports		
• Volume US $ million	17,975	42,295
• % Manufactures	71	79
Merchandize imports		
• Volume US $ million	23,642	50,455
• % Food	3	7
• % Fuels	27	31
• % Manufactures	51	51
Exports of commercial services		
• Volume US $ million	4,610	17,670
• % Others*	45.4	71.4
Imports of commercial services		
• Volume US $ million	5,943	19,601
• % Others*	35.9	45.8
Exports of goods and services		
• Volume US $ million	23,028	63,764
• As % GDP	7	14
Imports of goods and services		
• Volume US $ million	31,485	75,656
• As % of GDP	10	17
External debt		
• Volume US $ million	83,628	100,367
• Debt service as % of GNI	2.6	2.2
• Debt service as % of exports of goods and services	32.4	12.8
Foreign direct investment (FDI)		
• Volume US $ million	162	2315
• % of world's total FDI	0.08	0.20
Gross private capital flows		
• % of GDP	0.8	3.0
Stock market		
• Volume US $ million	38,567	110,396
• % of GDP	6.9	48.4
Gross international reserves		
• US $ million	5,637	41,059
Tariff barriers		
• Simple mean tariff	80.2	32.8
• Weighted mean tariff	69.9	32.7

Source: World Development Indicators, 2002.
* Others include such activities as insurance and financial services, international telecommunications, courier services, computer data, professional and technical services and the like.

limited. In 1990, India's merchandise imports formed 0.67% of the world's merchandise imports; exports were even lower, 0.52% of the world's total exports. Foreign direct investment (FDI) in 1990 amounted to US $162 million.[2] The average nominal tariff on imports was 125%, with a peak rate of 353%. Domestically, the public sector controlled and managed the key strategic sectors of the Indian economy.

In 1991, triggered by large and unsustainable spending during the 1980s and a sharp fall in foreign exchange reserves, combined with the possibility of

[2]See for figures.The World Bank (2002) World Development Indicators. Washington D. C.

Table 2. Distribution of foreign director investment (FDI) and foreign technical collaboration (FTC) approved between August 1991 to April 2002 (major)

States	Amount approved (Rs.million)	% of total approved amount
Andhra Pradesh	130,377	4.69
Bihar	7,395	0.27
Gujarat	183,523	6.60
Haryana	35,193	1.27
Karnataka	214,470	7.71
Kerala	15,245	0.55
Madhya Pradesh	92,273	3.32
Maharashtra	485,342	17.45
Orissa	82,290	2.96
Punjab	19,684	0.71
Rajasthan	30,047	1.08
Tamil Nadu	232,095	8.34
Uttar Pradesh	47,903	1.72
West Bengal	87,304	3.14
Delhi	334,933	12.04
Other smaller states and territorics	–	1.37
Others (state not indicated)	–	26.80
Total	2,781,806	100.00

Source: Secretariat for Industrial Assistance, Government of India. Newsletter XI (1): May 2002.

a default on repayment of external debt, the Government of India opted in favor of a policy of macroeconomic stabilization and structural adjustment. A stabilization policy meant reducing the fiscal deficit, improving the balance of payments position, and controlling inflation, without causing any adverse impact on real income and output. Accordingly, the Indian rupee was devalued and a program of fiscal retrenchment and credit squeeze was undertaken. Several import controls were kept in place so as not to affect the balance of payments position. However, as a part of structural reform, policies governing external trade were liberalized, initially by moving from a system of quantitative restrictions to price-based mechanisms, and later by introducing a negative list that described goods which were subjected to import controls, and reducing the import tariff. Industrial licensing except for a short list of industries relating to security and strategic concerns was abolished. Conditions for foreign direct investment were relaxed. The Statement of Industrial Policy (1991) reduced the number of industries reserved for the public sector, and introduced what it called a flexible location policy for cities of more than one-million population where industries required "industrial regeneration". Other measures such as restructuring of public enterprises, privatization of public services, and dismantling of the publicly-administered pricing regime were simultaneously introduced in order to improve productivity and enhance competitiveness of industrial enterprises.[3]

[3]For a fuller discussion of the process of globalization in India see. Jagdish Bhagwati and T. N. Srinivasan (1993) India's economic reforms, Government of India; and Vijay Joshi and I. M. D. Little (1996) India's economic reforms, 1991–2001. Oxford University Press, Delhi.

Table 3. Share of seven metropolitan cities in foreign direct investment (FDI) January 1994 to March 2002

City	Amount (Rs.million)	% in total FDI
Delhi	324,360	12.22
Mumbai	256,514	9.67
Bangalore	163,750	6.17
Chennai	118,580	4.47
Hyderabad	37,961	1.43
Kolkata	30,739	1.16
Ahmedabad	21,679	0.82

Source: ibid. 2002.

The impact of these policy changes was swift and substantial. The value of external trade increased from US$17.9 billion in 1990, to nearly US$35 billion in 1996, and US$42 billion in 2000. Annual foreign direct investment (FDI) rose to US$3.2 billion in 1997, and has since then ranged between US$2.1 billion and US$2.5 billion. Trade and foreign direct investment have become an important source of economic growth. The volume of stock market transactions increased to nearly US$110 billion in 2000. Foreign exchange reserves are currently placed at US$59.2 billion (2002).

The size of the Indian economy has grown substantially over the past decade. The country's GDP growth rate has been consistent in the period following 1992–1993, and is being maintained at an average annual rate of 6.0%, although concerns have been expressed about falling growth rate in the last two years. The current account deficit which peaked to 3.2% of GDP has declined, and is being maintained at about 1% of GDP. Global recessionary trends have not affected the Indian economy in a substantial way.

Trade and foreign direct investment (FDI) which are core measures of globalization are important factors in economic growth and development. States and cities compete for opportunities created by the expanding trade and foreign direct investment (FDI). How has globalization spread out to different states and cities? While public accounts for exports, imports and balance of trade are reported and compiled at the national level, it is possible to analyze the state-level distribution of FDI. Table 2 that provides information on the distribution of FDI shows that nearly US$27.8 billion of FDI has been approved for India since August 1991.[4] Of this, 58% has been garnered by six states, namely, Maharashtra (17.45%), Delhi (12.04%), Tamil Nadu (8.34%), Karnataka (7.71%), Gujarat (6.60%) and Andhra Pradesh (4.69%). Several other states, notwithstanding their size and larger markets, have not able to take advantage of the globalization process.

Special tabulations covering the period 1994 to 2002 show that within the states, cities compete for opportunities provided by foreign direct investment (FDI). The shares of seven largest metropolitan cities in FDI, shown below, are substantial, being around 36%. Mumbai's share in the total FDI

[4]This level of FDI is a fraction of the total world's foreign direct investment. In 2000, it formed only 0.08% of the world's total FDI. It is now estimated to be 0.2 to 0.25% of the world's total FDI.

approved during January 1994 to March 2002 was placed at 9.67% of the total which was exceeded only by Delhi whose share was 12.22%. Bangalore accounts for 6.2% of the total approved FDI which has contributed to the development of competency and specialization in software and information technology. Globalization as measured by FDI has thus been spatially uneven, with several states and cities having garnered a larger share compared to others. The locational pattern of FDI in India has followed the trend of domestic investment. Several scholars have attributed the regional unevenness in growth and development to globalization and recent macroeconomic policies.[5] This paper does not propose to examine this aspect of globalization; rather it focuses on presenting the changes that have taken place in cities, and later exploring the links of these changes with the globalization processes.

3. Cities and city-level policies: A survey

A considerable body of literature addressing the urban and city-level impacts of globalization has been published in recent years, suggesting that globalization has a profound impact on cities. Many cities are sites of international transactions. Moreover, as Savitch has noted, "one way or another, all major cities are affected by globalization and its paradigmatic motif".[6] As markets become larger and more open, the agglomerative features of cities make them the natural and strategic centers in the development process. Cities provide the necessary critical spaces and possess the infrastructure to support the new activities. The ability to process capital, availability of financial services, access to capital markets, and proximity to the sources of information and investment have become important characteristics of major cities.

Cities have historically been viewed as part of a hierarchical system of settlements, and are rank-ordered according to population size. As economies have opened up, and are in the process of adapting economic activities and land uses to globalism, the key factors are the capacity of cities to generate new activities and develop synergies with capital, high technology, and information. In what way have the hierarchical system of settlements changed since the opening up of the Indian economy? To what extent have cities been able to adapt their economies and spatial structures to meet global needs? To what extent have they restructured and realigned their infrastructure related policies? This section addresses these issues.

3.1. Urban growth in the post-1991 era

India has a larger network of cities and towns. In 1991, the network consisted of twenty-three cities with a population of over one million, 300 cities with a population ranging between 100,000 and one million, and nearly 4290 towns.

---

[5]N. Singh and T. N. Srinivasan (2002) Indian federalism, economic reform and globalization, Draft mimeo

[6]H. V. Savitch, "Cities in a Global Era: A New Paradigm for the Next Millennium", in Michael Cohen et al. (eds), 1996. Preparing for the Urban Future. Published by the Woodrow Wilson Center Press, Washington D. C.

Table 4. Urban growth, 1991–2001

Year	Urban population (million)	% of total	% change
1991	217.61	25.71	–
2001	285.35	27.78	31.13

Table 5. Share of city's population in national and regional urban population

City	% of national urban		% of state urban	
	1991	2001	1991	2001
Mumbai	5.79	5.74	41.20	39.92
Kolkata	5.06	4.63	48.55	58.78
Delhi	3.87	4.48	89.96	92.96
Chennai	2.49	2.25	28.19	23.57
Bangalore	1.90	1.99	29.40	31.75
Hyderabad	2.00	1.94	23.99	26.97

Categorized as a low-urbanized country, India has been urbanizing at an average annual growth rate of 3.1 to 3.2% which, although comparable with the growth rate observed for the less developed countries, is 1.1 percentage points lower compared with the average for Southeast Asia.

In 2001, the network of cities and towns expanded to comprise thirty-five cities with over one million population, 388 cities in the population size category of 100,000 and one million, and approximately 4700 towns. The emerging pattern of urban growth is characterized by three features:

1. *Declining urban population pressures*. Urban population growth during the 1991–2001 period dipped to 31.13% from 36.47% registered in the decade proceeding 1991. The level of urbanization which was projected to cross the 30% threshold, inched up to 27.78% in 2001.
2. *Lowering of the population growth rates of cities with over one-million population*. Although the number of cities in this size category rose from 23 to 35 and the population share from 32.6 per cent in 1991 to nearly 38 per cent in 2001, their overall growth rates in the post-1991 period have been lower compared to the earlier decade. The average annual growth rate of Mumbai declined sharply to 2.62 per cent from a high of 4.24 per cent in 1981–91. Similarly, the population growth of Hyderabad during the 1991–2001 decade was nearly 55 per cent lower in comparison with the earlier decade. Delhi, however, recorded a high annual growth of 4.18 per cent, surpassed by the growth of five other cities of which three acquired the one-million status for the first time in 2001.
3. *Absence of primacy*. Unlike most developing countries where a single city commands a disproportionately large proportion of population and economic activities in relation to the second largest city, India's urban system is spatially dispersed, and is not characterized by primacy. Moreover, the primacy factor has weakened in the country. Mumbai's population weight in the country's total urban population has declined from 5.79 in 1991 to 5.74 in 2001, and that of Kolkata from 5.06 to 4.63 during the same period.

Table 6. Sectoral break-up of foreign direct investment, August 1991 to April 2002

Sector	% of with total FDI approved
Metallurgical industry	5.54
Fuels (Power & Oil Refinery)	27.74
Electrical equipment (Incl. S/W & Elec.)	9.83
Telecommunications	19.87
Transportation	7.40
Services	6.25
Hotel and Tourism	1.75
Others	21.62

The importance of Chennai and Hyderabad, in population terms, has also dipped in the post-1991 period. In the context of the region of their location, however, larger cities with the exception of Mumbai and Chennai have reinforced their primate position since 1991.

The declining population pressures combined with the lower growth rates of large cities have given rise to the question as to why did the rate of urban population in India decline during a period of relatively high economic growth, outward looking economic policies, and greater reliance on market forces for development? Apart from recognizing that an open economy and globalization do not necessarily accelerate urban growth or push the growth of large cities, two explanations – still untested – have been advanced. One: the nature of globalization in India itself. It is argued that the nature of globalization in India has been such that it has led to selective migration as distinct from the commonly observed rural-urban and urban-urban migration. The composition of FDI as would be seen from Table 6 is weighed in favor of such sectors as power and oil refineries, electrical equipment including computer hardware and software and electronics, telecommunications, and the service sector including hotel and restaurants and the transportation sector. These sectors have accounted for nearly 73% of the total approved FDI. None of these sectors are likely to generate a high level demand for unskilled migrant labor.

Second, urban population growth occurred during the 1991-2001 period, not wholly within the legal jurisdiction of cities but along transport axes and corridors. Emergence of urban corridors[7], particularly originating from Mumbai, Ahmedabad, Chennai, Bangalore and Hyderabad, linking several important urban centers, and absorbing new investments is an extremely important feature of urban growth of the post-1991 period. As noted in a recent study, "the location of new investments in industry and infrastructure in the context of liberalization of the economy after 1991 is shaping the spatial pattern along the corridors".[8] These corridors are composed of a set of

[7]Important corridors are Mumbai-Thane-Ahmedabad; Mumbai-Pune-Ahamadnagar-Aurangabad-Jalgaon; Mahesena-Gandhinagar-Ahmedabad-Vodadara-Bharuch-Surat-Valsad; Chennai-Krishnagiri-Hosur; Bangalore-Belgaum; and Hyderabad-Vijaywada. See for details, Centre for Policy Research (2001) The future of urbanization. New Delhi.

[8]Centre for Policy Research (2001). The future of urbanization: Spread and shape in selected states. New Delhi.

smaller scale urban corridors and account for a significant proportion of new investments. In Maharashtra, Greater Mumbai together with adjoining districts whose boundaries overlap with the urban corridors accounted for nearly 61% of new investments. In Gujarat, about 50% of the investments are in the central-south corridor which runs through Ahmedabad-Vadodara-Surat and Valsad. In Tamil Nadu, Chennai together with Chengalpattu have attracted the largest share of the total investment (32%) in industry, manufacturing, and services. This pattern of urban growth has raised new questions about the relevance of city size as a measure of determining the importance of a city.

3.2. Urban economic structure

The alignment of the Indian economy to global and regional markets has important implications for urban and city-level economic structure. Cities are in the process of adapting to new economic realities. City-level economic development is slowly shifting away from industrial activities to more sophisticated knowledge base systems. Several cities have built on newly developed technologies to emerge as major financial services centers.

The post-1991 period is marked by a significantly slower growth of formal sector employment.[9] Compared to an average annual growth of 2.04% in the 1983–1993 period, the employment growth since 1993 has been around 1% annually. Although much of it is explained by the withdrawal and downsizing of the public sector from several sectors, the private sector employment too has shown little buoyancy in the post-1993 period. Private sector employment is reported to have registered an average annual growth of 1.87%. In line with the global trends, much of the new employment generation (73%) has taken place in the services sector. Fifty per cent of new employment has taken place in manufacturing activities, while primary sector employment has declined by 23% during this period.

The Economic Census of 1998 shows significant shifts in the country's urban economic structure. First: while the share of manufacturing in total urban employment continues to be high, it is no longer the growth sector of the country's urban economy. Compared to a 45% increase in aggregate urban employment during 1990–1998, employment in manufacturing rose by 22%. Second: retail trade has registered an extraordinary growth of over 180 per cent, with the result that from a relatively small share of urban employment in 1990, the share of retail trade has risen to nearly 25% in 1998. Noticeable gains are noted in construction, transport and communication sectors.

The mobility of the factors of production alters the structure and location of employment, use of technologies, and pattern of trade and investment. This means that because of technological advances in communications, information exchange, and transportation, domestic and multinational companies are free to locate anywhere. Some cities are able to retain the manufacturing base and generate additional activities and promote high technology. Ahmedabad and Delhi have not only retained but reinforced the

[9]A. Mathur and P. S. Raikhy (2002) Economic liberalization and its implications for employment. Deep and Deep Publication Pvt. Ltd., New Delhi.

Table 7. India's urban economic structure (Non-primary sector employment)

Sector	% Share in urban employment		% Change 1990–1998
	1990	1998	
Mining and quarrying	0.56	0.40	4.8
Manufacturing	30.16	25.43	22.5
Electricity, gas & water	0.82	0.74	30.8
Construction	0.61	0.82	97.9
Wholesale trade	3.06	3.18	51.4
Retail trade	12.81	24.90	182.4
Restaurant and hotels	4.23	4.28	47.1
Transport	2.51	2.95	70.5
Storage & warehousing	1.05	0.47	64.8
Communications	1.36	1.55	65.3
Financial, insurance & real estate	6.30	5.51	27.3
Community social and personal services	36.38	29.75	18.8
Others	0.17	0.01	56.8
Total	100.00	100.00	45.29

Table 8. Economic structure of cities: Selected sectors

Cities	Manufacturing sector		Communications		Financial, insurance & real estate service sector	
	1990	1998	1990	1998	1990	1998
Ahmedabad	11.99	27.94	0.70	0.96	11.00	5.03
Bangalore	24.22	23.87	0.81	1.40	6.58	11.64
Chennai	16.75	15.67	1.66	1.87	9.89	13.62
Delhi	30.62	41.78	2.56	2.86	9.64	6.03
Kolkata	22.51	18.20	1.54	1.53	13.95	7.50
Mumbai	28.91	17.89	1.70	2.51	1.12	13.82

manufacturing base, the former by upgrading the old manufacturing industries and the latter by the most extraordinary expansion in building up the new generation, information base and white goods industries. On the other hand, there has occurred a major transformation in the employment base of Mumbai. Financial, insurance and real estate services account for nearly 13.8 per cent of total employment, affirming the place of Mumbai as an overwhelmingly dominant financial centre not only for India but for Asia as well. Also, the triangle Mumbai-Pune-Nashik provides a dispersed industrial region that sustains the service economy of Mumbai. The services involved are classified as accountancy, law, advertising, finance, banking, research and development. Bangalore has acquired, since the 1991 reform, the status of India's Silicon Valley, with an extraordinarily large concentration of activities relating to software, communications, and information technology. Hyderabad's economic structure is orienting itself towards high value added export and research functions.

4. Globalization and spatial structure

The forces which shape and determine the organization and allocation of space in cities are necessarily constrained by the existing built environment.

The development and the flexibility with which changes can be affected in the built environment are crucial to the relative success or failure of the competitive position of cities in the emerging global economy. Moreover, the dismantling of barriers to the international movement of capital, liberalization of financial markets, and developments in information technology have made investment in real estate development property a viable option. In terms of the competitive global economy, locational characteristics are perhaps the most important factor in the investment decision.

Cities in India are in the midst of restructuring of space, in terms of both use and form. Residential areas in the central and sub-central districts of such cities as Delhi, Bangalore and Hyderabad are being transformed into commercial spaces. Shopping malls have sprung up replacing the old pattern of retail trading. Commercial and office space has been added to accommodate the branch offices of multinationals and domestic companies and financing institutions. In Bangalore, nearly 92,000 sq. meters of work space and 200,000 sq. meters of living space were added between 1994–2001.

As interesting feature of the impact of post-1991 developments is the mushrooming of high quality residential and office space bordering major cities. In Delhi, several new settlements consisting of 500–1,000 residential dwelling units with quality infrastructure and back-up services and office space have been developed to accommodate the offices of multinationals, airlines, and financial institutions. In Bangalore, at least seven such townships in sizes ranging between 15 and 220 acres have been established during the post-1994 period. Specialized parks for software and technology have come up in Hyderabad, Vashi and Mahapi near Mumbai, and Bangalore. Golf courses have been added around Delhi, Hyderabad and Bangalore.

Globalization has affected the land and housing markets of major cities. During the peak years of economic reform and the years during which the foreign investment flows crossed US$3 billion and trade as a proportion of GDP touched 19.5%, the land prices of commercial space in Mumbai's heartland reached a high of Rs. 32,500/ sq. feet.[10] Between 1992 and 1995, land prices of commercial space registered an increase of 360%, and of over 100% in residential space. In Delhi, during the same period, prices of land rose sharply, registering an increase of over 580% for commercial space in Mumbai and nearly 270% for residential space. While at one level, such a sharp increase in land prices reflects the scarcity value of commercial and residential space following the opening up of the Indian economy, at the other level it shows the constraints within the land and housing market operate in the country. Absence of appropriate reform in policies that govern land markets in India is noted to be one of the key constraints in reaping the fuller benefits of the globalization process.

5. City-related policies

City-related policies in India, i.e. policies relating to the allocation and development of land, provision of city-level services like water supply, sew-

[10]At the then prevailing exchange rate, land price was US$900/ sq. foot for commercial space in Mumbai and US$605/ sq. foot for residential space.

Table 9. Public sector engagement in city level services

Services/Tasks	City
Sanitation and public health	
• Conservancy/drain cleansing/sanitation/ maintenance of STP.	Guwahati, Bangalore, Jodhpur, New Bombay, Ludhiana
• Construction and maintenance of toilets.	Faridabad, Delhi, Hubli Dharwad, Aurangabad, Kalyan, Jaipur
• Mosquito control.	Cochin
Solid waste management	
• Garbage collection/disposal/street cleaning.	Guwahati, Ahmedabad, Rajkot, Baroda, Bangalore, Cochin, Bombay, Pune, Jalandhar, Amritsar, Ludhiana, Jaipur
• Compost plant, solid waste conversion.	Baroda, Kalyan
Water supply	
• Maintenance of water supply.	New Bombay
Roads and streets	
• Road maintenance	Bangalore, Cochin, Jaipur
• Street lighting	Faridabad, Ranchi, Rajkot, Jodhpur, New Bombay
Gardens and parks	
• Development and maintenance of garden/parks/ playgrounds/sports complex/swimming pools	Aurangabad, Rajkot, Baroda, Bangalore, Faridabad, Cochin, Bombay, Pune, Jalandhar, Amritsar, Ludhiana, Jaipur, Ranchi, Kalyan, New Bombay
• Social forestry, tree planting.	Baroda, Rajkot
Others	
• Maintenance of libraries	Faridabad
• Bus terminals/shelters	Ranchi, Cochin
• Market development	Ahmedabad, Kalyan
• Land development	Faridabad
• Maintenance of vehicles	Rajkot

erage systems, solid waste disposal, and citywide road systems are determined by state governments. The role of the Central government in matters relating to land or service-related policies is severely restricted. For reasons of externalities, the city governments hold the primary responsibility for service provision, often with financial support from the state governments.

The level at which the city governments are able to provide and maintain services, policies with respect to allocation of land for different uses and building permits and regulations with respect to change of land use constitute the base for the physical development of cities. Until 1991, city governments exercised this role, often with unsatisfactory and frustrating results. In 1991, for instance, the country reported a shortage of nearly 10 million urban dwelling units. It also reported that 18% of the households had no access to safe water and nearly 40% of the urban households were without basic sanitation. The finances of city governments were in shambles, and with the exception of a few, most urban governments depended on the state governments for meeting their recurrent account requirements. Few city governments, if any, had surpluses to contribute towards building new infrastructure and services.

Changes in the post-1991 period in city-related policies have sprung up out of recognition that first, the public sector does not have the needed capacity to deliver and manage city-level services, and second, it does not have the required financial resources to meet the service deficits and provide incremental infrastructure. Buoyed by the changes in the macroeconomic policies, important directional changes have taken place in city-level policies:

1. *Engagement of the private sector in city infrastructure development and management.* Several cities have entered into contracts and partnerships with the private sector in such services as solid waste management, water billing, maintenance of street lights, and local tax collection in the expectation that it will result in greater efficiency. A sample of cities which have begun to use the private sector is shown in table below.
2. *Accessing capital markets.* Faced with resource compression and the inability on the part of the state governments to continue to finance city-level infrastructural services, a number of cities have entered the capital market. For city governments which have historically depended on public financing of city-level infrastructure, accessing the capital market by pledging the future streams of revenues or putting their own assets as collateral is a watershed development of the post-1991 period. Although the number of cities which have financed their activities with capital market funds is few, it has opened up a new chapter in making use of markets for infrastructure financing.
3. *Establishment of funds for initiating structural changes at city levels.*[11] Starting from the proposition that economic growth and poverty alleviation efforts are dependent on the efficiency of cities, the Government of India have set up two dedicated Funds, called, the City Challenge Fund (CCF) and Urban Reform Incentive Fund (URIF). The purpose of the Funds is to create incentives for effecting changes at the city level in support of the national agenda of economic growth and poverty reduction. The Funds assume that restructuring the economy of cities is essential for sustained improvement in the delivery of city-level infrastructure and services. These

Table 10. Local government finance: A paradigm shift

From	To
Negotiated intergovernmental transfers.	Rule or formulae based intergovernmental transfers to allow financial stability and predictability to local governments.
Grant financing of municipal infrastructure.	Debt financing of municipal infrastructure.
Subsidized prices of basic municipal infrastructure and services on externality grounds	Application of the principle of cost recovery for pricing municipal infrastructure and services.
Land treated as fixed assets.	Sale of land use rights for raising resources.
Other municipal assets held on books.	Assets to be leveraged for mobilizing resources.
Municipal provision of services.	Public-private partnership in the provision of municipal services and infrastructure.
Rents to form the principal basis for estimating annual rateable value and property taxation.	Area characteristics or capital valuation to form the basis for property taxation.
Finances and functioning of municipalities based on directions of higher tiers of government.	Incentive funds for municipal governments to undertake reforms for improving finances and functioning.

[11]Government of India (2002) Urban sector reforms: A new paradigm. New Delhi, mimeo.

policy changes are a landmark development and reflect a paradigm shift in the functioning of cities. The following Table 10 attempts to capture the shift.

6. Conclusions: Exploring the links between globalization and cities

The sections above have reviewed the changes since 1991 in the country's macroeconomic policies, and correspondingly in the demographic, economic, and spatial profile of urban settlements and cities. Also reviewed are the changes in policies relating to the institutional and financing arrangements for service provision and management. Several questions arise: are the changes in macroeconomic policies and restructuring of cities linked? What has globalization done to cities? Has globalization accelerated urban growth or changed the pattern of urban growth? Has it affected the urban economic structure and economic and spatial structure of cities? Has it influenced city-related policies?

As a preface to attempting to explore the links between globalization and cities, it is necessary to take note of the fact that the scale of globalization in India as measured by trade and foreign direct investment has been small compared with most Asian countries. In 2000, while the foreign direct investment (FDI) to India amounted to US$2.3 billion, the same was US$38 billion for China, US$9.2 billion for the Republic of Korea, US$2.0 billion for the Philippines, and US$3.4 billion for Thailand.[12] In terms of external trade too, a similar situation is observed.

Second: globalization of the Indian economy in the sense of the opening up of the sectors to external influences and competition has focused on trade, capital and technology inflows, and balance of payments. It has not percolated to other sectors, mainly on account of the federal character of the Indian economy where other sectors fall within the jurisdiction of state governments, with little or no federal control. Thus, globalization has not been extended to land and water which are crucial for freeing the city economies from the rigidities of the existing laws and regulations and which would help realize the globalization goals and objectives. Absence of reforms in these spheres has slowed down the participation of cities in the process of globalization.

Third: much of the external trade transactions and foreign direct investment are concentrated in six states, namely, Maharashtra, Delhi, Tamil Nadu, Karnataka, Andhra Pradesh, and Gujarat and, within these states, in major cities of Mumbai, Delhi, Chennai, Bangalore, Hyderabad, and Ahmedabad. Globalization has followed the locational directions of domestic investments. Given the small scale of globalization, the expected impact on restructuring of cities has, at best, been marginal.

Reviews of the post-1991 city-level changes show interesting results. One: expansion in trade, capital flows, and consistently high economic growth as embodied in GDP, has not led to any acceleration in the overall urban growth or growth of large cities. Two: globalization has not resulted in any expansion of overall employment opportunities. It has selectively led to expansion of opportunities in retail trade, communications, and financial, banking and real

[12]The World Bank (2002), op. cit.

estate services. Third: globalization has meant an increased demand for residential, office and commercial space. On a limited scale, residential space has been converted into commercial malls; new shopping plazas have sprung up, and townships with quality infrastructure have been developed around major cities to accommodate the branch offices of multinational and domestic companies. Four: globalization has influenced city-level policies wherein new institutional and financial arrangements are being forged to improve service delivery and management and enhance city-level productivity.

An overall assessment of city-level changes is that these are few and limited. City transformation has not occurred. With the exception of new physical development and some spatial restructuring, no landmark shifts have occurred in urban form. Moreover, the changes appear to be isolated and "add-on", rather than signaling a structural shift in the economy of cities. The basic postulate that major improvements in infrastructural services can occur only if they are undertaken within the context of city economies is still in an infant stage.

This paper provides a preliminary assessment of the links between globalization and cities. Unlike in other countries where systematic research on the impact of globalization on cities has been conducted for nearly 5–7 years under the aegis of the United Nations University[13], and where a much better level of understanding has been reached on the linkages, no such research has been done in India and other South Asian economies. In what different ways can globalization reshape the economy of cities, and, in turn, be reinforced by cities is a subject which is neither acknowledged as important nor adequately understood.

References

Cohen MA (1990) Macroeconomic adjustment and the City. Cities. February 1990

Cohen MA, Ruble BA, Tulchin JS, Garland AM (1996) Preparing for the urban future global pressures and local forces. The Woodrow Wilson Center Press, Washington DC

Fuchs RJ, Brennan E, Chamie J, Lo F-c, Uitto JI (1994) Mega-City growth and the future. The United Nations University Press, Tokyo

Hall P (1988) Cities of tomorrow. Blackwell Publishers. Oxford, UK

Harris N, Fabricius I (1996) Cities and structural adjustment. UCL Press, London

Knight RV, Gappert G (eds) (1989) Cities in a global society (Urban Affairs Annual Reviews. Vol. 35). Sage Publications, Beverly Hills, CA

Lo F-C, Marcotullio PJ (eds) (2001) Globalization and the sustainability of cities in -the Asia Pacific Region. The United Nations University Press, Tokyo

Lo F-C, Yeung Y-m (eds) (1998) Globalization and the world of large cities. The United Nations University Press, Tokyo

Lo F-C, Yeung Y-m (eds) (1996) Emerging world cities in Pacific Asia. The United Nations University Press, Tokyo

McGee TG, Robinson IM (1995) The Mega-Urban regions of Southeast Asia. UBC Press, Vancouver

Rondinelli D et al. The changing forces of urban economic development: Globalization and city competitiveness in the 21st century. Cityscape, A Journal of Policy Development and Reseach

---

[13] F. Lo and P. J. Marcotullio (2001) Globalization and the sustainability of cities in the Asia Pacific Region. The United Nations University, Tokyo; and Fu-chen Lo and Yue-man Yeung (1998) Globalization and the world of large cities. The United Nations University, Tokyo.

Sassen S (1991) Urban impact of economic globalization. Woodrow Wilson International Center for Scholars,Washington DC
The World Bank (2002), World Development Indicators. Washington D.C
Yeung Y-m (2000) Globalization and networked societies: Urban-Regional change in Pacific Asia. University of Hawaii Press, Hwaii, USA

Appendix 1.

Table A1. Population growth rates of one-million cities, 1981–1991 and 1991–2001

City	Population (million)	Average annual growth rate %	
	2001	1981–1991	1991–2001
Mumbai	16.37	4.24	2.62
Kolkata	13.22	1.81	1.82
Delhi	12.79	3.85	4.18
Chennai	6.42	2.34	1.69
Bangalore	5.69	3.46	3.20
Hyderabad	5.53	5.34	2.41
Ahmedabad	4.52	2.62	3.11
Pune	3.75	3.92	4.08
Surat	2.81	5.08	6.15
Kanpur	2.69	2.14	2.82
Jaipur	2.32	4.02	4.24
Lucknow	2.27	5.05	3.08
Nagpur	2.12	2.45	2.42
Patna	1.71	1.79	4.42
Indore	1.64	2.86	3.96
Vadodara	1.49	4.04	2.90
Bhopal	1.45	4.61	3.10
Coimbatore	1.45	2.10	2.44
Ludhiana	1.40	5.11	3.25
Kochi	1.35	5.08	1.70
Agra*	1.32	2.38	3.31
Vishakapatnam	1.30	5.60	2.70
Varanasi	1.21	2.57	1.62
Madurai	1.19	1.86	0.84
Meerut*	1.17	4.48	3.20
Nashik*	1.15	4.93	4.61
Jabalpur*	1.12	1.60	2.31
Jamshedpur*	1.10	1.98	2.83
Asansol*	1.09	4.19	3.55
Dhanbad*	1.06	1.74	2.63
Faridabad*	1.05	6.24	5.31
Allahabad*	1.05	2.62	2.18
Amritsar*	1.01	1.75	3.54
Vijayawada*	1.10	3.21	1.78
Rajkot*	1.00	3.86	4.24
Average for 35 cities		3.33	2.92
Average for 23 cities**		3.36	2.88

* Cities which acquired the status of a one million city in 2001.
** Cities which had one million population in 1991 and also in 2001.

The impacts of globalization on the urban spatial-economic system in Korea

Sang-Chuel Choe

Graduate School of Environmental Studies, Seoul National University, Seoul 151-742, South Korea (e-mail: choesc@snu.ac.kr)

Abstract. This chapter discusses trends in Korean urbanization during the era of increasing globalization. Much of the earlier globalization bypassed Korea except in the sense that its industrial growth was propelled forward by export expansion. More recently, however, Korea has had to face the impacts of globalization on the internal dynamics of the Korean economy and its cities: trade liberalization, market opening and foreign direct investment. This has resulted in severe adjustment problems in terms of economic structure (the transition to high-order services has probably been too slow) and the urban hierarchy (reinforcing the larger cities, especially the Seoul metropolitan region). There are opportunities and goals, e.g. to attract global events (in sports and culture) and to build up Seoul as the symbolic land bridge linking China and Japan. However, the government has not yet developed a viable trade-off between the dispersal policies aimed at achieving balanced regional development and the implicit spatial consequences (benefiting the larger cities) of accommodating globalization.

1. Introduction

The Asian economic crisis of the late 1990s vividly illustrated the vulnerability of a country or a region to the forces of globalization. Many firms and even governments were forced to restructure, generating significant unemployment in Asian cities. Urban infrastructure building and housing construction were delayed because of a shortage of funds created by the financial crisis. Perhaps, it is the first time that ordinary citizens of Asia felt the impact of globalization in real and concrete terms. This does not mean that globalization came to Asia suddenly. Many Asian countries have been globalizing over two or three decades in the sense that their economies have become increasingly integrated with the world economy. Increasing trade and investment in Asia has indeed been the force behind Asia's rapid economic growth in the 1970s and 1980s. Korea and other Asian countries have liberalized their trade regimes and adopted policies of receiving foreign direct investment. However, globalization has taken a different track in recent years, involving a much broadened scope and velocity, especially of finance capital.

While globalization can be defined in such economic terms as increasing trade and investment, it has other dimensions, for example, the globalization of production and consumption. The rise of transnational corporations has been dramatic in the last decade or two. They have been creating and integrating global systems of production, distribution, finance and consumption. The rise of transnational corporations has been also accompanied by the spread of dominant cultures and institutions. Consumption patterns in remote villages tend to converge with global patterns. Business practices and institutions across the world now follow global standards at least on the surface. In sum, globalization is a process marked by historical transformations leading to new configurations in economic organization, in state-civil society-capital relations, and in the industrial landscape.

In Korea's economic transformation, globalization has two aspects: one is externalization (internationalization) of the Korean economy and the other is internalization of global challenges and pressures within the Korean economy. Even though Korea has been successful in the first aspect, it has been not as successful with respect to the second. In other words, the Korean economy and social institutions have not been flexible and open enough to accommodate global changes. This latter aspect could have been the principal cause of Korea's recent economic crisis. The externalization of the Korean economy in terms of increasing trade dependence and external orientation has occurred in its earlier stages of development up until the 1980s, whereas the internalization process, which includes import liberalization, market opening, and the adoption of global standards, has taken place at a much slower pace in its later stages of development.

Urbanization consequences of globalization have two facets, negative and positive. The former includes the acceleration of urbanization and mega-city growth, which have created so many problems that no government has successfully dealt with them. Another is the breakdown of the urban economic base which has been dominated by the labor-intensive export sector and non-traded service industries, while a new economic base has not yet emerged. However, there are also positive impacts. They include the speeding up of restructuring of inefficient industrial and administrative systems which have clogged the competitive edge in both countries and cities. A crisis mentality after the IMF bailout in late 1997 made it easy to reform stubborn labor-business relations, the hard-headed bureaucratic apparatus and the insolvent banking system in Korea.

Urbanization can be seen as corresponding to these changes and new configurations brought on by both aspects of globalization. In other words, urbanization and globalization have become interdependent. This interdependency grows and becomes more complex as the globalization process deepens. It is moving from simple trade interdependence to a complex interdependence of global production, distribution, consumption, and finance. The confluence of globalization and urbanization is more pronounced in East Asia where urbanization has been taking place in a very condensed fashion. Based on the experiences of Korea and other Asian countries, globalization in a broader sense has created four prominent features of urbanization (although any causal connections remain unclear). They are the dominance of large cities in the national urban hierarchy, spatial polarization and formation of mega-city regions and the internationalization of cities, urban restructuring, and deteriorating rural economies. This paper looks at and interprets these features in the context of global-local interplay. Then, it discusses policy responses to these features, often perceived to be problems. Finally, the paper discusses major policy issues arising from the recent globalization and urbanization interface.

2. Korea's urbanization path

Korea has experienced an unprecedented speed of urbanization, as indicated by a sharp increase in the level of urbanization from 39% to 91% in less than four decades. Korea's rapid urbanization was facilitated via a drastic change in its economic structure from an agrarian economy to an industrial economy, with 80% of the labor force employed in the agricultural sector in 1960 reduced to 8.7% by 2000 (Fig. 1). In 1960, per capita GNP was less than US$100, with the agricultural sector accounting for 45% of gross domestic product. The total value of exports accounted for only 1.5% of Korea's GDP in 1960. The only path, perceived at that time by the leaders, was to promote exports utilizing Korea's comparative advantage in cheap and relatively well-educated labor. The growth of labor-intensive manufacturing was very fast during the 1960s and 1970s. The abundant supply of rural labor supported Korea's rapid structural transformation and relative neglect of agricultural development as compared with Taiwan's accelerated rural to urban migration. Industrialization and urbanization often reinforced each other. Rural to urban migration responds to rural-urban wage differentials (explained by productivity differences) and income opportunities (Todaro 1969). The productivity differential hypothesis that labor moves from low productivity agriculture to the high productivity manufacturing sector strongly applies to Korea. The rapid growth of manufacturing employment during Korea's labor-intensive growth phase of the 1960s and the early 1970s triggered very high rates of rural-urban migration, primarily to Seoul and the southeastern coast. The primary destination of this massive rural to urban migration was large urban centers. The majority of rural migrants settled in Seoul and

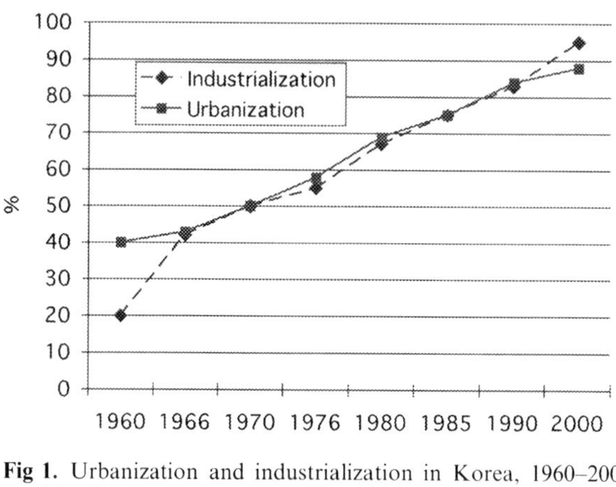

Fig 1. Urbanization and industrialization in Korea, 1960–2000. *Note*: Industrialization is the combined proportion of manufacturing and service industries in the total. *Source*: Author

southeastern coastal cities, where more jobs were created by the concentration of the labor-intensive manufacturing sector.

2.1. Dominance of large cities

The export-oriented growth strategy has resulted in a premium on large cities and port cities, leading to a rapid growth of these cities. The large cities of Seoul, Pusan, and Daegu were the magnets for rural migrant workers. Seoul's population more than tripled between 1960 and 1980, while Pusan and Taegu have more than doubled. In 1960, two cities, Seoul and Pusan, accounted for about 39% of total urban population. The rate of rural-urban migration was very fast. Between 1961 and 2000, 33 million people moved from rural to urban areas. In the 1960s, Seoul alone absorbed 60% of the total net rural-urban migration.

During this labor-intensive phase of economic growth, globalization in terms of capital mobility and trade liberalization did not have a significant and direct impact on the pace of Korea's urbanization. Rather, the process was primarily driven by the internal forces of industrialization. However, this industrialization process was conditioned upon the requirements of the world market. In this indirect sense, the earlier phase of Korea's urbanization was linked with globalization.

The capital-intensive growth phase of Korea during the late 1970s and the early 1980s can be seen as a period partially driven by an import-substitution strategy. Heavy and chemical industries were regarded as the new dynamos of the Korean economy (in addition to the labor-intensive industries of 1960s such as apparels, textiles, and footwear). The drive for heavy and chemical industries has given locational preference to port cities such as Incheon, Masan, Changwon, Ulsan, and Pohang. This somewhat relieved the trend of population concentration in the large inland cities. However, the continued growth of labor-intensive manufacturing and the rise of service employment in large cities during the 1970s and 1980s continued to contribute to the dominance of large cities in Korea's urbanization process. In 1980, for example, the six cities over one million accounted for 53% of Korea's urban population. In terms of size distribution of cities as shown in Table 1, Korea's top heavy structure of the urban system established during the 1970s did not change significantly. The decline of smaller urban centers than 100,000 was a notable feature of Korea's urbanization process.

Why is Korea's urban system so skewed toward large cities? Conventional urban theory suggests that the advantages of large cities consist of agglomeration economies: economies of scale and scope, a large pool of skilled labor and better infrastructure (Mills and Hamilton 1984). In addition, large cities are often gateways to the world, through which new information and technology first arrive and then subsequently disseminate. In other words, a city's global connection is an important economic benefit (Sassen 1991; Friedmann 1995). Although Seoul City's population began to fall in absolute terms in the early 1990s, its dominant position in the Korean economy has not been challenged. Localization economies and urbanization economies are important factors explaining the dominance of large cities and primacy (Moomaw 1988). But we should add one more factor common in Asian countries with a long tradition of a centralized political and educational system. The centralization of power in the capital city and the social rewards system emphasizing higher education are additional reasons for the primacy of Seoul in Korea.

2.2. *Spatial polarization and the formation of mega-city region*

The mega-city region, as well as the so-called "extended metropolitan region" (Ginsberg et al. 1991), emerging in Pacific Asia, is a result of the interdependency between globalization and urbanization. The expansion of Seoul into the surrounding areas accelerated during the 1980s and the early 1990s. Spatial polarization is a policymaking concern in Korea and in high-performance economies in Pacific Asia. In hindsight, Korea's policy of population dispersal began in the early 1970s to reduce population concentration in Seoul and from the 1980s on in the Seoul metropolitan region. It was less a skewed urban size distribution than spatial polarization that alarmed Korean central government policymakers (Table 2).

The capital region (or the Seoul metropolitan region) including Seoul, Incheon, and Kyonggi province had about 3.2 million people in 1960. Its population increased to 11.9 million in 1980, accounting for 44.3% of the total national population. In 2000, the capital region with more than 22 million (living within the relatively small area of 11,675 square kilometers) is home for almost one out of two Koreans. The capital region includes 35 cities and townships.

This massive agglomeration in the capital region is greater (certainly in terms of primacy) than in Tokyo, Jakarta, Shanghai and Hong Kong-Guangzhou. The key process behind mega-city region formation is growth spillovers. As the size of the central city grows, spatial expansion occurs and functional differentiation deepens. The growth spillover of Seoul has spread to adjacent areas, creating a network of cities centering around Seoul. This trend of suburbanization was enhanced during the 1980s and 1990s by the growth of car ownership and rising incomes. However, a severe housing shortage and the saturation of urban land in Seoul were push factors helping to relocate some of the intra-metropolitan population away from Seoul elsewhere in the capital region. Many low value-added activities with extensive land requirements have moved out of Seoul. Routine manufacturing functions and people (for better housing with lower prices) moved out to satellite towns, while continuing to maintain close links with Seoul. However, the centralization of headquarter functions, advanced services and international activities in Seoul intensified during the 1980s and 1990s with the advance of globalization.

2.3. *Internationalization of cities and urban restructuring*

A widely recognized feature of contemporary globalization is the centralization of global command functions in a few urban centers (Scott 1997). The growth of transnational corporations with associated global networks of production and distribution requires a complementary and compatible urban system to effect global management. To host global functions and to aspire to be a world city, inter-city competition in Asia has been increasing in recent years. Korea's large cities are not an exception. As investment becomes

Table 1. Distribution of cities by size, selected years

Number of inhabitants	1960			1970			1980			1990			1996			2000		
	Number of cities	Population (thousands)	Percent of Urban population	Number of cities	Population (thousands)	Percent of Urban population	Number of cities	Population (thousands)	Percent of Urban population	Number of cities	Population (thousands)	Percent of Urban population	Number of cities	Population (thousands)	Percent of Urban population	Number of cities	Population (thousands)	Percent of Urban population
5 million	0	0	0.0	1	5,536	35.0	1	8,367	31.3	1	10,628	29.5	1	10,470	29.5	1	10,373	23.2
1–5 million	2	3,609	39.1	2	2,963	18.7	3	5,852	21.7	5	10,051	27.9	5	11,374	27.9	6	12,723	28.5
0.5–1 million	1	676	7.3	2	1,149	7.3	2	1,379	5.1	5	3,054	8.5	10	6,899	8.5	10	6,861	15.4
0.1–0.5 million	6	1,291	14.0	13	2,209	14.0	29	5,514	20.5	29	6,369	17.7	53	11,028	17.7	55	11,951	26.8
Less than 0.1 million	101	3,653	39.6	106	3,952	25.0	211	5,805	21.6	213	5,899	16.4	133	2,874	16.4	131	2,732	6.1
Total urban population	110	9,229	100.0	124	15,809	10.0	246	26,917	100.0	253	36,001	100.0	202	42,645	100.0	203	44,640	100.00
Urbanization rate (percent)		36.9			50.3			70.6			82.9			91.8		93.0		
Total nation population		24,986			31,435			35,124			43,390			46,430		47,955		

Note: The number of cities has been reduced because of rural-urban integration implemented in 1995. The urbanization rate is the proportion of the population living in cities and towns.
Source: Ministry of Administration and Local Government (1971, 1981, 1991, 1997, 2001)

footloose and transportation costs have declined, a city's comparative advantage has shifted from natural resources–based industries to a new focus on created assets such as highly-skilled and professional workers, advanced transportation and communication infrastructure, and cultural amenities. This tendency was reinforced by Korea's decentralization of the political system. In 1995, for the first time in more than three decades, a full-fledged local autonomous system of electing mayors and council members by popular vote was introduced. Urban boosterism and politician-citizen coalitions pushed ahead with an ambitious drive for globalization. All major cities in Korea expressed their desire to host certain kind of international events, to establish international organizations, and to build inter-city networks beyond national borders. In sum, cities offer to use segments of global capital with investments in the built environment as a means to capture and sustain its presence and benefits. Hosting the World Cup in 2002 led almost to a war among Korean cities. International cultural events such as movie and animation festivals and biennale have become a major part of the agenda for the globalization drive of both politicians and residents.

Increased inter-city competition is accompanied by physical, economic and social restructuring. The industrial structure of major cities in Korea has changed from being manufacturing-centered service-centered (Kim et al. 1997). Seoul is the forerunner of this structural transformation. During the period from 1981 to 2000, the share of manufacturing employment in Seoul's total employment declined from 30.4 % to 18.9 %, whereas the share for the service sector especially in finance, insurance and producer services increased significantly. This is similar to Tokyo's industrial restructuring during the 1970s. The difference, however, lies in Seoul's continued high proportion of employment in the wholesale and retail trade sector (Fujita 1991). With the overall decline of the manufacturing sector, Seoul's industrial mix within the sector has also changed substantially. In 1975, labor-intensive industries such as textiles and apparel and assembly of electrical and electronic goods were the major industries in Seoul's economy. Fifteen years later, the importance of textiles has declined, while the apparel industry gained significance. This industrial restructuring has occurred in part because of spatial decentralization. The suburban areas of Seoul have gained a significant portion of industrial growth in assembly manufacturing including the electrical and electronic industries. On the whole, the data indicate that the trends of Seoul's industrial specialization in fashion-oriented apparel, printing, the assembly of electrical/electronic products, and machinery are common to many large, advanced cities (Park 1995).

Pusan and Taegu, the second and third largest cities in Korea are following the path of Seoul. However, like Detroit and Pittsburgh in the 1970s, Pusan and Taegu are having difficulties in industrial restructuring. Both cities' main industries are labor-intensive, challenged by firms in China and Southeast Asian countries with their much lower wages. Nike shoes once had its major production base in Pusan but has relocated its production facilities to China, Thailand, and Indonesia with much cheaper production costs (Lim 1995). The flight of transnational capital from one city to another can have substantial impacts on the urban economy. To prevent capital flight or to attract capital, cities in Korea and in Asia are refurbishing their infrastructure and trying to improve their traditionally hostile labor-management relations.

Table 2. Distribution of cities by region, selected years

Region	1960		1970		1980		1996		2000	
	Number of cities	Urban population (thousands)	Number of cities	Urban population (thousands)	Number of cities	Urban population (thousands)	Number of cities	Urban population (thousands)	Number of cities	Urban population (thousands)
Jeju	3	108	4	196	8	403	9	486	9	506
Jeonbuk	10	547	10	688	19	1,065	15	1,703	15	1,738
Chungbuk	7	287	8	389	13	662	13	1,095	14	1,174
Ganwon	12	488	14	758	29	1,165	26	1,275	26	1,321
Gwangju-Chonnam	19	957	20	1,299	36	1,969	34	2,706	32	2,839
Busan-Gyongnam	16	1,826	19	2,870	28	5,007	23	7,479	23	7,585
Seoul Metropolitan Region (Capital Region)	12	3,160	14	6,853	41	11,904	35	20,387	37	21,675
Daegu-Gyongbuk	17	1,242	18	1,829	46	3,253	26	4,823	26	4,905
Daejon-Chungnam	14	614	17	927	26	1,489	21	2,692	21	2,897
Total	110	9,229	124	15,809	246	26,917	202	42,646	203	44,640

Source: Ministry of Administration and Local Government (1971, 1981, 1991, 1997, 2001)

Large city regions equipped with modern infrastructure, professional workers capable of speaking dual and multiple languages, advanced business services, and cultural amenities are definitely the winners in inter-city competition, further enhancing the dominant position of large cities in domestic and international urban networks. Indeed, the mega-city regions in Asia, such as the Seoul metropolitan region, are the powerhouses of the Asian economies and they disproportionately host global functions and capital. But to succeed in the inter-city competition, many countries plan to embark on new mega-projects such as international hub airports, convention centers, and high technology parks (Douglass 1998). Financing these mega-projects often strain the government treasury. The post-1997 economic crisis put many of these projects on hold, although some are now being revived.

Obviously, these regions are where foreign direct investment is usually concentrated. In Korea's case, Seoul takes the lion's share of inward foreign direct investment. However, Korea is distinguished from other developing economies in the respect that it has not depended much on foreign direct investment for its economic growth (Table 3). Foreign direct investment during the 1970s and 1980s was predominantly in the manufacturing sector, although the share of foreign direct investment in the service sector has increased in the 1990s. Korea is no longer considered to be a cheap production site for transnational companies. Foreign investors are now more interested

Table 3. FDI and overseas investment

Year	FDI		Overseas investment	
	Number of contracts	Amount (million)	Number of contracts	Amount (million)
1962–80	1,440	1,713	400	251
1981	44	153	64	109
1982	56	189	54	121
1983	75	269	67	83
1984	104	422	49	67
1985	127	532	43	219
1986	203	355	73	364
1987	362	1,063	109	367
1988	343	1,284	250	475
1989	336	1,090	368	943
1990	296	803	515	1,611
1991	286	1,396	527	1,511
1992	233	895	631	1,206
1993	273	1,044	1,049	1,876
1994	414	1,317	1,946	3,581
1995	556	1,941	1,561	4,949
1996	596	3,203	1,795	6,220
1997	638	6,971	1,579	5,822
1998	798	8,853	716	5,246
1999	1,464	15,542	1,265	4,654
2000	3,073	15,697	2,257	4,956
Total	11,717	64,732	15,317	44,630

Note: The number of contracts refer to new contracts, while the amount is sum of both new and expansion investment.
Source: Ministry of Finance and Economy, Investment Promotion Bureau data.

in Korea's potential as a market. The service sector, especially non-traded service industries such as eateries, beauty parlors and neighborhood general stores which were once thought to be safe niches for domestic incubators have been encroached by multinational outlet chains since the early 1990s. Local eateries have now to compete with KFC, Coco's and McDonald. The entry of Walmart and Costco has resulted in panic among domestic shopping outlets.

While inward foreign direct investment did not play a significant role in the national economy, Korean firms' overseas investment has been increasing since the late 1980s. Korean multinational companies began to make overseas investment mainly to cut production costs. Wage hikes and labor disputes in the late 1980s were the primary reasons for the surge in overseas investment. China and South East Asia are the major destinations for overseas investment seeking lower production costs. The major centers of both inward and outward foreign direct investment were large cities. With a stronger trend toward the service economy, large cities are subject to an earlier economic restructuring than smaller cities, primarily because of their global connections. There has been a great concern with de-industrialization and the industrial hollowing-out of large cities in Korea. It is this dimension of globalization that will generate more urban changes in Korea in the near future.

2.4. Deteriorating rural economies

Globalization, especially after the Uruguay Round in 1994, has had major impacts on rural areas via the lifting of tariff barriers on agricultural products. On the top of the intrinsic weakness of the Korean agricultural sector, the opening of agricultural products to the world market has resulted in near panic. The price competitiveness between domestic products and imports has become substantial (e.g. meat from the US and Australia, tropical fruits from Southeast Asia, and vegetables and fish from China). Consequently, many Korean farmers have abandoned cultivation and sought out alternative work. For example, Jeju Province had two-thirds of its regional income from growing tangerines and tropical fruits, but these have been replaced by Californian oranges and Philippino bananas. Hence, the Province has shifted its economic base from agriculture to tourism, and has been designated as a free trade zone to promote international tourism.

The government has intervened to relieve the Uruguay Round's shock on the rural economy since 1994 through more than 200 policy packages including land reform, rural cooperative schemes, marketing strategy to stabilize the price of agricultural products, rural public works, rural industrialization and outright subsidies for succeeding generations of farmers, costing about 57 billion won for the eight-year time span. But they have not had any visible impact, and the debt ratio of farm households had worsened even before the implementation of rural policy packages. Eventually, most rural development strategies have resulted in trickle-up to urban groups either through increases in the demand for urban goods or through cheaper food, or both. This has led to a deterioration in the agricultural terms of trade which are extremely sensitive to changes in the supply of agricultural products domestically produced or imported. However, rural-urban migration has not been great as expected. One of the main reasons might have been that the reservoir of potential rural migrants had dried up before the Uruguay Round shock.

In sum, globalization has severely hit rural areas, further accentuating the agricultural terms of trade against agricultural products and marginalizing rural areas. In response to this irreversible trend of globalization, both policymakers and farmers (who have been very supportive of agricultural protectionism) seem to accept that indiscriminate efforts to avoid globalization may only serve to aggravate rural problems. Recently, the government has taken a step towards "rurbanization" policies, allowing non-farmers to own limited farmland for uses other than farming, introducing a contract system to buy agricultural products from farmers at the fixed price, and relaxing rural land use controls (which protected agricultural land).

3. Policy responses

The above three prominent features of urbanization in Korea have been partly the result of globalization. Although initial conditions and domestic political and economic factors have contributed to shaping the structure of Korea's urbanization path and urban system, there have been and still are several policies that intervene in the on-going urban process. These policies more or less correspond with the aforementioned four features, namely the dominance of large cities, spatial polarization, urban restructuring, and the deteriorating rural economy. However, policies implemented during the past two or three decades have been designed to achieve the goals of balanced regional development, optimal urban growth, and efficient urban service provision.

3.1. From interregional dispersal to intra-regional relocation

Policies to combat the polarization tendencies of urban growth have targeted the decentralization of population and industry away from the capital region. There was an attempt to develop countermagnets to Seoul in the late 1960s and the early 1970s. But it failed. The attractiveness of the capital region was so strong that repeated policy attempts to decentralize population and industrial activities away from the capital region have failed. However, the central government has not given up its efforts. Decentralization policies centered on the capital region are probably the most elaborate in Asia. The establishment of manufacturing plants is strictly controlled in the congested areas of the capital region. Also, other actions to promote population growth are discouraged within the capital region via tax penalties and the withholding of development permits.

A comprehensive plan, called the First Capital Region Management Plan (1984–1996), was introduced by the central government to curb the concentration of population and industrial activities in the Seoul metropolitan region. The plan defined the jurisdictions of Seoul Special City, the City of Incheon, and the Gyonggi province as the Capital Region. This region was subject to the Capital Region Management Law, which overrides all other laws related to development activities in the region. The major tools of the plan were laws and decrees regulating development activities inducing pop-

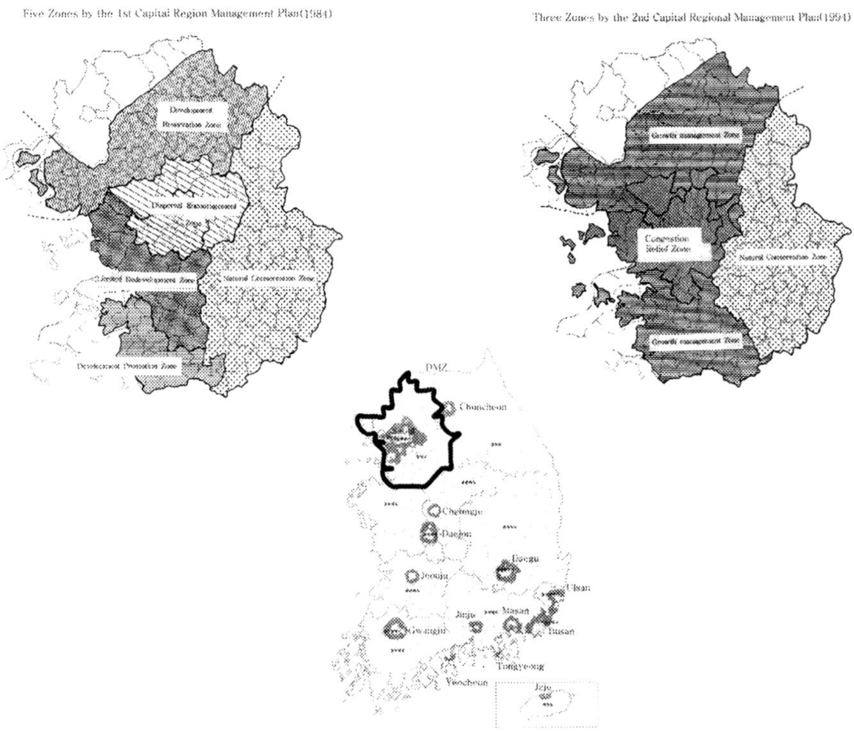

Map 1. Development control zones (The 1st and 2nd capital region managements plans)

ulation concentration. The region was divided into five zones with varying degrees of development control.[1] In addition to this designation of a broad geographical region with zoning instruments, two important policy instruments were adopted. They were congestion charges and an aggregate development ceiling system. Congestion charges are levied on those development activities that are likely to induce population concentration within the dispersal encouragement zone. Business offices, department stores, and public facilities above a certain size are subject to congestion charges, usually ten percent of total construction costs. The aggregate ceiling system is designed to control the growth of industrial activities. With an aggregate ceiling of factory construction set by the Capital Region Management Review Committee for the beginning of each year, a portion of this total development ceiling is allocated to different localities and then the local governments have power to screen applications and permit factory construction.

These policies, however, have been criticized on the ground that they are not very effective, while creating unnecessarily high costs of urban development. Critics also cite the location of unregistered factories without permits.

[1] The five zones are: Dispersal encouragement zone, limited redevelopment zone, development reservation zone, growth promotion zone, and natural conservation zone. Later in the Second Plan, these five zones were consolidated into three zones, i.e., congestion relief, natural conservation, and growth management (refer to Map 1).

Across the capital region, small-scale factories which could not afford high land costs and emission charges have mushroomed. For a variety of reasons, these factories had to be given legal recognition with only promises of future improvement (Hwang 1996). More seriously, these restrictions are claimed to have resulted in a shortage of land for factory construction, thereby raising industrial land prices. Furthermore, the policy as a whole did not succeed in decentralizing population and industrial activities away from the capital region. An argument for the policy, however, remains, considering the counterfactual situation on the ground that there would have been more population and industrial concentration in the capital region without the policy.

Although the effects of these policies were dubious, the policy goals were reluctantly tolerated during Korea's high growth phase because of strong job generation. As a matter of fact, manufacturing employment growth over 5% per annum during the heyday of Korea's high-speed growth had contributed somewhat to the alleviation of population concentration in Seoul and other million-plus cities. The industrial estates that developed across the country during the 1970s and the 1980s generated many manufacturing jobs, absorbing a significant number of migrants. Industrial location policy, another major arm of government intervention in the urbanization process, has contributed somewhat to the decentralization of industrial activities away from the capital region. The industrial estates developed according to the policy have been located outside the million-plus cities and hence helped to mitigate the dominance of large cities in Korea's urban system. In addition, Korea's rural industrialization policy (including the promotion of rural industrial estates) has had some positive effect in holding down rural out-migration and raising rural incomes.

In order to abate population concentration in the large cities, the Korean government in 1971 introduced a strong land use control policy. The greenbelt policy was implemented to control urban sprawl near the large cities. Uncontrolled growth was believed to undermine urban efficiency and to increase the burden of providing urban infrastructure provision. Seoul was the first target but other major cities were also subject to the greenbelt policy. Despite good intentions of the government, the greenbelt policy generated complaints from the modest number of residents in the greenbelt areas who were deprived of their property land rights. It also drew criticisms from neo-liberal economists. They argued that the greenbelt policy simply resulted in the distortion of urban development pattern, without decentralizing population away from the large cities. This leap-frog pattern increased infrastructure and commuting costs. On the other hand, urban planners and environmentalists have argued in favor of the environmental benefits of the greenbelt. Without it, the urban environment would have deteriorated more. After three decades the greenbelt policy has been relaxed: Abolished in the seven smaller cities with the development of some modest areas permitted in the larger cities. These changes, while limited, have been strongly welcomed by greenbelt residents as well as by economists, who considered the greenbelt policy as an indirect reason for Korea's declining international competitiveness (Lee 1998).

Globalization pressure has also resulted in a shift in policy for the capital region. This shift is reflected in the Second Capital Region Management Plan (1997–2011). Regulations restricting certain development activities have been changed in favor of price disincentives such as congestion fees and penalties imposed primarily to accommodate the increasing space demand for advanced services and for information and research functions. High-tech industries are now allowed to locate freely in the capital region. However, the major focus of the Second Plan was the reorganization of spatial structure of the capital region. The previous single-core structure centered on Seoul is planned to be transformed into a multi-core structure. For this purpose, a region-wide transportation system based on rapid transit has been designed and much of it built. In sum, the primary objective of the Second Plan is to enhance the agglomeration economies of the capital region with the intra-metropolitan redistribution of economic activities and an improved transportation system. Although population concentration in the capital region is still discouraged, the main concern has shifted from the interregional redistribution of population and economic activities to intra-regional relocation within the capital region itself.

This policy shift has aroused concerns from regions other than the capital region. These policy changes were interpreted as a setback from two respects: Balanced regional development and environmental quality. City and provincial governments outside the capital region perceive that the relaxation of development control and more infrastructure investment in the capital region would exacerbate the existing development differentials between the capital region and the rest of the country. They argue that the central government should have adhere to the former restrictive policies to enable other regions to catch up with the capital region. Policy changes in the Second Plan were considered to be a step backward from both a balanced and a sustainable development perspective. Some argue that enhancing economic efficiency via the logic of agglomeration economies in the capital region would damage the long-run competitiveness of the capital region because environmental quality is a key component in the region's future competitiveness.

In sum, Korea's urbanization policies are forced to compromise between their original stance of strictly controlling the growth of the capital region and the goal of creating a global city that competes internationally at a high level. In other words, the domestic logic of balanced regional development has to be weighed against the continued promotion of Seoul (the recent, if abortive, proposal to relocate the capital out of Seoul in the interests of balanced regional development shows that the first objective has not been abandoned).

3.2. From inward to outward development

Urban restructuring is the task of the local governments. The central government, however, has been providing support when it comes to the industrial restructuring of cities and major infrastructure construction such as subways. Rising wages, capital costs and land prices are among the main reasons for Korea's weakening position in the global market. Currency appreciation that began in 1985 also contributed to the decline in industrial competitiveness. Industrial restructuring, compelled by globalization of production, began in earnest in the late 1980s. A few large cities, especially Pusan and Taegu, were vulnerable because of their specialization in traditional labor-intensive industries such as textiles and footwear. Recognizing the local impact of industrial decline, the central government has attempted to render support through the provision of industry rationalization funds and general policy support for small and medium-sized enterprises. However, the timing of the policy was too little and too late (Kim 1995).

Another dimension of urban restructuring directly addresses the issue of enhancing international functions of large cities, especially Seoul. Hosting the 1988 Olympic game was an epochal event that raised the consciousness of both policymakers and citizens about globalization. Given the trend of de-industrialization in Seoul, policymakers and city planners were preoccupied with the transition toward the service economy with global functions. Many ideas and schemes were proposed to make Seoul a global city, including the construction of a new international hub airport in Incheon (now open). Other large cities followed the suit. For example, both Pusan and Incheon want to become the major center of maritime transport and logistics in Northeast Asia, while Taegu wishes to become an Asian Milan. All these efforts to adjust to external changes are examples of how individual cities respond in the global era. However, their success depends on external factors beyond the control of individual cities.

The globalization drive of Korean cities for international events has been a mandate since the successful hosting of the 1988 Summer Olympic Games in Seoul. Taejon succeeded in attracting the 1993 International Exposition but an overall evaluation of the event was negative in terms of urban boosterism and economic impact. More recently, the 2002 Korea/Japan World Soccer Cup was held in ten cities in Korea. It certainly helped the creation of image-building and promote place-marketing. Pusan held the Asian Games in September 2002. Although many positive impacts on image-building and the enhancement of civic spirit should not be overlooked, there are also negative consequences. The most tangible legacy of the World Cup is 10 new or re-furbished stadiums in Korea, leaving a $2.7 billion bill for infrastructure at the expense of local needs. Taegu spent its entire annual budget to build Korea's largest World Cup stadium, and had to postpone the completion of the subway line under construction. Although there was euphoria about the Korea team's success, some Koreans have complained that the hosting the World Cup is an example of globalization going too far.

It is very doubtful that Korea can continue its historical 5% or more annual job growth rate. The manufacturing sector, once the major source of employment, has been declining in absolute and relative terms. Although the service sector is still growing, policymakers have not much room to maneuver. First, the size of low-order service employment is proportional to population size. Second, advanced services such as accounting, design, law firms, and R&D tend to locate disproportionately in large international cities, where global connections are already established. The transition of the Korean economy toward the service economy began in the late 1980s. As Korea's urbanization becomes more closely intertwined with globalization, it is more difficult for the government to exercise power in urban transformation.

3.3. Decentralization, deregulation and governance

With the restoration of fully-fledged local autonomy in 1995 and a broad democratization trend set begun in the late 1980s, there is an increasing demand for citizen participation and local policy discretion. Local governments, awakened by the challenges of global competition, are expressing their demand for the devolution of power from the central to the local level.

Concerns with the international competitiveness of cities are intermingled with the broader trends toward deregulation, privatization, and democratization of Korean society in the 1990s. However, the interpretation of alternative measures to increase urban competitiveness vary widely. Neo-liberal economists call for the dismantling of the government regulatory system in the firm belief that the invisible hand of the market will take care of everything. On the other hand, city planners and environmentalists, more conscious of social justice and urban environmental sustainability, are much more cautious about the radical withdrawal of public intervention in urban management and planning. The current debate about hosting more foreign direct investment in Korea is focused on whether the central government should remove restrictions on the types of foreign direct investment within the capital region. Local governments strongly argue for the removal of restrictions to the national economy.

For both urban efficiency and quality of life reasons, the demand for better housing, clean water, and improved transportation has been increasing in the cities of Korea and elsewhere in Asia. With limited government budgets, the public sector alone cannot provide all the necessary urban services. Big city subways under construction (or being expanded) have become a major burden on local government finance. A few cities have tried to issue bonds in foreign markets, but bringing in foreign funds for urban infrastructure financing is difficult. Under the IMF bailout, attracting foreign investment was considered to be a major solution. Even before the financial crisis, the rapid increase in demand for urban infrastructure posed problems for the public sector. Privatization and public-private partnerships have been proposed as a solution. The Korean government passed a law to encourage private investment in infrastructure in 1994. The main areas proposed for private participation were roads, ports, rail and airports. This emphasis was based on the recognition of the importance of transportation costs in national and international competitiveness. The concept failed because of the lack of rational and objective criteria in selecting target projects. There was no guarantee of profitability or mechanisms to spread risks. Most of all, private initiatives and management were not fully permitted. Nevertheless, other policy measures at the central and local levels of government are under consideration to increase private participation and to solicit foreign investment in urban infrastructure.

One of the most pronounced features of contemporary urbanization in Asia is the extensive growth of core metropolitan regions well beyond administrative boundaries and into distant hinterlands, the so-called "extended metropolitan region" (Douglass 1998). As the expansion of the Seoul metropolitan region suggests, planning and management of this giant region becomes more and more difficult. With a strong tradition of a centralized political system, Korea has been slow in creating new forms of governance, particularly metropolitan governance. The central government is reluctant to yield decision making power on the grounds that local administrations lack the ability to manage their cities and to resolve inter-jurisdictional conflicts. As long as inter-governmental cooperative mechanisms remain undeveloped, many important issues such as clean water supply, waste management, transportation, and air pollution abatement await solution. However, a consultative committee composed of upper-level local governments in the capital region is making progress in resolving conflicts in the management of region-wide urban problems. A search has begun to find a more inclusive, responsible, transparent, and collaborative form of metropolitan governance in Korea.

3.4. The emerging transnational urban coalition

Given the advances of the new telecommunication technologies and the global economic market, the time-space dimension is shrinking, especially after reconciliation between the capitalist and socialist countries in Northeast Asia. Ideological confrontation has now been replaced by economic competitiveness. Changes in the world economic order have brought pressure on the Northeast Asian countries to develop a new economic regionalism similar to the EU and NAFTA. In addition to the economic superpower of Japan, the recent striking performance of the Chinese economy and its entry into the WTO has forced Korea to redefine its role in Northeast Asia. Korea has historically played a role of land bridge between the maritime hegemony of Japan and continental power of China. It now hopes to become a logistic hub linking Pacific Rim countries to the Eurasian continent. To this end, Korea has built a state-of-art international airport in Incheon, a container hub port in Gwangyang, and is reconnecting the trans-Korea railway through North Korea. The four countries of China, Japan and both Koreas share many

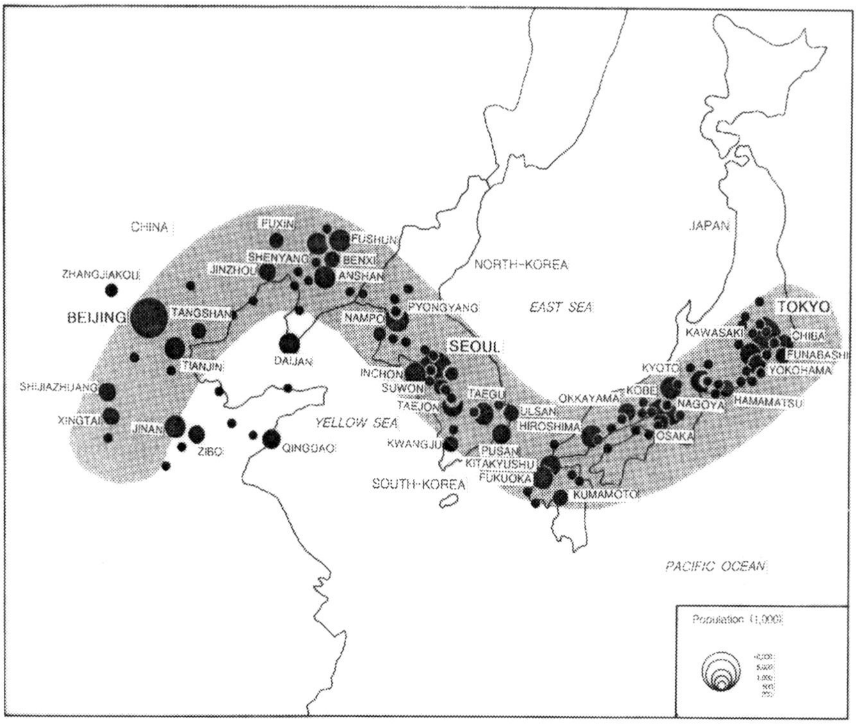

Map 2. Beijing-Seoul-Tokyo (BESETO) transnational urban corridor

historical legacies and cultural affinities beyond being simply neighboring states, although the relationship between the two Koreas remains problematic.

In the inverted S-shaped corridor from Beijing to Tokyo via Pyongyang and Seoul there are about 100 million urban inhabitants, and 112 cities with population greater than 200,000 that are almost contiguous along a 1,500 kilometer strip of densely populated land (Map 2). This could be called an "ecumenopolis" (using the term of the Greek urbanologist (C.A. Doxiadis) or the BESETO transnational urban corridor (Choe 1996). We can find European counterparts. In Europe, the transnational conceptualization of socio-spatial formation has been variously described as a polynucleated urban field (Dieleman 1998), the Blue Banana or the Pentagon (ESDP 1999). Some of these concepts have been criticized for its over-simplification of a complex and changing reality. The relevance of the core-periphery model has also been challenged for failing to acknowledge the pockets of deprivation with the core and pockets of development within the periphery (DETR 2000). The concept of the BESETO transnational urban corridor has also been evaluated from a functional point of view (McGee 2000). Although the concept of cross-border urban development is not yet realized, there is a strong sentiment in Northeast Asia to develop it, e.g. the North-South Korean railroad, and the ambitious project of an undersea tunnel between the Japanese archipelago and the Korean peninsula across the Korea Straits. Even before fully fledged transnational urban coalitions are in place, inter-city coalitions on a small scale are being actively developed in cross-border areas such as the Tumen River Area Development Program which promotes the development of the triangular zone covering Rajin-Sonbong in North Korea, Hunchun in China and Khasan in the Russian Far East. Regular conferences and exchange programs are actively taking place in the East Sea (Japan Sea) Rim and the Yellow Sea Rim. They are collectively exploring the possibility of linking maritime and inland transportation, creating free trade trade zones for foreign direct investment, and promoting tourism in the region as a whole.

4. Concluding remarks

With the development of information and communication technologies, competition is further intensified, and the world is shifting to a new free market system that transcends national ideologies and levels of development. Increasing openness is accelerating movement between cities not only in products but also in capital, technology and management. Globalization has posed opportunities as well as threats to Korean cities. Opportunities include the hope to share in the globalization benefits offered by the prospects offered by the locational advantages of being a land-bridge country between the two great hegemonic powers, Japan and China. All large coastal cities aim to become logistics hubs for Northeast Asia and the Pacific Rim. Large cities want to have international functions of one kind or another to exploit their competitive edge. On the other hand, threats are always there, such as the marginalization of peripheral cities outside the core city region; this accelerated growth of the mega-city region. Also, the hollowing-out of manufacturing base in the Korean cities has had an impact, especially because some high-order economic functions have been slow to catch up. Nevertheless, many urban Koreans are slowly realizing that globalization is an irreversible trend and that they have to live with it.

However, national urbanization policies are still very much ambivalent. The dispersal of industry and population from large cities has been continued to soothe regionalism and to buy political legitimacy. However, this has also heralded open competition and market-orientedness among regions and cities. Korea's globalization drive has been dominated by state catch-up policies with one-sided global involvement. In this respect, globalization is at stake in Korea and the rest of Northeast Asia because they have not experienced globalization with the same vigor as in many of the European and Atlantic Rim countries. The Hanseatic spirit of the free city, mercantilism and global consciousness has not yet emerged because the Northeast Asian countries and their cities have closed themselves off from the outside world for long.

References

Choe S-C (1996) The evolving urban system in Northeast Asia. In: Lo F-c; Yang Y-m (eds) Emerging world cities in Pacific Asia. United Nations University, Tokyo

DETR (Department of the Environment, Transport and the Region) (2000) European spatial planning and urban-rural relationship : The UK dimension. DETR, London

Dieleman F, Faludi A (1998) Polynucleated metropolitan regions in Northwest Europe : Theme of the special issues. European Planning Studies 6(4): 365–377

Douglass M (1998) Globalization and extended metropolitan regions in Pacific Asia. Paper at the workshop on comparative policy framework for managing the expansion of the extended metropolitan regions in Pacific Asia, Bellagio, Italy, May 27–June 2

Friedmann J (1995) Where we stand: a decade of world city research. In: Knox P, Taylor P (eds) World cities in world system. Cambridge University Press, Cambridge, UK

Fujita K (1991) A world city and flexible specialization: restructuring of the Tokyo metropolis. International Journal of Urban and Regional Research 15: 269–284

Ginsberg N, Koppel B, McGee T (1991) The extended metropolis: Settlement transition in Asia. University of Hawaii Press, Honolulu, Hawaii

Hong SW (1997) Building a power house. KRIHS, Anyang

Hwang M-I (1995) The status of unregistered factories and improvement measures. Planning Information Bulletin, pp 34–41 (in Korean)

Kim WB (2005) National competitiveness and governance of the capital region of Seoul, Korea. Environment and Planning A (forthcoming)

Kim WB (1995) Patterns of industrial restructuring. In: Clark GL, Kim WB (eds) Asian NIEs and the global economy: Industrial restructuring and corporate strategy in the 1990s. Oxford University Press, Oxford

Kim WB, Kwon YS, Lee YA (1997) Strategies for local competitiveness of large cities. KRIHS, Kyonggi, South Korea

Lee BS (1998) Land use regulations and efficiency of Seoul's economy. International Journal of Urban Sciences 2: 48–72

Lim JD (1996) Pusan, Korea: second-city blues. In: Clark GL, Kim WB (eds) Asian NIEs and the global economy: Industrial restructuring and corporate strategy in the 1990s. Oxford University Press, Oxford

McGee T, Pang X, Shin D-H (1999) From corridor to intercity networks: The role of emerging urban system in building regional networks in Northeast. The Korean Journal of Regional Science 15(2): 21–38

Mills ES, Hamilton BW (1984) Urban economics, 3rd ed. Scott, Foresman and Company, Glenview, Illinois

Moomaw RL (1988) Agglomeration economies; localization or urbanization? Urban Studies 25: 150–161

Park SO (1995) Seoul, Korea: city and suburbs. In: Clark GL, Kim WB (eds) Asian NIEs and the global economy: Industrial restructuring and corporate strategy in the 1990s. Oxford University Press, Oxford
Sassen S (1991) The global city: New York, London, Tokyo. Princeton University Press, Princeton, New Jersey
Scott AJ (1996) Regional motors of the global economy. Futures 28: 391–411
Todaro MP (1969) A model of labor migration and urban unemployment in less developed countries. American Economic Review 59: 138–148
Yang Y-m (ed) (1998) Urban development in Asia: Retrospect and Prospect. The Chinese University of Hong Kong, Hong Kong

Trade openness and regional development in a developing country

Ernesto M. Pernia, Pilipinas F. Quising

Economics and Research Department, Asian Development Bank, 6 ADB Avenue, Mandaluyong City, 0401 Philippines (e-mails: {epernia; pquising}@adb.org)

Abstract. This paper examines how economic openness influences regional development in a developing country, with the Philippines as a case study. It first looks at the disparities in economic and social indicators across the country's 14 regions and over time. Metro Manila continues to tower over the national economic landscape, although economic dispersal especially in adjacent regions appears to be expanding. The paper then analyzes the determinants of regional development, using five-year panel data. Trade openness appears to be beneficial to regional economic growth and, via growth, poverty reduction. However, it cannot by itself be expected to bring about more balanced regional development.

JEL classification: I32, 018, R11

1. Introduction

External influences on a country's urban and regional development are not new. Records of such influences date back at least to colonial times when cities became the strategic contact points of the colonizer with the colony. The evolution of ports and local transport systems were strongly shaped by the trade and investment decisions of the colonial authorities. Indeed, the geographic location of ports had a decisive impact on the choice of what were to become the primary and secondary urban centers.

The Philippines had a relatively high degree of urbanization early in the 20th century, compared with other countries at similar levels of development, and this can be attributed to historical circumstances (Pernia 1976). For instance, the Spanish colonial tradition of urbanism through *reducción* meant that, for purposes of christianization, the natives were resettled from scattered *barangays* (villages) into compact settlements (Phelan 1959). The strategy of "reduction" was earlier applied to Hispanic America, resulting as well in

The authors thank Emma Fan, Jesus Felipe, Rana Hasan, and participants in the conference on the Impacts of Globalization on Urban Development, Bellagio, Lake Como, Italy, 19–23 August 2002, for their helpful comments.

relatively high urbanization levels (Reed 1967). The evolution of urban primacy or spatial concentration can be ascribed to international forces. This is true of Manila and several megacities elsewhere in the developing world (Pernia 1994; Lo and Yeung 1996).

Recent and ongoing globalization trends exert stronger and probably different types of impacts on national urban and regional development (Lo and Yeung 1996; Lo and Yeung 1998). Economies are inexorably becoming more open, subjecting them to all kinds of global forces, such as trade, capital, technology, economic policy, information and knowledge. Also, while external influences during colonial times were almost exclusively one-way – from colonizer to colony, with the economic benefits arguably going mostly to the former – these influences are becoming more two-way, with developing countries benefiting as well.

Urban primacy that characterizes the Philippine space economy appears to have been heightened, not lessened, by recent external influences, specifically investment and trade (Solon 1996). Capital and trade flows, supported by new communications and transportation technologies, operate in the world economy via the national capitals that evolve as megacities. This view is backed by evidence on the tendency of foreign direct investment (FDI) to locate in and around the metropolises of East Asian countries (Fuchs and Pernia 1987).

In the Philippines, more recently, a few regional centers such as Cebu in Central Visayas, Davao-General Santos in Southern Mindanao, and Subic-Clark in Central Luzon appear to be growing faster than Metro Manila, partly because of increased levels of investment and exports. Can this be an indication that globalization could lead to more dispersed spatial development?

In this paper, we attempt to address the general issue whether or not economic openness is beneficial to regional development and poverty reduction. This issue can be broken down into more specific questions. What is the effect of external economic forces on regional and urban development in the Philippines? How is their effect on the evolution of regional poverty transmitted? How significant is the impact of these external forces relative to that of domestic factors? Do they contribute to more balanced regional development (i.e., narrower interregional disparities) or reinforce spatial concentration?

Regarding the last question, there are essentially two views. First, based on cross-country regression analysis, Henderson (2002) finds a strong negative correlation between international trade and urban primacy. The conceptual underpinning is the new economic geography models which posit that economic openness tends to spur growth of the countryside (Krugman and Livas 1996). The idea is that because exports are not linked to the domestic market, producers may locate outside major urban centers as land, labor and congestion costs escalate in megacities. Such relocation may be further induced if basic infrastructure requirements are provided.

The second view is that in a developing country where economic activity is typically highly concentrated in the capital metropolis and inter-city infrastructure is inadequate, foreign direct investment and trade could reinforce urban primacy (Fuchs and Pernia 1987). Spatial development patterns are often set by domestic market forces and public policy, and investment and trade tend to follow these set patterns for efficiency reasons.

The paper is organized as follows. In the next section, we briefly describe the data used in the study. We then look at the patterns of regional development, other regional economic and social indicators, and differences in poverty levels across regions. We next analyze the factors affecting regional development and living standards of the poor to see the relative importance of external influences. We conclude with implications for policy and further research.

2. Data and approach

We use data on the country's 14 regions over the period 1988–2000, consisting of five 3-year sub-periods. Significant liberalization measures were introduced into the economy over this period, thus making it particularly suitable for our purposes. The national economy grew at an annual average rate of under 3% in 1988–1991, a period of political instability, dipping further to 2.3% in 1991–1994 as a consequence of the Middle East crisis-triggered global economic slowdown. Gross domestic product (GDP) growth picked up sharply to over 5% annually in 1994–1997 as market-based reforms kicked in amid a buoyant global economy, but fell back once more to 2.3% per annum during 1997–2000 in the wake of the Asian financial crisis. Across the regions there was considerable variation in economic performance during these different growth episodes.

The data on gross regional domestic product (GRDP) are from the national income accounts, various socioeconomic and fiscal data are from records of relevant government agencies, and household data are from the Family Income and Expenditure Survey (FIES) conducted by the National Statistics Office every three years. To represent external economic impacts, we use data on exports and investments which are the best available at the regional level; specifically, trade openness is defined as the ratio of regional exports to GRDP. We have two indicators for poverty from the FIES: poverty incidence (headcount ratio) – the proportion of population below the poverty line, and mean consumption expenditure of the bottom quintile. For theoretical and practical reasons, mean consumption expenditure is deemed superior to mean income as a measure of welfare (Deaton 1997). The theoretical basis is the permanent income hypothesis; at the same time, in practice, current income is more difficult and costly to measure in developing countries where the majority of the poor are self-employed and engaged in agricultural activities with fluctuating incomes.

We first examine the data to discern general patterns across regions and over time before applying more rigorous analytical techniques.

3. Patterns of regional development

Earlier studies have shown the highly uneven spatial distribution of economic activity in the Philippines, with Metro Manila towering over all the other regions (Pernia et al. 1983; Lamberte et al. 1993; Pernia and Israel 1994). While such spatial concentration or urban primacy may be desirable initially to minimize infrastructure expenditures and achieve agglomeration economies, it can become excessive and costly. The costs are all too familiar, such as time lost to traffic congestion, health costs owing to air and water pollution, flooding, and traffic accidents. Thus, dispersed spatial development remains an important goal in the government's agenda, although regional policy has been in the national plans for more than three decades.

3.1. Economic indicators

The spatial imbalance appears to be persisting. Metro Manila (also referred to as the National Capital Region or NCR) continues to have by far the highest per capita income (Table 1). Though this is expected, what is striking is the increasing income differential relative to the national average and to those of the other regions. In 2000, NCR's GRDP per capita was close to 2.5 times the national average, about double that of the next highest in the Cordillera Autonomous Region (CAR), and more than 5.5 times that of the poorest region (Bicol). CAR's relative development has picked up in recent years as a result of special attention from the government. More importantly, this region includes Baguio which is a popular tourist destination and the site of a major export processing zone. By contrast, Bicol has traditionally been the most backward region and continues to have the lowest growth rate, partly because destructive typhoons pass through it several times a year.

The continuing dominance of Metro Manila is also evidenced by its regional share of GDP which rose further to 36% in 2000 from 30% in 1988 (Table 1). The second largest share is less than half and belongs to Southern Tagalog, which is adjacent to the NCR. Central Luzon, which borders the NCR to the north, has roughly under 8% of GDP, while Central Visayas which includes the country's second largest city, Cebu, claims just under 7% of national output. CAR was the fastest growing and is among the few regions that have increased their GDP shares. What explains the relative economic buoyancy of these regions?

There is no doubt that the regions bordering Metro Manila benefit from spillover effects. Nevertheless, it can be argued that part of the economic

Table 1. Gross regional domestic product (GRDP) per capita, regional shares, and growth of GRDP (*constant 1985 prices*)

	Region	GRDP per capita (pesos)		Regional share of GDP (%)		GRDP growth rate (annual %)	
		1988	2000	1988	2000	1988–1994	1994–2000
A	Metro Manila or NCR	26,090	29,577	29.95	35.68	2.40	4.55
B	Cordillera Autonomous (CAR)	11,066	14,952	1.85	2.30	4.55	5.75
I	Ilocos	5,675	6,873	2.92	3.06	2.49	5.26
II	Cagayan Valley	5,942	7,150	2.12	2.15	1.64	5.77
III	Central Luzon	10,546	10,673	9.39	7.42	3.36	2.99
IV	Southern Tagalog	12,784	13,179	14.93	13.92	1.12	5.50
V	Bicol	4,789	5,227	3.05	2.72	2.33	1.95
VI	Western Visayas	8,586	9,869	7.09	6.53	3.40	2.72
VII	Central Visayas	9,696	11,118	6.55	6.81	2.39	4.60
VIII	Eastern Visayas	5,334	5,828	2.63	2.47	1.02	3.77
IX	Western Mindanao	6,393	7,494	2.97	2.85	3.36	4.02
X	Northern Mindanao	10,356	11,659	5.41	4.65	1.84	3.02
XI	Southern Mindanao	11,784	11,181	7.39	6.19	1.29	3.23
XII	Central Mindanao	8,800	7,786	3.74	3.25	0.56	3.68
	Philippines	11,215	12,178	100.00	100.00	2.56	3.73

Source: National Statistics Office. Philippine Statistical Yearbook (various years).

Table 2. Number of special economic zones by region as of July 1, 2002

		Operating	% Share	Proclaimed	% Share	Dev't in progress	% Share	Total	% Share
A	NCR	9	19	2	7	8	11	19	13
B	CAR	1	2	2	7	0	0	3	2
I	Ilocos	0	0	1	3	3	4	4	3
II	Cagayan Valley	0	0	0	0	0	0	0	0
III	Central Luzon	5	10	3	10	5	7	13	9
IV	Southern Tagalog	25	52	10	33	28	39	63	42
V	Bicol	0	0	1	3	6	8	7	5
VI	West Visayas	0	0	1	3	6	8	7	5
VII	Central Visayas	5	10	2	7	6	8	13	9
VIII	East Visayas	1	2	2	7	0	0	3	2
IX	West Mindanao	0	0	1	3	0	0	1	1
X	North Mindanao	1	2	4	13	1	1	6	4
XI	South Mindanao	1	2	1	3	6	8	8	5
XII	Central Mindanao	0	0	0	0	3	4	3	2
	Philippines	48	100	30	100	72	100	150	100

Source: Philippine Economic Zone Authority, 2002. List of approved/proclaimed special economic zones, http://www.peza.gov.ph/ecozone_frmset.htm.

influence comes from international factors, such as investment and trade. Table 2 shows that most of the special economic zones (SEZs – largely export processing zones [EPZs]) are located in four regions: the NCR, Southern Tagalog, Central Luzon, and Central Visayas. In the 1980s, there were only four EPZs owned and operated by the government located in Bataan and Cavite (Southern Tagalog); Mactan, Cebu (Central Visayas); and Baguio (CAR). Then in 1992, the *Bases Conversion and Development Act* was signed into law, converting the former U.S. bases, Clark and Subic in Central Luzon, into SEZs. This marked a sharp rise in foreign direct investments and greater private sector involvement in the economy.

To further spread the benefits of industrialization to areas beyond Metro Manila, the Special Economic Zone Act of 1995 was signed into law to:

> … encourage, promote, induce and accelerate a sound and balanced industrial, economic and social development of the country in order to provide jobs to the people especially those in the rural areas, increase their productivity and their individual and family incomes, and thereby improve the level and quality of their living conditions through the establishment, among others, of special economic zones in suitable and strategic locations in the country and through measures that shall effectively attract legitimate and productive foreign investments.

Enterprises located in the ecozones are granted fiscal incentives. According to the SEZ ACT, each ecozone shall be provided with transportation, telecommunications, and other facilities needed to generate linkage with industries and employment opportunities for its own inhabitants and those of nearby towns and cities. Thus, from six ecozones in the early 1990s, the number has burgeoned to 150 to date. Of this total, 48 are currently operating, 72 are under development, and 30 additional sites have been officially proclaimed as ecozones. More than two of five of the existing ecozones are located in Southern Tagalog, mostly in the provinces of Laguna and Cavite which are located near to Metro Manila.

As expected, the four regions hosting the SEZs are the main recipients of both foreign and domestic investments (Table 3). Also, Table 3 shows that the share of investments going to the NCR has been declining while that going to Southern Tagalog has been expanding significantly. By contrast, all four Mindanao regions suffered noticeable drops in investment shares because of peace and order problems in a few areas, resulting in adverse publicity for the whole of Mindanao.

A look at the regional pattern of exports reveals essentially the same relative dominance of the four regions (Table 4). Similar to the spatial pattern of investments, the NCR's prominence in exports appears to be waning, from more than half of total exports in 1988 to just below a quarter in 2000. At the same time, Southern Tagalog's share shot up dramatically from less than 4% in 1988 to over half of total exports in 2000. Other remarkable increases in export shares are those of the CAR and Central Luzon. By contrast, all four Mindanao regions experienced marked falls in export shares. Overall, exports tend to be more evenly distributed spatially than investment because agricultural regions also export, as shown by earlier data (Solon 1996).

Table 3. Approved investments by region (value in million pesos)

	Region	1988	1994	2000	Regional share (%)		
					1988	1994	2000
A	NCR	13,122.91	42,325.91	16,963.04	45.76	28.22	18.81
B	CAR	8.59	653.08	1,575.16	0.03	0.44	1.75
I	Ilocos	77.69	19,679.93	911.62	0.27	13.12	1.01
II	Cagayan Valley	–	321.20	–	0.00	0.21	0.00
III	Central Luzon	6,580.11	24,990.74	14,464.03	22.94	16.66	16.04
IV	Southern Tagalog	4,577.46	29,390.49	50,415.44	15.96	19.59	55.91
V	Bicol	77.99	338.43	1.47	0.27	0.23	0.00
VI	West Visayas	640.56	247.68	1,130.92	2.23	0.17	1.25
VII	Central Visayas	1,171.31	16,890.83	4,158.81	4.08	11.26	4.61
VIII	East Visayas	31.86	5,229.73	19.55	0.11	3.49	0.02
IX	West Mindanao	362.20	2,708.65	9.22	1.26	1.81	0.01
X	North Mindanao	1,283.29	2,853.78	82.88	4.47	1.90	0.09
XI	South Mindanao	745.26	1,006.74	432.96	2.60	0.67	0.48
XII	Central Mindanao	–	3,367.50	–	0.00	2.24	0.00
	Philipines	28,679.23	150,004.68	90,165.09	100.00	100.00	100.00

Source: Board of Investments; Philippine Economic Zone Authority; National Statistics Coordination Board.

Table 4. Exports by region (FOB in million U.S. dollars)

	Region	1988	1994	2000	Regional share (%)		
					1988	1994	2000
A	NCR	4,038.49	9,178.35	8,998.87	57.09	68.07	23.63
B	CAR	–	654.74	2,477.56	0.00	4.86	6.51
I	Ilocos	260.83	40.26	34.68	3.69	0.30	0.09
II	Cagayan Valley	6.96	0.06	1.01	0.10	0.00	0.00
III	Central Luzon	325.76	346.87	2,761.37	4.60	2.57	7.25
IV	Southern Tagalog	259.71	337.40	19,904.16	3.67	2.50	52.27
V	Bicol	28.65	39.74	39.46	0.40	0.29	0.10
VI	West Visayas	89.11	91.77	59.53	1.26	0.68	0.16
VII	Central Visayas	475.94	793.58	2,141.01	6.73	5.89	5.62
VIII	East Visayas	414.72	769.96	361.90	5.86	5.71	0.95
IX	West Mindanao	129.05	155.56	171.52	1.82	1.15	0.45
X	North Mindanao	358.05	364.30	297.36	5.06	2.70	0.78
XI	South Mindanao	508.23	580.47	724.27	7.18	4.31	1.90
XII	Central Mindanao	178.69	129.83	105.55	2.53	0.96	0.28
	Philippines	7,074.19	13,482.90	38,078.25	100.00	100.00	100.00

Note: Exports are computed as the sum of domestic exports and re-exports.
Source: National Statistics Office. Foreign Trade Statistics of the Philippines (various years).

3.2. Social indicators

Typically, the social development of a country's regions is predictable from their economic performance. However, social disparities across regions may also reflect the relative effectiveness of public spending in the social sectors at the local level.

Metro Manila has the highest functional literacy at over 90%, followed by Southern Tagalog and Central Luzon. Central Visayas also has a relatively high literacy at more than 80%, but other regions that are not as economically well-off, such as Ilocos and Cagayan Valley, have slightly higher literacy rates. As expected, the Mindanao regions generally have the lowest functional literacy rates (70% for Western Mindanao, the poorest of the group). A related indicator is the cohort survival rate for secondary education which shows a similar spatial pattern, although the regional differentials are much narrower (Table 5). The highest rates at around 80% are, as expected, in Metro Manila and the more advanced regions, as well as in two lower-income ones (Ilocos and Cagayan Valley), while the lowest at 63% is in Western Mindanao.

Health indicators, such as infant mortality rate and life expectancy at birth, are similarly the best for Metro Manila and the more economically advanced regions (Table 6). However, as with the education indicators, the disparities across regions are smaller, ranging from 70 years of life expectancy in the NCR to 62 years in Western Mindanao. Life expectancy is a composite indicator of physical safety, nutritional level, and the efficacy of health interventions.

3.3. Poverty indicators

Based on spatially consistent poverty lines, as suggested by Balisacan (2001), applied to the distribution of per capita consumption expenditures, poverty

Table 5. Cohort survival rate for secondary education by region (%)

	Region	1990	1995	2000	Annual % change	
					1990–1995	1995–2000
A	NCR	79.78	82.12	75.56	0.58	−1.65
B	CAR	74.17	83.44	77.25	2.38	−1.53
I	Ilocos	84.46	81.69	78.3	−0.66	−0.84
II	Cagayan Valley	75.07	77.44	77.9	0.62	0.12
III	Central Luzon	76.65	75.57	76.23	−0.28	0.17
IV	Southern Tagalog	79.11	76.17	78.05	−0.75	0.49
V	Bicol	70.62	68.09	71.73	−0.73	1.05
VI	Western Visayas	87.84	76.63	68.01	−2.69	−2.36
VII	Central Visayas	70.76	72.05	74.41	0.36	0.65
VIII	Eastern Visayas	67.16	65.26	64.99	−0.57	−0.08
IX	Western Mindanao	67.67	48.26	63.23	−6.54	5.55
X	Northern Mindanao	70.52	53.93	69.07	−5.22	5.07
XI	Southern Mindanao	71.28	59.82	70.43	−3.44	3.32
XII	Central Mindanao	76.42	55.38	65.73	−6.24	3.49
	Philippines	76.41	72.97	73.05	−0.92	0.02

Notes: For 1995 and 2000, values for regions 9 and 12 are the averages of these regions and ARMM.
For 1995 and 2000, values for regions 10 and 11 are the averages of these regions and CARAGA.
Source: Philippine Institute for Development Studies Website (http://dirp.pids.gov.ph/eismain.html).

incidence (headcount ratio) at the national level appeared to be on the downtrend. From 41.5% in 1985, the headcount ratio fell to 32% in 1994, then to 25% in 1997, before rising to 27% in 2000 in the aftermath of the Asian economic crisis exacerbated by the El Niño drought.[1]

At the regional level, poverty incidence varies widely, with Metro Manila having the lowest at 5.6%, followed by Central Luzon, Southern Tagalog, and CAR at just under 20% (Table 7). As expected, Western Mindanao and Bicol have the highest poverty incidence at over 50%. What appears surprising is the relatively high poverty rate in Central Visayas (39%), despite its relatively high-income level and favorable social indicators. This probably reflects sharper intra-regional inequality, implying that aggregate economic and social benefits may not be trickling down fast enough to the poor (Monsod and Monsod 1999). This suggests the need for a subregional or more micro approach to poverty reduction. It could also reflect the below-average performance of the agricultural sector on which the majority of the poor depend, implying the need for appropriate investments in this sector.

Another poverty indicator (mean consumption expenditure per capita of the poorest quintile, reflecting the poor's living standards) tells the same story (Table 7). This indicator is closely associated with GRDP per capita,

[1] These estimates are different from the officially published figures which are higher. The official figures are based on current income, rather than consumption expenditure, as the welfare indicator, and on poverty lines that vary in real terms across regions and between urban and rural areas. This approach, as Balisacan (2001) shows, fails the consistency test for poverty lines. Accordingly, it is not suitable for poverty monitoring at the national or subnational levels, if the policy objective is to reduce absolute poverty.

Table 6. Life expectancy by region (in years)

	Region	1980	1990	2000	Annual % change	
					1980–1990	1990–2000
A	NCR	59.7	66.6	70.1	1.10	0.51
B	CAR	57.8	61.1	66.1	0.56	0.79
I	Ilocos	63.9	65.5	69.5	0.25	0.60
II	Cagayan Valley	59.6	63.1	67.6	0.57	0.68
III	Central Luzon	65.2	67.5	70.7	0.35	0.47
IV	Southern Tagalog	63.4	65.6	69.5	0.34	0.57
V	Bicol	59.3	64.0	68.3	0.77	0.65
VI	West Visayas	61.5	64.3	68.7	0.45	0.66
VII	Central Visayas	64.1	66.4	70.1	0.35	0.55
VIII	East Visayas	56.8	60.6	65.6	0.65	0.80
IX	West Mindanao	54.7	57.0	62.0	0.41	0.85
X	North Mindanao	60.7	62.3	67.1	0.26	0.74
XI	South Mindanao	60.0	63.7	68.1	0.60	0.67
XII	Central Mindanao	53.9	57.1	62.1	0.58	0.85
	Philippines	60.6	64.8	68.9	0.67	0.62

Note: The value for Regions 9 & 12 computed as averages of these regions and ARMM.
Source: National Statistics Office, 2001. Philippine Statistical Yearbook; Asian Development Bank, 1998. Compendium of Social Statistics in the Philippines.

although the link is not as tight as suggested by other studies. For example, Dollar and Kraay (2001), employing cross-country regressions, estimate a growth elasticity of poverty of 1.0, suggesting that the average incomes of the poor move one-for-one with overall average incomes. The elasticity estimate from our cross-regional regression is 0.42, implying that a 10% increase in regional incomes is associated with a 4.2% rise in the well-being of the poor.

In sum, Metro Manila remains pre-eminent in the country's economic and social landscape, although a few regions are thriving more visibly in recent years.[2] Regional disparities are revealed more sharply in economic indicators than in social indicators. To some extent, the narrower differentials in terms of social indicators suggest that there is not much regional variation in the effectiveness of social policy and spending at the local level, given that fiscal decentralization is still in its nascent stage. Regional poverty rates vary widely and are more closely associated with economic indicators than with social indicators.

4. Determinants of regional development and poverty reduction

This review of regional development patterns leads to two key hypotheses regarding factors influencing regional development and poverty reduction. First, we expect economic openness to affect regional economic growth positively in a significant way, in addition to the impact of domestic factors. In

[2] Based on cross-country regressions, Henderson (2002) finds that urban primacy (population in the largest city) increases as GDP per capita rises from low levels up to $5,300 (approximate average world GDP per capita in 1990), after which it declines. The Philippines' GNP per capita was $1,040 as of 2000.

Table 7. Poverty incidence and expenditure per capita of poorest quintile

	Region	Poverty incidence %		Annual change in poverty %	Expenditure per capita poorest quintile (1985 = 100) PhP		Annual change in exp. per capita of poorest quintile %
		1988	2000	1988–2000	1988	2000	1988–2000
A	Metro Manila	9.48	5.6	−4.29	3,183	3,680	1.22
B	CAR	24.13	19.85	−1.61	2,021	2,063	0.17
I	Ilocos	28.4	20.31	−2.76	2,087	2,236	0.58
II	Cagayan Valley	43.22	29.57	−3.11	1,849	2,344	2.00
III	Central Luzon	24.7	16.13	−3.49	2,535	2,924	1.20
IV	Southern Tagalog	38.2	19.56	−5.43	1,917	2,516	2.29
V	Bicol	53.84	53.32	−0.08	1,546	1,487	−0.32
VI	Western Visayas	37.58	28.15	−2.38	1,785	1,949	0.74
VII	Central Visayas	47.57	39.3	−1.58	1,256	1,365	0.70
VIII	Eastern Visayas	53.44	46.82	−1.10	1,433	1,493	0.34
IX	Western Mindanao	48.03	55.48	1.21	1,536	1,446	−0.50
X	Northern Mindanao	30.62	30.24	−0.10	1,722	1,703	−0.09
XI	Southern Mindanao	34.84	25.29	−2.63	1,797	2,089	1.26
XII	Central Mindanao	30.45	36.16	1.44	1,813	1,709	−0.49
	Philippines	34.31	27.27	−1.90	2,002	2,266	1.04

Source: National Statistics Office, Family Income and Expenditure Surveys; authors' own calculations.

other words, regions that produce tradable goods grow faster than those that do not. Second, given that economic growth at the national or regional levels is good for poverty reduction, as shown by several studies (e.g., Dollar and Kraay 2001; Balisacan and Pernia 2002; Balisacan et al. 2002), we expect that trade openness contributing to growth should also help improve the welfare of the poor. Such an impact may be expected to be not only indirect (via growth) but also direct on poverty itself. The direct effect can occur because investments and exports typically generate a host of ancillary economic activities that benefit the poor. Moreover, to the extent that many of these activities are in the informal sector, they are not captured in GDP accounts and, therefore, would not be reflected in the growth effect on poverty.

5. Empirical model

We adopt a simple model based on theoretical expectations but, at the same time, is conditioned by data availability.

$$\mathrm{PCEPOOR}_{rt} = \mathrm{PCEPOOR}_{rt}(\mathrm{GRDP}_{rt}, \mathrm{LOCAL}_{rt}, \mathrm{ICOND}_{r}) \tag{1}$$

$$\mathrm{GRDP}_{rt} = \mathrm{GRDP}_{rt}(\mathrm{LOCAL}_{rt}, \mathrm{LOCAL}_{rt-1}, \mathrm{OPEN}_{rt}) \tag{2}$$

$$\mathrm{OPEN}_{rt} = \mathrm{OPEN}_{rt}(\mathrm{LOCAL}_{rt}, \mathrm{LOCAL}_{rt-1}, \mathrm{OPEN}_{rt-1}, \mathrm{GRDP}_{rt}) \tag{3}$$

where

$\mathrm{PCEPOOR}_{rt}$ = per capita expenditure of the poor in region r at time t
GRDP_{rt} = income of region r at time t

Table 8. Determinants of economic openness, GRDP per capita, and welfare of the poor

Variable	Ln exports/ GRDP (1)	s.e.	Ln GRDP per capita (2)	s.e.	Ln mean exp. per capita of bottom quintile (3)	s.e
Endogenous						
Ln GRDP per capita	−0.165	0.410			0.198**	0.079
Ln Exports-GRDP Ratio			0.044**	0.019		
Lagged Ln Exports-GRDP Ratio	0.869**	0.044				
Lagged Ln Investment-GRDP Ratio	−0.022	0.047				
Local factors						
Ln social Expenditures per capita					0.031*	0.016
Lagged Ln Social Exp. per capita			0.142**	0.058		
Lagged Ln Dev't Exp. per capita	0.184**	0.087	0.016	0.050		
Number of special economic zones	0.047**	0.010				
Terms of trade	2.204**	0.898				
Average schooling years of household heads			0.115**	0.039		
Initial conditions						
Cohort survival rate for secondary education					0.010**	0.003
Road density					0.125**	0.027
% of Households with electricity					0.009**	0.001
Primacy (NCR = 1; 0 otherwise)	2.411**	1.081	0.570**	0.185		
Constant	−1.907	3.629	7.870**	0.351	4.336**	0.671
Equation	R^2	chi^2				
Ln Mean Exp. of Bottom Quintile	0.828	366.543				
Ln GRDP per capita	0.682	133.097				
Ln Exports	0.908	636.847				

* Significantly different from zero at 10% level.
** Significantly different from zero at 5% level or lower.

$OPEN_{rt}$ = economic openness (exports-GRDP ratio) in region r at time t
$LOCAL_{rt}$ = local factors in region r at time t
$ICOND_r$ = initial conditions of region r

Equation 1 shows how the welfare of the poor is influenced by the region's income, local factors, and initial conditions. Equations 2 and 3 take into account the endogeneity of GRDP and economic openness as both are affected by each other and by local factors.

Equations 1–3 are estimated using the three-stage least squares (3SLS) method. The 3SLS estimation procedure takes into account not only the endogeneity of the three variables (per capita expenditure of the poor, regional income, and exports) but also the interaction between equations via the covariance matrix of the equations' disturbances.

For the estimation, we use panel data on the 14 regions for the years 1988, 1991, 1994, 1997, and 2000, i.e., five 3-year intervals. The empirical model is constrained by the available data. To test for dynamic effects, current as well as lagged values are used. Appendix Tables 1 and 2 present the detailed description of the variables and their descriptive statistics, respectively. The three endogenous variables were described briefly above. Now, we need to say something about *local factors* and *initial conditions*.

5.1. Local factors

These include public expenditures on economic development services and on social services. The former refers to local government unit (LGU) outlays for agriculture, agrarian reform and natural resources, trade and investment, and tourism (including power and energy, water development and flood control, communication, roads and other transport). The latter is public spending for education, health, housing and community development, and land distribution. These two variables measure output rather than outcomes. According to Solon et al. (2000): "Expenditure outlays directly imply the relative priority given to different types of public services ... local officials can readily influence the allocation of public resources, more than they can local welfare." During the period 1985–2000, LGUs spent about PhP 201 per person on economic services and PhP 69 per person on social services.

Other local factors refer to physical infrastructure, such as paved roads, electricity, international port and airport facilities, and telephones. SEZs not only represent major infrastructure investments but also receive important fiscal incentives from the government. The agricultural terms of trade is the ratio of the price of agricultural products to the price of non-agricultural output. Local educational attainment is represented by the mean schooling years of household heads, which measures the capacity of the local population to take advantage of the economic opportunities arising from economic growth. The crime rate is the monthly average of incidents for every 100,000 population in the region.

5.2. Initial conditions

These refer to time-invariant factors. Recent discourse on poverty points out the increasing disparities across states or regions in various countries. In India, for example, Datt and Ravallion (2002) find that states with relatively low levels of initial physical and human capital development are less effective in reducing poverty in response to economic growth. As initial conditions, we use infrastructure (electricity and paved roads) and human capital (education and health).

Further, we introduce into the model a dummy for primacy (NCR = 1) to capture the distinct economic and political advantages of Metro Manila over the other regions. As rightly articulated by Hill (2000, 13):

the (national) capitals are where major infrastructure projects are awarded, where business licenses must be obtained, where major foreign and domestic firms are headquartered, and where foreign aid flows first before it enters the domestic economy.

5.3. Empirical results

The estimation results are mostly in accord with expectations. Column (1) of Table 8 shows that the significant determinants of trade openness are previous export performance, agricultural terms of trade, previous-period local development expenditures, and the number of SEZs. The agricultural terms-of-trade variable suggests that price incentives favor regions with a comparative advantage in agriculture. The significance of the primacy dummy implies that the NCR remains an important source of exports and re-exports.

Column (2) of Table 8 shows that regional development is significantly driven by trade openness, as hypothesized. A 10% increase in the exports-GRDP ratio raises GRDP per capita by 0.44%. Regional economic growth also appears to be strongly influenced by lagged public spending for social sectors. Human capital (average schooling years of household heads) has a positive and significant effect. The primacy dummy implies that Metro Manila maintains dominance over all other regions, as mentioned above.

Finally, Table 8, column (3) supports the well-established view that the well-being of the poor is significantly influenced by economic growth. The growth elasticity of poverty is 0.2, implying that a 10% rise in regional incomes per capita raises the incomes of the poorest by 2%. This elasticity value is smaller than the OLS estimate of 0.42 mentioned above, and smaller still than the 3SLS estimate of about 0.5 based on provincial data (Balisacan and Pernia 2002).[3]

In addition to growth, the welfare of the poor is strongly affected by current public spending for social sectors including agrarian reform and better initial conditions, such as availability of electricity and roads, and human capital stock (secondary-education survival rate).

As a further point, our analysis provides no empirical support to the hypothesis of a direct link from exports or investments to the incomes of the poor other than through economic growth. This is consistent with the findings of a recent survey on trade, growth, and poverty by Krueger and Berg (2002). They argue that, while trade openness does not have systematic effects on incomes of the poor, openness is good for growth. Also, such growth is equally pro-poor as other growth; they add that trade reforms positively influence other reforms and lead to a wider constituency for reforms.

6. Conclusion and policy implications

Economic and social development varies markedly across the Philippines's 14 regions, with Metro Manila towering over the national economic landscape. However, the emergence of Southern Tagalog and Central Luzon (both adjacent to Metro Manila), the Cordillera Autonomous Region (CAR), and

[3] A region is made up of provinces. As of 2000, there were 81 provinces making up the Philippines' 14 regions.

Central Visayas is notable. This emergence can be partly attributed to the influence of such external factors as exports and investments.

On the whole, it appears that economic openness, as represented here by the exports-GRDP ratio, is beneficial to regional economic growth and, via growth, poverty reduction. Nevertheless, it seems that trade openness by itself cannot be relied upon to bring about more balanced regional development, i.e., narrower disparities in regional incomes and poverty, which is an important policy objective in many developing countries. In the post-colonial era, domestic market forces and public policy set spatial development patterns. Global influences tend to follow these set patterns. For instance, foreign direct investments go to where there is good infrastructure, human capital, a favorable policy environment, and where economies of agglomeration can be achieved. In addition, non-traditional exports tend to originate in areas with adequate physical and human capital, e.g., the export processing zones (EPZs).

To foster more balanced regional development, public policy will have to take the lead and encourage the private sector to play an active role in that pursuit. It cannot be overstressed that good physical and social infrastructure is crucial (as represented by the EPZs), as is a conducive investment climate. Those in charge of implementing the decentralization policy must take these into account.

In this paper, we have dealt with economic openness in a rather limited fashion. There are several other cross-national influences, besides trade and capital, such as technology, information, knowledge, and economic policy that could be as powerful. Further analytical work should incorporate these additional factors. Moreover, more disaggregated data, e.g., at the provincial level, are likely to lead to better insights. Finally, longer time-series data should allow a distinction between the short-term and long-term effects of economic openness.

References

Balisacan AM (2001) Poverty in the Philippines: An update and reexamination. Philippine Review of Economics 38(1):16–51

Balisacan AM, Pernia EM (2002) Probing beneath cross-national averages: Poverty, inequality, and growth in the Philippines. ERD Working Paper No. 7, Asian Development Bank, Manila

Balisacan AM, Pernia EM, Asra A (2002) Revisiting growth and poverty reduction in Indonesia: What do subnational data show? ERD Working Paper No. 25, Asian Development Bank, Manila

Datt G, Ravallion M (2002) Is India's economic growth leaving the poor behind? Policy Research Working Paper Series, The World Bank, Washington, D.C

Deaton A (1997) In: The analysis of household surveys: A microeconometric approach to development policy. Johns Hopkins University Press, Baltimore

Dollar D, Kraay A (2001) Growth is good for the poor. World Bank Policy Research Paper No. 2587, The World Bank, Washington, D.C

Fuchs RJ, Pernia EM (1987) External economic forces and national spatial development: Japanese Direct Investment in Pacific Asia. In: Fuchs RJ, Jones GW, Pernia EM (eds) Urbanization and urban policies in Pacific Asia. Westview Press, Boulder and London, pp 88–111

Henderson V (2002) Urbanization in developing countries. The World Bank Research Observer 17(1):89–112

Herrin AN, Pernia EM (1987) Factors influencing the choice of location: Local and foreign firms in the Philippines. Regional Studies 21(6):531–541

Hill H (2000) Intra-country regional disparities. Paper presented at Second Asia Development Forum, Singapore, June 6–8

Krueger A, Berg A (2002) Trade, growth, and poverty: A selective survey. Paper presented at the World Bank's Annual Bank Conference on Development Economics, Washington, D.C., 29–30 April

Krugman PR, Livas RE (1996) Trade policy and the third world metropolis. Journal of Development Economics 49:137–150

Lamberte MB, et al. (1993) Decentralization and prospects for regional growth. Philippine Institute for Development Studies, Manila

Lo F, Yue-man Y (eds) (1996) Emerging world cities in Pacific Asia. United Nations University Press, Tokyo

Lo F, Yue-man Y (eds) (1998) Globalization and the world of large cities. United Nations University Press, Tokyo

Makabenta MP (2002) FDI location and special economic zones in the Philippines. Review of Urban and Regional Development Studies 14(1):59–77

Monsod SC, Monsod TC (1999) International and intranational comparisons of Philippine poverty. In: Balisacan AM, Fujisaki S (eds) Causes of poverty: Myths, facts and policies. University of the Philippines Press, Quezon City, pp 51–96

Pernia EM (1976) Urbanization in the Philippines: Historical and comparative perspectives. Papers of the East-West Population Institute No. 40. East-West Center, Honolulu

Pernia EM, Paderanga CW, Hermoso V (1983) The spatial and urban dimensions of development in the Philippines. Philippine Institute for Development Studies, Manila

Pernia EM (1994) Issues of urban and spatial development. In: Pernia EM (ed) Urban poverty in Asia: A survey of critical issues. Oxford University Press, Hong Kong pp 53–80

Pernia EM, Israel RC (1994) Spatial development, urbanization, and migration patterns in the Philippines. In: Balisacan AM, Medalla FM, Pernia EM (eds) Spatial development, land use, and urban-rural growth linkages in the Philippines. National Economic and Development Authority, Manila, pp 13–46

Reed RR (1967) Hispanic urbanism in the Philippines: A study of the impact of church and state. Journal of East Asiatic Studies 11:1–222

Solon OJ (1996) Global influences on recent urbanization trends in the Philippines. In: Lo F, Yeung Y (eds) Emerging world cities in Pacific Asia. United Nations University Press, Tokyo, pp 268–285

Solon OJ, Fabella RV, Capuno JJ (2000) Is local development good politics? Philippine Center for Policy Studies, Manila (Processed)

Appendix

Table A1. Description of the variables

Variable	Definitions
Mean expenditures of poor	Ln of mean consumption expenditure per capita of bottom 20% of population of the region.
Regional income	Ln of real GRDP per capita of the region.
Exports	Ln of ratio of exports to GRDP; exports computed as sum of exports and re-exports (1988–2000).
Lagged exports	Ln of previous period export-GRDP ratio.
Lagged investments	Ln of previous period investments-GRDP ratio.
Social expenditures per capita	Ln of social services expenditures per capita (i.e., education, culture and manpower, health, social services, housing and community development, land distribution, other social services, subsidy to LGUs) of LGUs in the region.
Lagged social expenditures per capita	Ln of previous period social services expenditures per capita.

Table A1 (continued)

Variable	Definitions
Economic development expenditures per capita	Ln of economic development exp. per capita (i.e., agriculture, agrarian reform and natural resources, trade and investments, tourism, power and energy, water dev't and flood control, communication, roads and other transport, others) of LGUs in the region.
Lagged economic development expenditures per capita	Ln of previous period economic development expenditures per capita.
Terms of trade	Ratio of price of agriculture to price of non-agriculture.
Special economic zones	Number of SEZs in the region.
Crime rate	Monthly average incidents of crimes reported per 100,000 population in region (1990 data).
Educational attainment of adult population	Average schooling years of households heads in region computed from the 1988–2000 FIES.
Initial roads	Ratio of total length of concrete and asphalted roads to total land area in region (1989 data).
Initial cohort survival rate	Cohort survival rate for secondary education level in region (1990 data).
Initial electrical connections	Percent of households with electricity in region (1988 data, FIES).
Primacy	NCR = 1; 0 for all other regions.

Table A2. Descriptive statistics

Variable	Obs.	Mean	Std. dev.	Minimum	Maximum
Ln mean expenditures of poor	70	8.84	0.22	8.50	9.48
Ln real GRDP per capita	70	9.13	0.43	8.47	10.29
Ln export-GRDP ratio	81	−2.55	1.81	−10.01	0.65
Lagged Ln export-GRDP ratio	81	−2.59	1.75	−10.01	−0.16
Lagged Ln investment-GRDP ratio	65	−4.50	1.73	−8.67	−0.93
Ln social expenditures per capita	70	3.71	1.09	1.60	6.20
Lagged Ln social expenditures per capita	70	3.46	1.01	1.60	6.20
Ln economic development expenditures per capita	70	4.84	1.09	2.93	6.41
Lagged Ln economic development expenditures per capita	70	4.34	1.08	2.85	6.33
Agricultural terms of trade	70	0.86	0.26	0.00	1.12
Schooling years	70	6.57	1.12	4.38	9.66
Special economic zones	70	2.80	7.42	0.00	46.00
Crime rate	70	12.20	6.57	4.32	31.61
Initial road density	70	0.37	1.01	0.02	4.00
Initial electrical connections	70	52.06	14.08	35.11	84.56
Initial cohort survival rate	70	75.11	5.93	67.16	87.84
Primacy	70	0.07	0.26	0.00	1.00

Do the donors have it right? Decentralization and changing local governance in Indonesia

Christopher Silver

Department of Urban and Regional Planning, University of Illinois at Urbana-Champaign, 111 Temple Buell Hall, Urbana-Champaign, IL 61820, USA
(e-mail: silver@uiuc.edu)

Abstract. Indonesia has initiated an ambitious decentralization program since 1999 spurred on by the international donor community (earlier decentralization measures were more like "deconcentration" under strong central control). This paper examines the degree to which Laws 22/1999 and 25/1999 are working. Local government employment has been expanded (not fully offset by a decline in central government employment) and training has been provided. Many functions have been transferred to the local level, but this was not matched by adequate funding transfers. Those localities that fare best have revenues available from their own natural resources. The results, therefore, are very mixed, and it is much too early to determine whether decentralization is a success.

JEL classification: H, R

1. Introduction

Decentralization is a global reform movement that has had far-reaching implications for urbanization in the developing world over the past two decades. This illustrates the point that globalization is not only about the exchange of goods and services or factors of production, but embraces many other phenomena including ideas and modes of governance. According to a 1994 World Bank commissioned study, more than 80% of developing nations with a population of greater than 5 million were engaged in a process of devolving responsibility and power to local governments (Dillinger 1994). While there are many explanations for the pervasiveness of the decentralization movement in the developing world, one important factor has been the consensus within the international donor community that a decentralized governance structure is the preferred model among nations struggling to provide basic services in the face of rapid urbanization. The donor community involvement in promoting decentralization began in the 1970s through efforts to strengthen local government capacity by exposing managers to new planning and management tools. By the 1980s and extending into the 1990s, the international aid community propagated a broad-based critique of central government planning and management and pushed decentralization through a combination direct technical assistance and policy reform, with improved local fiscal performance being the overarching objective (World Bank 1988; Rondinelli 1989).

Approaches such as privatization of urban service delivery, improved tax collection, utility and service pricing based upon willingness to pay, the introduction of long range capital planning, enhanced local revenue generation (to counter reliance upon central government transfers), and transfer of responsibilities from central to local government were the common elements in the donor driven decentralization model, although there were differences in approach as applied to different nations. Yet, the 1990s also found advocates of decentralization placing emphasis on political outcomes, most notably expanded democratization and strengthened civil society in nations ruled by authoritarian regimes and where indigenous political forces were present to utilize outside assistance. As Crook and Manor (1998) remind us, decentralization itself does not necessarily imply democratization. The legacy of international donor assistance in support of decentralization has often had an opposite effect. In its earliest manifestation, donor-assisted decentralization was pursued as a counterforce to attempts to dismantle authoritarian regimes. According to Siddique (1997), this was the case with the decentralization experiment in the authoritarian regime of Bangladesh in the 1980s. "Whether judged on managerial grounds, or in terms of its democratic political rationale, or from a 'developmentalist' perspective," Siddique continues, "the performance of the upazila decentralization has fallen short of expectations and reinforced authoritarians." (p. xii) The case of Indonesia, which is the focus of this study, also demonstrates how an authoritarian regime initially embraced decentralization as a way to improve public sector performance in the face of rapid urbanization but without relinquishing control from the center. In its most basic form, Indonesian decentralization reforms prior to 1999 reforms actually increased local dependency on the central government.

Yet an important aspect of the donors' decentralization agenda of the 1990s was democratic governance, including empowerment of community organizations and strengthening civil society. In Indonesia, the local government strengthening and democratic governance strains ran along parallel tracks during the 1990s and the Suharto government seemed to tolerate (but not condone) donor assistance to non-governmental pro-democracy organizations while readily accepting assistance in support of local financial reform. When the indigenous political side of decentralization after 1998 produced new fiscal and management practices, the result was fundamental change in Indonesia's local governance structure beyond what even the donors were advocating. Whether the structural reforms inherent in this broader approach to decentralization are likely to produce the sort of fundamental change in the way cities or local governments are managed is an issue that this paper seeks to illuminate. To put it simply, has the decentralization movement in Indonesia laid the foundation for an administratively and politically responsive local governance system?

The interface between the global decentralization movement pushed by international donors as a solution to the unique circumstances of developing nations and the changing structure of local governance in Indonesia is the crux of the matter. The competition between proponents of decentralization and centralization in Indonesia, an ideological tug of war that dates back to the 1950s, has been a crucial factor affecting governance processes in urban areas. In the case of Indonesia, the international donor community pursued a consistently pro-decentralization agenda from the 1970s onward. All of the major donors, The World Bank, the Asian Development Bank, the United Nations Development Program, the German Development Agency (GTZ), the U.S. Agency for International Development, the Ford Foundation and the British Aid Agency (to name just the most prominent participants) pushed decentralization (and more subtly, democratization) strategies. The unanticipated demise of the Suharto regime in 1998 in "one of the most centralized countries in the world (Beier and Ferrazi 1997, p. 1), and subsequent passage of radical decentralization legislation (Law 22/1999 and Law 25/1999) under the Habibe administration (which will be discussed fully below), advanced Indonesia's local government reform process so rapidly that some of the international donors and government leaders responded, in the aftermath of the 1999 laws, not so much with applause or even self-congratulations but with worried calls for retrenchment and even recentralization. The International Monetary Fund was the most concerned, fearing that "decentralization could expand Indonesia's debt as a result of localities borrowing separately from the [central] governmental" (Cawley 2001). Donors grouped under the Consultative Group on Indonesia, led by the World Bank, expressed concern shortly after implementation of the new decentralization laws in January 2001 that "the country could face serious threats to its economy without clear guidelines to manage the transfer of power to its regions." (*Dow Jones News Letter* 2001) Resistance to the full implication of decentralization still persists in Indonesia, although most analysts recognize that any attempt to abort the process of devolving responsibility and resources to local government would plunge Indonesia into a deep political crisis, no less destabilizing than the first few years following the demise of Suharto's authoritarian New Order in 1998. Indeed, several recent proposals to tinker with the formula for distributing funds to localities have brought vociferous protests from local governments who have benefited from the new system.

Yet as deeply entrenched as decentralization has become within Indonesia's political culture, the form and substance of the changes taking place continue to be guided by the international donor community. Indonesia continues to draw upon outside assistance in fashioning a workable decentralization program. In the meantime, there is an increasingly vocal political element critical of external interference by the International Monetary Fund and the World Bank because of fear that these institutions might derail the current reform movement. The Minister of Settlement and Regional Infrastructure, Erna Witoeloc stated it most dramatically: "Giving money and power to more than 350 districts across the country is the only way Indonesia can survive as a nation-state." (South China Morning Post 11/22/00).

2. Pre-1999 decentralization

In the pre-1999 era, even at the height of power and legitimacy of Suharto's New Order government, there were those within the regime who recognized that strengthened (but certainly not autonomous) local government units could improve the quality of service delivery without jeopardizing the authority of the center. Resistance to full-scale decentralization on the part of the Suharto government was based, in part, on "concern that such moves [would] encourage ethnic tensions and undermine national unity and centrally-defined priorities" (Walker, p. 94). Yet the most salient factor is that the Suharto government expended considerable effort over several decades to fashion a centralized system to consolidate its political power. Moreover, donors praised the many noteworthy accomplishments of the New Order, such as nearly universal primary education, a national network of basic health care, a vigorous urban slum improvement program (Kampung Improvement Program), rising incomes, improved infrastructure, and solid economic progress particularly as measured by annual growth rates. These stood in stark contrast to the dismal experience under the Sukarno government when the call for greater local autonomy had limited central authority.

Between independence in 1949 and the imposition of Sukarno's Guided Democracy in 1959, the basis of a decentralized administrative structure with an elected local head and a powerful local legislative body (*Dewan Perwakilan Rakyat Daerah* – DPRD) was devised but not implemented. The notion of empowering local governments set forth in a 1957 law but was abandoned by 1959. Only after the Suharto government came to power in 1966 were the key components of the centralized system put into place. Ironically, passage of a 1974 law on decentralization marked the beginning of the new relationship between central and local governments that crippled rather than empowered local authority. The New Order system required all local government officials be tied to a line ministry of central government for budget and responsibility, and employees of the Ministry of Home Affairs for their salary. The district head (*bupati*), city mayors (*walikota*) and governors of the provinces were appointed by the national government, not elected by the citizens or even appointed by the local legislative body. Although the local and provincial legislatures were based upon votes of citizens, there were only three legal political parties and Suharto's Golkar party was the one to support in order to retain a public sector job.

In addition, central government ministries operated offices at the local level (often duplicating local agencies) and revenues for these offices (*dinas*) came directly from central government. The real planning and implementation for local services took place in the *dinas*. Overall, roughly 75% of all local revenues were controlled either by these deconcentrated units or were earmarked grants prescribed in their use by central government regulations and not locally controlled. According to Walker (1991), the donor community accepted this structure and sought to strengthen the capacity of the 3500 local offices by funding training centers throughout the nation. The short-lived training initiative did little to enhance local capacity for two reasons: first, those trained were recruited from the entry level ranks; and secondly, the donor community (in this instance, the U.S. Agency for International Development) dropped the program because the central government Ministry of Home Affairs (MOHA) opposed it (USAID, 1980). Why train local officials, MOHA reasoned, when they only acted on direct orders from Jakarta?

The deconcentrated system became the entrenched model in Indonesia during the 1980s and 1990s despite the intentions of the international donor community to strengthen the local units. The funding mechanism for local government reinforced this tendency. All of the major local revenue streams, including DIPs (*Daftar Isian Proyek*) for sectoral expenditures, SDO (*Subsidi*

Daerah Otonom) to cover wages of all local government officials and staff (including teachers), and INPRES (*Instruksi Presiden*) development funds for a variety of small local development projects, were drawn from the national budget and controlled by central government ministries. The extent of local reliance on intergovernmental transfers to finance routine activities as well as new projects underscored the increasing centralization of local governance and the structural weakness of localities. Rather than challenging the deconcentrated system, international donor assistance focused on modernizing the local finance system. Their focus was on increasing the degree of local discretion in intergovernmental transfers (especially INPRES), pushing central government to use measurable and transparent criteria to allocate funds to localities, encouraging the use of intergovernmental transfers to reduce regional disparities, and advocating improved revenue generation at the local level to decrease dependence on the center. Right up until the unanticipated demise of the Suharto regime in 1998, this was the prevailing strategy of two major proponents of Indonesia's decentralization, the World Bank and the U.S. Agency for International Development (Shah and Quereshi 1994; Aten 1997).

The inefficiencies of the system of dual responsibilities for local affairs in the deconcentrated system and the need for increased local involvement in allocations of routine and development funds were already acknowledged by the New Order government in the early 1990s. In 1994/95, Indonesia created a pilot program involving one district (kabupaten) in each of twenty-six provinces (Jakarta was excluded) to experiment with an approach "to increase autonomy throughout the nation." (Beier and Ferrazzi 1997, p. 3) The essence of the program was to transfer central government sectoral ministry functions, as well as some regional level functions to the district level (cities were to be included in the next round of pilot localities). The pilot program was intended to determine if local government officials were prepared to handle greater responsibilities and how the devolution of responsibilities should take place. In one of the pilot areas, the district of Minahasa in North Sumatra, there were no difficulties absorbing the central government employees into the local office and maintaining the basic serves, but the funds transfer only covered salaries, with no funds for development expenditures. (Alm and Ball 1999, p. 7)

Another case examined by Beier and Ferrazzi (1997) involved the Badung regency in Bali, where a total of 165 functions and 353 tasks were transferred to the locality from the central and regional governments. The most significant transfers involved the public works sectors (especially roads and irrigation), tourism and education. Yet in Badung, like in Minahasa, the principle that transferred functions would be "accompanied by attendant resources, including staff, assets and routine and development funds" was not followed, "especially in relation to the development budget." (Beier and Ferrazzi 1997, p. 8) Beier and Ferrazzi concluded that the top down guided District Autonomy Pilot Program (DAPP) was a modest but symbolically important "departure from the pattern of delay and uncertain progress in realizing the objective of increasing regional autonomy at the second regional level..." (p. 10) Yet they noted quite perceptively that real change is unlikely to come from the top down, that "pressure on the bureaucracy must come principally from the bottom" and that "non-government organizations and the donor community...must seek to organize the lower levels of government to more effectively and forcefully channel their aspirations to the political/administrative apparatus." (p. 10) The crises that struck later in 1997 provided that impetus, and proved the power of the lower levels of government, non-government organizations and new political factions in a democratic climate.

3. Decentralization after 1998

The economic and political crises (not to mention related environmental and social upheavals) that hit Indonesia in 1997 toppled the seemingly indomitable Suharto in May 1998 (Forrester and May 1999) and accelerated the process of decentralization in central/local government relations (McAndrews 1986; Leigland 1993; Ranis and Stewart 1994). Two laws enacted in 1999 under the shortlived government of B.J. Habibe (Suharto's Vice-President) framed the imminent radical transformation of central and local government relations in Indonesia. Law 22/1999 eliminated the hierarchical governance system where localities were under the control of the provincial and central governments with a system that granted substantial autonomy to the city (*kota*) and district (*kabupaten*) levels. Mayors and district heads were no longer appointees of the provincial government but selected by the local parliament and responsible to that body. The new law also devolved substantial new responsibilities to local governments that had previously been carried out by central government sectoral ministries. Under Law 22, central government functions would be limited to international policies, defense and security, the judiciary, monetary and fiscal policies, religion, national planning, natural resource utilization and the state economic institutions. All other government responsibilities, including health, education, public works, agriculture, environmental protection, and other urban services, all of which previously had been under the domain of central government ministries, were now the responsibility of local governments. The one remaining link between local and central government was the requirement that all decisions from the local legislatures and local administrators be reported to the Ministry of Home Affairs. What was significant about this component of Law 22 was that it removed provincial government from its traditional oversight of local affairs, and left their status under the decentralized governance structure much less precisely defined than under the old system. The new law failed to specify exactly what role the central government would exercise in reviewing local decisions, although the assumption among local officials was that they now possessed unlimited discretion so long as local decisions were consistent with national laws.

Probably the most significant change was the transfer of sectoral ministry personnel to local offices (a move anticipated in the DAPP) and the conversion of all local personnel, including schoolteachers, from central government to local employees. This change, which had surfaced in different forms from a variety of donor-sponsored projects related to restructuring local/central relations from the 1980s onwards, was the one reform proposal that had previously been dismissed out of hand. Clearly, the links between government employees and the continued dominance of Suharto's Golkar party was an obvious factor in earlier rejection of administrative reform. So long as all government employees were controlled from the center, then

Golkar could be assured of a consistent voter base at the central, provincial and local levels. When the Habibe government included the dismantling of this key pillar of the central government bureaucratic dominance of localities, it unleashed not only an organizational transformation but a political metamorphosis that saw Indonesia change from a rigidly controlled three party systems to a chaotic assemblage of more than one hundred political parties trying to shape the new agenda of a new society. According to Rya'as, who briefly headed a ministry created in 1999 under the Wahid administration to oversee implementation of Law 22 (and in 2002 created a new political party devoted to accelerating decentralization), the impact of the decentralization legislation was a "new paradigm" in Indonesia's governance.

The other component of Indonesia's decentralization, Law 25/1999, changed the fiscal structure of central/local relations through the establishment of four types of intergovernmental transfers, including a new general allocation fund to support the expanded functions of local government. In addition, it included a natural resources revenue sharing provision, which applied to those provinces and districts with strategic assets. In addition, there were changes in property tax sharing, especially with regard to metropolitan areas. Finally, there were special allocations for those districts with significant forestry activities. But the general allocation fund was the most significant feature of Law 25 since it combined the multitude of earmarked central government transfer grants into a single discretionary grant. According to Law 25, the general allocation fund (*Dana Alokasi Umum* or DAU) would be no less than 25% of domestic revenues (total domestic revenues excluding natural resources revenue sharing), which in 2001 (which was the first year of implementation) amounted to 60.5 trillion rupiah. Ninety per cent of the DAU would be distributed through a formula based upon local fiscal capacity and local fiscal needs to all districts, with the remaining 10% going to the provinces (Brodjonegoro 2001, p. 11). No longer would local governments get SDO for staff and teacher salaries, INPRES for development expenditures, or DIPs to support sectoral projects through the deconcentrated central government offices. The assumption was that the new DAU would be at least comparable to the transfer funds provided under these programs, although at no point in the development of the formula for the block grant was there any attempt to make a financial comparison between these two methods of distribution as it applied to specific localities. In fact, it became apparent to many local officials that shifting central government staff to the localities was not accompanied by the salary funds previously managed by the central government ministries. This was the major complaint that local governments had with the new system. Without auxiliary sources of funding, such as local own source revenue or funds from the natural resources transfers, the new system might provide the basis for local discretion but it also put local governments under new and severe fiscal strains.

4. Impacts of decentralization

In order to determine how decentralization affected the governance system in support of national development in Indonesia, it is necessary to examine a variety of evaluative criteria. One obvious measure relates to the expectation that decision-making is brought closer to those most directly impacted by government programs through decentralization, and that those constituencies are able to influence the allocation of both routine and development expenditures. This is reflected in the notion of local discretion, since as Devas (1998) puts it, "one of the main reasons for having a system of local government is the difficulty, indeed impossibility in many cases, of making all decisions about local expenditures centrally." (p. 9) The centrally-focused decision-making under the New Order regime was what Devas was referring to, and this system abruptly changed with the implementation of Laws 22 and 25 in January 2001.

The establishment of the DAU itself signifies the change to an intergovernmental financial transfer system, which significantly expands the scope of local government discretion. The overall amount of the national domestic budget allocated to DAU grew from 17% in 2000 (34 trillion rupiah) to 28.5% (344 trillion rupiah) in 2002 (Firman 2000, p. 11–12). Those localities which received large transfers under the former system continue to benefit from DAU, since the so-called "balancing factor" (*faktor penyeimbang*) stipulates that the allocations for each province and local government should be at least as great as the amount received the previous year. On this basis, the size of the discretionary fund for each local government, (which will be discussed further) is a predictable amount so long as the balancing factor persists, even though it maybe inadequate to the new level of responsibility. What is not clear is if the real value of intergovernmental transfers for local government increased under the new system. In those localities that receive natural resources revenues in addition to DAU, the local financial situation improved substantially under the decentralized system. Kabupaten Kutai in East Kalimantan, a predominantly rural and sparsely populated district, had the largest budget in 2001 based upon over 1 trillion rupiah from oil revenues (see Table 1). A proposal by central government to reduce the local share of oil and gas revenues in 2002 led to the establishment of a political lobby, the Coordinating Forum of Oil and Gas Producing Areas (FKPDM) to fight the move. (Firman 2002, p. 18)

The obviously positive impacts of the new financial transfer system on the amount of discretionary funds for local governments must be balanced against two related factors, one being increased fiscal dependency on central governments and the other being the higher cost of local government. Under the pre-1999 donor-led initiatives, the objective was to reduce dependency on intergovernmental transfers by strengthening local revenue generation. Improved property tax collection was one strategy that produced positive results in some localities. Another was introducing real costs for local public services to improve own-source revenues. Under the new decentralized financial system, local own-source revenue became a smaller proportion of local budgets because total budgets are now larger. According to Simanjuntak (2002), the contribution of own source revenue (*Pendapatan Asli Daerah*, or PAD) to local governments overall is approximately 15% whereas previously it amounted to nearly 25% of local revenue (Municipal Finance Monitoring Indicators 1996). Thus while local governments are presently better off, they are increasingly dependent on central government transfers to maintain their fiscal viability. This growing fiscal dependency is not what was conceived when donors pushed decentralization as an alternative to the centralized system. Moreover, these figures do not necessarily accurately gauge the impact of new responsibilities, particularly the salaries of former central

Table 1. Kabupaten and Kota received oil and gas revenue sharing > 100 million Rupiahs, 2001 and 2002 (in billion Rupiahs)

No.	Kabupaten	Province	2001	2002 (estimated)
1.	Aceh Utara	Aceh	413.39	305.58
2.	Bengkalis	Riau	695.96	682.67
3.	Indragiri Hilir	"	111.92	n.a.
4.	Indragiri Hulu	"	113.08	n.a.
5.	Kampar	"	258.97	242.41
6.	Karimun	"	111.91	n.a.
7.	Riau Kepulauan	"	111.91	n.a.
8.	Natuna	"	111.92	100.15
9.	Pelalawan	"	114.37	n.a.
10.	Rokan Hilir	"	476.29	346.92
11.	Rokan Hulu	"	117.80	n.a.
12.	Siak	"	461.76	380.35
13.	Batam City	"	111.92	n.a.
14.	Dumai City	"	111.92	n.a.
15.	Pekanbaru City	"	111.92	n.a.
16.	Musi Banyuasin	South Sumatera	188.71	262.27
17.	Bulungan	East Kalimantan		156.92
18.	Kutai	"	1077.89	1040.85
19.	Kutai Barat	"	142.10	n.a.
20.	Kutai Timur	"	143.34	156.92
21.	Nunukan	"	143.29	161.84
22.	Pasir	"	147.57	178.78
23.	Bontang City	"	142.09	162.06
24.	Samarinda City	"	145.94	163.16
25.	Tarakan City	"	146.27	163.14
26.	Balikpapan City	"	142.09	n.a.

Source: Firman (2002).

government ministry staff transferred to the local payroll. Strategies to strengthen local financial capabilities such as the use of debt financing (which had never been used by local governments in Indonesia) or service tariff reforms, were part of the reform agenda pushed by donor consultants that was scuttled by the Asian financial crisis after 1997. As previously noted, donors in the current economic climate adamantly approve the idea of local government adding to the national debt through borrowing.

Another measure of decentralization effectiveness is how local governments addressed the organizational restructuring called for in Law 22. An assessment conducted in thirteen districts and municipalities in 2001 by a Jakarta research group (Usman 2001) found that implementation of governmental restructuring under decentralization was uneven. Some local governments maintained the dual system of government services, with autonomous agencies (those under local rule) co-existing with vertical agencies connected to central government ministries. All but one sample local government experienced an increase, rather than the anticipated reduction, in the number of government work units after implementation of Law 22 (see Table 2). The impact of the transformation is most apparent in the expanded size of the civil service corps at the local level owing to the absorption of former central ministry staff, and the reluctance of local leaders to reduce its work force despite the excess. Some local governments have reduced staffing

Table 2. Number of government work units in selected districts and municipalities

District & municipality	Before the new law	After the new law	Change
1. Minahasa	20	34	+14
2. Bolaang Mangondow	16	25	+09
3. Gorontalo	13	25	+12
4. Banjarmasin	25	33	+08
5. Sanggau	18	25	+07
6. Magetan	22	26	+04
7. Kudus	16	16	0
8. Karo	15	19	+04
9. Simalungun	39	28	−11

Source: Usman (2002).

and departments, such as the provinces of Yogya Konta and West Java, and the district of Sleman. Yogya Jakarta is implementing a program to reduce staffing by two-thirds, through attrition, early retirement, outsourcing services, and training courses for released staff to take up new careers or start business enterprises. But the example of successful adaptation of a streamlined local public section workforce is still the exception.

Another measure of the impact of decentralization relates to the enduring problem of reducing inter-regional inequities. One of the advantages of a centralized governance system is the potential to address regional inequities through the allocation of intergovernmental transfers. A common criticism of the Indonesian intergovernmental financial transfer system in the 1980s and 1990s was the so-called Java-bias, whereby its populous provinces benefited more than others via the centralized system. Financial data from the Ministry of Finance in 1990s suggests that the Java-bias was probably overstated, especially on a per-capita basis. The New Order government used the INPRES transfers to reallocate central government revenues to poorer localities that did not enjoy the benefits of the higher level of development in Java.

The revised financial transfer structure set in motion by Law 25 continued to reduce inter-regional fiscal disparities. Per capita allocations were substantially greater off-Java as under the former INPRES system (see Table 3). According to Brodjonegoro (2001), the allocation formula for the GAF was designed to reduce the disparities in regional economies, more than under the previous allocation of SDO and INPRES. Based upon a simultaneous econometric model using cross-section data from 26 provinces (there are now 32 provinces), University of Indonesian economists found that "if GAF is the only intergovernmental fiscal transfer scheme as a replacement of SDO and INPRES, then the regional disparity becomes much better..." (p. 25) Yet, as was also noted, sharing revenues from natural resources counteracts some of the positive effects of the GAF. Nonetheless, the results are still better than under the pre-1998 transfer system (see Table 4).

5. Conclusion

On one level, implementation of decentralization in Indonesia since 1999 represents the fulfillment of a donor-driven reform agenda dating back to the 1970s. Yet, it is also apparent that the distinctive character of the changes

Table 3. General allocation fund (DAU) for provincial, cities, and district governments in Indonesia, by province, 2001 (in billion Rupiahs)

No.	Province	Prov. govt.	City and district govts.	Total	Total/capita[1]
1.	Aceh	165.80	1986.63	2152.43	0.00053
2.	North Sumatera	264.42	2958.43	3222.85	0.00028
3.	West Sumatera	140.73	1023.10	1663.83	0.00039
4.	Riau	251.94	2015.21	2267.15	0.00048
5.	Jambi	109.29	904.00	1013.29	0.00042
6.	South Sumatera	153.17	1493.62	1646.79	0.00023
7.	Bangka Belitung	65.64	255.89	321.53	0.00039
8.	Bengkulu	82.74	527.15	609.89	0.00043
9.	Lampung	180.30	1568.56	1748.86	0.00026
10.	Jakarta	587.14	185.84	773.02	0.00009
11.	West Java	521.23	5701.46	6222.69	0.00017
12.	Banten	142.15	1123.77	1265.92	0.00015
13.	Central Java	647.21	7216.47	7863.68	0.00025
14.	Yogyakarta	110.36	857.32	967.68	0.00031
15.	East Java	449.57	8349.47	8799.04	0.00025
16.	West Kalimantan	194.38	1342.29	1536.67	0.00041
17.	Central Kalimantan	153.31	881.10	1034.41	0.00057
18.	South Kalimantan	122.52	1014.91	1137.43	0.00038
19.	East Kalimantan	257.11	1596.99	1854.10	0.00076
20.	North Sulawesi	75.58	706.30	781.88	0.00039
21.	Gorontalo	45.35	317.38	362.73	0.00043
22.	Central Sulawesi	126.45	959.78	1086.23	0.00052
23.	South Sulawesi	232.73	2566.53	2799.26	0.00035
24.	Southeast Sulawesi	101.38	764.95	866.33	0.00049
25.	Bali	91.17	1093.38	1184.55	0.00038
26.	West Nusa Tenggara	122.61	1098.13	1220.74	0.00032
27.	East Nusa Tenggara	150.93	1948.74	2099.67	0.00053
28.	Maluku	101.29	582.65	683.94	0.00051
29.	North Maluku	74.11	399.25	473.36	0.00075
30.	Papua	331.03	2525.72	2856.75	0.00135
Total		6051.64	54465.06	60516.70	0.00030

Source: Brodjonegoro (2001).

reflects the emerging power of political reform elements in Indonesia in the post- Suharto era that do not necessarily embrace this lineage. In any event, the 1999 decentralization laws have brought significant change to local governments throughout the nation. There is a new funding mechanism that provides significant discretionary authority to local governments in the expenditure of public funds. A powerful new institution overseeing the allocation process is the local legislative assembly (DPRD), which approves local budgets and no longer needs to look to Jakarta for guidance.

At the same time, the responsibilities of the local government head, both the district head (*bupati*) and the mayor (*walikota*), have expanded in functional terms. But, as many local leaders contend, the resources to get the job done have not accompanied this added responsibility. Not all are complaining, however. In those localities that receive revenue sharing from oil, gas, forestry, or mining, there has been a virtual avalanche of new revenues (see Table 5). In one case, the *bupati* has proposed (and the DPRP agrees) that the new wealth be used to plan and build an entire new capital city, an

Table 4. Model simulation results on regional disparities (in Rp./person)

Province	GRDP per CAP SKO + INPRES	GRDP per CAP NATURAL RESOURCE	GRDP per CAP GAF	GRDP per CAP GAF + NAT.RES
Aceh	1,460,076	1,463,384	1,463,600	1,472,071
North Sumatera	1,812,230	1,812,305	1,815,013	1,815,596
West Sumatera	1,280,758	1,280,859	1,282,964	1,283,633
Riau	6,114,932	6,123,381	6,118,403	6,139,304
Jambi	1,591,307	1,591,691	1,595,157	1,596,772
South Sumatera	2,412,556	2,413,605	2,414,738	2,417,654
Bengkulu	1,942,040	1,942,145	1,945,777	1,946,810
Lampung	1,045,071	1,045,299	1,047,137	1,048,010
Jakarta	7,124,956	7,124,975	7,127,962	7,128,646
West Jawa	1,437,755	1,437,835	1,440,051	1,440,533
Central Jawa	1,446,126	1,446,138	1,448,598	1,448,939
Yogyakarta	1,559,839	1,559,856	1,563,078	1,563,682
East Jawa	1,647,075	1,647,121	1,649,758	1,650,200
Bali	1,959,170	1,959,220	1,960,933	1,964,562
West Nusa Tenggara	1,183,633	1,183,872	1,186,038	1,187,044
East Nusa Tenggara	1,023,727	1,023,961	1,030,413	1,031,818
West Kalimantan	1,492,906	1,493,013	1,497,640	1,498,579
Central Kalimantan	1,811,462	1,812,558	1,822,512	1,826,541
South Kalimantan	1,432,496	1,432,589	1,435,098	1,435,908
East Kalimantan	6,064,034	6,079,414	6,074,510	6,112,876
North Sulawesi	1,340,184	1,340,302	1,343,570	1,344,365
Central Sulawesi	1,451,038	1,451,358	1,457,188	1,458,909
South Sulawesi	1,189,987	1,190,041	1,191,929	1,192,412
Southeast Sulawesi	1,386,333	1,386,431	1,390,845	1,391,913
Maluku	1,408,563	1,408,626	1,414,023	1,415,047
Irian Jaya	1,670,250	1,671,784	1,691,300	1,697,496
Standard deviation	1,637,247	1,639,470	1,637,623	1,643,048
Average	2,088,019	2,089,299	2,092,624	2,096,397
Coefficient of variation	78.41	78.47	78.26	78.37

Source: Brodjonegoro (2001).

amusement park (supposedly to attract tourists – Disney in Kalimantan) and a variety of other expansive capital projects previously unimaginable as an initiative of local government. But most Indonesian localities are not so fortunate, and face more difficult choices in managing new responsibilities with additional (but inadequate) financial resources. In both cases, however, the evidence points to a new decentralized system that actually has increased the dependency of local governments on central government financial transfers and a recognition that adjustments to funding formula will be an ongoing concern as the decentralization system in Indonesia matures.

The diminution of the central government role in national development projects at the local level has potentially significant implications for reducing inter-regional disparities in the vast Indonesian archipelago. As shown here, the evidence available suggests that the distribution of the DAU has continued a process begun in the waning years of the New Order government to use intergovernmental transfers to reducing regional disparities. But as we have also seen, there are sharp imbalances because of the ability of some

Table 5. Districts (Kabupaten) and municipalities (Kota) in Indonesia received revenue sharing (> 100 billion Rupiahs) from the general allocation fund (DAU), 2001

Kabupaten/Kota	Province	General allocation fund (DAU)	DAU/capita	Total revenue sharing	Revenue sharing/capita
Aceh Utara	Aceh	245.55	0.00025	452.61	0.00046
Bengkalis	Riau	206.72	0.00016	754.12	0.00059
Indragiri Hilir	"	203.82	0.00036	134.87	0.00024
Indragiri Hulu	"	162.26	0.00035	134.29	0.00029
Kampar	"	185.11	0.00021	294.91	0.00034
Kariumun	"	117.65	n.a.	140.84	n.a.
Riau Kepulauan	"	131.60	0.00023	139.69	0.00025
Kuantan Singingi	"	118.23	n.a.	127.37	n.a.
Natuna	"	147.58	n.a.	125.94	n.a.
Pelalawan	"	109.95	n.a.	141.42	n.a.
Rokan Hilir	"	91.85	n.a.	519.18	n.a.
Rokan Hulu	"	104.15	n.a.	143.53	n.a.
Siak	"	95.61	n.a.	492.28	n.a.
Batam City	"	104.20	0.00024	151.45	0.00035
Dumai City	"	93.48	n.a.	129.34	n.a.
Pekanbaru City	"	143.01	0.00024	148.03	0.00025
Musi Banyuasin	South Sumatera	249.92	0.00020	216.52	0.00017
Bandung City	West Java	734.07	0.00034	114.60	0.00005
Surabaya City	East Java	332.08	0.00013	166.47	0.00006
Kutai	East Kalimantan	297.81	0.00036	1148.28	0.00142
Kutai Barat	"	116.62	n.a.	199.37	n.a.
Kutai Timur	"	103.06	n.a.	294.56	n.a.
Nunukan	"	81.63	n.a.	175.46	n.a.
Pasir	"	148.55	0.00055	221.03	0.00082
Balikpapan City	"	135.09	0.00033	214.28	0.00053
Bontang City	"	75.72ä	n.a.	184.30	n.a.
Samarinda City	"	194.48	0.00037	186.50	0.00035
Tarakan City	"	72.99	n.a.	175.61	n.a.
Jakarta City	Jakarta	773.02	0.00009	2518.55	0.00030

Source: Presidential decree 181/2000 for general allocation fund and ministry of home affairs and regional autonomy for revenue sharing. See Brodjonegoro (2001).
Note: Population estimates are based on the results of the 2000 National Census.
n.a.: Population data are not available for new districts.

localities to capture a large share of the revenues from national resources that happen to lie within their borders and these localities are likely to progress rapidly ahead of those areas without similar assets. To redress this imbalance will require continued efforts by the central government, but these may invoke opposition from localities. Recurring threats of succession (which have accompanied the decentralization process since 1999) remain a credible threat to the nation. How to achieve the proper balance between national objectives and strong local governments will constitute a major challenge in the years to come. The need for responsive and responsible local management in the face of rapid growth of cities throughout Indonesia is greater now that the decentralization dreams of the donors have come to pass and there is no turning back.

References

Alm J, Bahl R (1999) Decentralization in Indonesia: Prospects and problems. USAID Working Paper

Aten R (1997) Why increased local democratic decision making would aid Indonesian economic development. USAID Working Paper

Beier C, Farrazzi G (1997) The district autonomy pilot program: A new approach to decentralization in Indonesia. Policy Paper, Indonesian-German Technical Cooperation Project

Brodjonegoro B (2001) Indonesian intergovernmental transfers in decentralization era: The case of general allocation fund. Paper presented at an International Symposium on Intergovernmental Transfers in Asian Countries: Issues and Practices, Hitotsubashi University, February 9–10

Cawley T (2001) Indonesia's reform hits trouble. Financial Times, January 3

Crook RC, Mann J (1998) Democracy and decentralisation in South Asia and West Africa: Participation, accountability and performance. Cambridge University Press, Cambridge

Devas N (1998) The subsidi daerah otonom: A review of the issues, Unpubl. paper. School of Public Policy, University of Birmingham, U.K

Dillinger W (1994) Decentralization and its implications for urban service delivery. Urban Management Discussion Paper, #16. The World Bank, Washington

Dow Jones Newsletter (2001) Indonesia's donors concerned about decentralization. April 24

Firman T (2002) Potential impacts of Indonesia's fiscal decentralization policy reform on city and regional development. Institute of Technology, Bandung, Indonesia

Forrester G, May RJ (eds) (1999) The fall of Suharto. Select Books, Singapore

Leigland J (1993) Decentralizing the development budget process in Indonesia: Progress and prospects. Public Budgeting and Finance 13:85–101

McAndrews C (1986) Central government and local development in Indonesia. Oxford University Press, New York

Ranis G, Stewart F (1994) Decentralization in Indonesia. Bulletin of Indonesian Economic Studies 30:41–72

Rondinellit DA (1989) Decentralizing public services in developing countries: Issues and opportunities. The Journal of Social, Political and Economic Studies 14(Spring):77–98

Shah A, Qureshi Z (1994) Intergovernmental fiscal relations in Indonesia. World Bank Discussion Paper 239

Siddique NA (1997) Decentralization and development: Theory and practice in Bangladesh. University of Dhaka, Dhaka

Simandjuntak RA (2002) Sixteen months of fiscal decentralization journey in Indonesia. Ekonomi Indonesia di Era Politik Baru, pp 164–174

South China Morning Post (2000) Regional autonomy needed to keep country united. November 22

United States Agency for International Development Local Government Training II (1980) Project No. 497-0308. USAID, March 4

Usman S (2002) Regional autonomy in Indonesia: Field experiences and emerging challenges. SMERU Research Institute, Jakarta, Indonesia, June 20–21

Walker M (1991) Decentralized planning for sustainable development: The case of Indonesia. Review of Urban and Regional Development Studies 3:94–102

South Africa in the global context: The view from above and below

Hermanus S. Geyer

Urban and Regional Planning, School for Environmental Sciences and Development, Potchefstroom University, Potchefstroom, South Africa (e-mail: ssbhsg@puknet.puk.ac.za)

Abstract. Perceptions differ on the positive impact globalization has on the economic environment of the developed and developing world. This paper identifies elements of the African economic make-up that could hinder or assist in the reconnection of the region into the global economic society. It then discusses structural changes that have occurred in South Africa's economic and demographic profile over the past two decades to demonstrate how different sections of the country's population have reacted to threats and opportunities posed by changing local, regional and global circumstances in recent years. Particular emphasis is placed in the latter part of the paper on the dominant role that the Greater Johannesburg urban agglomeration plays nationally and internationally and the way in which changing agglomeration forces have influenced the relocation of multinationals in the metropolitan region.

JEL classification: R

1. Africa in the global perspective

For centuries, two major factors have influenced Africa's economic development, one externally and the other internally induced. Since the Portuguese became involved in North Africa during the early fifteenth century, but especially since the seventeenth century, Africa has become increasingly exposed to the dynamic world trading system dominated by Western Europe. Although the continent was exposed to advanced technologies and Western forms of government, exploitative policies and paternalism enforced upon the continent by colonial powers early on inhibited its peoples' political and economic emancipation. It was only after the tide started to turn against colonialism, around the middle of the twentieth century, that Africans were really given the opportunity to take decisions on their own. Soon after independence, government models forced upon Africa by the colonial powers started to wither while African nationalism began to flourish. Single party elective bodies increasingly began to replace parliaments. Elections became little more than processes in which majority party leaders rallied popular support by demonstrating their Afro-centric focus and their resolve to resist colonial dependency, while opposition leaders were often branded as traitors and colonial collaborators (Fage 1995). In the process some countries slipped back into a state of stagnating development (from a developed world perspective). As a result, socio-cultural traditions – in which people tend to focus on the past rather than the future (Potgieter 1998) – and a traditional subsistence way of life still predominate in large parts of Africa today.

Most of the continent has been unable to attract large volumes of direct foreign investment, (compared to regions such as South East Asia), except in specific instances and locations where the return on investments justified the risk, such as in the production of petroleum products and the precious stones and metal industries in Northern and Southern Africa. This has left most countries in Africa acutely dependent on financial assistance and struggling to survive on the fringe of the global economy (Amin 2001). Despite efforts to loosen their ties with their ex-colonial rulers, economic development and the improvement of living standards in many countries of Africa depend on exports of primary products and imports of processed products to and from developed nations (Stewart 1997). Also of importance is their ability to obtain foreign aid for food and the provision and maintenance of social and civil infrastructure (Lipschutz 1991).

Although representative democracies have increasingly replaced single party governments in Africa in recent years, and despite the continent's new economic direction as professed by the NEPAD (New Partnership for Africa's Development) agreement, almost insurmountable difficulties still need to be overcome over the short term before Africa could successfully engage in the global economy.

First, extreme levels of poverty are one of the main stumbling blocks. One-half the population lives on less than $1 per day, most of them concentrated in rural areas and informal urban settlements. Because of factors such as under-nourishment, pandemic levels of HIV/AIDS infection, lack of good quality drinking water, and poor health services, the life expectancy of people in Africa at birth is 48.9 years compared to 77.7 years in developed countries. Only 58% of the people have access to safe and drinkable water and there are only 16 doctors per 1000 of the population compared to an average of 253 per 1000 in developed countries. This helps to explain the mortality rate of juveniles of 169 per 1000 compared to 7 per 1000 in the developed world (NEPAD 2001).

The current low level of education of the African population is another factor that prevents the continent from engaging in the global economy. While the newly industrialized economies of Asia are maintaining high economic performances because they have invested massively in education for a long time (Marshal 1995), Africa with an illiteracy rate of 41% of people over 15 (NEPAD 2001) is lagging far behind.

A major inhibiting factor is the lack of infrastructure to engage in the New Economy. While there are 567 telephones per 1000 people in the developed world, there are only 18 lines per 1000 people in Africa. The improvement of communications infrastructure is hampered by relatively high service provision costs in Africa – i.e., 20% of GDP per capita compared to the world average of 9% and 1% in developed countries (NEPAD 2001).

Perhaps the most important factor that negatively influences Africa's economic participation globally is its unacceptable levels of violence, crime, and human rights violations. Many nations in Africa are still plagued by internal strife, abrupt policy changes, insecure property rights and weak judicial systems, resulting in unrest and political instability. These factors make the risks for foreign investors unacceptably high.

Indications are, however, that NEPAD, a new African initiative that was launched in July 2001, followed by the formation of the African Union in July, 2002 may bring positive changes in all the negative areas mentioned above. The main objective of these initiatives is to improve the negative image of the continent and to enable it to reconnect to the global economic community. Important goals of the organizations are the promotion of peace, human rights and sound economic management principles, as well as regional cooperation and economic integration. Priorities listed in the NEPAD Report include: Bridging the gaps in infrastructure; improving competencies in the mastering of current information and communication technologies; improving health and education standards; diversifying production and exports; and gaining access to global markets.

2. South Africa's image as a global player

In many respects, South Africa is a contradiction in terms of the role it played in the global market place over the past few decades. Although the country was officially ostracised economically, financially and socially by the world for many years, it had always been able to attract relatively large amounts of FDI throughout the period compared to its neighbours to the north that were not burdened by sanctions. This has vividly been demonstrated by current attempts to bring large multinationals that supported the apartheid system to justice. Areas in which South Africa managed to attract significant amounts of investments from abroad (often indirectly) lay in the fields of real estate, motor manufacturing, finance, mining, weapons production and the aviation industry. Although reasons given by multinationals to justify their investments in South Africa during the years of apartheid, often revolved around their concern for its disadvantaged sufferers, an important factor in the flow of FDI always lies in whether the trade-off between security risks and potential profits in a country is positive, whatever the political conditions. However, if one compares the amounts of FDI that have been attracted by developing countries in South East Asia compared to South Africa, sanctions (apartheid) have prevented the country from realizing its full potential as a global player.

South Africa's position as a potential global player has worsened in certain respects, but in other respects its readmission to the global community has had positive effects since the first democratic elections were held in 1994. First, the country clearly plays an important role as a global gateway to Africa, and the South African government has been playing a leading part in remodelling Africa's new approach to global economic-politics since its readmission. Second, after many years of intrusive monetary policies in which local South African investors were completely fenced in, the government has shown its willingness to allow global investment interaction in both directions, outwardly and inwardly. As a result of the government's balanced approach to macroeconomic planning and the opening up of its financial system it has repeatedly been given high grades in the World Bank's assessment of the economic policies of developing countries. Third, South Africa has been making significant progress in bringing its full range of economic, social and environmental policies in line with global standards. Finally, the country's full entrepreneurial potential can now be cultivated compared to only a small section of the population during the years of apartheid. However, despite these positive changes, South Africa still faces formidable challenges if it wants to overcome the backlog built up over apartheid years.[1]

One area in which South Africa has improved significantly since the apartheid era is its economic policy. Immediately after the government of national unity came into power in 1994 it started implementing its Reconstruction and Development Programme (RDP). The programme covered a wide spectrum of social and economic issues (ANC 1994). Soon after the potentially constricting effects of some of the static[2] economic elements of this program became evident,[3] the government immediately shifted its focus to the neo-liberal oriented Growth, Employment and Redistribution (GEAR) policy in 1996.[4] The safeguarding of tenure and property rights in the constitution and the adoption of a multifaceted approach to the redistribution of land (in which the replacement of productive agricultural land, for instance, is linked to market-related mechanisms) was a positive shift in emphasis towards a more dynamic productivity-related model of redistribution of wealth.

Subsequent reductions in tariffs, quotas and surcharges have accelerated South Africa's entry into the global business arena (Edwards 2001). Some believe that liberalizing and privatizing market forces will remove the stigma of a country plagued by underlying threats of political instability, lack of accountable government, poor infrastructure and a massive brain drain (Jordaan 2001). The Congress of South African Trade Unions (COSATU), on the other hand, believes that GEAR will only lead to more privatization and result in job losses among disadvantaged groups (Nevin 2001).[5] Afro-centrists and cultural fundamentalists also believe that it is neo-liberal policy forced upon Africa by Western imperialists who only want to perpetuate the standard capitalist ethic based on privatization and the promotion of market economic principles. Simultaneously, they prevent the continent from

---

[1] South Africa is listed along with Egypt as the only two African emerging market economies among developing countries. The others include Argentina, Brazil, Chile, China, Columbia, the Czech Republic, Hong Kong, Hungary, India, Indonesia, Israel, Malaysia, Mexico, Peru, the Philippines, Poland, the Russian Federation, Singapore, Thailand, Turkey and Venezuela (Loots 2002).

[2] According to Killick (1980) the static redistribution of wealth refers to the redistribution of wealth without an increase in productivity, while a dynamic redistribution takes account of economic growth and productivity increases.

[3] Chapters 2 and 4 of the RDP (ANC 1994) are long on issues of redistribution of land, the monitoring of race-related labor arrangements of local and international investors, income levels and affirmative action but short on ways in which this could be achieved without a decline in the levels of output. Nowhere can the devastating effects of a static policy of redistribution of wealth on an economy be more clearly demonstrated than in Zimbabwe.

[4] This puts South Africa in Kreuger's (1992) promising category of developing countries whose policy reforms had not yet had enough time to achieve appreciable results.

[5] This view has been confirmed empirically (Edwards 2001).

becoming African auto-centred and achieving collective African objectives (Tsheola 2002; Sihlongonyane 2001).

In order to realise the goal of opening up the economy and at the same time address the legacy of apartheid, South Africa therefore has to fight scepticism on both fronts. Most importantly, it needs to overcome the scepticism of the First World that first wants to see the positive resolutions implemented before the continent's bona fides are accepted. A clear signal to this effect was sent by developed countries at a G8-meeting on African development. The African representatives indicated that they need $10 billion per year to overcome backlogs in the competitive engagement of Africa in the global economy. Only $3 billion over a three-year period, i.e. 10 per cent of the amount initially requested, was approved.

South Africa was always plagued by high (disguised) unemployment during the years of apartheid. In 1997 the unemployment rate stood at 38.5%. The most recent official unemployment rate stands at 14.4% (Statistics South Africa 2003), an indicator of the increasing importance of the informal sector. The last official household survey has indicated that although large businesses remain an important provider of employment opportunities (Statistics South Africa 1995), the focus is clearly shifting towards the survivalist, micro, and very small enterprises (DTI 1995). Most of these businesses are located in the region around the largest metropolitan areas. Unless this tendency is reversed, the declining share of the South African business sector in global economic activity has negative consequences for the country's ability to remain connected to the global economy. This fact is confirmed by attempts by the government in recent years to make small, medium and micro enterprises aware of current exporting opportunities (DTI 1997).

Two related sets of factors have left their mark on the country's competitiveness: the backlog in entrepreneurship and employment creation during the years of apartheid and the ostracising effects of the sanctions on the economy. Based on the eight major categories that determine a nation's competitiveness, South Africa was ranked as one of the least competitive of the first 46 nations in the world in 1996 (World Competitiveness Yearbook 1996). However, since the liberalization of the country's economy its overall ranking first stabilized around rank 42/43, and now has improved to rank 39 (World Competitiveness Yearbook 2003). Also, the efficiency of South Africa's government and its business sector has improved steadily since the year 2000. On the other hand, since 1998 the quality of the country's infrastructure has worsened, despite a minor improvement since 2001 (World Competitiveness Yearbook 2003).

During the apartheid years South Africa's labor productivity was very low. From 1972 to 1990, productivity in the manufacturing sector grew by only 0.9% annually, while that of China grew by 7.6%, Indonesia by 8.2%, with Korea and Taiwan by 5.9% (Potchefstroom 2001). In terms of labor quality South Africa ranked 46 in 1996, and the declining manufacturing capacity since 1995 (Fig. 1) show that the country's labor productivity has not increased since the end of the apartheid era. In fact, the decline in manufacturing capacity is confirmed by the relative decline in the importance of this sector in the economy overall from 1990 to 1999 (compare Figs. 1 and 2).

A key change necessary for the country to become integrated in the post-Fordist global economy is a shift in emphasis from an import-oriented

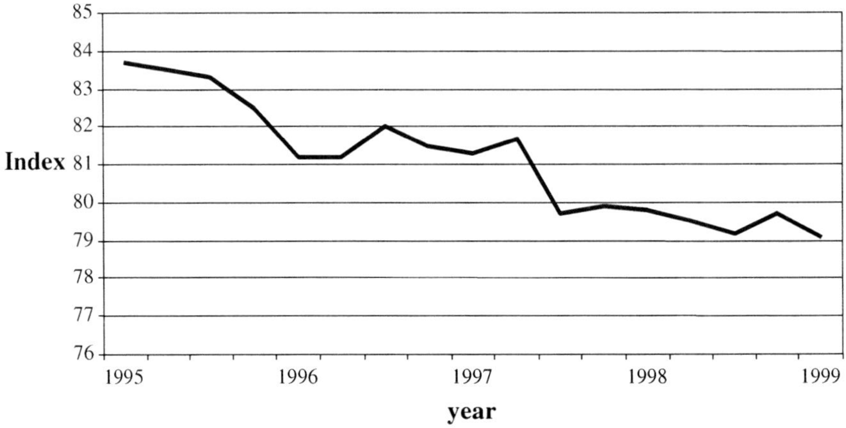

Fig. 1. Manufacturing capacity in SA

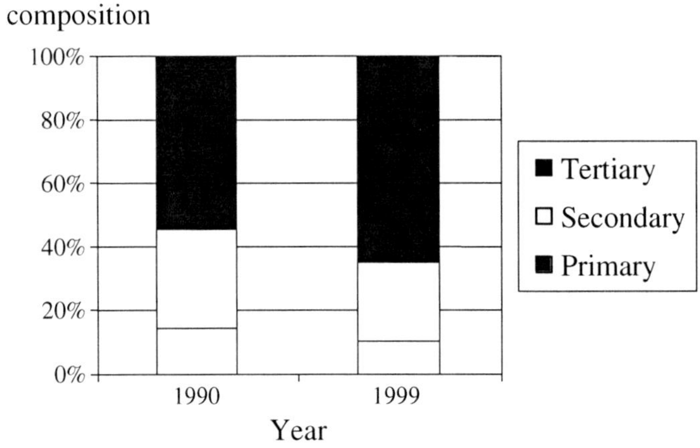

Fig. 2. Shifts in GDP in SA

economy towards one focused on labor-intensive export production (coupled with a realistic exchange rate). The newly industrialized countries of East and South East Asia show that liberalization can create a positive investment climate attracting manufacturing and boosting exports. However, South Africa's corporate tax system of 36% and a maximum tax holiday of six years compares unfavorably with Botswana (its close neighbour) with a corporate tax maximum of 15% and a 10-year tax holiday.

In recent years South Africa's balance of payments has worsened considerably, changing from surpluses in the mid-1990s to deficits in recent years.[6]

[6] Very recently, the SA Rand has fluctuated between R8-R10 to the US Dollar. The latest improvement in the South African exchange rate, according to currency analysts, can be more ascribed to the weakening of the Dollar than the strengthening of the Rand.

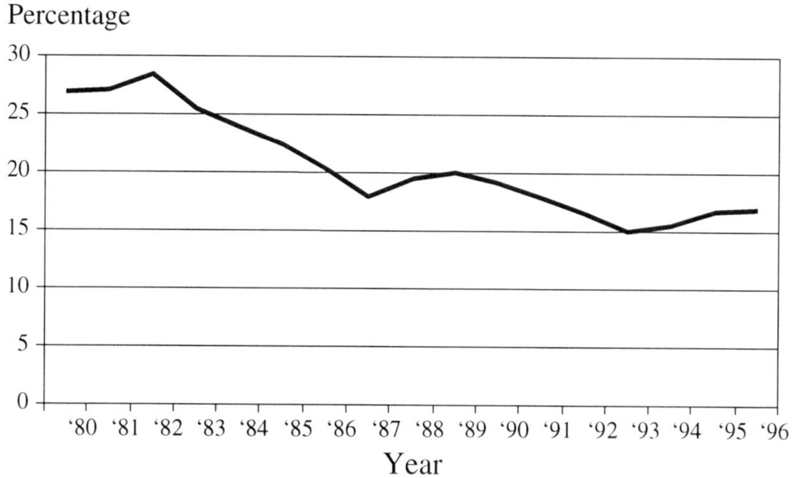

Fig. 3. Fixed investment in SA as a percentage of GDP

Many factors account for this. Negative signals in the RDP initially,[7] a subsequent decline in foreign direct disinvestment, coupled with an increase in local capital flight and excessive manufacturing capacity contributed directly and indirectly to the deficits. On the other hand, a massive decline in the Rand exchange rate in recent years has helped to moderate these negative trends by promoting exports.

To promote international investor confidence in a country positive economic policy changes need to be accompanied by a positive political climate. Crime is probably the country's worst economic enemy at present. In 2002 South Africa's crime rate was 52 times higher than that of England (Geyer 2002b). At least 68% of all small businesses in South Africa have been robbed or burgled and in the national cost of crime exceeds $3 billion (Potchefstroom 2001). Also, when major political forces are in continuous conflict, capital flight is likely. COSATU, an organization strongly associated with the South African Communist Party, has increasingly crossed swords with the ANC government since the implementation of its GEAR policy (Nevin 2001). This trend resulted in more labor disputes, from 315 in 1995 to 1324 in 1997 (SARB, 2001),[8] with a net outflow of FDI. Although there have been brief periods when fixed investment as a percentage of GDP increased (all of them associated with cyclical growth periods) the trend has been generally downward since the early 1980s (Fig. 3), an indication that there is still a lack of confidence among investors in the long-term political-economic prospects of the country.

International migration is a potentially important indicator of how the local and international communities perceive a country's political-economic climate. Factors that induce migration include unequal distribution of wealth, political

[7] See Footnote 3.

[8] The implementation of the GEAR policy may also have contributed to the increase in labour disputes.

Table 1. A comparison of SA's competitiveness in the global economy

Region	Trade (as % of GDP)	FDI (as % of GDP)	Financial flows (as % of GDP)
Emerging markets	82.9	2.8	1.8
Asia	129.7	3.3	2.3
Latin America	37.9	3.2	1.7
Eastern Europe	74.0	3.1	1.5
South Africa	49.0	−0.2	2.8

(Loots 2002).

and economic pressure, ethnic and religious pressure, and a lack of economic freedom (Sandercock 1998). These factors currently exist in urban South Africa. They impact negatively on both the developed and lagging sections of the population. Overwhelming numbers of rural migrants who do not have the ability to compete for urban employment are streaming into the major cities. The added pressure from these migrants on urban infrastructure and on financial resources, combined with policy initiatives have led to escalations in the property tax. Increasing numbers of the more educated section of the population (mostly whites) in cities are losing jobs or are struggling to find employment, and this has prompted many of them to emigrate since the mid-1990s.

Similar trends are visible on an international scale. Legal immigration of people to South Africa declined from around 14500 in 1990 to 4800 in 1998 (Van Rooyen 2000), with the most rapid decline from European immigrants, from 7600 in 1990 to 1600 in 1998 (Jürgens 2002). On the other hand, the inflow of illegal immigrants from Africa has been staggering. Up to 170,000 are deported each year (Beeld 2003). Of course, many of the deportees return. These two sets of migration streams, the former being dwarfed by the latter, are indicative of an international pattern of differential urbanization (Geyer 1998) where many unskilled migrants from Africa migrate to South Africa, while the highly skilled migrate from South Africa to developed countries in Australasia, Europe and North America.

The AIDS crisis in South Africa also poses a significant threat. Because the young and sexually more active section of the population is the most susceptible, a significant proportion of the population is already infected and is threatened by a disease with pandemic proportions (Geyer and van der Merwe 2002), in spite of serious attempts to try to curb it.[9] Also, there are early indications that the South African population is aging prematurely. While the aging process occurs naturally in the developed world, leaving it with an older but literate population, the combined effect of AIDS and the current brain drain in South Africa could soon leave it with an older but much less literate population.

Despite these negatives, there are some encouraging factors. Loots (2002) estimated South Africa's comparative standing relative to other countries in the global economy (Table 1). In the study, exports plus imports were used as

[9] See the Integrated Development Plan (IDP 2003) of Greater Pretoria (Tshwane), for instance (www.pimss.net).

a proxy for participation in international trade,[10] portfolio investment (equity and bonds) as a measure of participation in international financial flows, and FDI as an indicator of international investment, with each indicator presented as a percentage of the real GDP of the countries. When these indicators are aggregated, South Africa ranks 16 out of 23 countries, with seven of the first 10 countries located in the Pacific Rim, and two in Central Europe.

3. The megalopolis of Gauteng

The Greater Johannesburg-Pretoria-Vereeniging[11] megalopolis is the economic core of South Africa. In the national context the city is located in a province that covers only 2% of the total area of the country, yet the city accommodates around 18% of the country's total population and contributes 37% to its GDP (DWAF 2000). In an international context, six studies on global cities list the megalopolis as an emerging world city (Beaverstock et al. 1999; Finnie 1998 (in Beaverstock et al.); Keeling, 1995; Petrella 1995 (in Beaverstock et al.); Knox and Agnew 1989; Friedmann 1986).[12] Looking at the emerging global city of Southern Africa from below, however, no prospective investor can escape the impact of the current economic-demographic dynamics of the country.

Since a significant increase in the influx of Black migrants occurred from rural areas and neighbouring countries to cities of all sizes in South Africa towards the end of the apartheid era, significant spatial and structural changes occurred throughout the country (Geyer 2002a). Black migrants often had to settle in townships located on the outskirts of cities because central locations had already been occupied by higher-income groups. This is especially true in the large metropolitan areas (Cross et al. 2000; Gilbert and Crankshaw 1999; Geyer 1993). Subsequently, however, large numbers of Blacks tried to move to more central locations because available housing in residential areas on the metropolitan outskirts is far removed from their workers' areas of employment (Nathan and Spindler 1993; Cross et al. 2000).[13] In this process, places such as Hillbrow (in Johannesburg) and Sunnyside (in Pretoria) have completely transformed from cosmopolitan areas before the 1980s into predominantly Black residential areas today.

Although most metropolitan areas of the country are not overcrowded, parts of them have become so in recent years. Parts of the Johannesburg, Pretoria, and Germiston metropolitan centers (to name only three metropolitan areas in the megalopolis), as well as adjacent residential areas such as Hillbrow, Doornfontein, Yeoville, Ellispark, Troyville, Jeppe, and Fordsburg

[10] This measure could be somewhat misleading because although imports could increase the value, it could also be regarded as a negative factor with respect to economic independence.

[11] In this section the focus is on the megalopolitan area, hence its title. Gauteng, the province in which the megalopolis is located, contains large areas that are non-urban in character.

[12] In most of these 'tip-of-the-iceberg'-studies global cities are looked at from above. They mainly focus on the global oriented corporate sector in the upper layers of their economies while the impact of the lower layers of business, i.e., the businesses that operate 'below the iceberg's waterline', are ignored.

[13] It must be stressed, however, that substantial numbers of black migrants had already infiltrated central locations long before the demise of apartheid (Hart 1988).

(in the Johannesburg area), and Sunnyside, Arcadia and Pretoria-west (in Pretoria) show clear signs of overcrowding. People in these areas are living under squalid conditions on the streets, in makeshift shelters or in buildings not suitable or designed as housing and showing clear signs of structural neglect (Crankshaw and White 1995).

The urban poor have to do whatever it takes to survive. Because of an increase in competition in manual labor and the low skill levels of most new arrivals in South African cities, they cannot effectively compete for formal sector employment. This results in an increase in informal urban activities, associated with a decrease in the viability of formal business locations not invaded by the informal sector. The increase in informal activities in central city areas is frequently associated with rising crime levels. This significantly reduces the potential of such areas to attract investments from prospective investors, locally and internationally, and is contributing to current trends of capital flight from some core locations to secure nodes within the CBD and/or to outlying suburban nodes. Over the past decade this has led to significant capital shifts in urban South Africa. Informal business activities start moving into the CBD, while the formal business and service sectors are moving out. As a consequence, some local authorities have made attempts to restrict informal businesses to certain locations or buildings, but these attempts have not been successful because informal vendors depend on formal business clients for their survival. Isolating them reduces their viability.

This sequence is associated with seven major trends in urban areas in South Africa.[14] First, there is an increase in informal business activities throughout central city areas, although at scattered locations. Almost without exception, this leads to premature economic deterioration of parts of CBDs. As a result, new security controlled shopping, office, and industrial parks have sprung up inside core areas. Significant numbers of smaller service-oriented businesses, especially professional services that were formerly located in office buildings inside the CBD, now are moving in larger numbers to suburban home offices. This is resulting in visible sprawl on the urban fringe. Some businesses, many of them highly specialized services, have relocated deep into residential areas. Also, the development of new up-market security controlled shopping centres in suburban nodes is gaining momentum because they are regraded as much safer and more economically viable. Finally, there has been an upsurge in corridor development in South African cities. Most of these are home-business conversions along major transport routes leading towards the CBD or collector roads linking residential areas with suburban shopping centers.

Since the invasion of central city areas by the informal sector over the past decade, major economic shifts have occurred in urban areas throughout South Africa. Formal businesses remaining in central areas are primarily those catering for low-income Black households. On the other hand, the corporate sector and professional services catering for more sophisticated local and global markets are relocating to shopping and office parks in higher-income areas or along arterial roads leading out to the suburbs.

These trends are also occurring in Johannesburg. They have significantly influenced the spatial arrangement of the financial and global business sector

---

[14] Some of these trends are not new in South Africa, but what is new is the how rapidly parts of city centers are deteriorating, and how it has affected capital flight.

in the city in recent years. Just as the dim lights of the favelas on the hillsides of Rio de Janero stand in contrast to the bright lights of Copacabana, and the overwhelming informal settlements encroaching upon the high rises of central Bombay, the invasion of Johannesburg's city center by the informal sector[15] has forced many formal businesses (especially multinationals) to escape from the central city and find refuge in security office complexes, most of them located in the safer high- income suburbs of northern Johannesburg (Paulling 2002). Financial institutions such as the Johannesburg Stock Exchange, Investec, Citibank and Nedcor and multinationals such as Ernst and Young, Nashua, M-Tel and a host of other companies have shifted location to new peripheral office parks. Certain locations in Johannesburg and Pretoria long popular with the professional and corporate sector have become more attractive in the past decade. These include the Sandton area, the Midrand strip near the Grand Central airport, the motorway from Midrand to Germiston, the motorway from Johannesburg to the Johannesburg International airport, and the corridor from Pretoria centre to the eastern bypass of Pretoria. This has left many traditional businesses in the core city struggling.

It may be argued that the spatial economic restructuring that Johannesburg and Pretoria (as well as most other larger urban centers of South Africa) have experienced over the past decade is one of the legacies of apartheid, because of the attempts to prevent informal vendors from doing business in the Johannesburg and Pretoria CBDs. This is partially true, but it is also an oversimplification because the invasion of formal business areas by informal businesses is not unique to South Africa. Many developing (and some developed) countries are experiencing the same situation (Brown and Connell 1993; King 1996; Sandercock 1998). Perhaps it is largely a feature of post-modern urban development, a phenomenon with possible long-term effects on urban economic sustainability in developed and developing countries that have yet to be determined.

Looking at the Johannesburg megalopolis as a global city in Africa from below stands in stark contrast to the typical "tip of the iceberg" approach from above. Although the Johannesburg megalopolis still contains many regional head offices for a wide range of multinationals, because it serves as the gateway to Southern Africa, it is less conducive to global economic interaction than most comparable cities in the newly industrialized world.

4. Conclusions

South Africa may have to bear the brunt of the negative impacts of globalization. Just as the United States has become a prime migration destination, and Miami and Los Angeles are regarded as the new capitals of Latin America, South Africa has become the core state in Southern and Central Africa with the Johannesburg megalopolis the magnet. Large numbers of unskilled (or semiskilled) migrants from other Sub-Saharan countries are flocking to South African cities to find new hope, many of them finding their

---

[15] Pamuk et al. (1998) refer to the planning policy of the previous populist government of Brazil that allowed the uncontrolled mixing of informal and formal urban activities, 'perverse integration'.

way to the Johannesburg megalopolis. At the same time, large numbers of Black migrants from rural areas within South Africa are also moving to its major cities. The deteriorating central city of Johannesburg, directly and indirectly resulting from the additional pressures of these two migration streams on infrastructure in the urban core, together with the negative stereotyping of Africa by the international economic community, are two forces influencing South Africa, and specifically Johannesburg, as a global investment destination. Despite the newly formed African Union and the positive wording of the NEPAD accord, much will have to be done if Africa's,[16] and especially South Africa's standing, is to improve in the global economy community.

Until now, most globalization research about the possibility of Johannesburg as an emerging global city has not taken these changing socioeconomic conditions into consideration. Neither has it been able to provide answers to most of the underlying issues of this paper. Perhaps it is because we have only been able to scratch the surface of a very complicated phenomenon and we are only now beginning to understand the intricacies of the concept. Obvious questions about globalization and global city research that need to be addressed in the future include:

How applicable are the criteria that are being used in the compilation of current rosters of world cities, i.e., the status of other large cities of the world that enjoy global status in fields other than those that have been used as criteria in thc first attempts at classification?
How applicable are current definitions of world cities?
How can the dynamism of the concept be captured in the measurement of the global significance of cities?
How can the vertical depth of globalization be measured, especially the relationship between 'local', 'multinational', and 'global' businesses in the upper and lower layers of business strata and the logic and social and economic consequences of the depth and width of the current emerging local divisions of labour?
What role does the immediate hinterlands (core regions) of global cities (or the lack of it in the case of certain emerging global cities) play in their sustained (or waning) status as global cities?
How can the core-peripheral relationship inside and between global regions be brought into the equation?
What advantages and disadvantages exploitative and collaborative relations inside and between global regions hold for such regions?

It seems unlikely that 'tip-of-the-iceberg-approaches' to the study of globalization will provide answers to these questions. But neither would the view from below suggested in this paper. Both approaches are bound to portray a distorted picture of some element of a city's position in the global economy. To present a more balanced image of globalization, a more concerted effort will have to be made to study the concept more comprehensively

[16] See Shaw's (1995) views on what Africa needs to do to successfully re-engage in the global economy.

from both ends. Only then will we be able to uncover the obvious intricacies of the concept.

References

Amin S (2001) Africa: Living on the fringe? Africa Insight 31:3–7
ANC (1995) The reconstruction and development programme. Johannesburg, Umanyano Publications
Beaverstock JV, Smith RG, Taylor PJ (1999) A roster of world cities. Cities 16:445–458
Beeld (2003) Repatriasie kos SA jaarliks miljoene rande. May 1, p 9
Brown RPC, Connell J (1993) The global flea market: migration, remittances and the informational economy in Tonga. Development and Change 24:611–647
Crankshaw O, White C (1995) Racial segregation and inner city decay in Johannesburg. International Journal of Urban and Regional Research 19:622–638
Cross C, Bekker S, Eva G (2000) En waarheen nou? Migration and settlement in the Cape Metropolitan Area (CMA). Occasional Paper No. 6a, University of Stellenbosch, Stellenbosch
DTI (1995) Government reports on small business. Department of Trade and Industry, Pretoria
DTI (1997) A guide to exporting for small, medium and micro enterprises. Department of Trade and Industry, Pretoria
DWAF (2000) Gauteng province: macroeconomic overview. Department of Water Affairs and Forestry
Edwards L (2001) Globalization and the skills bias of occupational employment in South Africa. The South African Journal of Economics 69:40–71
Fage JD (1995) A history of Africa. London, Routledge
Friedmann J (1986) The world city hypothesis. Development and Change 17:69–83
Geyer HS (1993) Urban infusion as a policy option for future urban development in South Africa: the Witwatersrand metropolitan area as an example. Geographica Slovenica 24:243–257
Geyer HS (1998) Differential urbanization and international migration: An urban systems approach. In: Gorter C, Nijkamp P, Poot J (eds) Crossing borders: regional and urban perspectives on international migration. Ashgate, Aldershot pp 161–184
Geyer HS (2002a) Notes on entrepreneuship in South Africa, International symposium on Entrepreneuship. The University of Buckarest, July 21–28
Geyer HS (2002b) Südafrikanische Städte im Wandel – Stadtentwicklungspolitik von Verwoerd bis Mandela. Petermans Geographische Mitteilungen 146:48–49
Geyer HS, van der Merwe IJ (2002) Current perspectives on urban change in South Africa. In: Geyer HS (ed) International handbook of urban systems: studies of urbanization and migration in advanced and developing countries. Edward Elgar, Cheltenham, Aldershot, UK
Gilbert A, Crankshaw O (1999) Comparing South African and Latin American experience: migration and housing mobility in Soweto. Urban Studies 36:2375–2400
Hart GHT (1988) The emergence of grey areas in South Africa, a critical assessment. Paper presented at the bienniel conference of Development Society of Southern Africa, University of Durban-Westville, Durban, 6–8 July
IDP (2003) Integrated Development Plan of Tshwane. www.pimss.net
Jürgens U (2002) Soziale und demographische Entwicklungen in Südafrika Ende der 1990er Jahre. Petermans Geographische Mitteilungen 146:48–49
Jordaan AC (2001) The challenges of globalization for development in Southern Africa. Development Southern Africa 18:79–92
Keeling, DF (1997) Transport and the world city paradigm. In: Knox PL, Taylor PJ (eds) World cities in a world-system. Cambridge University Press, Cambridge, UK, pp 115–131
Killick T (1980) Policy economics: a textbook of applied economics on developing countries. Heinemann, London
King K (1996) Microenterprise: macroeconomic environment: Revisiting Kenya's informal (Jua Kali) sector against the background of the formal globalising economy. International Journal for Educational Development 16:417–426
Knox PL, Agnew J (1989) The geography of the world economy. Edward Arnold, London

Krueger AO (1992) Global trade prospects for the developing countries. The World Economy 15:457–474
Lipschutz RD (1991) One world or many? Global sustainable economic development in the 21st century. Bulletin of Peace Proposals 22:189–198
Loots E (2002) Globalisation, emerging markets and the South African economy. The South African Journal of Economics 70:263–286
Marshal (1995) The global job crisis. Foreign Policy 100: 50–68
Nathan CD, Spindler ZA (1993) Squatting as rent-seeking and pressure-group competition: a South African case-study. Urban Studies 30:477–494
NEPAD (2001) New partnership for African development. www.polity.org.za/misc/mapomega.html
Nevin T (2001) SA's Cosatu and ANC square up, the gloves are off. African Business, 269:1–2
Pamuk A, Fernando P, Cavallieri PFA (1998) Alleviating urban poverty in a global city: new trends in upgrading Rio-de-Janeiro's favelas. Habitat International 22:449–462
Paulling C (2002) Looking around: an overview of the Johannesburg office market. Planning 180:6–11
Petrella R (1995) A global agora vs. gated city-regions. New Perspectives Quarterly. RIIA, New York
Potchefstroom (2001) Land development objectives: Potchefstroom City Council (Unpublished)
Potgieter FJ (1998) Sub-Saharan Africa's inability to compete economically. In: Eichorn P, Friedrich P Policies of regional competition. Schriften zur Öffentlichchen Verwaltung und Öffentlichen Wirtschaft 161:139–162
Sandercock L (1998) Towards cosmopolis. Wiley, Chichester, West Sussex
SARB (South African Reserve Bank) (1995–2001) Annual reports. Pretoria
SARB (South African Reserve Bank) (2001) Quarterly bulletins. www.resbank.co.za
Shaw TM (1995) Africa in the global political economy at the end of the Millennium: what implications for politics and policies? Africa Today 42:7–30
Sihlongonyane M (2001) Eurocentric values are playing a role in the underdevelopment of African societies. Africa Insight 30:18–25
Statistics South Africa (1995) Household survey. Pretoria
Statistics South Africa (2003) www.statssa.gov.za
Stewart DJ (1997) African urbanization: dependent linkages in a global economy. Tijdschrift voor Economicshe en Sociale Geografie 88:251–261
Tsheola J (2002) South Africa's form of globalisation: a continental posture paradox for insertion and dependence. Political Geography (Science Direct)
Van Rooyen J (2000) The new Great Trek – the story of South Africa's white exodus. Pretoria
World Competitiveness Yearbook (1996) IMD International: Lausanne, Switzerland
World Competitiveness Yearbook (2003) IMD International: Lausanne, Switzerland www02.imd.ch/wcy

III. City-Specific Studies

The Rio/São Paulo Extended Metropolitan Region: A quest for global integration

Hamilton Tolosa

Department of Economics, Candido Mendes University, Rio de Janeiro, Brazil
(e-mail: htolosa@openlink.com.br)

Abstract. This paper explores whether the Rio/São Paulo Extended Metropolitan Region, an area with 36 million and accounting for one-third of Brazil's GNP, can successfully integrate into the global economy. Analysis of private investment projects in different sub-regions over the period 1995–2002 suggests that most of the investments are in high-tech or average technology rather than in low technology projects. Decentralization into the Paraiba Valley appears to be taking place rapidly. However, in the region as a whole, severe imbalances between the Rio and the São Paulo remain, and these are an obstacle to the region's attempt to climb up the global urban hierarchy rankings.

1. Introduction

The third globalization wave has brought out striking new patterns of developing countries exports. Since the mid eighties a large group of developing economies broke into global markets. In 1980 25% of developing countries exports were manufactures; by 1998 this share had risen to 80%. Likewise, there has been a substantial increase in the exports of services[1]. Several of these developing countries have undertaken reforms involving stabilization, investment liberalization and property rights. As they reformed

[1] According to the World Bank (2002 Ch. 1), there have been three waves of globalization in modern economic history. The first wave comprised the years from 1870 to 1914. After the First Great War the world retreated to nationalism, anti-immigrant sentiment and drastic restrictions to trade. During the second globalization wave (1945–1980) most developing countries did not participate in the growth of global trade, in other words, "trade was selective both in terms of which countries participated and which products were included" (p. 28). Finally, the third wave of globalization, which began about 1980, has been quite distinctive in the sense of: i) incorporating a large group of developing economies into global markets, while ii) "other developing countries became increasingly marginalized in the world economy and suffered declining incomes and rising poverty and iii) international migration and capital movements, which were negligible during the second wave of globalization, have again become substantial" (p. 31).

and integrated with the world market, the "more globalized" developing economies started to grow rapidly, accelerating steadily from 2.9% in the 1970s to 5% through the 1990s. They found themselves in a virtuous circle of rising growth and rising penetration of world markets. It seems likely that growth and trade reinforced each other, and the policies of educational expansion, reduced trade barriers, and strategic sectorial reforms reinforced both growth and trade"[2]. In middle income economies, globalization has also given birth to new forms of industrial relations and brought forth unparalleled spatial changes associated with the production side of metropolitan economies.

The major purpose of this paper is to inquire into the nature of globalization induced spatial changes. It tries to explain the behavior of some "typical" high-rank world city industries and services located or capable of being located in Brazil. More precisely, I intend to analyze the nature of changes in product mix, technological innovation, investment portfolios and location preferences coming about as a consequence of competitive integration in international markets.

With these questions in mind, the paper looks into recent structural adjustments taking place in the Rio/São Paulo Extended Metropolitan Region (RSPER). In addition to the official[3] Rio and São Paulo Metropolitan Areas, the Extended Region is here defined as encompassing most of the medium-sized cities located along the Rio/São Paulo transport axis and the significant industrial area dominated by the city of Campinas (see Map 1)[4]. As a whole, the Extended Region accounts for almost one third of Brazil's Gross Domestic Product and commands an overwhelming share of modern services, technological innovations and leading investments.

The Extended Metropolitan Region represents a fairly unusual case among developing countries, in the sense of raising a set of unique policy issues associated with the economic integration of two large metropolitan agglomerations only 219 miles apart from each other. In addition to its geographical proximity, the Rio/São Paulo region stands for an economic size (Gross Regional Product) comparable to countries such as Poland or Norway[5]. The region also offers diversified infrastructure facilities and has a production capacity similar to some of the largest world cities.

In order to improve its competitive standing in international markets, the metropolitan economies of Rio de Janeiro and São Paulo ought to be able, in the first place, to strengthen their reciprocal complementarities. In spatial terms this implies that some activities have to be internally relocated, new technological processes introduced and actual production scales revaluated. From a supply side standpoint, global integration also requires the definition of sector clusters distinctively associated with world cities, that is, exhibiting a

---

[2] Ibid., p. 36.

[3] In 1973, a federal law established the first group of eight metropolitan areas (São Paulo, Porto Alegre, Curitiba, Belo Horizonte, Salvador, Recife, Fortaleza and Belém). One year later, a new law was issued creating the ninth area, the Rio de Janeiro Metropolitan Area (RJMA). Since their creation, the boundaries of the nine most important metropolitan areas remained basically unchanged.

[4] Presently Campinas and the Santos seaport are themselves metropolitan regions. See www.seade.gov.br.

[5] See World Bank: Data and statistics; quick reference tables; www.worldbank.org.

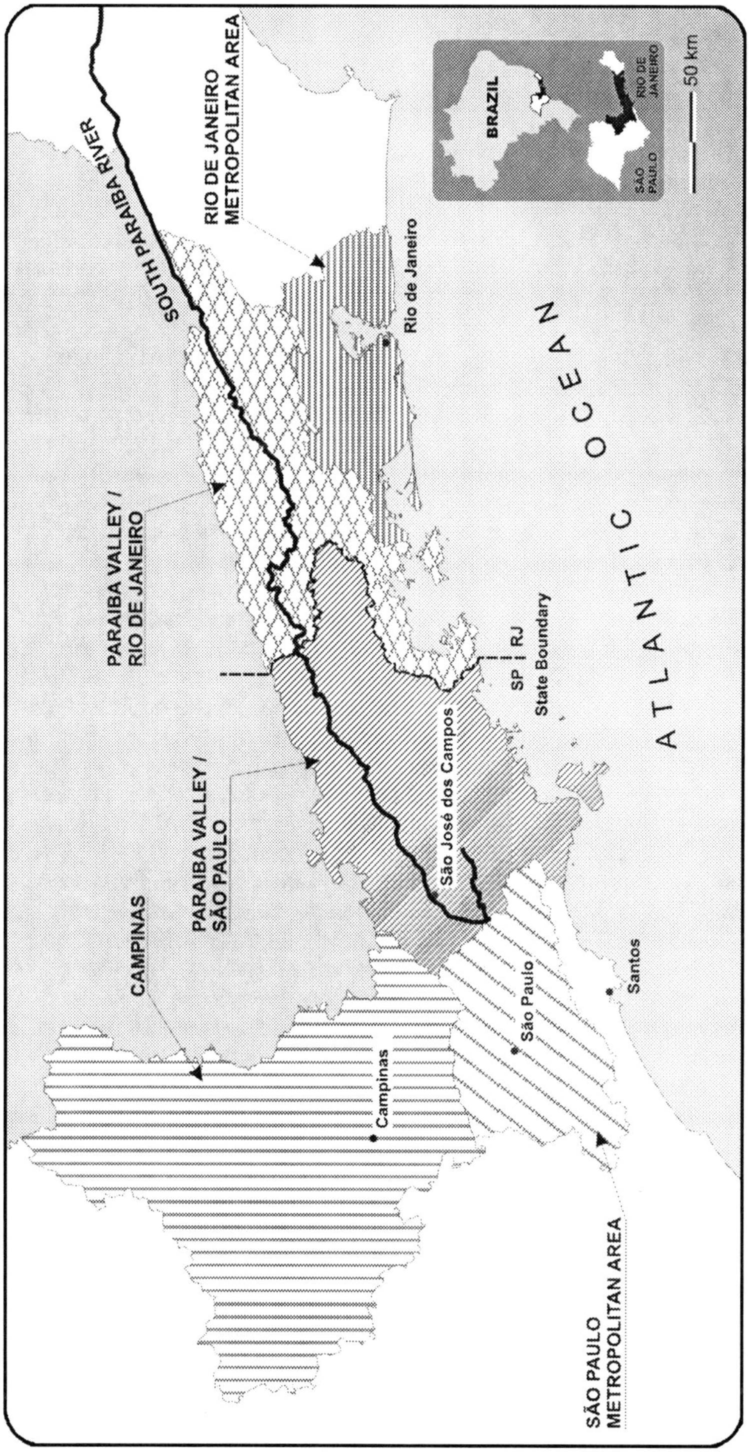

Map. 1. The Rio/São Paulo Extended Metropolitan Region

set of production features regarded as representative or "typical" of high-rank world cities. Along these lines, Sect. 2 briefly reviews the behavior of "typical" world city industries and services and their potential contribution to internal restructuring and global integration. Section 3 examines some of the Extended Metropolitan Region major economic and demographic characteristics. Next, Sect. 4 looks into the relationship between invesment portfolios and the production restructuring process in the Extended Region three major sub-regions, namely: i) the São Paulo Metropolitan Area (SPMA) and Campinas; ii) the South Paraíba River Valley and iii) the Rio de Janeiro Metropolitan Area (RJMA). Finally, Sect. 5 discusses the Extended Region competitive integration trends and its growth prospects over the next decade.

2. Technical complementarities and the shaping of a global urban system

Urban systems are simultaneously defined by sets of cities of different sizes and locations and by spatially oriented flows of goods, services, market and technological information among cities. As a result, any urban system can be uniquely defined by a hierarchical set of urban nodes and dependency vectors.

In a closed economy, a system of cities is always referred to in terms of national or regional boundaries. To the extent that economies open up their frontiers to international trade, distinct national urban systems progressively interact on one another and the aggregate of national systems converges to a system of cities defined on a worldwide basis. Along the transition path from national to global, hierarchies and interdependency relations among cities are redefined according to changes in urban competitive advantages. At any point along such a path the high-ranked nodes in the global hierarchy are known as world cities and play a crucial function of trickling-down market and technological information to lower-rank urban centers. According to such a model, the Extended Rio/São Paulo Metropolitan Region (RSPER) is seen as a single node in the system of high-ranked world cities.

The planning literature[6] has tried to devise empirical criteria capable of ranking cities in a world urban system. Friedmann, for instance, suggests that world city rank will depend upon three major factors: i. the presence of leading international corporations; ii. its role as a large financial center; and iii. its manufacturing production scale and innovation ability.

High-Technology Clusters and Knowledge-Based Complexes are loosely defined concepts commonly used in the literature to highlight the leading role played by technology and information-intensive activities in modern world city development. The Organization for Economic Co-Operation and Development (OECD) defines knowledge-based industries and services as the set of intensive activities in technology and human capital[7]. "The effective use of knowledge and information is becoming the most important factor for international competitiveness, as well as for the creation of wealth and improved social well-being"[8].

[6] See, Friedmann (1986, p. 71).

[7] The technology and human/intellectual capital embodied in the complexes tend to grow along their life cycle. Likewise, some of production stages tend to be decentralized and subcontracted.

[8] Thurow (1999) and OECD/World Bank (2000, p. 31).

The basic proposal for a complex is to strengthen inter-sectorial linkages[9] in a cost-effective manner. From a spatial standpoint, most of the market and technological changes brought about by globalization tend to strongly favor the location of knowledge and information-intensive complexes in prime world cities. Among these changes, the most remarkable involve both the centralization of investment decisions and the decentralization of goods and services production. The dissemination of new technologies has weakened the importance of economies of scale in modern industries and has enabled these activities to bring parts and components together in assembly-nodes scattered all over the world. In other words, production activities are spatially dispersed whereas investment decisions are a world city privilege.

"Typical high-rank world city complexes" exhibit a set of major technical and market features worth referring at this point:

- "Typical complexes" play a dominant role in regional growth and command high value-added coefficients.
- Display strong technical and market linkages with the foreign located activities. It follows that "typical complexes" tend to be especially vulnerable to international cycles and external shocks.
- Are highly intensive in knowledge, technology and R&D.
- Play the role of key technology transfer agents, which include the absorption, adaptation and transmission of technological innovations and new managerial methods.
- Are low direct-users of local primary factors and inputs. Their local impact depends upon the implementation of policies specially designed to increase local multipliers. The direct impact on local employment is usually low although its indirect production and labor effects may be significant.
- Exhibit spatially concentrated decisions patterns (decision nodes) and scattered spatial distribution of production sites (assembly nodes[10]).

3. The Extended Metropolitan Region: Major demographic and economic features

The Extended Metropolitan Region, as defined above, has an elongated shape parallel to the South Paraiba River (see Map 1) and spreads over a geographical area of 80,739 square kilometers. It also displays some of the highest demographic and economic densities in Latin America. According to the latest Brazilian Demographic Census (2000), the Extended Region population amounted to over 36 million urban residents, roughly 22% of the

[9] Technical complementarities are expressed as variable production coefficients a_{ij}, for sectors i and j and are written as functions F of the state of technology Φ_j in sector j; production scale Q_j in j, and relative prices p_i/p_j; that is, $a_{ij} = F(\Phi_j;Q_j; p_i/p_j)$. In the constant coefficient (linear) case F is written simply as $a_{ij} = \alpha_{ij} \cdot p_i / p_j$ where the α_{ij} are technical coefficient measured in physical units.

[10] Referring to the recent historical experience of industrialized countries, the World Bank writes: "The second wave of globalization introduced a new type of trade: rich country specialization in manufacturing niches that gained productivity from aggomerated clusters. Most trade between developed countries became determined not by comparative advantage based on differences in factor endowments but by cost savings from agglomeration and scale. Because such cost savings are quite specific to each activity, although each individual industry became more and more concentrated geographically, industry as a whole remained very widely dispersed to avoid costs of congestion", World Bank (2002, pp. 28–29).

national urban population. Furthermore, according to Table 1, its estimated Gross Regional Product in 2000 amounted to more than one hundred and seventy billion dollars, about one third of the Brazilian Domestic Product in that same year. In order to illustrate the degree of spatial concentration in the Brazilian Southeast it could be noted that the geographical area contained within a semicircle of 500 km. radius centered at the RJMA accounts for nearly two thirds of the National Product.

In spite of its current size, the Extended Region population growth has been slowing down for the last two decades. As a matter of fact, average growth rates have remained fairly stable in the Greater São Paulo (1.7% in 1980/1991 and 1,65% in 1991/2000) and have grown slightly in the Greater Rio (0.8% in 1980/1991 and 1,1% in 1991/2000). Most of the demographic growth occurred in the large metropolitan peripheries and in the Paraiba River Valley medium-sized cities, possibly a lagged response to the deep recession of the eighties and the slow economic recovery afterwards.

Column seven on the right-hand side of Table 1 deserves special attention for trying to measure the Extended Region economic size. The Gross Regional Products (GRP) estimates are based on local value added taxes and carry methodological differences, which most certainly bias[11] downwards the São Paulo estimates. Despite these shortcomings, the GRP figures ascribe an order of magnitude to local economic activities and are useful to depict the sub-regional shares in the RSPER production effort.

The Extended Region average yearly per capita income is estimated to have a value in the upper neighborhood of US$ 4.6 thousand dollars per urban resident and reaches its highest value (over seven thousand dollars) in the São Paulo Section of the Paraiba River Valley. All these figures are much above the average Brazilian per capita Gross Domestic Product[12] (US$ 2.9 thousand dollars) for that same year.

Regardless of its demographic and economic size, the Extended Region's major characteristics have to do with its internal structural imbalances. First of all, as shown by the last four columns of Table 1, the sub-regions display a wide variation of sector shares. On one hand, the SPMA, Campinas and the Paraiba River Valley, specially its São Paulo Section, rely heavily on industrial activities. On the other, nearly 80% of the Greater Rio GRP primarily depends upon services, including commerce. In the latter case, the RJMA shares expose the longstanding inequity between a high-income center and its impoverished periphery.

4. Investment choices and structural adjustment

The investment variable measures positive or negative changes in capital stock[13]. Sets of investment projects with distinct characteristics normally produce different structural adjustment patterns. The relevant investment

[11] The value added tax leaves out most personal and business services and includes goods, in general, and certain services such as transport and communications. The São Paulo value-added data refers to year 2000 and the Rio de Janeiro Gross Product are 1999 estimates. Exchange rates refer to July first of these same years.

[12] See, "Most Requested Series/Per Capita Gross Domestic Product" (www.ipeadata.gov.br).

[13] For accounting purposes it can also be associated with inventory changes.

Table 1. The Rio/ São Paulo Extended Metropolitan Region (RSPER) demographic and economic indicators (2000)

Sub-regions of the RJ/SP Extended Metropolitan Region	Urban population (10^3)	Urbanization ratio (%)	Average yearly growth rate (1991/2000)	Area (km^2)	Density (Inhab./ km^2)	Gross[1] Regional Product (US$ 10^9)	GRP sector share (%)			
							Ind.	Comm.	Serv.	Other
São Paulo Met. Area	17119.4 (46.9)	95.7	1.65	8051	2126.3	66.54 (39.3)	42.6	23.3	15.6	18.5
Campinas area[2]	5007.2 (13.7)	92.8	2.29	7079	184.9	27.68 (16.4)	48.6	15.2	9.8	26.4
Paraíba River Valley	3547.3 (9.8)	90.7	1.73	9916	77.6	21.41 (12.6)	45.2	7.1	23.2	24.5
São Paulo Section[3]	1851.9	92.9	2.13	6268	113.8	13.39	54.0	8.6	6.5	30.9
Rio de Janeiro Section	1695.4	87.4	1.16	3648	52.8	8.02	32.7	5.0	46.2	16.0
Rio de Janeiro Met. Area	10792.5 (29.6)	96.0	1.14	693	1895.7	53.70 (31.7)	14.6	8.0	70.1	7.3
RJ/SP Extended Region	36466.4 (100.0)	94.9	1.59	80739	446.13	169.33 (100.0)	34.3	15.0	34.1	16.6

Sources: State of São Paulo Data Analysis Foundation, (SEADE/SP), www.seade.gov.br and State of Rio de Janeiro Information and Data Center (CIDE/RJ); *Rio de Janeiro State Yearbook* – 2001.

[1] Estimated at factors prices. Numbers in parentheses indicate relative shares;

[2] Refers to the Campinas Administrative Region, as defined by SEADE/SP;

[3] Refers to the São José dos Campos Administrative Region, as defined by SEADE/SP.

features include: sector choices, project location, scale of production, technology mix, gestation periods, input sources and consumer markets. Investment portfolio analysis can be mostly helpful in explaining prospective production changes and in evaluating the effectiveness of regional restructuring and global integration policies.

Assume a given urban center of rank j in a worldwide system of cities[14] Assume further that the variable $V_j(t)$ stands for its typical production profile and at point $t = t_0$, local authorities start a series of policy actions capable of improving city rank from j to g ($g > j$) in the positive time interval $(T - t_0) > 0$. The policy target vector is written as $V^*(T)$. Policy actions assume the form of alternative investment portfolios which, in turn, are themselves functions of the time horizon $(T - t_0)$. The sequence of structural adjustments required to achieve[15] target $V^*(T)$ at point T will depend both on the amount of resources invested along the period $(T - t_0)$ and the technology embodied in the investment portfolios.

Thereby, "structural adjustment"[16] is defined as an incremental variable Δ_j of vector $V_j(t)$ and a competitive structural adjustment process can be seen as a sequence of changes leading to improvements in the global integration of j.

It is also reasonable to assume that the higher the technological intensity of an industry or service the better will be its chance of successful integration in international markets. In other words, technology intensity is taken as a proxy for global integration. For practical purposes the target vector $V^*(T)$ is seldom known. However, if technical and market information on investment portfolios is available it is usually feasible to conjecture on V_j global integration prospects.

[14] Assume a city size distribution $V = \{V_{ij}\}$ where V_{ij} represents the production profile of city i and rank j. Each profile describes features as production scale, technology, activity mix and location preferences of existing sectors in city i of rank j. Next, define $V_j = E(V_{ij})$ as the first moment (expected value) of V_{ij}. Under this condition, vector V_j may be seen as a representative or typical production profile of rank j cities. Thus, city size distribution V can be written as $V = E(V_{ij}) = \{V_j\}$ where $j = 1,\ldots,n$.
In the case where $k \leq j$ the relation (1) below holds,

$$V_j = V_k + \Delta_j \text{ where } j = 1, \ldots, k, \ldots, n \tag{1}$$

That is, all the production characteristics present in typical profile V_k are also present in V_j plus a component Δ_j describing specific production characteristics present only in j-rank cities. In other words, profile k is contained in j (written as $V_k \subset V_j$) and the latter can be differentiated due to its new characteristics embodied in Δ_j. If, instead of just describing general production characteristics, vector V_j stands for a "typical" production profile of rank j cities, β_j represents marginal output/capital ratios observed in j and I_j is the investment portfolio of j, then equation (1) above can be rewritten as;

$$V_j = V_k + \beta_j I_j \quad j = 1, \ldots, n. \tag{2}$$

According to relation (2) the incremental variable Δ_j is simply written as $\Delta_j = \beta_j I_j$ and says that the structural adjustment required to change a k-rank typical profile into a j-rank typical profile depends upon: i) – the investment values I_j and; ii) – the state of the technology embodied in the marginal output/capital ratios β_j .

[15] In the case of a successful policy the condition $V^*(T) - V_j(T) = 0$ holds at terminal point T.

[16] Generally speaking, the structural adjustment process is defined as a monotonic function $\Delta_j = F(I_j; \Phi_j; t)$ where I_j measures investment value, Φ_j is the state of technology in j and t is the time axis.

The Extended Region data single out two key investment features: i. private investment project values scheduled[17] to be carried out in each of its five sub-regions; and ii. sector investments ordered by classes of technological intensity. The information on the São Paulo Metropolitan Area, Campinas and the Paraiba Valley/São Paulo Section was collected by SEADE/SP (State of São Paulo Data Analysis Foundation)[18] over the period 1995/ May 2000 and is based on business newspapers and other financial publications. The original data was further validated and reviewed by SEADE/SP in order to avoid duplication. Investments associated with privatizations, mergers and capital markets were removed from the data set as well as expenditures on human resources, residential dwellings, durable goods, marketing, business fairs, meetings and auctions.

In the two remaining sub-regions: Rio de Janeiro Metropolitan Area and the Paraiba Valley/Rio de Janeiro Section, planned private investment values and the technological intensity index were obtained from aggregation of FIRJAN (Rio de Janeiro State Federation of Industries) data at the project level.[19] The original data identify each project as a new plant unit, expansion or modernization. In order to avoid duplication only specific sequences of projects types were accepted. For instance, if a potential investor announces a new production unit at a given location in 1997, only expansion and/or modernization expenditures at that same location and later dates are regarded as distinct projects. In turn, if the same (or a very similar) new unit shows up more than once along the 1997/2002 period, it is likely that the original project has been postponed and only its earliest planned value should be accounted for.[20]

The investment portfolio analysis comprises three aggregation levels. First, investment portfolios are analyzed in each of the following sub-regions: i. SPMA and Campinas; ii. Paraiba River Valley; and iii. RJMA. Second, at the micro level, major investment projects are listed and their relevant project features examined. These features include: corporation name; country of origin; project location; project type (new unit, expansion or modernization); investment value; and project share in total sector investment. Third, at the most aggregate level, the Extended Region is envisaged as a single spatial unit.

---

[17] In portuguese, "investimentos anunciados" can be literally translated as "announced investments", however it seems more appropriate to use commonly accepted words such as "planned", "programmed" or "expected".

[18] See, SEADE/SP (2000) and SEADE (2001). Both references are available from the site: www.seade.gov.br.

[19] See, FIRJAN(The State of Rio de Janeiro Federation of Industries) "Decisão Rio", three issues dated: 1997/1999; 1999/2001; 2000/2002.

[20] This statistical procedure will prevent duplication and, at the same time, underestimates planned investment values. Investment portfolio analysis actually assumes that most planned investments are carried out during the given five year period, i.e., project mortality rate is small. Projects with gestation lags longer than five years or projects implemented in the later years of the five year period will bias upwards the investment values.

Table 2. São Paulo Metropolitan Area (SPMA) planned private investments (1995/May 2000)

Ranking of planned investment values	Productive activities	Industry or service	Planned investment values (10^6 US$)	Planned investment share (%)	Degree of technological intensity[1]
1	Real estate	Serv.	6785.82	20.77	L
2	Manuf. and assemb. of motor vehicles	Ind.	5688.07	17.41	AH
3	Chemical products	Ind.	3191.85	9.77	AH
4	Retail and repair of domestic appliances	Serv.	2318.03	7.10	L
5	Telecommunications	Serv.	2025.50	6.20	H
6	Food and lodging	Serv.	1519.40	4.65	L
7	Air transport	Serv.	1404.65	4.30	AH
8	Electronic and communication equip.	Ind.	1244.74	3.81	H
9	Pulp, paper and paper products	Ind.	872.53	2.67	L
10	Culture, recreation and sports	Serv.	863.61	2.64	L
11	Electricity and gas	Serv.	831.86	2.55	AL
12	Publishing and printing	Ind.	616.57	1.89	L
13	Basic metallurgy	Ind.	500.20	1.53	AL
14	Financial intermediaries	Serv.	494.38	1.51	AH
15	Services rendered to business	Serv.	385.65	1.18	AH
16	Health and social work	Serv.	377.96	1.16	AL
17	Food products and beverages	Ind.	305.96	0.94	L
18	Electric machinery and materials	Ind.	297.12	0.91	AH
19	Textiles	Ind.	236.60	0.72	L
20	Computing and data processing	Serv.	226.31	0.69	H
21	Coke, refined petroleum and alcohol	Ind.	220.61	0.68	AL
22	Machinery and equipment	Ind.	218.40	0.67	AH
23	Education	Serv.	216.54	0.66	AL
24	Nonmetallic mineral products	Ind.	205.07	0.63	AL
25	Rubber and plastics	Ind.	198.94	0.61	AL
26	Aux. transport and travel agencies	Serv.	177.30	0.54	L
27	Wood products	Ind.	166.60	0.51	L
28	Trade and repair of motor vehicles	Serv.	158.02	0.48	L
29	Metal products exclusive machinery	Ind.	140.71	0.43	AL
30	Extraction of crude oil and related serv.	Ind.	140.00	0.43	AL
31	Office and computing machinery	Ind.	113.64	0.43	H
32	Construction	Ind.	108.53	0.33	L
33	Furniture and related products	Ind.	89.72	0.27	L
34	Land transport	Serv.	60.08	0.18	L

Table 2 (continued)

Ranking of planned investment values	Productive activities	Industry or service	Planned investment values (10^6 US$)	Planned investment share (%)	Degree of technological intensity[1]
35	Wholesale trade	Serv.	56.04	0.17	n.a.
36	Sanitation and related activities	Serv.	54.48	0.17	n.a.
37	Medical and surgical equipment	Ind.	52.20	0.16	H
–	Other activities	–	102.34	0.31	–
Total		–	32665.73	100.00	–

Sources: SEADE/SP, "Investimentos Privados Anunciados no Estado de São Paulo: 1995 a maio de 2000" (Planned private investments in the state of São Paulo: 1995 to May 2000), São Paulo State Government, June 2000.

[1] H = High; AH = Average High; AL = Average Low; L = Low; n.a. = not available.

4.1. The São Paulo Metropolitan Area and Campinas

From a geographical point of view, the SPMA and Campinas make up a nearly continuous metropolitan space. However, in economic and demographic terms, the two cases show quite distinct features. The SPMA Gross Regional Product is twice as large and the urban population is three times larger than Campinas. In both cases industrial activities play a dominant role (roughly 45% of GRP) but services are now growing faster and are highly diversified.

As far as total investment values are concerned, the SPMA figure (US$ 32.6 billion) more than doubles the value estimated for Campinas (US$ 15.6 billion). The top ten activities (fifth column of Tables 2 and 3) planned investment shares in both areas seem to follow a fairly similar pattern, accounting for 78% of total planned investments.

About one-half of the SPMA total planned investment value (US$32.6 billion) can be allocated to Services and Commerce (US$17.1) and US$ 15.5 billion is assigned to Industry and other sectors. According to Table 2, the three largest planned investment values (real estate, assembly of motor vehicles and chemical products) accounted for almost 50% of total investment expenditures in the five-year period 1995/May 2000. This share rises to 78.9% when the ten largest sectors are considered.

Among the service activities[21] in Table 2 at least five: – telecommunications, air transport, financial intermediaries, services rendered to business,

---

[21] Among the major investment projects in services located in the SPMA it is worth mentioning the following:
Telecommunications: – BCP; Brazil/USA; New Unit; São Paulo/ SPMA; US$ 600 million [30.0%]
– Metrophone; Brazil/USA; Expansion; São Paulo/SPMA; US$ 400 million [19.7%]
– MetroRed; USA, New Unit, São Paulo/SPMA; US$ 200 million [9.8%].
Air Transport: – TAM; Brazil; Expansion; São Paulo/SPMA; US$ 1095 million [78.0%].
From left to right each project information includes: company name; country of origin; location (county and sub-region); investment project value and project share (in square brackets) in its corresponding sector investment value.

Table 3. Campinas region[1], Planned private investments (1995–May 2000)

Ranking of planned investment values	Productive activities	Industry or service	Planned investment values (10^6 US$)	Planned investment share (%)	Degree of technological intensity[2]
1	Coke, refined petroleum and alcohol	Ind.	2677.65	17.08	AL
2	Manuf. and assembly of motor vehicles	Ind.	1912.88	12.21	AH
3	Electricity and gas	Serv.	1756.50	11.21	AL
4	Chemical products	Ind.	1558.43	9.94	AH
5	Electronic and communications equip.	Ind.	905.98	5.78	H
6	Food products and beverages	Ind.	880.82	5.62	L
7	Real estate	Serv.	659.22	4.21	L
8	Rubber and plastics	Ind.	650.39	4.15	AL
9	Textiles	Ind.	643.96	4.11	L
10	Machinery and equipment	Ind.	838.12	4.07	AH
11	Culture, recreation and sports	Serv.	577.91	3.69	L
12	Pulp, paper and paper products	Ind.	458.82	2.93	L
13	Retail and repair of household goods	Serv.	400.36	2.55	L
14	Basic metallurgy	Ind.	395.84	2.53	AL
15	Food and lodging	Serv.	239.72	1.53	L
16	Office and computing machinery	Ind.	1471	0.94	H
17	Nonmetallic mineral products	Ind.	123.74	0.79	AL
18	Agro-industrial prod. and related activities	Ind.	118.11	0.75	L
19	Metal products exclusive machinery	Ind.	111.91	0.71	AL
20	Air transport	Serv.	100.53	0.64	AH
21	Telecommunications	Serv.	88.64	0.57	H
22	Construction	Ind.	85.50	0.55	L
23	Retail and repair of motor vehicles	Serv.	79.75	0.51	L
24	Medical and surgical equipment	Ind.	45.50	0.29	H
25	Publishing and printing	Ind.	40.50	0.26	L
26	Services rendered to business	Serv.	38.94	0.25	AH
27	Aux. transport. and travel agencies	Serv.	37.37	0.24	L
28	Wood products	Ind.	32.79	0.21	L
29	Electric machinery and materials	Ind.	32.42	0.21	AH
30	Computing and data processing	Serv.	29.20	0.19	H

Table 3 (continued)

Ranking of planned investment values	Productive activities	Industry or service	Planned investment values (10^6 US$)	Planned investment share (%)	Degree of technological intensity[2]
31	Other activities	–	4.59	–	–
Total		–	15672.80	100.0	–

Sources: SEADE/SP, "Investimentos Privados Anunciados no Estado de São Paulo: 1995 a maio de 2000" (Planned private investments in the State of São Paulo: 1995 to May 2000), São Paulo State Government, June 2000.
[1] Refers to Campinas Administrative Region, as defined by SEADE/SP; see www.seade.gov.br.
[2] H = High; AH = Average High; AL = Average Low; L = Low; n.a. = not available.

computing and data processing command either a H (High) or an AH (Average High; the other categories are Average Low and Low) technology rating. All the above services are listed among the top twenty investment values, strong evidence of the leading role played by these sectors in the regional adjustment process since the mid nineties.

Similarly, industrial activities such as: the assembly of motor vehicles[22], chemical products, electronic and communications equipment, pulp and paper, publishing and printing and basic metallurgy, all long-standing industries[23] in the Greater São Paulo area, show up near the top in the local investment portfolio. As regional restructuring proceeds, other technology-intensive industrial sectors (e.g., electric materials, office and computing machinery, medical and surgical equipment) are expected to increase their share in the SPMA investment portfolio.

According to Tables 2 and 3, the top ten activities both in Campinas and in the Greater São Paulo are very similar. However, coke, refined petroleum and related products such as rubber and plastics have been considered traditional activities in Campinas for some time and, unlike the SPMA, still rank as the area top investment priorities. Furthermore, the assembly of motor vehicles, chemicals, electronic and communications equipment,

[22] The Assembly of Motor Vehicles is a good example of a highly concentrated industrial activity in the São Paulo Metropolitan Area (SPMA). The sum of its four major investment projects accounts for 78.4% of the sector total planned investment value in the period 1995/2000, namely:
i) Mercedes-Benz; Germany; Expansion/Modernization, São Bernardo/SPMA; US$ 1206 million;
ii) Volkswagen; Germany; Expansion/Modernization; São Bernardo/SPMA; US$ 2275;
iii) General Motors; USA; Expansion; São Caetano/SPMA; US$ 724,15 million;
iv) Scania; Sweeden; Expansion; São Paulo/SPMA; US$ 255 million.

[23] In these latter five industries the major projects are:
Chemicals: – Petroquímica União; Brazil; Expansion; Santo André/SPMA; US$ 558.8 million [17.5%].
Electronic and Communications: – ITC Net; USA; New Unit; São Paulo/SPMA; US$ 470 million [38.0%].
– Nextel; USA; Expansion; São Paulo/SPMA; US$ 250 [20.0%].
Publishing and Printing: – Grupo Abril, Brazil, New Unit; São Paulo/SPMA; US$ 323 [52.4%].

machinery and equipment (all with H and AH ratings) are prominent among the top ten in both areas, suggesting similar industrial restructuring[24] patterns.

4.2. *The Paraiba River Valley: São Paulo and Rio de Janeiro Sections*

The South Paraiba River Valley encompasses 59 small to medium-size highly urbanized counties distributed over an area of forty thousand square kilometers. The Valley makes up a fairly heterogeneous geo-economic aggregate. The São Paulo section is highly industrialized (54%) while its Rio de Janeiro counterpart is dominated by services (51%), mostly of the informal or low productivity type.

According to Tables 4 and 5, the São Paulo Section private investment value amounted to 11.2 billion dollars in the period 1995-May 2000, that is, almost three times larger than the corresponding investment value estimated[25] for the Rio de Janeiro section, in a nearly equivalent period (1997–2002).

The Valley is the site of the busiest traffic corridor in the country, having transported a cargo load of 162 million tons/year in 1997 and estimated to reach 211 million tons/year by 2005, the majority of which is via road (96%). The Paraiba Valley multi-modal transport corridor also includes the largest cargo airport complexes[26] (São Paulo/Guarulhos; Campinas/Viracopos and Rio de Janeiro) and seaports[27] (Santos/Sepetiba/Rio de Janeiro) complexes in the Brazilian economy.

[24] In Campinas the major projects are:
Assembly of Motor Vehicles: – Honda; Japan; New Unit; Sumaré/Campinas; US$ 350 [18.3%].
– Toyota; Japan; New Unit; Indaiatuba/Campinas; US$ 150 [7.8%].
Chemicals: – Rhodia; France; Expansion; Campinas; US$ 348.2 [22.3%].
– Elekeiroz; Brazil; New Unit; Varzea Paulista/Campinas; US$ 204 [13.1%].
Electronic and Communication Equip.: – Motorola; USA; Expansion; Campinas; US$ 371.5 [41.0%].
– Lucent; USA; Expansion; Campinas; US$ 190 [21.0%].
Textiles:-Du Pont/Fibra; USA/Brazil; New Unit; Campinas; US$ 297.4 [46.2%].
Coke and Refined Petroleum:- Petrobras/CPP/Elekeiroz; Brazil; New Unit; Campinas; US$ 2500 [94.0%].
Pulp and Paper.- Ripasa; Brazil; Expansion; Limeira/Campinas; US$ 250 [54.5%].
Rubber and Plastics: – SVJ; Brazil; New Unit; Sumaré/Campinas; US$ 200 [30.7%].
Food Products: – Cervejaria Cintra; Portugal; New Unit; Mogi-Guaçu/Campinas; US$ 136.3 [15.4%].

[25] Most likely the Rio de Janeiro figure is underestimated due to differences in statistical coverage and criteria.

[26] In charge of 94% of the international air cargo.

[27] The so-called Southeast seaport complex handles 21% of the total long distance sea cargo.

Table 4. Paraíba River Valley, São Paulo Section[1], Planned private investments, (1995 – May 2000)

Ranking of planned investment values	Productive activities	Industry or service	Planned investment values (10^6 US$)	Planned investment share (%)	Degree of technological intensity[2]
1	Manuf. and assemb. of motor vehicles	Ind.	3124.21	27.69	AH
2	Other transport equipment	Ind.	1852.40	16.42	AH
3	Basic metallurgy	Ind.	1129.98	10.02	AL
4	Eletronic and communication equip.	Ind.	912.82	8.09	H
5	Pulp, paper and paper products	Ind.	811.42	7.19	L
6	Chemical products	Ind.	784.18	6.95	AH
7	Electricity and gas	Ind.	642.83	5.70	AL
8	Food products and beverages	Ind.	418.16	3.71	L
9	Nonmetallic mineral products	Ind.	332.77	2.95	AL
10	Retail and repair of household goods	Ind.	244.85	2.17	L
11	Extraction of crude oil and related serv.	Ind.	165.52	1.47	AL
12	Metal products exclusive machinery	Ind.	162.47	1.44	AL
13	Telecommunications	Serv.	136.55	1.21	H
14	Recreation, culture, and sports	Serv.	74.40	0.66	L
15	Rubber and plastics	Ind.	74.26	0.66	AL
16	Textiles	Ind.	64.84	0.57	L
17	Machinery and equipment	Ind.	61.14	0.54	AH
18	Electrical machinery and materials	Ind.	44.05	0.39	AH
19	Construction	Ind.	40.00	0.35	L
20	Aux. transport. and travel agencies	Serv	34.11	0.30	L
21	Food and lodging	Ind.	32.04	0.28	L
22	Coke, refined petroleum and alcohol	Ind.	19.21	0.17	AL
23	Publishing and printing	Ind.	17.53	0.16	L
24	Furniture and related products	Ind.	15.42	0.14	L
25	Real estate	Serv.	15.00	0.13	L
26	Trade and repair of motor vehicles	Serv.	12.85	0.11	L
27	Education	Serv.	12.13	0.11	AL
28	Waste and scrap recycling	Ind.	7.10	0.06	n.a.
29	Medical and surgical equipment	Ind.	5.50	0.05	H

Table 4 (continued)

Ranking of planned investment values	Productive activities	Industry or service	Planned investment values (10^6 US$)	Planned investment share (%)	Degree of technological intensity[2]
30	Other activities	Serv.	34.26	0.30	AH
Total			11282.00	100.00	–

Sources: SEADE/SP, "Investimentos Privados Anunciados no Estado de São Paulo: 1995 a maio de 2000" (Planned private investments in the State of São Paulo: 1995 to May 2000), São Paulo State Government, June 2000.

[1] Refers to São José dos Campos Administrative Region, as defined by SEADE/SP; see www.seade.gov.br.

[2] H = High; AH = Average High; AL = Average Low; L = Low; n.a. = information not available.

Table 5. Paraíba River Valley, Rio de Janeiro Section[1], Planned private investments (1997/2002)

Ranking of planned investment values	Productive activities	Industry or service	Planned investment values (US$ 10^6)	Planned investment share	Degree of technological intensity[2]
1	Basic metallurgy	Ind.	1033.0	35.44	AL
2	Manuf. and assemb. of motor vehicles	Ind.	700.0	24.02	AH
3	Rubber and plastics	Ind.	220.0	7.55	AL
4	Other transport equipment	Ind.	204.5	7.02	AH
5	Food and lodging	Serv.	183.3	6.29	L
6	Food products and beverages	Ind.	161.0	5.52	L
7	Nonmetallic mineral products	Ind.	136.0	4.67	AL
8	Chemical products	Ind.	85.9	2.94	AH
9	Electric machinery and materials	Ind.	50.0	1.72	AH
10	Machinery and equipment	Ind.	41.0	1.41	AH
–	Other activities	–	100.0	3.43	–
Total		–	2914.7	100.00	–

Source: FIRJAN (State of Rio de Janeiro Federation of Industries) "Decisão Rio", (Rio Decision), three issues dated: 1997/1999; 1999/2001; 2000/2002.

[1] Comprises 32 counties located in four Rio de Janeiro State sub-regions: Mountains, Center South, Center North and Low Lands.

[2] H = High; AH = Average High; AL = Average Low; L = Low.

As shown in Table 4, 94.6% of the São Paulo Section total planned investment value is allocated to industrial activities. The top five Industries (assembly of motor vehicles, other transport equipment, electronic and communications equipment, basic metallurgy and pulp and paper products) account[28] together for 70% of that total, and the first three activities carry either an H or an AH technology mark.

A comparison between Tables 4 and 5 also shows that the Rio de Janeiro Section not only invests smaller amounts of resources than its São Paulo counterpart but also relies on more traditional (L or AL) industries and services, namely: Metallurgy (steel and nonmetallic minerals); food and lodging, and food products. The Rio de Janeiro Section of the valley has been a traditional producer of flat-rolled, both coated and uncoated steel products. The CSN (Companhia Siderúrgica Nacional), one of the oldest steel mills in Latin America, has a rolling installed capacity of 4.6 million tons/year and is the only tinplated producer in the country, with a 1.1 million tons/year capacity. Its major operational investment (US$ 670 million) in the period 2000–2002 involved the revamping and modernization of Blast Furnaces and Hot Strip Mills to improve its competitiveness abroad[29].

Among the High Tech sectors located in the Paraiba Valley/RJ Section (namely chemical products; electric machinery and materials; machinery and equipment; other transport equipment and the assembly of motor vehicles), only motor vehicles activities are new to the region, especially the new Peugeot/Citroën Car and Truck Plant. Other units[30] include Michelin (Rubber), Galvasud (Metallurgy), the expansion of Xerox (Machinery), and the modernization of Nestlé (Food products).

4.3. Rio de Janeiro Metropolitan Area

The Rio de Janeiro Metropolitan Area (RJMA) is the second largest urban agglomeration in the country. It is also characterized by

[28] Among the major investment projects in the top five industrial activities one can mention:
The Assembly of Motor Vehicles: General Motors; USA; New Unit; SJ dos Campos/SP Section; US$ 1238,4 million [39.6%] Ford; USA; Expansion/Modern.; Taubaté/SP Section; US$ 582.3 million [18.6%] Volkswagen; Germany; Expansion; Taubaté/SP Section; US$ 411 million [13.1%].
Other Transport Equipment:- Embraer; Brazil; Expansion/Modern.; SJ dos Campos/SP Section; US$ 1850 million (of which US$ 1300 million refers to R&D expenditures) [100%].
Electronic and Communication Equip.:- Philips; Holland; Expansion; SJ dos Campos/SP Section; US$ 275 million [30.1%]. Ericsson; Sweeden; Expansion/Modern.; SJ dos Campos/SP Section; US$ 281 million [30.8%].
Basic Metallurgy:- Alcan; Canada; Expansion; Pindamonhangaba/SP Section; US$ 419 million [37.0%] Usiminas; Brazil; New Unit; Taubaté/SP Section; US$ 320 million [28.3%].
Pulp and Paper:- Votorantin; Brazil; Expansion; Jacareí/SP Section; US$ 660 million [81.4%].

[29] Presently 1.1 million tons or 22% of CSN total production is exported.

[30] The major investment projects in the Paraiba Valley/Rio de Janeiro Section are:
Assembly of Motor Vehicles:- Peugeot/Citroën; France; New Unit; Porto Real/RJ Section; US$ 600 million [85.7%].
Chemicals:- Instituto Bioquímico; Brazil,;New Unit;Itatiaia/RJ Section; US$ 20 million [23.5%].
Cyanamid:- USA; Expansion/Modern.;Resende/RJ Section; US$ 12.4 million [14.4%].
Rubber:-Michelin; France; New Unit; Itatiaia/RJ Section; US$ 220 million [100%].
Basic Metallurgy:- Galvasud; Brazil/Germany; New Unit; Porto Real/RJ Section; US$ 290 million [28.0%].
Machinery:- Xerox; USA; Expansion; Itatiaia/RJ Section; US$ 41 million [100%].
Food Products:- Nestlé; Switzerland; Modernization; Barra Mansa/RJ Section; US$ 8 million [5.0%].

unfavorable topographical conditions, exponential infrastructure costs, rising land prices and by an extremely impoverished periphery. According to the most recent Brazilian Census, the RJMA urban population was almost 10.8 million residents in 2000, 54% of which lives in its central city, Rio de Janeiro.

The RJMA economy has been attempting to recover from a long period of decline during the eighties, when some of its most important basic production activities were severely stricken. This was especially the case with the local machinery, metallurgy and shipbuilding industries. There were also some relevant losses in services such as banking, computer services and related activities. On the positive side, the area still retains some its comparative advantages in quaternary activities such as higher education, oil-related R&D, engineering, business tourism, leisure and landscape-based activities. Lately, the region has been specializing in high value-added transport modes, in particular, containerized sea cargo.

Services and Commerce activities account for more than 78% of the area GRP, a much higher share than the average 50% estimated for the Extended Region as a whole (see Table 1). Personal and domestic services prevail among tertiary occupations, a proxy for a large informal labor market.

As mentioned in Sect. 3, the local sector shares also expose a long-term structural imbalance between a high-income center and its impoverished periphery. Rising incomes in the center and poverty in the periphery combine to produce a proliferation of slums and a rapidly growing socially excluded population[31].

Chemicals[32], especially petrochemical products, have been a traditional industrial activity in the RJMA as well as pharmaceutical products[33], transport equipment (mostly Shipbuilding[34]), rubber and plastics, the first three sectors bearing high technological intensity ratings (see Table 6). As for services, large planned investments value allocated to food, lodging, hotels, resorts and trade centers confirm a long-standing metropolitan tradition in tourism and landscape-related activities, with an emphasis on professional and business meetings and conferences.

5. Conclusion: Competitive integration trends in the extended metropolitan region

"Typical world city complexes" are notable for their strong international market linkages and high-technological content. Moreover, the growth of the

---

[31] See Tolosa (1996), pp. 203–223.

[32] *Chemicals*:- Riopolímeros; Brazil; New Unit; Duque de Caxias/RJMA,US$ 990 million [51%].
Reduc/Petrobrás; Brazil; Expansion; Duque de Caxias/RJMA; US$ 850 million [43.7%].

[33] *Pharmaceuticals*:- Smithkline; USA; New Unit; Rio/RJMA; US$ 134 million [33.4%].
Bayer, Germany; Expansion/Modern.; Belfort Roxo/ RJMA; US$ 25 million [6.4%].
Belfan Wella; Germany; Expansion; Rio/RJMA, US$ 30 [7.7%].
GlaxoWellcome; England; New Unit; Rio/RJMA; US$ 29 million [7.5%].
Knoll/Abbott; USA; Expansion/Modern.;Rio/RJMA; US$ 29.3 million [7.5%].
Sanofi Winthrop; Brazil/USA; Modern.; Rio/RJMA; US$ 25 million [6.4%].

[34] *Transport Equipment/Shipbuilding*:-
Estaleiro Mauá; Brazil; Expansion; Rio/Niterói/RJMA, US$400 million [89.0%].

Table 6. Rio de Janeiro Metropolitan Area (RJMA), Planned private investments (1997/2002)

Rank of planned investment values	Productive activities	Industry or service	Planned investment values (US$ 10^6)	Planned investment share	Degree of technological intensity[1]
1	Chemical products	Ind.	1945.0	31.74	AH
2	Food and lodging	Serv.	1877.1	30.63	L
3	Transport equipment	Ind.	449.0	7.33	AH
4	Pharmaceutical products	Ind.	389.3	6.35	H
5	Business and trade centers	Serv.	322.2	5.26	AL
6	Basic metallurgy	Ind.	310.0	5.06	AL
7	Electric machinery and material	Ind.	245.3	4.00	AH
8	Food products and beverages	Ind.	178.6	2.91	L
9	Publishing and printing	Ind.	120.0	1.96	L
10	Rubber and plastics	Ind.	116.0	1.89	AL
11	Non-metallic mineral products	Ind.	110.6	1.80	AL
12	Textiles	Ind.	25.0	0.41	L
–	Other activities	–	40.0	0.65	–
Total			6128.1	100.00	

Source: FIRJAN (State of Rio de Janeiro Federation of Industries) "Decisão Rio" (Rio Decision), three issues dated: 1997/1999; 1999/2001; 2000/2002.
[1] H = High; AH = Average High; AL = Average Low; L = Low.

"typical complex" depends upon a selective number of rapidly expanding technology-intensive and knowledge-based activities. This is specially true in the cases of some fast growing business and financial services, such as auditing, managerial consulting, engineering, R&D, advertising, computer and data processing, insurance, legal services, commercial and investment banking, savings and loans, foreign currency markets, international finance and the stock exchange.

High-rank nodes in the global system of world cities have a keen competitive advantage with respect to the location preferences of knowledge-based activities. Furthermore, high-tech industries and services often display volatile location patterns and tend to be less sensitive to changes in local economic cycles.

In order to achieve global integration, the Rio/São Paulo Extended Metropolitan Region depends upon a far-reaching effort to foster a set of technology-based activities distinctively associated with the growth of high-rank world cities. For the sake of evaluating how far the region as a whole has advanced along its competitive integration path, Table 7 presents the planned investment data consolidated by sub-regions and organized according to different levels of technological intensity.

If one accepts the technology intensity index as a proxy for international competitiveness, the last column figures on the right of Table 7 clearly point to an overall improvement in the global integration of the Extended Region. As of the year 2000, almost one-half of the total private investment

Table 7. RJ/SP Extended Metropolitan Region, planned private investment values by degree of technological intensity (SP: 1995/May 2000; RJ:1997/2002; US$ millions)

Degree of technological intensity	Sub-regions					RJ/SP Extended Region
	São Paulo Metropolitan Area	Campinas	Paraiba River Valley/ SP Section	Paraiba River Valley/ RJ Section	Rio de Janeiro Metropolitan Area	
High	3662.1	1216.1	1058.6	0.0	389.3	6326.1
	(11.2)	(7.8)	(9.4)	(0.0)	(6.3)	(9.2)
Average high	11680.0	4281.3	5869.7	1081.4	2639.3	25551.7
	(35.8)	(27.3)	(52.0)	(37.1)	(43.1)	(37.2)
Average low	2831.7	5759.0	2539.2	1389.0	858.8	3377.7
	(8.7)	(36.7)	(22.5)	(47.7)	(14.0)	(19.5)
Low	14278.6	4278.7	1780.6	344.3	2200.7	22881.9
	(43.7)	(27.3)	(15.8)	(11.8)	(36.0)	(33.4)
n.a.	212.5	137.7	33.9	100.0	40.0	524.1
	(0.6)	(0.9)	(0.3)	(3.4)	(0.6)	(0.7)
Total planned Investment	32664.9 (100.0) [47.6]	15672.8 (100.0) [22.9]	11282.7 (100.0) [16.4]	2914.7 (100.0) [4.2]	6128.1 (100.0) [8.9]	68662.5 (100.0) [100.0]

Sources: SEADE/SP, "Investimentos Privados Anunciados no Estado de São Paulo: 1995 a maio de 2000" (Planned private investments in the State of São Paulo: 1995 to May 2000), São Paulo State Government, June 2000 and FIRJAN (The State of Rio de Janeiro Federation of Industries) "Decisão Rio"(Rio Decision), three issues dated: 1997/1999; 1999/2001; 2000/2002.
n.a. = information not available.
The numbers in parentheses and square brackets denote relative share (%).

expenditures had been allocated to high and average-high technology activities. In addition, these high-tech industries and services tend to be closely associated with large investment projects and high capital-output ratios. Thus, the production restructuring process is concentrated in technology-intensive and large high-value investment projects[35].

Turning next to the last row of Table 7, it can be seen that the SPMA and Campinas together account for a planned investment of more than 48 billion dollars or more than 70% of total private investments in the whole region. The Paraiba Valley/ São Paulo Section is second with 11.2 billion dollars or 16.4% of total investments. Far behind, the RJMA and the Rio de Janeiro Section of the Valley account together for less than 13.5% of the regional total. The conclusion is that from a spatial standpoint the regional restructuring process is very imbalanced and fails to meet the conditions required to improve existing intra-regional complementarities.

According to the investment figures in Table 7, the most striking structural changes have taken place in the São Paulo Section of the Paraíba Valley where 61.4% of local planned investments are in high and average-high

[35] Brazilian-owned projects account for the major investment share (30 to 35%) in the region, followed, in decreasing order, by projects of American, German and French origin. However, joint capital (Brazilian/foreign) ventures are expected to increase their share in investment financing. In the State of Rio de Janeiro, 47% of the projects refer to New Plant Units, 25% to Expansions, 20% to Modernization and 8% to Expansion and Modernization.

technology activities. SEADE/SP data show that in the year 2000, for the first time the Paraiba Valley/São Paulo section investment value superseded Campinas, taking second place among the five sub-regions. In the same year, the SPMA investment value sustained a 25% fall, weakening its relative position[36].

The investment values in the Paraiba Valley, both in the São Paulo and the Rio de Janeiro sections, have been concentrated in large projects located in a small number of counties. In the São Paulo section, for instance, 30 projects in the top five sectors accounted for 94% of total private investment value in 2000.

The main purpose of this paper has been to inquire into the nature of recent structural changes taking place in the Rio/São Paulo Extended Metropolitan Region (RSPEMR). It has also tried to evaluate to what extent the regional adjustment process is leading towards global integration.

From a macro-regional standpoint, the empirical evidence points to an overall improvement in the Extended Region's global integration. Second, from a micro approach, the available data point out structural deficiencies that may hamper the pace of regional integration. Among these deficiencies is the highly concentrated nature of the production adjustment process, both in terms of size and location. These imbalances impair the cost-effective use of actual and potential intra-regional complementarities.

The lack of a concerted institutional effort to foster[37] local comparative advantages is perhaps the major hindrance to effective global integration. Very often, myopic decisionmaking at the federal, state and municipal levels fails to envisage the region as a system of interdependent units, thus resulting in further imbalances and delaying the Extended Region's competitive global integration.

References

Araújo M, Fátima I (2001) Reestruturação produtiva e transformações econômicas: Região Metropolitana de São Paulo. Perspectiva 15(1):20–30

CIDE/RJ (2001) Rio de Janeiro state yearbook. State of Rio de Janeiro Information and Data Center

FIRJAN (1997–2002) Decisão rio. State of Rio de Janeiro Federation of Industries. 1997/1999; 1999/2001; 2000/2002

Friedmann J (1986) The world city hypothesis. Development and Change 17(1):69–83

Gilbert R (1995) Rio de Janeiro: the make-up of a modern megacity. Habitat International 19(1):91–122

Hall P (1998) Globalization and the world cities. In: Lo F-C, Yeung Y-M (eds) Globalization and the world of large cities. United Nations University Press, Tokyo, pp 17–36

Krugman P (1994) Competitiveness: a dangerous obsession. Foreign Affairs 73(2):28–44

Krugman P (1994) Location and competition: Notes on economic geography. In: Rumet RP, Schendel DA, Teece DJ (eds) Fundamental issues in strategy: A research agenda. Harvard Business School Press, Boston, pp 463–493

Krugman P (1995) Increasing returns and economic geography. Journal of political economy (99):483–499

---

[36] See SEADE/SP (2001); p. 7.

[37] According to the World Bank, "The newly globalized countries helped their firms to break into industrial markets by improving the complementary infrastructure, skills and institutions that modern production needs"; World Bank (2002), p. 34.

Meyer D (1998) World cities as financial centers. In: Lo F-C, Yeung Y-M (eds) Globalization and the world of large cities. United Nations University Press, Tokyo, pp 410–432
Santos M (1996) São Paulo: A growth process full of contradictions. In: Gilbert A (ed) The mega-city in Latin America. United Nations University Press, Tokyo, pp 224–240
Sassen S (1991) The global city: New York, London, Tokyo. Princeton University Press, Princeton
Sassen S (1998) The impact of new technologies and globalization of cities. In: Lo F-C, Yeung Y-M (eds) Globalization and the world of large cities. United Nations University Press, Tokyo, pp 391–409
SEADE/SP (2000) (State of São Paulo Data Analysis Foundation) Investimentos privados anunciados no estado de São Paulo. 1995 a maio de 2000 Governo do Estado de São Paulo, Secretaria de Economia e Planejamento, Pesquisa de Investimento no Estado de São Paulo
SEADE/SP (2001) (State of São Paulo Data Analysis Foundation) Investimentos privados anunciados no estado de São Paulo em 2000. Governo do Estado de São Paulo, Secretaria de Economia e Planejamento, Pesquisa de Investimento no Estado de São Paulo
Thurow LC (1999) Building Wealth: New rules for individuals, companies, nations in a knowledge based economy. Harper Collins, New York
Tolosa H (1998) Rio de Janeiro as a world city. In Lo F-C, Yeung Y-M (eds) Globalization and the world of large cities. United Nations University Press, Tokyo, pp 203–227
Tolosa H (1996) Rio de Janeiro: Urban expansion and structural change. In: Gilbert A (ed) The mega-city in Latin America. United Nations University Press, Tokyo, pp 203–223
Tolosa H (1997) Redistribution des revenus, marché du travail et pauvreté urbaine au Brésil. In: Joussemet A (ed) La Recherche sur la ville au Brésil. CNRS Editions, Paris
Tolosa H (1999) A reestruturação produtiva do Rio e São Paulo e a viabilidade das cidades mundiais Brasileiras. In: Rezende F, Lima R (eds) Rio-São Paulo cidades mundiais: Desafios e oportunidades. IPEA, Brasília, pp 91–113
World Bank (1999) Knowledge for development. In: World development report 1998/99. co-publication by World Bank and Oxford University Press, New York
World Bank (2002) Globalization, Growth and Poverty: Building an Inclusive World Economy. co-publication by World Bank and Oxford University Press, New York
World Bank Institute/OECD (2000) Korea and knowledge-based economy. In: Dahlman C, Anderson T (eds) World Bank, Washington, Paris

Mexico City as a peripheral global player: The two sides of the coin

Boris Graizbord[1], **Allison Rowland**[2], **Adrian Guillermo Aguilar**[3]

[1] El Colegio de México, Camino al Ajusco No. 20, Colonia Pedregal de Sta. Teresa, 10740 México, D.F., México (e-mail: graizbord@lead.colmex.mx)
[2] CIDE, División de Administración Pública, Carretera México-Toluca 3655, Colonia Lomas de Santa Fe, 01210 México, D.F., México (e-mail: allison.rowland@cide.edu)
[3] Universidad Nacional Autónoma de México, Instituto de Geografia, Ciudad Universitaria, Circuito 2, 04510 México, D.F., México (e-mail: adrian@servidor.unam.mx)

Abstract. This article considers the effects of globalization on Mexico City, as well as whether this urban area, one of the largest in the world, can be considered a "global city." We base our arguments on a number of scales of analysis suggested in the literature on these topics. At the international scale, we look at the increased concentration of corporate headquarters and air traffic flows in the city. In terms of its role in the national urban system, we argue that while domestic migration patterns have shifted toward other destinations, the majority of domestically produced merchandise continues to find its way to the capital. At the metropolitan scale, our analysis suggests increasing spatial segregation, as well as longer commutes. At the intraurban level, we find that the sectoral composition of jobs has shifted toward commercial and service sectors, the informal sector has expanded, the labor force is polarizing, and that high-level service sector growth is spatially concentrated. In view of these findings, we suggest that the effects of globalization on Mexico City are mixed, as it consolidates its position as a second-tier global city. We also argue that, in spite of welcome steps toward democratization, pre-existing income inequalities in the country have accentuated the socio-economic polarization predicted by the literature on global cities and globalization, giving rise to a megacity with two very distinct sides.

1. Introduction

Mexico City, with over 18 million inhabitants, has historically been the main destination of migrants from the rest of the country, the prime location for all types of economic activity and the center for coordination, decision-making and most economic development efforts by the Mexican government. Explicit adoption by the federal government in the 1980s of liberal fiscal and monetary policies, including privatization and the opening of the economy to

The authors would like to recognize Emelina Nava and Raul Lemus at El Colegio de México and Irma Escamilla and Josefina Hernández at the Institute of Geography, UNAM, for their participation in data management and producing tables and maps.

regional and global markets, accentuated the importance of the national capital as the center of high-level financial and other service activities, as well as for entertainment and electronics-related industries.[1] During the same period, however, the city started to lose population and certain types of economic activities to the medium-sized cities in the national urban hierarchy, as infrastructure capacities expanded outside the capital and congestion costs began to rise within it.

The city still contains the country's highest paid jobs and high-skilled labor. In addition, the network of factories, offices and service firms, as well as government offices, may be evolving in the direction of a high quality environment for the inter-firm coordination and face-to-face interaction needed by the expanding sectors of the economy. At the same time, Mexico City offers opportunities for unskilled workers from rural areas and small towns to find employment as low-paid support to service industries, as well as in personal services, primarily in the informal sector. In this sense, the occupational structure and labor market in Mexico City, as in other global cities (Sassen 1991), has become polarized both in the growing service sector and in the troubled manufacturing sector, where most remaining jobs have evolved into routinized processes in assembly plants. Polarizing trends have also increased during the last twenty years because the loss of formal jobs in manufacturing, and to a lesser extent in government, imply the termination of social security benefits, particularly healthcare, for former employees and their families.

The polarized social structure is reflected in the fragmented urban landscape, where differentials in local government capacity to provide public services and to raise public revenue affect the quality of life of the population between and within each jurisdiction.[2] Contrasts are especially marked between the 16 delegaciones or areas of the city, which are located within the Federal District (DF) and municipalities (the number varies according to criteria of metropolitan delimitation) which fall under the jurisdiction of the neighboring State of Mexico.

Thus, we encounter two sides of the coin in Mexico City's recent past, as the historical gap widens and deepens between winners and losers, rich and poor, haves and have nots. In the process of integration into the international economy and the world system (Parnreiter 1998: 47–48), the shiny side of the coin reveals high-paid jobs that lead to conspicuous consumption. The flip side consists of poverty, subsistence-level wages, and families without access to health services, educational opportunities and basic public infrastructure.

The purpose of this paper is to review recent data for Mexico City, and to reflect on a number of questions raised by these changing patterns. Will Mexico City suffer from all the disadvantages of globalization while

[1] The adoption of liberal economic policies and an open economy as well as a relative spatial concentration of high-level financial services and high-tech related industries have produced some changes in the urban economy in several Latin-American countries. See Sabatini (2000) for Santiago, Gilbert (2002) for Bogota, Tolosa (2002) for what he terms the Rio/Sao Paulo Extended Metropolitan Region.

[2] Since the 1990 census, data is published at the AGEB level (essentially, census tract) which allows analysis of spatial distributions within municipalities and *delegaciones*.

reaping few advantages in terms of improved quality of life, both for local residents and the rest of the national population? Is reaching the status of global city a desirable public policy objective for Mexico City, that is, one which can justify massive public investment in physical infrastructure demanded by the new service industries but is possibly of little direct benefit to most residents? We do not pretend to answer these questions in a definitive way. Rather, we hope to shed light on whether the evolving social, economic and spatial structure of Mexico City, as seen in light of theories of global cities and the urban impacts of globalization, could represent a glimpse into the future of other large cities, perhaps even in the richest countries. We divide the paper into three additional sections. The first refers to the process of worldwide trade expansion and the transformation of international organizations and also identifies different scales and variables that heuristically can serve our description of the impact of globalization on some features of Mexico City. The second section describes some social, economic and spatial changes affecting Mexico City on these different scales. The final section identifies some general and particular issues for further research.

2. The changing global context and world cities

The emergence of what was considered "global society," based on the expansion of the global economy, the growth of international organizations of all kinds[3] and the global restructuring of industry, was discovered by the media and became a cliché in the 1980s (Knight and Gappert 1989). According to Wallerstein (1984), these patterns were the result of the second wave of colonialism starting in the nineteenth century when imperial countries viewed their colonies as immense supply depots for the cheap production and direct extraction of raw materials from which their economies could profit. In this sense "world system theory" suggests that the key to understanding the waves of colonialism is the changing structure of core regions. Periods of stability and instability in the core coincide with periods of contraction and colonial expansion in the periphery.

In economic terms, globalization implies that borders between nation-states and differences between financial markets have become much less important. Some of the reasons for this (Stutz 2002) are trends including:

i. The globalization of finance;
ii. the increasing importance of transnational companies;

[3] Apart from "nation-state," a concept dating back to the end of the Thirty Years War in 1648, and a growing phenomenom largely due to de-colonization after World War II (67 nations in 1945 grew to close to 190 sovereign nation states at the end of the twentieth century), other organizations have appeared and developed in the last century. Intergovernmental organizations (IGOs) are those formed by governments to fulfill common purposes or attain common objectives. Non-governmental organizations (NGOs) are not-for-profit institutions established to promote special interests or concerns, to influence IGOs, and to inform the general public. Multinational corporations (MNCs) are centrally-controlled multilocational enterprises for profit-making and dedicated not only to trading but also to governing technology (Knight 1989).

iii. global direct foreign investment (DFI) from North America, Western Europe, and East Asia (mainly Japan);
iv. global specialization in the location of production (the new international division of labour);
v. globalization of the tertiary sector of the economy;
vi. globalization of office functions;
vii. global tourism.

Two additional dimensions of globalization are occurring at the same time as the globalization of the economy: the globalization of culture (Sklair 1991) and the globalization of environmental change (Young 1997: 2). In cultural terms, it implies the following four processes:

i. Increasing levels of shared beliefs, social forms and material tracts worldwide;
ii. fewer cultural differences displayed among societies than in the past;
iii. globalization of cultural preferences created by improved telecommunications worldwide;
iv. penetration of global culture occurring at different places and at different rates, and therefore not all peoples sharing the same access to globalization.

Even in developed countries, these processes have ambivalent results (Hamelink 1984, cited in Sklair 1991: 80): utilization of information offers new job opportunities, but also creates more unemployment. It offers some decentralization in social decision-making, but at the same time, reinforces centralized administration. It enhances citizen participation in local government, but reinforces local dominant coalitions. It offers more security for data processing, but threatens privacy. It offers more social equity, but adds to existing social disparities.

Taking into account Simon's (1995: 146) concerns about complexities, and the difficulty or inadequacy of criteria to provide a straightforward definition of "world city" (see Table 1), Godfrey and Zhou's (1996) arguments related to data biases, or Smith and Timberlake's (1995) observance about lack of data as the main reason for eclecticism, we would like to simplify our Mexico City description as a peripheral global player based on the "two sides of the coin" metaphor. To do that, in the remainder of this paper, we will describe these trends at different levels (scales):

i. At the international level, this megacity is the privileged location of a majority of national and international corporations operating in the country, as well as the air terminal of international flights, reflecting its semi-peripheral world-level category.
ii. At the national level, all kinds of products (although no longer migrants) overwhelmingly are destined for the capital city, reinforcing its status as primate city and the most important market place in the national urban system.
iii. At the "city region" level, decentralizing trends are affecting the urban hierarchy in the functional region dominated by Mexico City, while at the metropolitan level, changes in the urban structure result from a readjustment in the housing and labor markets through changes of residences and journeys to work.

Table 1. A comparison of world city attributes

Hall (1966)	Friedmann (1986)	Sassen (1991, 1995, 2000)
Major centers of political power	Integration in the world economy; its functions in the new international spatial division of labour	Centers of political-economic control and influence over global marketing and production
National centers of trade	Basing points in the articulation of production and markets	Nodes for the management and regulation of the new space economy
Principal nodes of the transportation network	Global control functions reflected in structure and dynamics of economic sectors and employment	Location of top-level multinational headquarter functions and the growth of advanced corporate service
Banking and finance centers	Major sites for concentration and accumulation of international capital	Sites for the production of services for firms
Professional service centers	Points of destination of domestic and international migrants	Concentrate command functions
High income concentration	Spatial and class polarization	Post-industrial production sites for the leading industries, finance and specialized services
Overcrowding and congestion	Generators of social costs exceeding fiscal capacity of the state	National or transnational market places where firms and governments can buy financial instruments and specialized services

iv. Finally, at the intra-urban level it is easy to see the city as a mosaic and show the spatial differentiation of socio-demographic variables, social polarization and income inequalities.

3. Globalization trends in Mexico City

One of the most interesting aspects of the study of the effects of globalization on cities is its complexity. We choose to organize and simplify our efforts to look at the case of the Mexico City Metropolitan Zone (MCMZ) by examining trends at four different levels of analysis: international, national, metropolitan, and intraurban. The empirical evidence available varies considerably among these "city region" levels of analysis (see Simmonds and Hack 2000), but the idea is to paint as detailed a picture as feasible of the multiple ways of looking at a wide variety of recent changes.

3.1. International scale: Corporate headquarters

At the international level, Mexico City continues to be the privileged location of the majority of national and international corporations operating in the country, as well as the destination and point of departure of most international flights, including many which use the city as a stopover from the US and Europe on their way to Central and South America. This reflects Mexico City's semi-peripheral status in the hierarchy of world cities. However, it should be noted that in both of these variables, the capital's dominance over other cities in the national hierarchy has begun to erode in recent years.

The 500 top Mexican corporations produced 3.4 billion dollars in 2001, equivalent to more than half the country's GDP (Expansion 2002: 340); more than two thirds of these firms were located in Mexico City. But while these data suggest that the national capital continues to dominate the country's corporate life, some interesting changes have occurred within the list of largest companies. These serve to underline the massive changes in the Mexican economy in the past two decades.

In 1980, topping the list of largest companies were three state enterprises: PEMEX, SIDERMEX, and CFE (oil, steel and electricity, respectively), and two private ones with ownership in Monterrey, the main industrial city in the north of the county (Grupo ALFA and Valores Industriales, beer and steel production). With the beginning of privatization in 1988, other sectors and firms surpassed these traditional leaders of the economy. Communications (the first industry to be privatized), automobile companies, and food producers strengthened their positions, so that by the year 1990, with PEMEX still in the lead, General Motors, Ford, Volkswagen and TELMEX, occupied the first five positions, and three of these were foreign-owned. By 2000, two corporations in the communications sector were just behind PEMEX, the national oil company: CARSO (global telecom) and TELMEX, as well as automobile manufacturers, including Chrysler, in one of the top positions.

In spatial terms, of the top 25 firms in 1980, 19 were located in the MCMZ, with oil, electricity, automobile, steel, beer and food production at the top. Only three were of foreign origin. In 1990, eighteen companies were located in Mexico City, among them, one in telecommunications (TELMEX) and two in transportation (rail and air); seven of these were foreign-owned. By the year 2000, the 25 companies at the top of the list were mainly foreign (automobiles, communications and media), and 17 were located in Mexico City. Still, a decentralization trend was evident by 2000 in the manufacturing industries. Among these top 25 firms, eight were headquartered outside the capital: Monterrey (6), Puebla (1) and Torreón (1). Among the top 500 companies in 2002, 32% of corporate headquarters were located outside the MCMZ, mostly in the states of Nuevo Leon (Monterrey), Jalisco (Guadalajara), Chihuahua (Ciudad Juárez), Puebla, San Luis Potosí, Sinaloa and Coahuila (22% of the total).

3.2. International scale: Air traffic

In the context of rapidly expanding air traffic, Mexico City strengthened its position as an international hub, while diversifying its linkages in the international air network. This was true of both passenger and air freight services.

The total number of passenger arrivals (national and international) in the country amounted in 1980 to 13.5 million, with Mexico City accounting for around one third of the total.[4] Only two decades later, in 1999, the Mexico

[4] Data from Iracheta 2000: 321–332, Tables 4.11.1–4.

City International Airport (MCIA) alone received 20.4 million arrivals. Its nearest competitor in terms of volume was Cancún's International Airport, which specializes in the tourist service, with 12 million passengers. Annually, the MCIA now handles 71,712 domestic and 80,244 international flights. Main domestic links in the national network are Monterrey with 6,480 annual flights followed by Guadalajara (5,616), Tijuana (4,806), and Hermosillo (4,212).[5]

In 1994, among the international arrivals to the MCIA that accounted for more than 1% of the total, origins were in 23 cities, 14 of those in the US, one in Canada (Toronto), five in Europe, and three in Central America and the Caribbean. Arrivals amounted to a total of 2,837,246 passengers, of whom 43% originated in Los Angeles, Dallas, Houston and Miami and 13% in New York and Chicago. In fact, more than 70% of the arrivals were from passengers coming from a city in the US. However, this figure may be distorted by the hub structure of the airline industry, since there are an unknown number of passengers from Asian and European origins with connecting flights in US airports, mainly Los Angeles and San Francisco for the former, and New York and Atlanta for the latter.

Three years later, the volume of passengers had grown 10%, reaching 3,119,884. Los Angeles, Houston, Dallas and Miami remained the most important origins followed by New York and San Francisco. As in 1994, Madrid was the next most important point of origin. The number of cities accounting for more than 1% of the total flow increased to 27, with the addition of Panama City, Las Vegas, Washington, DC, and Lima, Peru. In addition, Atlanta, Phoenix and Detroit appeared in the 1997 list, as did Santiago, Chile, and San Salvador.

In 1994, airfreight received in the MCIA amounted to 110,846 tons, and it increased 10%, to 120,677 tons in 1997. Airfreight leaving the airport was a mere 50,943 tons in 1994, rising to 79,449 tons in 1997. This represents an extraordinary increment of 56%, and demonstrates an important change in Mexico's export basket: light, high-value manufacturing goods are replacing oil and mineral-based products. The main origin and destination of these commercial flows have not changed drastically, but the number of cities, which sent one ton or more goods, increased from 18 to 21 during the period considered, with half of those in the US. Miami and Los Angeles are outstanding contributors, but sources also include Paris, Amsterdam and Frankfurt in Europe, and Rio de Janeiro and Sao Paulo in South America. Three cities (Miami, Paris and Amsterdam) account in both years for one third of the total air freight imports, while more than a third of the total air freight exports handled in the MCIA in 1994 went to Los Angeles, Paris and Miami in 1994. In 1997, the same portion went to Los Angeles, Miami and New York in 1997, followed by Paris, Houston, Frankfurt, Amsterdam, Sao Paulo and Santiago, and Madrid. These ten destinations accounted for more than two thirds of all airfreight handled.

---

[5] See Aeromexico, Timetable, Effective April 7th, 2002. This source includes, in addition to Aeromexico and Mexicana subsidiaries, foreign air carriers in the SkyTeam Global Alliance (Air France, Alitalia, Czech Air Lines, Delta, El Al, Korean Air, KLM, Lan Chile, etc).

3.3. National scale

Although domestic migrants no longer view the MCMZ as the first and best destination, all kinds of products still overwhelmingly arrive there, reinforcing its status as primate city, and as the most important market place in the national urban system. The potential examples of this pattern are numerous; here, we limit our discussion to the fresh fruits and vegetables that are produced in the rest of the country and find their way to Mexico City. For producers in all those states, Mexico City is the main national market and first choice. For some of these producers, it also represents an alternative market for those products that do not fit to international export standards.

The trend of developing new international destinations for fresh produce is likely to continue, as foreign capital investment in the sector expands beyond the traditional US-based sources. Advanced technology in crop production and irrigation is concentrated in the northern states, which export to the US markets (mainly California and Texas, but also New York). However, as an example, Israeli companies are now investing in Jalisco's Ayuquila River Basin in large-scale greenhouse production of cherry tomatoes, mainly for export to the U.S. and European markets. In this sense, the primacy of Mexico City as a market for national production of all types is likely to decline as integration into international markets continues.

3.4. Metropolitan scale

At the metropolitan level, changes in urban structure result from a readjustment in housing and labor markets via changes of residence and journeys to work. In Mexico City, residential spatial segregation appears to be growing, but at the same time, decentralization of residential areas and employment in the high-income sectors has led to longer journeys to work for large segments of the population.

Spatial segregation patterns reflect human behavior mediated by variables such as family and individual migration history, income level, education, and other variables, as well as external forces related to cultural images and the physical context of daily life. Yet there is a general tendency of social groups to locate contiguous to their peers and to differentiate themselves from others, both socially and spatially. Mexico City displays an aggregated pattern of segregation, which appears to have been exacerbated by trends toward increasing socio-economic polarization. Considering income per capita of employed population in terms of minimum wages, 3.4% of the population receiving income >10 minimum wages in 1990 clustered in the western and southern local districts of the DF and the State of Mexico. In contrast, the poorest workers (18.3% of the population which earned the equivalent of less than 1 minimum salary) showed a more dispersed spatial distribution pattern. The low-income population (as in many developing country cities) has settled on the outskirts of the city, either in irregular, self-built housing on *ejido* land surrounding the consolidated areas, or has been incorporated into the MCMZ as small traditional towns and agricultural settlements were overtaken during the 1950–1970 period of population growth and physical expansion of the city (Negrete et al. 1993).

The spatial segregation of workers' residences from their jobs has received increasing attention since the 1950s, particularly from economists and geographers interested in transportation studies and changes in urban structure.[6] In the economic literature imbalances in this form of segregation are often referred to as *structural unemployment* and arise from slow adjustments to changes in the demand for and the supply of jobs. In geography this is known as the *spatial mismatch hypothesis* (Holzer and Vroman 1992; Simpson 1992), and it occurs either when the number of workers in an area surpasses the number of jobs offered, or when housing conditions and prices are not acceptable or affordable by workers with jobs in that area. In both cases the solution is long commutes.

With data from the 1994 Origin-Destination Survey of residents in the MCMZ, and the registered changes of residence during 1995–2000 in the 2000 Population Census, the relationship between net migration and commuting in the MCMZ's local units of government (*delegaciones* and *municipios*) shows that areas of the city with a negative net migration balance tend to show a positive net commuting balance (Map 1).

This explains much of the daily trip generation among metropolitan residential neighborhoods and major employment subcenters (Graizbord and Acuña 2002). Such interaction reflects changes in the urban structure as a result of suburbanization, physical expansion of the city and structural changes in the labor market.

A process of decentralization of employment and population, in addition to the physical expansion of the city, has been a general trend in the MCMZ during the last two decades. In 1970, 80% of the MCMZ population resided within the relatively better-off DF limits, with the remaining 20% in the metropolitan municipalities of the State of Mexico (MMEM). In 1995, the distribution was 50–50, and by 2000 the balance has shifted in favor of the MMEM.[7] These changes resulted, on the one hand, from economic activity, population and housing that "followed" manufacturing employment, and on the other hand, from employment in commerce and services that "followed" residential moves and expanding housing developments. At the same time, people moved with their jobs or tried to reduce their commutes by establishing their residence near their place of work (Table 2).

More than 7 million people are employed in the MCMZ, divided almost equally between the DF and the MMEM. But those who live in the latter tend to have longer commutes than those who live in the DF. The ratio of O-D flows between the DF and the MMEM is 1:5.8 in favor of the DF. In other words, for each journey to work originating in the DF and ending in a MMEM, there are 5.8 journeys originating in a MMEM and ending in the DF. On the other hand, O-D flows within the DF remain high with almost 1.5 million people, while there is a flow of about 500,000 within the metropolitan municipalities.

Of those living in the DF, 88% remain there for work, while of those living in the MMEM, 62% remain in the MMEM for work. Indeed, a high proportion of those residing in the DF and in the MMEM find jobs in the

[6] A classic is Kain (1962).

[7] See Graph II.B.1.2 in INEGI (1999: 95).

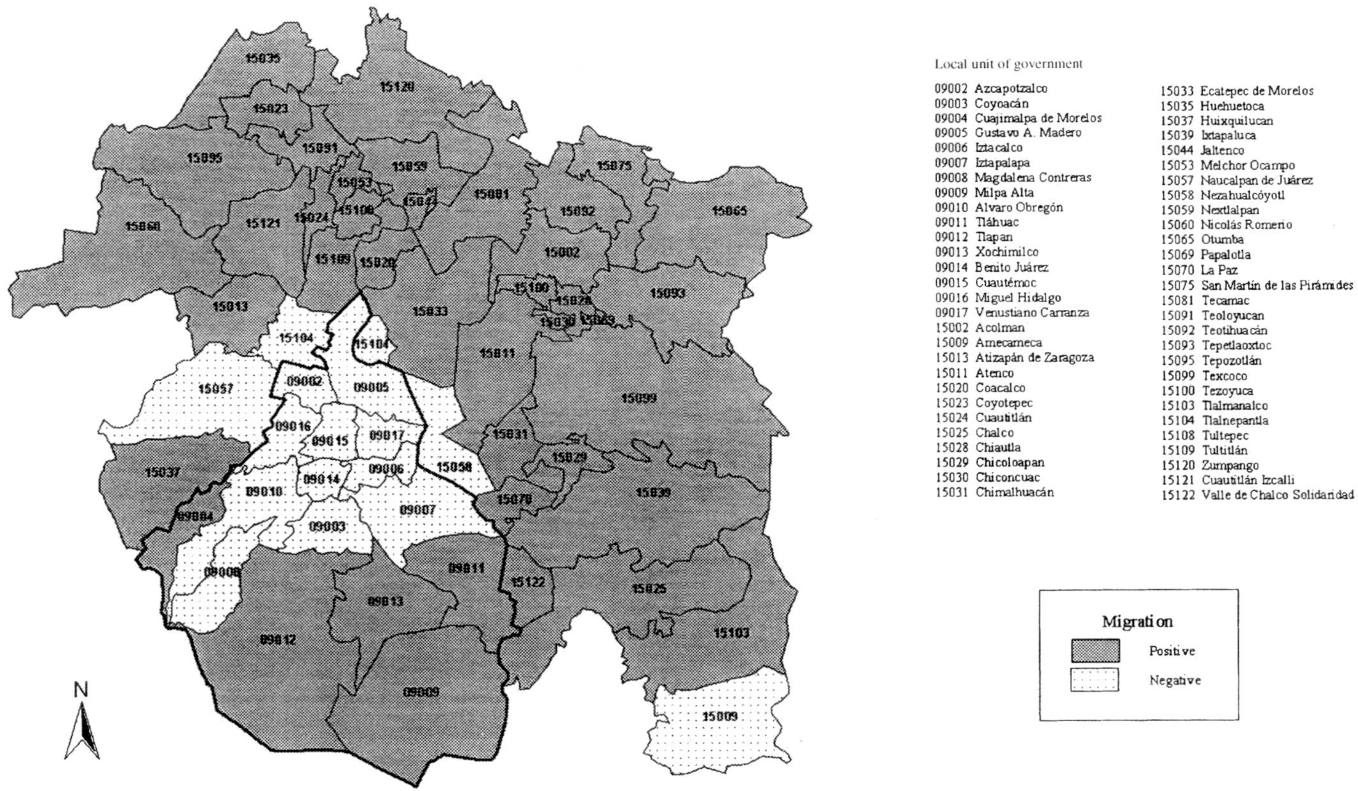

Source: Laboratory of Geographical Information Systems, El Colegio de México, with data of Graizbord and Acuña, 2000.

Map 1. Net migration balance

Table 2. MCMZ: Employed population by place of residence according to employment area, 2000*

	Employed population	Areas of employment							
		Federal District (DF)	Same residence and employment areas	Other *delegación*	State of Mexico (MMEM)	Metropolitan municipality	Other municipality	Other state	Insufficiently or non specified
Place of residence									
Federal District	3,671,925	3,226,875	1,790,070	1,436,805	176,707	114,451	62,256	28,390	237,299
Metropolitan municipalities of the state of Mexico	3,530,174	973,039	1,733,349	973,039	572,065	490,294	81,771	32,891	215,929
Metropolitan area totals	7,202,099	4,199,914	3,523,419	2,409,844	748,772	604,745	144,027	61,281	453,228
Percentages									
DF	100.0	87.9	48.8	39.1	4.8	3.1	1.7	0.8	6.5
MMEM	100.0	27.6	49.1	27.6	16.2	13.9	2.3	0.9	6.1
Total	100.0	58.3	48.9	33.5	10.4	8.4	2.0	0.9	6.3

Source: Estimated from INEGI. XII General Population and Housing Census 2000 (Extended questionaire). Mexico 2002.
* Local Administative Units are called *delegaciones* in the Federal District and municipalities in the State of Mexico.

same local government units in which they live: 49% in the DF and 49% in the MMEM. Of the remaining 51% of those living in the DF, 39% travel to work within the DF to another *delegación* and only 176,707 (4.8%) work outside the DF. Of the latter, 114,451 (3.1%) go to one of the MMEMs and 62,256 (1.7%) to another municipality in the State of Mexico, located outside the MCMZ limits. Close to 30,000 (less than 1%) travel to their jobs in another neighboring state (e.g., Morelos, Puebla, Tlaxcala, Hidalgo or Querétaro).

In contrast, of the remaining 51% of those living in the MMEM, 28% work in the DF and 16% work within the State of Mexico. Fourteen percent (almost half a million) have a job in another metropolitan municipality, 2% in a municipality outside the MMEM, and less than 1% in a neighboring state (in addition to those mentioned above, Guerrero and Michoacan might be included).[8]

Trips back home are almost symmetrical to journeys to work. More than 20 million trips a day, of which 25% are in private automobiles, also include trips for consumption and social purposes, which are more or less equal to the number of work trips. Metropolitan traffic makes up 75% of the total air emissions of more than 4 million tons a year in the MCMZ. Disaggregated figures show that transportation is responsible for 99.5% of CO (carbon monoxide), 71.3% of NO_x (nitrogen oxides), and 54% of all HC (hydrocarbons) produced in the Valley of Mexico (INEGI 1999: 61). Thus, emerging patterns of residential segregation and commuting not only affect productivity in Mexico City, because of time lost in traffic congestion, but also contribute to other serious problems such air pollution.

3.5. The intraurban scale

At the intra-urban scale, the city can be imagined as a mosaic, with spatial differentiation of socio-demographic variables resulting from social polarization and income inequalities. Here, we present evidence of sectoral changes in employment, shifts by size of establishment, and changes in occupational structure and labor force qualifications. These changes imply less stability in employment, replacement of permanent jobs by part-time occupations, and a growing use of subcontracting of small economic units by mid-size and large firms to avoid the costs imposed by Mexico's generous labor legislation. The general deterioration in labor conditions is revealed in the expansion of informal businesses, increasing use of unpaid workers, growth in the unskilled service sector, and a widening gap between economic sectors, income groups, size of firms and occupations. All these trends, in Aguilar's view, add up to greater social inequality (Aguilar 1997: 375). In this sense, the pattern of employment change in Mexico City appears to conform to the patterns defined in the literature on globalization and its impacts on cities.

---

[8] Almost 6% (453, 228) of the total is insufficiently or not specified in the census results, due probably to respondents not knowing the name of the area in which they work, or having more than one area of destination in their journeys to work.

Table 3. MCMZ: Sectoral changes in employment, 1991, 1995, 2000

Economic sector	Employed population			Net differences		Percentage growth	
	1991	1995	2000	1991–1995	1995–2000	1991–1995	1995–2000
Total MCMZ	5,763,655	5,984,770	7,269,910	221,115	1,285,140	3.84	21.47
Manufacturing	1,288,913	1,133,609	1,480,255	−155,304	346,646	−12.05	30.58
Public administration	479,202	431,221	527,451	−47,981	96,230	−10.01	22.32
Construction	261,975	220,448	364,490	−41,527	144,042	−15.85	65.34
Personal services	782,857	827,120	950,310	44,263	123,190	5.65	14.89
Wholesale	245,351	287,517	258,720	42,166	−28,797	17.19	−10.02
Retail	882,899	1,019,384	1,234,171	136,485	214,787	15.46	21.07
Tourism and recreation*	188,674	300,824	347,180	112,150	46,356	59.44	15.41
Street food sales	79,195	99,769	–	20,574	–	25.98	–
Transport and communication	382,418	441,472	525,407	59,054	83,935	15.44	19.01
Production services	1,063,806	1,164,172	1,466,262	100,366	302,090	9.43	25.95

* Hotels, restaurants and food preparation.
Source: Table 4 in Aguilar (*Op. Cit.*377) from INEGI, *National Survey of Urban Employment*, 1991, 1995 and 2000. México.

Between 1991 and 1995, employment grew by nearly 4% in Mexico City (Table 3), and from 1995 to 2000 by more than 20%. However, overall growth marks a substantial shift in both the sectoral composition of employment and in labor conditions. During the first period, the city was affected by job losses mainly in manufacturing, public administration, and construction, while other sectors, like retail and wholesale trade, and services in general, expanded in terms of employed population. The considerable growth from 1995 to 2000 was concentrated in production services. Together, production services, plus transportation and communication, combined with tourism and employment in recreation, accounted for one third of the total growth for Mexico City, while manufacturing jobs accounted for more than 25%. This high proportion is explained by an absolute loss of employment in manufacturing activities suffered the first half of the decade, and the positive impact of NAFTA in terms of industrial activities in the MCMZ since 1994. The second half of the 1990s, on the other hand, showed an increment in the number of establishments with only one worker, as well with more than five workers. But the percentage growth in the former category was more than 30%, while the second was nearer to 23%, showing the tendency of very small business to proliferate.

The expansion of small businesses (with fewer than 5 employees) provides one indicator of the growing importance of the informal sector. One-worker establishments decreased between 1991 and 1995 in manufacturing (−3,119), retail (−35,679) and transport and communications (−25,120), but these types of establishments proliferated in the personal services.

Employment data for the late 1980s and early 1990s in Mexico City show an increase in self-employed, piece-work, and non-wage workers, a trend associated with deteriorating labor conditions. The increase during the second half of the 1990s in all employment categories of laborers without fixed premises further suggests across-the-board expansions in informal work, either itinerant or based at home. This pattern was echoed in more than forty of the largest cities across the country, according to data from INEGI's National Surveys of Urban Employment. Formal jobs fell from 80% of the total in 1991 to 70% in 1995, with a corresponding decrease in the number of owners and wage workers. By then, one-third of Mexico City's independent activity (without fixed, non-residential premises) obtained income from mobile stalls, street vending, itinerant activities and work at home, practices which imply no employment benefits and often non-wage work by family members. Total employment with no fixed premises was 18% in 1991 but by both 1995 and 2000 the percentage had reached more than 27%. Non-wage workers without fixed premises, accounting for only 24% of total non-wage workers at the beginning of the 1990s, reached 47% in 1995, and 41% in 2000. However, in relative terms their weight fell from 4% to a little more than 3% of the overall employed population. In contrast, the self-employed population increased slightly from 16% in 1991 to 17% in 2000. The self-employed without fixed premises, in 1991 about 58% of all self-employed workers, reached 76% in 2000. In other words, although fewer people are willing to work without formal wages, at the same time more people enter the labor market as self-employed and without having fixed premises.

In the period 1991–1995, Mexico City's occupational structure moved (as in many global cities) towards divergence, with growth in the low-skilled commerce, services, and agricultural sectors, accompanied by a similar expansion of highly-qualified positions, including professional and technical workers, managers, and top level administrators (Aguilar 1997: 379–378). This pattern of polarization in the occupational structure is consistent with Sassen's (1991) argument about global cities in core countries, whose middle-level occupations are replaced with a growing low-skilled sector. The second half of the 1990s tells a different story. It is premature to accept a positive impact of the NAFTA in the MCMZ, but this possibility as an hypothesis has to be taken seriously in further analysis.

However, the processes of social polarization in the labor market structure and the precariousness of part of the labor force, as presented in the data above, show only one "side of the coin." The growth of tertiary employment also generated significant expansion in production services with high-wage, qualified personnel – people who can afford a life in upper-middle class neighborhoods, luxury consumption patterns and a cosmopolitan lifestyle.

Production services provide knowledge that adds to the value of goods produced in other economic sectors. These services are considered intermediate because they are inputs into other economic activities, and are produced either inside the plant or in the more general marketplace where they are purchased by firms. Professional and technical services are most representative of this sector, showing the highest and most intensive content of knowledge and information. They follow locational strategies based on proximity to other specialized services (Sassen 1998), access to information, and (perhaps) face-to-face interaction. The growth of the production service sector has been significant in the MCMZ since the mid-1980s. These services have tended to concentrate along the main commercial boulevards in high-income areas of the city reflecting a "growing service intensity in the organization of the economy" and give spatial form to the "process of economic globalization as concrete economic complexes situated in specific places"

(Sassen 2000: 269). Employment in the sector increased from 93,000 in 1980 to 297,000 in 1993, with jobs clustered mainly in areas surrounding the Central Business District (Cuauhtémoc), along the east-west axis formed by Reforma Boulevard. This street passes through the *delegaciones* of Benito Juárez, Miguel Hidalgo and Venustiano Carranza, and extends more than 20 kilometers, and through some traditionally high-income residential areas (Polanco, Lomas, Virreyes) that have been transformed in varying levels to offer up-scale offices, boutiques and restaurants catering to new high income urban elites. *Reforma* ends at the new Santa Fe commercial and office development on the west side of the metropolitan area. This new urban development, on the former site of a massive city garbage dump, has been promoted and patronized by many foreign companies, and now offers some of the highest real estate prices in the Western hemisphere. This zone is also the location of three of the finest universities in the country (the first two private): the *Universidad Iberoamericana* (UI), the *Instituto Tecnológico y de Estudios Superiores de Monterrey* (ITESM), and the *Centro de Investigación y Docencia Económicas* (CIDE).

Mexico City's north-south axis of high-end commercial and office development runs along Insurgentes Avenue, which stretches 15 kilometers from the central city to the most important and consolidated high-income residential areas in the south, as well as to the campus of the National University (UNAM).

4. Conclusions

After nearly two decades of increased integration with the rest of the world, Mexico City has consolidated itself as a second-tier global city. However, research suggests that the flip side of achieving this status is to suffer from the disadvantages of globalization, mainly social and economic polarization, while reaping few advantages in terms of improved quality of life. Clearly, Mexico City is not a global city in the same sense as New York, London and Tokyo, nor is it likely to become one. However, its importance as a megacity (Ward 1990) has increased since the 1980s, as international trade has expanded across Latin America.

The evidence of urban impacts on the MCMZ supports many of the predictions in the literature about globalization, especially in terms of the changing economic structure and polarization of socio-economic groups. Some of the urban patterns described in the literature for New York, London and Tokyo (especially polarization and segregation) are apparent in Mexico City, with the trade and service sectors replacing manufacturing as the principal sources of employment, and changes in the location of economic activity and population leading to the rise of major metropolitan subcenters. At the same time, in a context of pre-existing high levels of socio-economic inequality, most workers have experienced declining employment conditions in terms of stability, salary and benefits, while a small elite linked to the new economy has assumed the cosmopolitan consumption patterns of the traditional wealthy class.

There are some other urban changes predicted in the literature on impacts of globalization about which we have anecdotal evidence, but for which comprehensive data is unavailable. One is the conspicuous presence of an international capitalist class combined with a proliferation of street vendors and mobile informal activities. Another issue is the use of public funds to attract or maintain capital investment, for example, by planning the construction of a new, larger airport to the east side of the urban area. This national government project failed because of the violent opposition from local peasants in San Salvador Atenco. A city-sponsored program of this type is to build a second level for the *Periférico* (ring road) that is intended to facilitate the flow of private and commercial vehicles between the southern commercial, office and residential subcenter, the Santa Fe zone and the airport. Another effort, promoted by the DF government (with the support of private capital), aims to revitalize the city's historic architectural and artistic patrimony, primarily to attract more tourist revenue. The restoration of public urban spaces, such as plazas and streets (increasingly occupied by vendors and informal retail markets during the 1980s and 1990s), would benefit all residents, and is also on the local agenda.[9]

A current worry for the city authorities and for most residents of the MCMZ is the rapid increase in lawlessness, violence and crime since the mid-1990s. This has been accompanied by a growth in spending on police and private security, but the lack of tangible results threatens public confidence in city government and diminishes the attractiveness of the city for new private investment, both domestic and foreign.

Finally, the growth of secondary cities relative to the primate city may represent an interesting trend, especially in regard to globalization and long-term impacts. Both primary and secondary cities, and perhaps even small cities, are affected by global dynamics but are the impacts evident in the same way as in the MCMZ? How are these cities participating in the new economy? Are all urban economic activities part of the internationalization of the economy? Are these connected to globalizing forces? Far from increasing Mexico City's importance in the national urban hierarchy, the liberalization of the economy since the mid-1980s has allowed other cities, not only those on the northern border, to take advantage of previously suppressed comparative advantages and to grow at relatively rapid rates, both demographically and economically. Coupled with governmental decentralization and the improvements in the electoral process, these cities also increasingly define their own spheres of political action. Whether this trend implies that other cities in the country will eventually challenge Mexico City's primacy, and/or that they are part of an incipient transnational urban system (Sassen 2000: 271; Derudder et al. 2003) remains to be seen. The extent of these geographical, economic and political trends on residents and firms in the Mexico City Metropolitan Zone remains unclear.

References

Aguilar AG (1997) Metropolitan growth and labor markets in Mexico. Geo Journal 43: 371–383

[9] Restoration of urban public spaces (streeets and plazas) is central to a local approach to planning as proposed by Hack (2000: 191) and also Simmonds (2000: 194).

Aguilar AG (nd) Reestructuración económica y costo social de la Ciudad de México: Una metrópoli "periférica" en la escala global. Mimeo
Beaverstock J, Smith R, Taylor P (1999) A roster of world cities. Cities 16(6):445–458
Berry B (1976) Urbanization and counter urbanization. Sage, Beverly Hills, CA
Derudder B, et al. (2002) Hierarchical tendencies and regional patterns in the world city network: A global urban analysis of 234 cities. GaWC Research Bulletin 88. http://www.lboro.ac.uk/gawc/rb/rb88.html
Derudder B, et al. (2003) Beyond Friedmann's world city hypothesis: Twenty-two urban arenas across the world. GaWC Research Bulletin 97. http://www.lboro.ac.uk/gawc/rb/rb97.html
Expansión (2002) Las 500 empresas más importantes de México. Julio 24:340–442
Friedmann J (1995) Where we stand: A decade of world city research. In: Knox P, Taylor P (eds) World cities in a world system. Cambridge University Press, Cambridge
Friedmann J (1986) The world city hypothesis. Development and Change 17:69–83
Garza G (ed) (2000) La ciudad de México en el fin del segundo milenio. Gobierno del Distrito Federal y El Colegio de México, Mexico City
Geyer H, Kontully T (1993) A theoretical foundation for the concept of differential urbanization. International Regional Science Review 15:157–177
Gilbert A (2002) How does a non-global city fit into the global economy? Understanding the international links of Colombia's capital. Seminar paper: The Impact of Globalization on Urban Development, August 19–23, 2002, Villa Serbelloni, Bellagio, Lake Como, Italy. Mimeo
Godfrey B, Zhou X (1999) Ranking world cities: Multinational corporations and the global urban hierarchy. Urban Geography 20(3):246–281
Graizbord B, Acuña B (2002) Ajuste residencial en el Area Metropolitana de la ciudad de México. Seminar paper: La Población en la Región Centro: Situación Actual y Desafíos Demográficos. March 14 and 15, Toluca, Mexico. Mimeo
Graizbord B, Mina A (1994) Los ambitos geográficos del componente migratorio de la ciudad de México. Estudios Demográficos y Urbanos 9:609–628
Hack G (2000) Infrastructure and regional form. In: Simmonds R, Hack G (eds) Global city regions: Their emerging forms. Spon Press, London
Hall P (1966) The world cities. Werfenfeld and Nicholson, London
Hall P (1998) Globalization and the world cities. In: Lo FC, Yeung Y (eds) Globalization and the world of large cities. United Nations University Press, Tokyo
Hamer AM (1994) Economic impacts of Third World mega-cities: Is size the issue? In: Fuchs R, et al. (eds) Mega-city growth and the future. United Nations University Press, Tokyo
Holzer HJ, Vroman W (1992) Mismatches and the urban labor market. In: Peterson G, Vroman W (eds) Urban labor markets and job opportunity. The Urban Institute Press, Washington
Ibañez C (2001) Dinámica de la estructura sectorial y espacial del sector servicios en la Ciudad de México: El caso de los servicios al productor. Masters thesis, El Colegio de México, Mexico City
INEGI (1999) Estadísticas del medio ambiente del Distrito Federal y Zona Metropolitana 1999. Instituto Nacional de Estadística, Geografía e Informática, Mexico City
Iracheta J (2000) Globalización y flujos aereos. In: Garza G (ed) La ciudad de México en el fin del segundo milenio. Gobierno del Distrito Federal y El Colegio de México, Mexico City
Kain J (1962) The journey-to-work as a determinant of residential location. Papers and Proceedings of the Regional Science Association 9:137–160
Knight R (1989) The emergent global society. In: Knight R, Gappert G (eds) Cities in a Global Society. Sage, Newbury Park, CA
Lippman Abu-Lughod J (1995) Comparing Chicago, New York and Los Angeles: Testing some world cities hypotheses. In: Knox P, Taylor P (eds) World cities in a world system. Cambridge University Press, Cambridge
Negrete ME, Graizbord B, Ruíz C (1993) Población, espacio y medio ambiente en la Zona Metropolitana de la Ciudad de México. Serie Cuadernos de Trabajo 2, LEAD-México. El Colegio de México, Mexico City
Parnreiter C (1998) La ciudad de México: Una ciudad global? Anuario de Espacios Urbanos. Historia, Cultura, Diseño 21–52
Richardson H (1980) Polarization reversal in developing countries. Papers of the Regional Science Association 45:67–85

Rowland A, Gordon P (1996) Mexico City: No longer a Leviathan? In: Gilbert A, Lo F (eds) Megacities in Latin America. United Nations University Press, Tokyo
Ruiz Y (2002) Adios maquiladoras. Expansión 24 de julio-7 de agosto:82–91
Sabatini F (2000) The Santiago Region. In: Simmonds R, Hack G (eds) Global city regions: Their emerging forms. Spon Press, London
Sassen S (1991) The global city: New York, London, Tokyo. Princeton University Press, Princeton
Sassen S (1998) The impact of new technologies and the globalization of cities. In: Lo F, Yeung Y (eds) Globalization and the world of large cities. United Nations University Press, Tokyo
Sassen S (2000) Cities in the global economy. In: Simmonds R, Hack G (eds) Global city regions: Their emerging forms. Spon Press, London
Simmonds R (2000) Emerging cultures of governance. In: Simmonds R, Hack G (eds) Global city regions: Their emerging forms. Spon Press, London
Simmonds R, Hack G (eds) (2000) Global city regions: Their emerging forms. Spon Press, London
Simon D (1995) The world city hypothesis: Reflexions from the periphery. In: Knox P, Taylor P (eds) World cities in a world system. Cambridge University Press, Cambridge
Simpson W (1992) Urban structure and the labour market. Clarendon Press, Oxford
Sklair L (1991) Sociology of the global system. Johns Hopkins University Press, Baltimore
Smith D, Timberlake M (1995) Conceptualizing and mapping the structure of the world system's city system. Urban Studies 32: 287–302
Stutz F (2002) The world economy, class outline notes for chapters 8–12. Downloaded on Februrary 25, 2003 from http://www-rohan.sdsu.edu/faculty/fstutz/index.html
Tolosa H (2002) The Extended Rio/Sao Paulo Metropolitan Region: A quest for global integration. Seminar paper: The Impact of Globalization on Urban Development, August 19–23, 2002, Villa Serbelloni, Bellagio, Lake Como, Italy. Mimeo
Wallerstein I (1984) The politics of the world economy. Cambridge University Press, Cambridge
Ward P (1990) Mexico City: The production and reproduction of an urban environment. Belhaven Press, London
Ward P (1995) The successful management and administration of world cities: Mission impossible? In: Knox P, Taylor P (eds) World cities in a world system. Cambridge University Press, Cambridge
WRI (1996) World resources: A guide to the global environment, 1996–97. World Resources Institute, New York
Young O (1997) Rights, rules and resources in world affairs. In: Young O (ed) Global governance: Drawing insights from the environmental experience. MIT Press, Cambridge, MA

Globalization and Latin America: Understanding the global links of Colombia's capital

Alan Gilbert

Department of Geography, University College London, 26 Bedford Way, London, WC1H OAP, UK (e-mail: a.gilbert@geog.ucl.ac.uk)

Abstract. Although Colombia has been identified as one of the globalized countries in the developing world, it does not stand out among the countries of Latin America. However, the economy performed better after 1990 when liberalization reforms were introduced. Employment and economic growth were particularly strong, especially between 1993 and 1997, but then the economy collapsed. Bogota followed this cycle, but has disadvantages from the perspective of exploiting the opportunities of globalization: An interior location, a weak manufacturing base and negligible exports, and a tarnished reputation associated with the drug trade that discourages foreign direct investment and tourism. On the other hand, the city has been well managed under a series of mayors, although this is unlikely to have any major payoff in terms of globalization benefits.

1. What is globalization?

Globalization is a problematic term and one that is all too often abused. Too much of what goes on in the world is attributed to globalization and previous incarnations of globalization are frequently neglected. Without denying that the world has changed significantly over the last thirty years and that some parts of the global economy are more closely linked than ever before, I wish to explore how globalization is impinging on one, not insignificant, less-developed country and particularly on its national capital, Bogotá.

The World Bank (2002a) has recently defined globalization as "the growing integration of economies and societies around the world...." The current phase of globalization dates from 1980 but the Bank recognises that there have been two earlier phases of globalization, 1870–1914 and 1950–1980. However, no mention is made of that significant phase of globalization that began with the 'discovery' of the Americas, Africa and the Far East in the fifteenth century. Without the Conquest Latin Americans would not speak Spanish or Portuguese and the population's racial structure would be much more homogenous.

The most recent phase of globalization is arguably distinctive because of its depth and intensity: "Since about 1980 there has been unprecedented global economic integration" (World Bank 2002: 23). The Overseas Development Institute provides a somewhat fuller description of this process. "The common thread in most definitions of globalization is the idea that the world is facing a qualitatively new level of integration in a variety of economic and non-economic spheres, and that this is driven by communications and transport innovations. ... The term 'globalization' can be taken as having two broad dimensions. Firstly, factors causing accelerated global 'integration' of various kinds (liberalization of trade and capital flows, changing technology leading to changing patterns and growing volumes of exchange of information and knowledge), and secondly the institutional responses to such changes at various levels – global, regional, national and local" (ODI 2000: 1).

It is obvious that all parts of the world are not linked into the world economy in the same way or to the same extent. The Bank divides the developing world into two groups, 24 "more globalized" countries and the rest (World Bank 2001: 51). The list of 24 includes Colombia and eight other Latin American countries, as well as some rather odd countries: Bangladesh, Haiti, Rwanda and Zimbabwe. Chile is not included because it has been promoted to the developed-country category along with the 'Gang of Four'.

As the capital city of a 'more globalized' country, Bogotá is presumably doing well by developing world standards. And, if economic integration is meant to be good for a country's economic health, it is likely that its capital city will prosper. Whether that qualifies Bogotá, with its seven million or so inhabitants, into the ranks of world cities is uncertain. On some criteria it is often included, on others it is not. The paper will consider some of the major features of globalization make a brief estimation of where Colombia as a whole fits into the global equation and then assess whether Bogotá is benefiting or not from its relatively privileged position in the more highly integrated world economy.

2. To what extent and in what ways are Colombia and Bogotá part of the global economy?

2.1. Formal globalization

In several respects globalization is nothing new to Colombia. Colonization in the fifteenth century forcibly introduced it to Spanish, Catholicism and foreign trade. Along with the rest of Latin America, globalization occurred far more rapidly and intensely than in most parts of Africa or Asia. During the World Bank's first wave of globalization, 1870–1914, Colombia developed an important export product, coffee, which took it into the realm of partially successful developing countries. Later it managed to industrialize behind the protection afforded by import tariffs and quotas. Much of the finance for this industrial expansion came from foreign capital. Its 'globalization' was helped by the discovery of important quantities of oil, emeralds, coal and nickel.

Colombia did not participate immediately in the new wave of globalization that began in 1980. Prudent economic management and a reluctance to borrow excessively from abroad meant that it never plumbed the depths of the debt crisis in the way characteristic of most other Latin American countries in the 1980s. Its better than average economic performance dissuaded it from undertaking the kind of radical economic reforms required of Mexico or Bolivia and protected it from the kind of IMF agreements 'negotiated' with Argentina, Peru and numerous other Latin American countries. The first substantial attempt to restructure its economy came in 1986 when the incoming government sought to make Colombia more like an Asian Tiger. But the real thrust to reform the country and to integrate it more fully into the global economy came in 1990 with the arrival in power of César Gaviria.

Since 1990, successive national governments have tried to reform the Colombian economy following neo-classical economic guidelines. Economic 'opening' was initiated with a series of reforms in 1991 and 1992 that modified Colombia's trade, foreign investment, tax, financial and foreign exchange regulations (Ramírez-Ocampo 1998). Customs duties and import surcharges were slashed; in nominal terms overall protection fell from 36% in 1990 to 14% in September 1991. The central bank was made autonomous.

The basic economic model applied in Colombia is so close to recommended World Bank/IMF practice that little more needs to be said. But other elements of the globalization process in Colombia need a little more elaboration.

First, Colombia has attempted to follow the example of countries like Chile in reforming its pension, social security and health systems and in reducing the power of organized labour. Labor reforms introduced in 1990 sought to simplify Colombian labor laws and improve the functioning of the labour market. A new law allowed employers to dismiss workers who had been with a company for more than ten years, considerably reducing the cost of dismissal to the company (Hommes et al. 1994: 49). The law also modified the rules on short-term contracts, regulated the rules on strikes, improved the financial arrangements governing pensions and increased maternity leave to twelve weeks. The health, pension and social security systems have since been substantially privatized.

Second, privatization of state enterprises has been underway although it has not proceeded as quickly or successfully as had been hoped. Telecommunications garbage collection and some water companies have been privatized, although electricity production has continued to be something of a headache.

Third, the country introduced a new constitution in 1991 that attempted to liberalize its political institutions and to devolve government responsibility. The political equivalent of opening up the country to foreign investment and imports was to make government more efficient, more democratic and more responsive. This was deemed to be hugely important in the Colombian context as a means of combating the violence generated by the guerrilla movement and the drug business.

Fourth, although Colombia has long been open to foreign cultural influence, the reforms sought to go much further. Postgraduate students were encouraged to study abroad and nothing was done to stop the inflow of foreign music, film and television programs. Higher incomes and cheaper fares encouraged people to travel and the number of Colombians going abroad may well have trebled between 1991 and 2000. Most of these have headed for the United States, and Miami is today Colombia's preferred holiday resort. In return, Colombia has contributed to global culture. It has produced world famous pop-stars, Shakira; Nobel winning novelists, Gabriel García Márquez; internationally acclaimed artists, Fernando Botero and Rafael Obregón; and even footballers, Carlos Valderrama. It has established a reputation in certain branches of science and medicine. In sum, it is wholly understandable that the World Bank should classify Colombia as one of the developing world's 'more globalized' countries.

2.2. *Informal globalization*

If there are plenty of signs of formal globalization, globalization has also come through the back door. Colombia is, of course, most famous for fueling the addictive tendencies of many in the developed world. Marijuana and later cocaine and opium have generated considerably to the value of the export trade. Estimates differ on the value of this trade although the authorities tend to play the income effect down. It is true that much of the money generated does not come back to Colombia but, nonetheless, during the 1990s at least 2% of GDP may have been generated by drug monies (The Economist 2000; Fernández 1996; Steiner 1998; Thoumi 1995).

More important than the economic benefits, however, are the economic, political and social costs of drug production (Tirado 1998). The refusal of the OECD countries to contemplate legalizing drug use has caused many of Colombia's current difficulties. Illegality has encouraged high levels of violence and the city of Medellín was ravaged by the rivalry between drug gangs in the late 1980s and early 1990s. President Samper (1994–1998) was charged with receiving funds from the Cali drug cartel, a charge that severely weakened his presidency. The monies generated from drugs fund much of the military activity of the FARC guerrillas. The violence in the countryside is generated to a considerable extent by disputes over control over land used for the production of drugs or the laundering of drug monies.

Backdoor globalization is also reflected in the growing numbers of undocumented Colombians living abroad. We do not know how many there are but in 1999 and 2000 more than 10% of outward bound air passengers did not return to the country and in 2001 the proportion rose to 16.8%. In addition, there is a much poorer group of rural emigrants forced into neighboring Ecuador, Panama and Venezuela (Rojas-Rodríguez 2000). In two years, 2000 and 2001, some 565,000 Colombians appear to have left the country, 1.4% of the total population.

The drug trade, and the internal violence that it has helped to release, has also brought the dangers of international intervention. The United States has been playing an ambiguous role in Colombian politics for some years, helping to undermine the effectiveness of President Ernesto Samper and now being welcomed to help eliminate the guerrilla menace by President Alvaro Uribe. Plan Colombia is a dark cloud lying over Colombia. It is difficult to believe that the deadly cocktail of official, paramilitary, guerrilla, drug and private security power will not be accentuated by greater US involvement. Vietnam is a poor comparison; Nicaragua is possibly a more appropriate match. If this represents globalization through the back door, Colombia would be better without it.

3. How successful has globalization has been?

3.1. Economic growth

Relatively impressive economic growth rates between 1980 and 1997 put Colombia squarely into the realm of the "more globalized" developing countries. By Latin American standards, Colombia's growth record over the last fifty years has been very consistent. Most importantly, it suffered much less during the years of the debt crisis than most of the rest of the region. The deep recession that has hit the country since 1998 is causing many problems even if it has its parallels in many other countries of the region.

3.2. Foreign trade

If the extent of globalization is to be measured by the value of exports as a proportion of GDP, Colombia hardly qualifies as a new Tiger. It is true that Colombia increased its share of exports dramatically between 1965 and 1999 but that share has fluctuated greatly over the years. Significantly, the share has actually declined since economic opening in 1990.

Table 1. Economic growth by decade since 1950 (Annual growth in GDP)

Country	1950–1959	1960–1969	1970–1979	1980–1989	1990–1999	2000–2002
Colombia	4.7	5.0	5.7	3.7	3.3	1.8
Latin America	4.9	5.7	5.6	1.7	3.4	1.2

Source: United Nations (1998) and Inter-American Development Bank (2003).

Table 2. Export performance of Colombia and Latin America, 1965–2001

	Exports as % of GDP				
Country	1965	1980	1983	1990	2001
Colombia	11	16	10	15	15
Latin America	9	13	na	15	18

Source: World Bank (1982; 2000; 2003)

Table 3. Development of manufacturing exports, 1965–2001

	Manufactures as % of total merchandise exports			
Country	1965	1980	1990	2001
Colombia	7	20	25	34
Latin America	8	20	34	48

Source: World Bank (1982, 2000, 2003)

According to the World Bank the new phase of globalization has allowed poor countries "to harness the potential of their abundant labor to break into global markets for manufactured goods and for services" (World Bank 2002: 5). On this criterion, Colombia has not done badly. However, Table 3 suggests that this expansion has had little to do with the recent opening up of the economy – it is a longer established pattern. It is also notable that Colombia also appears to have done less well than Latin America as a whole, and much less well than Brazil or Mexico.

Currently, Colombia's exports are falling because of the world recession and particularly because of the crisis in Latin America. It is difficult to increase exports when your immediate neighbors, Ecuador and Venezuela, have such serious economic problems. Exporting is also complicated by the United States' reluctance to import agricultural imports and actively discriminates against many of the country's principal export products.

3.3. Foreign investment

According to Fernández-Arias and Hausmann (2000: 3) "foreign direct investment has been exploding" in Latin America and, for a while, Colombia benefited fully. FDI rose from US$457 million in 1991 to US$5.6 billion in 1997 (Banco de la República 2001: 8). Unfortunately, the combination of economic recession and increasing violence had cut this to only US$1.7 billion in 2001. Worse still, foreign debt has been increasing and reached US$36 billion in 2001, the equivalent of 44% of GDP (Banco de la República 2001: 9).

3.4. The role of government

Presidents Gaviria and Pastrana, and to a lesser extent President Samper, attempted to reduce the responsibilities of the national government. There has been some privatisation, many subsidies have been cut and some government activities have been severely pruned. Initially, this had a major impact on the government fiscal deficit, which fell from a high of 7.2% during the early 1980s to negligible proportions during the mid-1990s (Table 4). Unfortunately, an expansion in government social spending under Ernesto Samper, substantial increases in local government spending ordained in the 1991 constitution, combined with the severe recession that hit the country in 1998, resulted in a further massive deficit by the end of the 1990s. The intervention of the IMF has at best only partially

Table 4. Budget surplus/deficit in Columbia and Latin America, 1991–1999

Country	1991	1995	1999	2002
Colombia	0.2	−0.6	−4.6	−3.6
Latin America	−0.3	−1.5	−3.2	−2.0

Source: CEPAL (2003)

resolved the problem, and some believe that it has made it worse (Sarmiento 2002).

3.5. Employment

Other fears about globalization are that it either generates 'jobless growth' (UNDP 1993: 36) or creates jobs only for highly skilled and very low skilled people, accentuating inequality. Colombia demonstrates both of these tendencies. During periods of economic growth, the workforce has expanded rapidly, particularly in areas of low-skill work. During periods of recession, however, the liberalized labor regulations have allowed companies to lay workers off. Since 1990, the unemployment rate in the largest seven cities has fluctuated from a low of 7.6% in the third quarter of 1994 to a high of 20.5% in the same quarter of 2000 (Banco de la República 2002: 10).

In the 1980s, Colombian formal sector workers fare better than their compatriots in most other Latin American countries but in the 1990s, Colombia increasingly fitted the World Bank's (2002: 14) observation that: "Some of the important losers from globalization will be formal sector workers in protected industries". Certainly, several large banks and construction companies closed their doors during the late 1990s. There are also many signs that the informal sector has been expanding rapidly.

But whether globalization is really the cause of rising unemployment is an open question. Certainly the experience of Colombia, which only started to liberalize seriously after 1990 and seemed to be benefiting from that approach during the middle 1990s, does not help answer that question. Arguably the boom of the early 1990s, induced by property speculation, high commodity prices and the repatriation of drug monies, was not caused by liberalization. Similarly the severe recession that began to hit the country in 1998 was brought about largely by domestic policies. If liberalization opened up the economy to the financial instability that was affecting the Far East and Brazil, it did not affect the United States' decision to decertify the country nor explain the rising expenditure of the Samper government. Similarly, internal decisions made by the central bank and by the Constitutional Court have made the situation far worse than it needed to be. While some blame liberalization, it is difficult to place most let alone all of the blame there (Sarmiento 1999; Sarmiento 2002).

One other symptom of the impact of globalization on employment is the decline in union membership. In the six largest Latin American economies union membership in urban areas has fallen rapidly. In the middle 1990s, it had fallen to less than 20% in Colombia, Chile and Venezuela and varied from 20% to 30% in Argentina, Mexico and Brazil (The Economist 6/12/1997). Even here, however, globalization cannot explain the situation in Colombia for union membership in the country has never been very high.

3.6. Poverty and inequality

The World Bank (2002: 1) argues that: "globalization generally reduces poverty because more integrated economies tend to grow faster and this growth is usually widely diffused." Many other experts beg to disagree. In

Table 5. Poverty and inequality in Columbia

Year	Gini coefficient	% Population below poverty line	% Population lacking basic needs	Economic growth (%)
1980	0.54	59.1	55.4	
1991	0.55	57.7	35.6	2.0
1992	0.56	55.8	35.5	4.1
1993	0.58	56.4		5.4
1994	0.57	54.4		5.8
1995	0.56	55.0		5.2
1996	0.56	53.8		2.1
1997	0.54	54.2	26.9	3.4
1998	0.56	55.7	26.3	0.6
1999	0.59	60.1	26.1	−4.1
2000				2.8
2001	0.59	68.0		1.7

Source: Sarmiento (1999: 79), Banco de la República (2001), El Tiempo (2002b).

terms of inequality, while the World Bank (2002: 1) argues that growing integration does not usually heighten inequality within countries (p.5), it admits that: "in Latin America, due to prior extreme inequalities in educational attainment, global integration has further widened wage inequalities."

Colombian experience generally supports the World Bank's overall argument. While sustained economic growth has had little or no effect over the years in reducing inequality, it has substantially cut poverty, particularly in terms of the provision of basic needs. Since 1997, however, economic decline has led to an increase in inequality and to a substantial rise in the share of the population living below the poverty line. An official announcement in 2002 declared that 68% of Colombians were living in poverty (El Tiempo 2002b). If Colombia has long been one of the most unequal countries in the world, the recent trends cast doubt on what benefits integration brings even in a 'more globalized' country.

4. Bogotá's role in a more globalized developed country

Bogotá is not a typical Latin American mega-city. First, it is not a supra-primate city; it does not dominate Colombia in the way that Buenos Aires overshadows Argentina or Lima controls Peru. Second, unlike many of the primate cities of Latin America it is not a port, perhaps the reason why it generates a relatively small proportion of Colombia's export income. Third, while Bogotá's population growth rate is falling, population expansion has not slowed in the way that it has in most other major Latin America cities since 1980. During the 1980s, the city was growing annually at over 4%, a major fall from the 7% of the 1960s and 1970s, but a rapid rate nonetheless (Table 6). Fourth, because the Colombian economy was relatively healthy between 1980 and 1997, the incidence of poverty declined. It is only very recently that poverty has again become a really serious problem. Fifth, in recent years, Colombia's economy has become more centralized.

Bogotá is Colombia's largest industrial center and manufacturing contributed 21% of the city's domestic product in 1996 (DAPD 1999: 14). It is

Table 6. Bogota: Population growth, 1905–2001

Year	Population (thousands)	Annual growth (%)	Bogota/next three largest cities**
1905	100		0.80
1918	144	2.8	0.76
1938	356	4.6	0.84
1951	715	5.5	0.65
1964	1,697*	6.9	0.74
1973	2,855*	7.6	0.89
1985	4,268*	3.4	0.96
1993	5,898*	4.1	1.16
2001	7,223*	2.6	n.a.

* Includes Soacha. 2001 is based on my projection of the figures presented in González-Murillo (1998: 182).
** Medellín (including Bello, Envigado and Itagüi), Cali (including Yumbo) and Barranquilla

also the country's major financial center, and finance contributed a further 18% of the domestic product. As the administrative and political capital, government services are also important, contributing a further 13%. The bulk of the rest of the city's economic activity is contained in commerce, transport and personal services.

By comparison with most of the rest of the country, Bogotá's economy has been doing relatively well. In the late 1980s, economic growth in Bogotá and the surrounding department of Cundinamarca was faster than in the three other major metropolitan areas. In the early 1990s, the economic growth rate was exceeded only by that in Valle and Caldas, areas that undoubtedly benefited from drug monies (DAPD 1999: 144).

Bogotá's major weakness is that it produces little in the way of exports. In 1998 it generated only 1% of Colombia's exports, although the surrounding department contributed 14% (DAPD 1999: 75). The principal exports of Greater Bogotá are cut flowers, leather goods and textiles. To put the export situation in context, Latin America as a region exports US$816 per capita whereas Bogotá generates exports worth only $236 per capita (El Tiempo 2002a). Overall, the city has a large balance of payments deficit (DAPD 1999: 79).

5. To what extent has globalization in Bogotá been successful?

Since 1990, when neo-liberal policies were introduced in earnest, Bogotá has both prospered and suffered. Naturally, its economic experience has reflected that of the rest of the country; slow growth in the early 1990s as the reforms were introduced, a boom from 1993 to 1997, and then a severe recession. As explained above, some of the fluctuation can be explained in terms of external forces but internal changes are just as important. Arguably, the construction boom of the mid-1990s, a misguided exchange rate policy in the later 1990s, political crises and some bizarre decisions by the Constitutional Court were just as important in explaining these fluctuations as the Asian crisis, interventions by the IMF or the downturn in the US economy in 2001. Colombia and its capital are sufficiently globalized to benefit and suffer from changes in the wider world economy but internal factors are at least as important.

Until 1997, it might have been argued that Bogotá was doing rather well from the new regime. While poverty was all too common, it fell during the early 1990s and only increased in the latter years of the decade (Londoño 1995; Sarmiento-Palacio 1999). Until 1997, the economy was generating jobs at a rapid rate, keeping unemployment at a level lower than in the most of the other major cities, and raising the quality of life of the average citizen (Gilbert 1997).

Until 1997, the rate of job generation in Bogotá was very rapid. Between 1976 and 1995, the workforce increased from 1.1 million to 2.6 million people. Demographic growth, a maturing population and rising labor participation, particularly among women, boosted the labor supply remarkably (Gilbert 1997). Large numbers of older children joined the labor force and women began to work as never before. In 1976, one-third of women worked; twenty years later the proportion had risen to one-half. Despite the expansion in the economically active population, the unemployment rate in 1995 was lower than it had been in 1976, and very much lower than it had been in the middle 1980s. In March 1995, only 6.4% of the Bogotá labor force was out of work compared with an average of 11.5% during the 1980s (Table 7).

The combination of rising numbers of workers, rising labor participation and falling rates of unemployment, was highly unusual in a world where many criticize the impact of capital-intensive technology on employment creation (UNDP 1993; ILO 1995). Much of the expansion in employment had little to do with restructuring in the formal sense and was mainly fueled by a boom in the labor-intensive construction industry. Building activity increased dramatically during the early 1990s as a tax amnesty tempted Colombians to bring their capital back to the country and as drug monies were channeled into construction. The city was performing much better than most other Colombian cities in terms of job creation.

Unfortunately, the economic recession that hit the country in 1997 had a profound impact on Bogotá. With labor participation rates continuing to increase, 64% of adults were working in 2001 compared to only 51% in 1976, the recession led to a major increase in unemployment (Table 7). From a low

Table 7. Bogota: Employment and unemployment, 1976–2001

Year*	Gross participation rate	Global participation rate	Female global participation rate	Unemployment rate
1976	37.6	50.5	35.6	9.4
1980	42.0	54.8	42.1	9.5
1985	44.3	59.7	46.0	13.4
1990	44.4	59.7	46.6	7.9
1995	47.9	62.5	49.7	6.3
2001	49.1	63.7	49.7	18.9

* March of each year

Source: Gómez and Pérez, no date: 2–3, Revista del Banco de la República January 1995, and author's calculations.

Gross participation rate: Economically active population (PEA) over total population.

Global participation rate: PEA/PET (Population of working age).

of 6.3% in 1995, unemployment rose to 21.6% by July-August 2001. The incidence of unemployment was highest, as it always is in Bogota, among young, female and secondary-educated workers (Gómez and Pérez no date).

The impact of the recession on poverty and inequality in the city has been severe. Inequality has risen considerably and in 2000 the poorest 40% of the population were estimated to be earning only 8.1% of total income compared with 14.7% ten years earlier (Veeduría Distrital 2002: 45). Poverty has not been helped by the rural violence that has forced so many poor people out of the countryside to seek asylum in Bogotá.

Fortunately, there are signs that the city is being better run than in the 1980s (Gilbert and Dávila 2002). The city first began to elect its mayors in 1987 and rather than encouraging populism that change seems to have helped to improve government performance. The last four administrations have all made important contributions. Jaime Castro (1992–1994) inherited a virtually bankrupt city and put the finances on a sound footing and improved its external credit rating.[1] Antanas Mockus' (1995–1997) main aim during his first term was to improve civic culture in Bogotá, to increase citizen participation in local government and to improve governmental efficiency. Enrique Peñalosa (1998–2000) achieved much in his three years: establishing the Transmilenio bus system, improving the parks, reclaiming public areas of the city, introducing bicycle routes and establishing new cultural facilities for the poor such as mega-libraries. He left office with his ears ringing with praise: one columnist even calling him "the best mayor in the history of the capital" (*El Tiempo* 19 December 2000; Semana 2001a). Antanas Mockus returned to office in January 2001 committed to continuing the good work of his predecessor. His reputation for honesty remains intact and he reappointed many of Peñalosa's chief officials, a highly unusual gesture in support of administrative continuity. The only clouds on the horizon were the renewed financial problems of the city and the poor relationship between the mayor and the council (Semana 2001b).

As I have already emphasised, it is difficult to evaluate what degree of responsibility globalization has for any of these developments.

6. What chance has Bogotá of becoming a new Seoul or Taipei?

According to Colombia's authoritative weekly, Semana, Bogotá in the year 2010 will be "more peaceful, productive, mobile, and better planned" (Semana 2002a). Recent mayors have given it a new direction – improving the quality of its transport system, raising the quality of life, lowering its crime rate and generally raising its self-esteem. Certainly, more needs to be done and the city's elites are well aware of the need to generate more exports and to improve Bogotá's global competitiveness. The Chamber of Commerce contracted the Monitor Company to conduct a study of how productivity could

[1] In 1992, lenders were refusing to give it money; in October 1996 Bogotá was given a BBB risk rating by Standard and Poor's, something that had never previously been achieved by a Latin American city (Semana, 22 October 1996) In 1992, lenders were refusing to give it money; in October 1996 Bogotá was given a BBB risk rating by Standard and Poor's, something that had never previously been achieved by a Latin American city (Semana, 22 October 1996).

be improved in the city (Monitor 1997) and recently the Regional Council for Competitiveness was established for the city and its immediate region.

Nevertheless, Bogotá has a number of problems to overcome if it is to improve its competitiveness. First, its geography has granted it few advantages. Located high in the Andes, only its climate and flat terrain are positive factors. While the climate has permitted a highly competitive cut-flower industry to emerge, that industry's market position is now coming under challenge (Meier 1997; Rueda 1991). Otherwise, Bogotá's location poses a real problem. Hundreds of miles from the Pacific and Caribbean coasts, it is badly placed to export most kinds of manufactured products. The only hope is that high-value manufactures can be developed to take advantage of the fact that, "almost one quarter, by value, of global manufactured exports now travels by air" (UNRISD 1995: 29).

Unfortunately, Bogotá has several disadvantages in developing high-value exports. Currently only 7% of its exports are in high technology sectors, a much lower figure than in countries like Mexico or Costa Rica (El Tiempo 2002a), and its competitiveness is unlikely to improve in the immediate future because it has relatively few well-qualified workers. While it has some very good universities, the public primary and secondary education systems are sadly lacking in quality and badly need reform. In addition, although cyber-cafés are flourishing, the city does not have enough computers or Internet links. In July 2000, Colombia had only 33.7 personal computers per 1,000 people and 10.2 hosts per 10,000 people compared to averages of 37.7 and 29.6 for Latin America as a whole (World Bank 2001: 306–308). To underline the situation, a recent study of 75 countries, ranked Colombia only 57th in terms of the quality of its information and communication technology (Dinero 2002).

In principle, Bogotá could increase foreign earnings by attracting more overseas visitors. It is far more attractive than its dour image suggests and now has three world-class museums, a number of excellent hotels, a decent airport and attractive surrounding countryside. The problem is that few visitors are likely to visit a country with so much negative publicity hitting the news. The US Department of State recently announced that Colombia leads the world in the number of kidnappings - 2,800 during 2001 (*El Tiempo* 21 May 2002) - and Human Rights Watch announced that in 2001 Colombia was afflicted by a "tragedy in human rights" *El Espectador* 2002). The murder rate has dropped recently, but is still extremely high; in 2000 2,238 murders were recorded, a rate of 32 per 100,000 people (*El Tiempo* 10 May 2001). But the main problem lies in the state of almost civil war and the fear that the guerrillas may begin to unleash a war on the cities. In attempting to attract more tourists, Bogotá is bound to suffer from the general social and political instability of the country as a whole. In 1990 Colombia had a net positive balance of tourists but by 1999 this had disappeared.

On the positive side, a better future is more likely given that Bogotá is quite well run by Latin American standards (Gilbert 1996). The authorities are helped by the fact that, unlike Mexico City or Caracas, a single government authority has administered most of the metropolitan area ever since 1954 (Myers and Dietz 2002). The city has also benefited from some degree of administrative continuity. The constant arguments between the political parties, and between the different factions of those parties, have seldom been allowed to interfere with the long-term development of the city. Despite much evidence to the contrary, mayors have generally taken over responsibility for the implementation of major projects from their predecessors. In addition, the major public utilities have been largely insulated from the day-to-day bickering of local politicians. For decades, the building of dams and main roads, the installation of electricity and telephone lines have been considered to be far too important to the city's development to be damaged by the campaigning of councillors and local politicians. Bogotá's economic interests have been protected by an undemocratic and technical bureaucracy that was, for a time, highly effective in improving the city's services. If the quality of the city government declined during the 1980s, it undoubtedly improved during the 1990s as a succession of mayors built on the achievements of their predecessors and made genuine improvements to the quality of urban management.

However, despite vastly improved urban management, all is not well. Despite substantial organizational changes, Bogotá's public services are not in a wholly healthy state. There is an ambiguous attitude to privatization. The electricity system has been privatized, but there is a major dispute about whether or not the public telephone company should be sold and the water and sanitation company remains in public hands. Admittedly, after a bad period in the 1980s, the agencies seem again to be able to keep up with demand; water supply reached 95.1% of the population in 2001 compared to 89.3% six years earlier. But there is currently concern about the way in which tariffs are rising faster than wages (*El Espectador* 2002c). In 2001 and 2002, public protests have spilled onto the streets and the number of complaints is rising rapidly *El Espectador* 2001). The only partial consolation is that service provision seems to be much worse in most other parts of the country.

Bogotá is also suffering from a financial crisis, a consequence of the economic recession but certainly aggravated by the difficult relations between the mayor and the council (Gilbert and Davila 2002). Seemingly, there is currently no money for new investment. This is hardly new but is disappointing insofar as most people thought that the introduction of the Organic Statute in 1993 has solved the financial problems of the city (Castro and Garavito 1994). It is possible that the national government will give Bogotá a higher share of national revenues, something that it has never done in the past, but the city must also recognize the need to collect more taxes and to control expenditure more carefully. It also has the option of borrowing abroad. Indeed, over the last thirty years the city has financed several major projects with large loans from the World Bank and the Inter-American Development Bank. These projects have allowed the city to accommodate and service the growing population. Because the country has had a reasonable record of economic growth and has been highly responsible in repaying its foreign loans, this source of funding has rarely been threatened. It has been a critical ingredient in the city's development and will continue to be so.

7. Conclusion

The World Bank (2002: 40) argues that "there will be room for some new entrants to the market for global manufactures and services, and some well-located cities in countries that reform their policies, institutions, and infrastructure will surely develop successful clusters. Equally, it seems plausible that if all countries reformed, there would be more well-located sites than new clusters, so some would have missed the boat."

This is recognition that it is difficult for a city in the South to become a global economic player under normal circumstances. But Colombia and its capital city face a number of particularly difficult barriers. The country's image has been badly tarnished by its involvement in drugs. The attitude of developed countries, and particularly that of the United States, has helped to stimulate a civil war, undermine a previously healthy economy and increase political instability. Under the circumstances in which Colombia currently finds itself, Bogotá may well miss the boat. Is that Colombia's fault or a weakness of globalization?

References

Banco de la República (2001) Economic indicators: third quarter of 2001, Bogotá

Castro J, Garavito F (1994) Jaime Castro: tres años de soledad. Opticas Gráficas Ltda, Bogotá

CEPAL (2003) Situación y perspectives 2003. Estadística Económica de América Latina y el Caribe 2002–2003, Santiago

DAPD (Departamento Administrativo de Planeación Departamental) (1999) Observatorio de dinámica urbana, Bogotá

Dinero (2002) Conectarse hace la diferencia, Dinero, May 17

Economist (2001) Drugs, war and democracy: a survey of Colombia. The Economist 21 April

El Espectador (2001) Juicio a servicios públicos, 31 December 2001

El Espectador (2002) Colombia, Cuba, países con más violaciones a derechos humanos. El Espectador 16 January

El Espectador (2002c) Alza en tarifas de energía. 17 February

El Tiempo (2002a) La "chilenización" de Bogotá. 30 March, 1–14

El Tiempo (2002b) Pobres ponen en alerta las campañas. 9 February

Fernández J (1996) The impact of drugs on the Colombian economy. Paper presented at The Colombian Economic Model: Institutions, performance and prospects. ILAS, April 1996

Fernández-Arias E, Hausmann R (1999) Is FDI a safer form of financing? Inter American Development Bank, Research Department. Working Paper No. 416

Fernández-Arias E, Hausmann R (2000) What's wrong with international financial markets? Inter American Development Bank, Research Department Working. Paper No. 429

Gilbert A, Dávila J (2002) Bogotá: progress in a hostile environment. In: Myers DJ, Dietz DA (eds) Capital city politics in Latin America: democratization and empowerment, Lynne Rienner, pp 29–64

Gilbert AG (1997) Employment and poverty during economic restructuring: the case of Bogotá, Colombia. Urban Studies 34: 1047–1070

Gilbert AG (1998) The Latin American city, Latin America Bureau and Monthly Review Press, revised and expanded edition

Gilbert AG (ed) (1996) The mega-city in Latin America. United Nations University Press, Tokyo

Gómez A, Pérez MA (no date) El futuro de la capital; el mercado laboral, Misión Bogotá Siglo XXI

González-Murillo H (1998) La planificación y gestión metropolitana de las relaciones entre Bogotá y la Sabana. Desarrollo Urbano en Cifras 4: 177–193

Hommes R, Montenegro A, Roda P (eds) (1994) Una apertura hacia el futuro: balance económico 1990–1994. Ministerio de Hacienda y Crédito Público and Departamento Nacional de Planeación

ILO (International Labour Office) (1995) World employment: an ILO report: 1995. Geneva

Inter-American Development Bank (2000) Development beyond Economics, Economic and Social Progress in Latin America 2000. Washington DC

Londoño JL (1995) 25 años de cambios distributivos en Colombia. Coyuntura Económica 25: 61–63

Meier V (1999) Cut-flower production in Colombia – a major development success story for women? Environment and Planning A 31(2): 273–289

Monitor Company (1997) Fuerza Capital: estudio de competitividad para Bogotá: informe fase I. Cámara de Comercio de Bogotá
Montaña Cuéllar D (1963) Colombia: país formal y país real. Editorial Platina, Buenos Aires
Myers DJ, Dietz DA (eds) (2002) Capital city politics in Latin America: democratization and empowerment. Lynne Rienner
ODI (2002) Foreign direct investment: who gains? ODI Briefing paper April 2002
Ramírez-Ocampo J (1997) The Colombian apertura: an assessment. In: Posada-Carbó E (ed) Colombia: the politics of reforming the state. Macmillan, pp 187–205
Rojas-Rodríguez E et al. (2000) Esta Guerra no es nuestra: ninos y desplazamiento forzado en Colombia. CODHES and UNICEF, Bogotá
Rueda MC (1991) El mercado mundial de flores y las exportaciones colombianas. Coyuntura Económica 21: 113–134
Sarmiento-Anzola L (1999) Exclusión, conflicto y desarrollo societal. Ediciones Desde Abajo
Sarmiento-Palacio E (2002) En dónde están las causas del empobrecimiento? El Espectador 17 February
Semana (2001a) Peñalosa presidente, 16 August
Semana (2001b) Entre dos aguas, 1 November
Semana (2002a) Bogotá de 2010, 4 January
Semana (2002b) A la vanguardia, 4 January
Steiner R (1998) Colombia's income from the drug trade. World Development 26: 1013–1032
Thoumi FE (1995) Political economy and illegal drugs in Colombia, Lynne Rienner
Tirado A (1998) Violence and the state in Colombia. In: Posasa-Carbo E (ed) Colombia: the politics of reforming the state. Macmillan, pp 111–124
UNDP (1993) Human development report 1993. Oxford University Press, Oxford
UNRISD (1995) States of disarray: social effects of globalization. Geneva
Veeduria Distrital (2002) Vulnerabilidad social en Bogotá DC 2002. Indicadores Sociales 8
World Bank (1982) World Development Report, 1982. Washington DC
World Bank (2000) World Development Report, 2000. Washington DC
World Bank (2001) World development indicators 2001. Washington DC
World Bank (2002a) Globalization, growth, and poverty: building an inclusive world economy. World Bank and OUP
World Bank (2002b) World Development Report, 2002. Washington DC

Tijuana-San Diego: Globalization and the transborder metropolis

Chang-Hee Christine Bae

Department of Urban Design and Planning, University of Washington, Box 355740, Seattle, WA 98195, USA (e-mail: cbae@u.washington.edu)

Abstract. This paper explores the degree to which the Tijuana-San Diego metropolitan region functions as a transborder metropolis. It is shown that the border is quite porous, especially for work and shopping. In addition, the two metropolitan economies are much more complementary than competitive, with San Diego specializing in high-order services and the "new economy" while Tijuana primarily functions as a manufacturing center, based on *maquiladora*. However, much more cooperation and collaboration are needed in several areas: improving trade infrastructure; addressing the deficits in social infrastructure (especially in Tijuana); making the border crossings more user-friendly; expanding educational opportunities for Latinos in both areas; more priority to environmental problems, especially air quality and sewerage; attempting to reduce the public sector fiscal differentials between the two areas; and more attention to income distribution issues.

1. Introduction

This paper examines a very special transborder metropolis, the Tijuana-San Diego metropolitan region, to explore how it has responded to the challenges and opportunities of globalization. The area has received little national or international attention, apart from studies by local scholars, especially at the University of California at San Diego, San Diego State University and El Colegio de la Frontera Norte (COLEF) in Tijuana.

At the outset, it is necessary to make a few comments about the concepts of globalization and the transborder metropolis in this context. If globalization refers to increasing international flows of goods, capital and labor in the recent past, then the border has been "globalized" for many decades. The key determinant of *maquiladora* growth has been cross-border wage differentials rather than recent globalization trends (Gruben 2001). The idea of a transborder metropolis has to be treated with caution. While it is true that its physical development is more or less continuous, the two economies are far from integrated in economic and social terms. This is demonstrated by the continuously large price differentials in labor, land, goods and services between the two metropolitan areas. Furthermore, straddling two countries with very different government structures and institutions has made it almost impossible to develop even informal governance entities able to address the transborder issues effectively, although there is a long history of boundary-spanning institutions, usually with little or no implementation capacity.

Although there are many twin cities on the U.S.-Mexican border, the San Diego-Tijuana relationship is unique because of the extreme income differentials (a ratio of approximately 6.4 : 1, compared with an average of 3.9 : 1 in the other border twin cities; Gerber and Rey 1999). The income divide constrains the linkages between the two metropolitan regions, but nevertheless offers some scope for exploiting complementarities. Also, the links have become stronger in the 1990s, especially between Tijuana and the poorer towns closer the border south of San Diego (such as Chula Vista and San Ysidro).

Both San Diego and Tijuana have responded to globalization trends, but in different ways. San Diego is increasingly a high-order service economy that has taken advantage of the opportunities in the information technology sectors, while the Tijuana economy expanded as a manufacturing center benefiting from the incentives of the *maquiladora* program, a long-established promotion of assembly industries in the equivalent of export-processing zones (free of import and export taxes). The *maquiladoras* offered relatively high wages (but only by Mexican standards), especially for women. The future of the program in Baja California is now somewhat problematic because of the decentralization of *maquiladoras* away from the border cities, the reduction of the tax incentives in 2001 as part of the NAFTA implementation and the hiccup in Asian investments resulting from the post-1997 financial crisis.

The two economies are very unequal in size; at more than $110 billion, San Diego's gross regional product is about 11 times the size of Tijuana's. More serious than the difference in economic scale, however, are the differences in infrastructure endowments. Despite recent improvements, deficient infrastructure remains Tijuana's most serious problem. The hope is that cross-border cooperation and collaboration and the establishment of bi-national institutions can help to alleviate these deficiencies, although there are constraints on how actions can be implemented.

Another key element in this transborder metropolis is the porous border. Transmigrant workers move north across the border in large numbers for daily work, many of them without any legal rights to work. When they cross the border, they can take the light rail system (called the San Diego Trolley) or other forms of public transit to get to work at points north.

Even San Diego is not yet well placed to maximize its opportunities from globalization. For example, there are hardly any international banks in San Diego (only four). Its trade infrastructure (especially airports, seaports and rail service) cannot at the moment support a major globalization effort. On the other hand, its renowned quality of life is a major asset.

2. People

2.1. Population

The growth of this region has been a twentieth-century phenomenon. In 1900, there were only 18,000 people in San Diego while Tijuana was a tiny village of

Table 1. Population trends in San Diego and Tijuana Region, 1900–2020 ('000)

Year	San Diego County	Tijuana	SD-TJ regional Total	% in San Diego
1900	18	242	18	99
1930	210	11	221	95
1940	289	22	311	93
1950	557	65	622	90
1960	1,033	166	1,199	86
1970	1,358	341	1,699	80
1980	1,862	462	2,324	80
1990	2,498	747	3,245	77
2000	2,814	1,211	4,025	70
2010	3,437	2,256	5,694	60
2020	3,853	3,822	7,675	50

242 (in fact, the settlement did not even exist until 1848; Arreola and Curtis 1993). By 2000, the numbers are 2.814 million and 1.211 million respectively (i.e., San Diego accounts for 70% of the regional total). The forecast for 2020 makes them about the same size, 3.85 million in San Diego and 3.82 million in Tijuana (see Table 1 and Fig. 1). This is explained by a somewhat higher birth rate in Tijuana (a crude birth rate of 31 per 1,000 compared to 19 per 1,000) and higher immigration from elsewhere in Mexico.

Outside the core metropolises, there is a much smaller International Border Planning Area that straddles the border with a small population. The promotion of this zone is a key focus of some of the bi-national cooperation activities.

The San Diego-Tijuana axis is also a major path of illegal immigration. Sometimes, the major border crossing shifts east according to the changing loci of intense activity by the U.S. Border Patrol. However, the major illegal flows (apart from daily work) are not from Tijuana to San Diego but rather from all of Mexico and beyond (e.g., Guatemala, El Salvador) to Los Angeles. From this perspective, Tijuana is largely a "waiting room."

2.2. Transmigration

One of the most critical interactions between Tijuana and San Diego is the degree of transmigration (i.e., persons who live in one country and work on the daily basis in the other). Most of the transmigrants live in Tijuana and work in San Diego County, many of them in locations just across the border such as Chula Vista, San Ysidro, National City and Otay Mesa. As of 1998, about 36,000 out of a labor force of 414,000 (8% of the total) were transmigrants out of Tijuana (Alegria 2002). Four-fifths of the transmigrants were male, their average age was 38, most had a secondary education (but their educational profile is almost identical to that of non-transmigrants), they earned 2.84 times more than non-transmigrants (although a relatively modest average of $1,069 per month; the average manufacturing wage in San Diego was nine times greater than in Tijuana), three-quarters of them had formerly lived elsewhere in Mexico, and 28% had at one time been an international immigrant into the United States. Only a minority of the transmigrants have the legal right to work in the United States (14% are U.S. citizens, and 33%

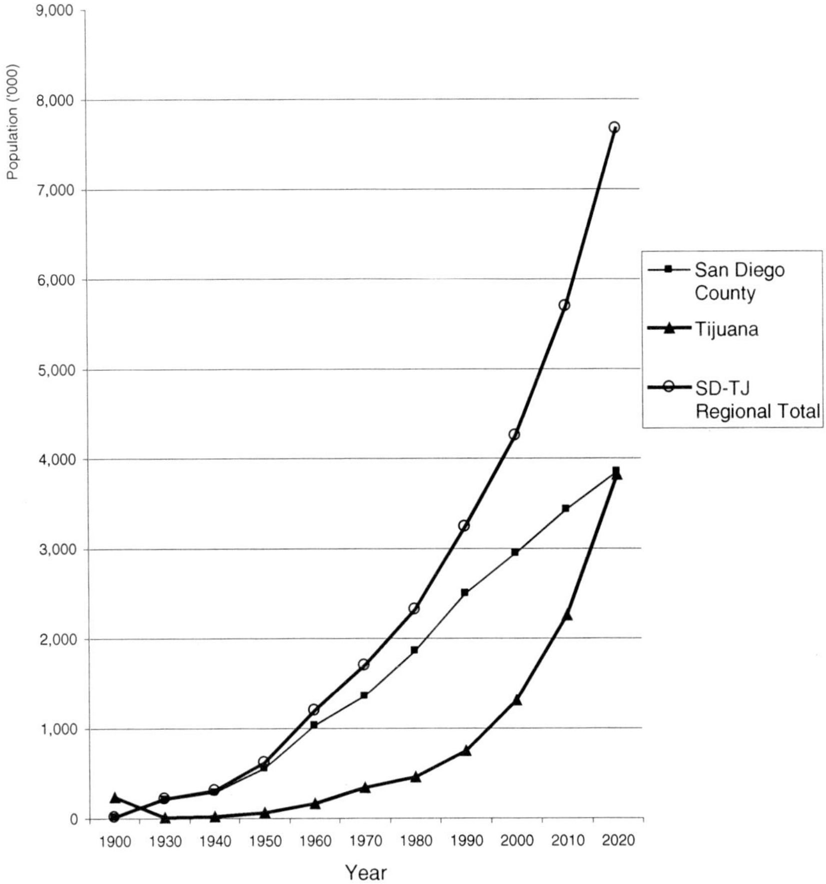

Fig. 1. Population trends in San Diego and Tijuana, 1900–2020

have Green Cards); the rest work illegally using a tourist or student visa or without a visa at all. However, 79% of Tijuana workers with Green Cards and 56% of the U.S. citizen workers work in the United States.[1] But the number of US citizens who work in Tijuana is quite small, not many more than 4,000.

A major factor influencing the rate of transmigration is the wage differential between San Diego and Tijuana: a one percent widening in the wage differential induces a 3% increase in transmigration. However, there are important structural differences between the San Diego and Tijuana's economy, and there are two distinct labor markets on each side of the border

[1] There are U.S. analogues to working in one jurisdiction and living in another on cost-of-living grounds. One example is found in the Pacific Northwest. Many who work in Portland, Oregon, live across the river in Clark County, Washington, to take advantage of cheaper housing and lower living costs. Of course, the monetary benefits are much smaller than between San Diego and Tijuana.

rather than a single cross-border labor market. Unemployment in San Diego has little impact on transmigration. The growth in two low-wage occupations (domestic service and personal services in establishments) rather than the growth of the San Diego economy as a whole dominated the rate of transmigration; there are very few commuters in professional and managerial occupations (less than 2%) who travel north. However, even the American-based Latino workers in San Diego are relatively scarce in the higher-status sectors, in part because of the lack of education; more than two-fifths did not graduate from high school, and their average earnings are about $12,500 (Mason 2000).

2.3. Other border crossers

Transmigrants account for only a minority of those who cross the border. Also, when other trips are accounted for the imbalance between northbound and southbound movements are much reduced. The most detailed survey is quite old (1992) and antedates NAFTA, and the numbers have changed since then, but this survey may not be far out in terms of proportions of trips. Shopping trips are the largest trip type to the north (42%), followed by worktrips (24%) and social visits (11%); tourism is minimal (4%), and 19% is for a miscellaneous category. On the other hand, social visits are the largest category moving south (40%), typically Mexicans and Mexican-Americans returning to visit family and friends. Tourism is the second largest category (20%), the number of shopping trips south is quite small (9%), and the number of worktrips is even smaller (4%); in this case, the miscellaneous category accounts for 24% of all trips. Northbound recreational trips tend to be weekend trips, usually to a restaurant, a movie and/or a sporting event (San Diego Dialogue 1994).

An interesting feature of the northbound traffic is that 80% of all trips are by "very frequent crossers" (defined as crossing the border more than 20 times a month) and another 16% are by "frequent crossers" (4–19 trips per month). Annual estimated expenditures by Tijuana residents are about US$2.8 billion. There are about one million shopping trips (mainly to shopping centers close to the border) from border crossers per month, involving about 150,000 individuals and generating about $120 million of sales taxes for California. At first sight, it might have been expected that the dramatic peso devaluation in December 1994 would have had a strong negative effect on cross-border shopping. However, it was estimated that a 10% fall in the value of the peso reduces total taxable sales in San Diego County by only one percent (Gerber 1999b). Moreover, negative effects can be offset in periods of peso volatility by increased shopping because of expectations of future depreciations.

3. Economy and infrastructure

3.1. The maquiladora

The *maquiladora* (originally assembly industries located on the border under special legislation that gave them equivalence to export processing zone status) were started in the 1960s and have been a major source of economic strength to the border cities, and especially to Tijuana (with direct employment almost one-third of total employment, which doubles when indirect and induced jobs are taken into account). Employment in Baja California *maquiladora* (overwhelmingly in Tijuana, but with a few jobs in Ensenada and other locations) increased by 260% between 1990 and 1999, and employment in Tijuana reached more than 190,000 in 2000, 62.4% increase over its level five years previously (Table 2).

However, their future expansion may be threatened by several factors. For example, a change in the law a few years ago made it easier for *maquiladora* to be extended nationwide. As a result, the *maquiladora* began to disperse (already anticipated in 1992 by Arreola and Curtis 1993, p. 220), less than 10% outside the border cities rising to more than 25% by the late 1990s (see Fig. 2). As an example, the number of *maquiladora* in the State of Yucatan has increased from 16 to 131 in the past decade. *Maquiladora* employment in Mexico as a whole reached more than 1.3 million in July 2000 (three times more jobs than a decade earlier) with jobs in several states increasing faster than in Baja California. Furthermore, the very advantage that promoted *maquiladora* growth (low wages) has now become a threat from China and Eastern Europe. In addition, as the free trade rules of NAFTA continue to kick in (e.g., the termination of the tariff waiver on imported inputs in 2001), the *maquiladora* are losing their special incentives, although NAFTA itself did encourage more foreign corporations to invest in Mexico. Firms, both domestic and foreign, now have close to free locational flexibility.

So, the issue increasingly becomes the comparative advantages and disadvantages of Tijuana for mobile firms compared to other Mexican cities (although much of the investment elsewhere in Mexico has been of Mexican

Table 2. *Maquiladora* employment in Tijuana, 1996–2000

1996	117,296
1997	133,975
1998	143,855
1999	165,696
2000	190,481

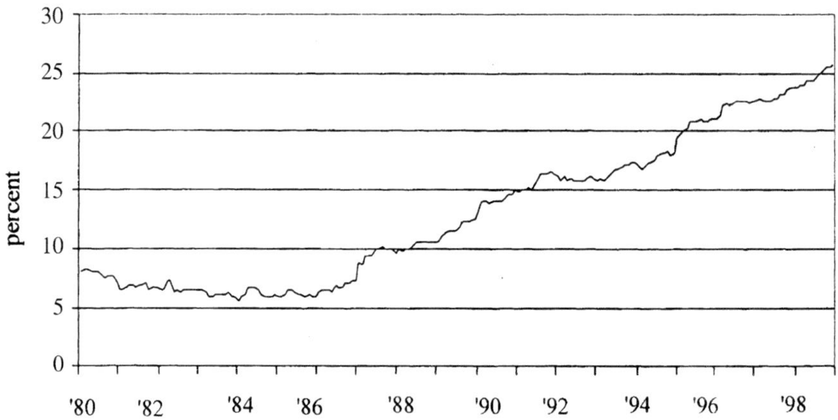

Fig. 2. Proportion of *maquiladora* outside the border cities

origin). In this inter-urban competition, Tijuana is handicapped by a tighter labor market (compared with other Mexican cities,) severe infrastructure deficits, and environmental degradation (Williams 1995). On the other hand, the Tijuana *maquiladoras* have some advantages (the NAFTA rules of origin, Mexico's bilateral trade agreements, proximity to the United States, and the low labor costs compared to the United States) that could favor continued growth. In fact, the U.S.- Baja wage differential and the business cycle in the United States are probably much more important than internal conditions in Mexico in determining the future of Tijuana's *maquiladora*.

Also, the manufacturing sector in Tijuana has the opportunity to go up-scale from low-skill assembly work to more advanced manufacturing (including software products and high performance lasers [already in production as a branch plant of the Laser Power Corporation, based in San Diego]) and to diversify export markets from the United States to the rest of the world. Much will depend on the extent to which Tijuana's manufacturing base can be adapted to the needs of San Diego's high-tech sector, and this depends in turn on the development of a contract manufacturing and supply logistics management system and on remedying the deficiencies in air cargo infrastructure (Curry 2000).

Furthermore, the involvement of Asian corporations in the Tijuana *maquiladora* industry is now considerable, despite the short-term concerns related to the post-1997 Asian financial crisis. By 1999, there were 131 Asian *maquiladora* in Tijuana (one-half of them Japanese, and one-fifth of them Korean), of which 56% were in the electronics industry.

In any event, the growth rate in employment in Tijuana barely slowed down in the 1990s (an annual growth rate of 12.6 percent, 1994–1998, compared with an annual rate of 14.2%, 1980–1993); however, there was a significant slowing down in new establishment formation (from 12.0% annually, 1980–1993, to 4.5%, 1994–1998; Gerber 1999). Moreover, unofficial statistics for 2000–2002 testify to the closure of more than 350 *maquiladoras* and the loss of 280,000 jobs in Mexico as a whole, but this was offset by job creation in existing and new firms. According to the New York Times (June 29, 2002), "(t)he closure of so many *maquiladoras* reflects the harsh economics of globalization." However, the births and deaths of firms can be interpreted as normalcy in a dynamic and flexible national (and global) economy. There were 3,653 registered *maquiladora* plants in December 2000, an increase of about 10% over the previous year.

3.2. Transportation

The San Ysidro Port of Entry is the main Tijuana-San Diego gateway. Northbound traffic consists of 41.4 million people, 15 million automobiles and 110,000 buses per year. The facilities are woefully inadequate: nine gates, secondary inspection areas for only 40 vehicles, severe staff shortages in the Immigration and Naturalization Service (which may or may not be alleviated by the recently announced reorganization), and increased emphasis on drug interdictions and terrorist threats rather than on illegal immigration. Vehicle delays at peak hours are often more than one hour. Matters are likely to get worse with the two-way daily flow expected to increase from 90,000 vehicles per day to 160,000 by the year 2020. The popular SENTRI program (an electronic express lane that allows cross-border travelers who have paid for an annual pass to cross the border in two minutes) is languishing because of long INS application processing delays; eventually, the scale of SENTRI will be limited by congestion in the lane. These problems at the San Ysidro Port of Entry inhibit successful commercial interaction between San Diego and Tijuana (44% of San Diego's exports go to Mexico compared with only 23% to Asia; in fact, the Asian presence is more noticeable in Tijuana). There may be some relief when the new East Otay Mesa Port of Entry opens in 2007, facilitated by the expansion of a State highway (SR 905) on the U.S. side linking I-5 and I-805 directly with the border.

The light rail system (the San Diego Trolley) takes people from downtown and other locations in San Diego to the border where they can change to the "Blue Bus" or to taxis. This is very important for the tourist trade to Avenida Revolucion, although it is possible to walk from the border (about 3/4 mile). Taxis (about 6,250) are the main source of transport, although Tijuana has about 800 buses and more than 1,500 microbuses. Traffic problems in Tijuana remain severe because of an unfavorable topography, unpaved roads, rapid growth, congestion and inadequate facilities.

A 7.5 mile light rail trolley system is planned from the San Ysidro border to the Tijuana business center. Also, there are planned extensions of the San Diego Trolley to San Diego State University, University of California – San Diego and National City; these would significantly improve public transit access in the San Diego-Tijuana region.

Another component of the Tijuana region transportation system is the toll road from Tijuana to the beaches south (Carretera Cuota) paralleled by a slower free road (Carretera Libre). There is a similar setup to the East to Tecate and Mexicali. The latter toll road is privatized, expensive and empty like many in Mexico (the system of toll roads was built primarily to serve trucks and American tourists, but has been less successful than expected because of the high tolls needed to recoup costs).

Although there is a freight rail line passing through San Ysidro, there are only 200 northbound trains a year. There has also been some discussion about the reopening of the San Diego and Arizona Eastern railroad. However, almost 90% of the freight travels by truck, and more than 5 million trucks cross from Mexico to the United States each year. This has created some political problems with the labor unions in the United States, ostensibly on safety grounds but more realistically as part of a "rent seeking" exercise. Most of the trucks cross at the nearby Otay Mesa special crossing, and since 1994 border wide commercial traffic has increased by 170%.

The San Diego International Airport (Lindbergh Field) is too small and too close to downtown (for example, it cannot handle the large planes, if fully loaded, that fly to Asia). One idea to handle this problem was to build a bi-national international airport at Otay Mesa to the east of San Diego. Had this been implemented, it could have been a landmark in bi-national cooperation. The project failed for many reasons, but the most important was institutional incompatibilities. In the United States decisions about airports are primarily local, while in Mexico every issue has to be referred to the Federal government in Mexico City. An example of overcoming difficulties to build a tri-national airport is the Basle Airport in Basle, Switzerland, although it must be admitted that the institutional differences among the three European countries (Switzerland, France and Germany) are minor compared with those between the United States and Mexico.

As for seaports, until very recently (the mid-1990s) the San Diego Unified Port District gave much more attention to waterfront development to promote tourism (and lease income) rather than to seaport expansion planning to enhance regional development and international trade. There has been some limited success developing the 24th Marine Terminal at National City as a niche port, specializing in autos and a few other products. The 10th Avenue Marine Terminal has now no regular container traffic since the Chicken of the Sea tuna company closed down its facility and moved to Los Angeles. Some deepening of the channel has been recommended, but the prospects remain bleak until multi-modal facilities, such as a reopening of and a direct link with the San Diego and Arizona Eastern railroad, are developed.

In Baja California, the Port of Enseneda has been privatized, directly as a result of globalization given that the new owner is a Philippine company, International Container Terminal Services. A 1992 Master Development Plan called for channel deepening, a 50% increase in breakbulk cargo by 2003 and a 10-fold increase in container traffic by 2015. Some investments have been made (a new berth and two quay cranes), but hitherto amounting to only about one-third of the original planned investments (Erie 1999). However, it is too soon to tell whether privatization will make a major difference to the Port in terms of its expansion and efficiency.

3.3. Trade infrastructure

An important element in an assessment of the transportation sector in Tijuana-San Diego is the extent to which it contributes or inhibits the expansion of trade opportunities. The 10% export share of gross regional product of the region is less than two-thirds of the share in Los Angeles, while trade infrastructure investment plans are less than one-tenth of those in Los Angeles. Erie and Nathanson (2000) have identified three major issues: the historical neglect of trade infrastructure investments in the region; a possible over-reliance on Los Angeles for air freight and business travel, its ports and its rail network; and the prospects for both short-term and long-term investments in trade infrastructure. With respect to the first issue, major problems include: the orientation to the global economic system in San Diego-Tijuana has been very recent, mainly in the post-NAFTA era; the fragmented governance structure for organizing trade infrastructure; devolution in Baja California has not been matched by decentralization of financial resources, but has been associated with Federal spending cutbacks in the region. As for the dependence upon Los Angeles, access to its world-class facilities has been a cost-saving advantage (90% of container cargo to and from the cross-border region passes through the twin Ports of Los Angeles and Long Beach). On the other hand, some parts of the Los Angeles trade infrastructure system (e.g., Los Angeles International Airport) are reaching capacity, although the port expansion plans are ambitious. With respect to trade infrastructure needs in San Diego-Tijuana, the most critical requirement is a new international airport and supporting air cargo infrastructure if the goal of building a high-value added manufacturing sector is to be successful (Erie and Nathanson 2000, suggest that Lindbergh Field's limited international, long-haul and air freight capacity costs the region \$4–5 billion a year, equivalent to 3.33–4% of gross regional product and 87,000 potential jobs). This airport could be located on either side of the border so perhaps the concept of a bi-national airport should be revisited to explore whether the institutional obstacles that led to its earlier failure can be overcome. The other main problem highlighted by the discussion in the previous section is the defects in completing an interconnected multi-modal transportation system (covering air, roads, rail, ports-of-entry and ports).

3.4. Energy

The major energy problems in the San Diego-Tijuana region are: the very limited indigenous energy resources in the region; expensive electricity rates in San Diego (a problem aggravated by the recent deregulation energy debacle in California); a sharply increasing demand for energy in Tijuana, fueled by manufacturing growth, population growth and extensions of electricity service to more and more households; no natural gas pipeline in Tijuana (gas supplies in Mexico largely rely on non-piped propane gas) and the lack of connection between the Baja California power grid and the rest of Mexico (Sweedler 1999). The United States has three companies that plan to import liquefied natural gas from Bolivia and Peru that will dock at Tijuana, Rosarito and Enseneda; this is a potential new source of natural gas for Baja but initially most of the gas would be sold in California.

The main source of electric power in Tijuana is the 620-MW plant at Rosarito (only 15 miles from the border), but it burns heavy oil and is one of the largest stationary source polluters in the region. Electricity consumption in Tijuana is increasing three times faster than in San Diego, even though 83% of households have electricity connections (relatively high by developing country standards) and per capita electricity consumption is only one-quarter of that in San Diego. The rate of growth is severely straining the capacity of the CFE (Federal Electricity Commission) to supply the metropolitan area. However, there are possibilities for energy exchanges between San Diego and Tijuana because Baja California's transmission grid connects to California at two points (San Diego-Tijuana and Calexico-Mexicali). In addition, there are prospects for non-fossil sources. There has been significant use of geothermal power in San Diego in the past under contract with the Cerro Prieto plant near Mexicali, but there is minimal reliance on solar energy – despite its huge potential. There are several capacity-increasing projects underway, but the expansion in supply is lagging behind the growth in demand. One idea is to expand the use of natural gas (a less polluting source) by exchanging natural gas from Mexican pipelines into Texas for imports into Tijuana from San Diego pipelines.

4. Environment and resources

4.1. Air pollution

Given the income differentials between San Diego and Tijuana, attitudes towards environmental protection vary widely in the two cities. This reflects the high income elasticity of demand for environmental quality. Air quality standards are similar in the two countries, but the levels of non-attainment vary significantly as do the degree of enforcement. Because San Diego and Tijuana share the same air basin, emissions are transmitted over the national border (and substantial pollutants frequently drift down from the Los Angeles area, dependent upon wind patterns). PM_{10} is a particular problem, especially on the Tijuana side: emissions from factories and automobiles, wood burning for fuel, dust from the large number of unpaved roads (almost two-fifths of Tijuana's total), and sand and dirt from the surrounding desert. In addition, automobiles in Mexico are not as clean as those in California, and there are high emission levels associated with the long stop-and-go lines at the San Ysidro border crossing. With respect to the latter, the San Diego Air Pollution District found that 7,000 vehicles registered in Mexico and driven daily to the U.S. accounted for 14% of the region's total air pollution. This led to the Border Smog Reduction Act of 1998 that allows Federal border agents to turn back commuter cars not registered in California (that requires them to undergo frequent smog tests).

One interesting idea, discussed by Alegria (2000) is to find a mechanism for the United States that is far wealthier than Mexico to help to improve air quality in Tijuana. The rationale for this approach is that the bad air in Tijuana does move over the border. Furthermore, the transmigrants who work in the United States pay taxes that they do not receive back in services. Alegria makes an interesting calculation (based on 1996 data) that transmigrant taxes would cover the costs of paving for 246 kilometers of streets in Tijuana. Of course, there are sovereignty issues on both sides: the transfer of U.S. federal resources to Mexico, while the Mexican constitution places constraints on bilateral transfers, especially at the local level. However, there is a mechanism whereby it could be implemented. The NADBank (the North American Development Bank) receives funds from both the U.S. and Mexican governments for improvements in border environmental infrastructure certified by the BECC (the Border Environment Cooperation Commission) without the need for matching funds. A key argument is that the benefits of improved air quality would accrue on both sides of the border, and would have an important pro-equity impact (Bae 1997).

4.2. Sewage

San Diego has an adequate collector and treatment infrastructure, although parts of the system are aging. There are problems in Tijuana because there are piped sewerage facilities in the Central Zone, but not in the eastern squatter settlements. Another major issue in Tijuana is that sewage has to be pumped over the hills from Pump Station 1. However, the system often breaks down and diverts raw sewage to San Diego via the Tijuana River Valley. New investments and upgrading are sorely needed, and this is an important area for bi-national cooperation.

4.3. Water

The combined water demand of the San Diego-Tijuana region was 683,000 acre-feet (1996), 90% of the demand being in San Diego. The expected demand by 2010 will rise to about 848,000 acre-feet. Hence, there is a severe water supply problem to be address by conservation, reclamation, reuse, improved storage capacity, and investing in a new aqueduct to the Colorado River. An agreement signed on April 1998 (but still not implemented because of incomplete environmental review and local concerns about the potential negative economic impact) would allow water voluntarily conserved by Imperial Valley farmers to the East to be transferred to San Diego in return for an annual payment of about $50 million (Forum Frontizero 2001). San Diego has been emphasizing reclamation (at the South Bay Water Reclamation Plant), but its most notorious program "From the Toilet to the Tap" has been a major failure. Tijuana, on the other hand, has been looking at desalination. However, for a large developing country city, Tijuana has a reasonable water distribution system; about 85% of its population has piped water. The rest, however, buy from truck vendors at 2–3 times the price of the public water tariff.

5. Governance

Attempts at bi-national cooperation are constrained by the very different governance systems and institutions in the United States and Mexico. There is a striking contrast between the traditional centralization of power in Mexico and the high degree of decentralization in the United States. It is true that Mexico, like many developing countries, has attempted to devolve power to the local level in recent years (Shirk 1999). However, these efforts look more important on paper than in practice because local access to significant financial resources were never granted on any scale, and public sector resources remain scarce, although in 2002 the City of Tijuana received a loan of 800 million pesos from a local bank for infrastructure and institutional development. In general, Erie and Nathanson (2000) summarize the problem very well: "limited capacity for long-term planning and development on the Baja side, highly fragmented local planning on the San Diego side, and no mechanisms for effective joint planning."

Cross-border issues have to be dealt with boundary-spanning institutions. They have a long history. The first was the International Boundary and Water Commission (IBWC) established in 1893 and reconfigured in 1944. Another major step was the La Paz Agreement of 1983 that provided for federal coordination. This eventually resulted in what is called the Border XXI program of 1996, primarily to address environmental concerns. Most of its efforts have focused on bi-national environmental cooperation under NAFTA.

The Border Liaison Mechanism (BLM) was established in 1992, initially as a local substitute for the diplomatic contacts that were used to provide means of preventing the escalation of day-to-day problems into international incidents. Later, it became an umbrella institution organizing sectoral working groups and fostering informal cross-border cooperation (San Diego Dialogue 2000b).

The most recent trend in the post-NAFTA era has been an emphasis on cooperation between the twin cities and other local institutions. This was initiated by the Letter of Agreement signed between the Cities of San Diego and Tijuana in 1993. However, the most important institutions, at least potentially, established via NAFTA side agreements are BECC (the Border Environmental Cooperation Commission), its local counterpart (Cal/BECC), and its financing counterpart, NADBank (the North American Development Bank).

The Committee on Bi-national Regional Opportunities (CCBRC) is yet another coordinating institution for all levels of government on both sides of the border, focusing on policy recommendations. A major institutional problem is that neither the US nor the Mexican constitutions permit *local* funds to be spent outside the country. This severely constrains cooperation. As a result, financial support from San Diego to Tijuana is minimal and indirect; for example, the sale of old fire engines at a very low price. There are severe weaknesses in the Mexican local government fiscal system. Local governments cannot issue bonds. They depend on meager handouts from the Federal government or on overseas financing (which are usually pass-throughs of funds loaned to the Federal government by multilateral or bilateral agencies). Two promising options to get around the institutional constraints on cross-border actions are the development of public-private partnerships and more involvement by non-government organizations (NGOs).

6. Conclusions

The border economy of San Diego-Tijuana is unique in the world because of the huge income differentials between the two components of the metropolitan region. It provides an interesting example of the impacts of globalization, but has few lessons for elsewhere.

Contacts between downtown San Diego and downtown Tijuana are stronger at the official rather than at the more informal level. However, if we look at the social and cultural interactions between the cities in Southern San Diego county and Tijuana this is the same world not different worlds. The border fence is artificial, and the border is porous, although less so than in the past. In the 1920s almost anyone could cross the border without documents; now, about one-half of Tijuana's population have the legal right to cross the border.

The San Diego and the Tijuana economies are much more complementary than overlapping or competitive. San Diego specializes in high-tech industries and services, while Tijuana specializes in manufacturing and daily tourism. These differences have been accentuated by globalization. Cross-border linkages between a rapidly changing manufacturing base of Tijuana and the "information age" economy of San Diego need to be improved.

As argued by Ohmae (1995), globalization offers opportunities for regions to make their own destinies with an unprecedented degree of independence from the control of nation states. If this is the case, then national borders should not be an overwhelming constraint on the development of a "new regionalism" (Shirk 2000). The bi-national metropolis has better prospects than ever before. However, its leaders and its entrepreneurs need to foster a consciousness of the interconnectedness of the areas on both sides of the border. It is arguable that Tijuana is much more aware of this mutual interdependence than San Diego. That would need to change if San Diego-Tijuana is to maximize its potential for taking advantage of globalization.

This paper has referred to many areas where more cooperation and collaboration are needed: improving the trade infrastructure that is so essential for expanding the region's trade to both export and their home national markets: addressing the deficits in social infrastructure (especially in Tijuana); making the border crossings easier and more user-friendly; improving access to better education for Latinos, both in San Diego County and in Tijuana; giving more attention to environmental problems (especially air quality and sewerage); developing mechanisms to reduce the public sector fiscal differentials on the two sides of the border; and more attention to social equity concerns.[2] It remains unclear whether there is either the political will or the institutional innovations needed to make progress in these critical areas.

References

Alegria T (2002) Demand and supply among Mexican cross-border workers. Tijuana, El Colegio de la Frontera, Departamento de Estudios Urbanos y Medio Ambente

Alegria T (2000) Transmigrants, NAFTA, and a proposal to protect air quality on the border. In: Herzog L (ed) Shared space: Rethinking the U.S.-Mexico border environment. Center for U.S.-Mexican Studies, University of California, San Diego

Arreola DD, Curtis J (1993) The Mexican border cities: Landscape anatomy and place personality. The University of Arizona Press, Tucson

Bae C-HC (1997) The equity impacts of Los Angeles' air quality policies. Environment and Planning A 29:1563–84

Benitez G (1995) Latin American perspectives: The maquiladora program: Its challenges ahead. The Wharton Journal 11

Curry J (2000) San Diego/Tijuana manufacturing in the information age. Paper prepared for San Diego Dialogue's Forum Fronterizo series on The Global Engagement of San Diego/Tijuana

Erie SP, Nathanson C (2000) The challenge of developing the cross-border region's trade infrastructure. Paper prepared for San Diego Dialogue's Forum Fronterizo series on The Global Engagement of San Diego/Tijuana

Erie SP (1999) Toward a trade infrastructure strategy for the San Diego/Tijuana region. Paper prepared for the San Diego Dialogue's Forum Fronterizo policy series

Forum Frontizero (2001) A Vision and Strategy for the Sustainable Development of the San Diego/Tijuana/Mexicali "Macro-Region." San Diego Dialogue

Gerber J (2001) Uncertainty and growth in Mexico's maquiladora sector. Borderlines 9(3)

Gerber J (1999a) Whither the maquiladora? A look at the growth prospects for the industry after 2001. San Diego Dialogue, Working paper $ E-99-1

Gerber J (1999b) The effects of a depreciation of the peso on cross border retail sales in San Diego and Imperial counties. Department of Economics, San Diego State University

Gerber J, Rey SJ (1999) The employment dynamics of regional economies on the U.S.- Mexico border. San Diego State University

Gruben WC (2001) Was NAFTA behind Mexico's high maquiladora growth? Economic and Financial Review 3rd quarter(11)

Mason C (2000) Latino employment patterns in San Diego county. California Employment Development Department

Ohmae K (1995) The End of the Nation State: The Rise of Regional Economies. Free Press, New York

Pastor M (2000) Regions that work: How cities and suburbs can grow together. University of Minnesota Press, Minneapolis

Rondinelli DA, Johnson JH, Kasarda JD (1998) The changing forces of urban development: Globalization and city competitiveness in the 21st century. Cityscape: A Journal of Policy Development and Research 3:71–105

San Diego Dialogue (2000a) The global engagement of San Diego/Baja California. San Diego Dialogue Forum Fronterizo, Final Report

San Diego Dialogue (2000b) Governance and public finance in the San Diego/Baja California Region. Paper prepared for San Diego Dialogue's Forum Fronterizo series on The Global Engagement of San Diego/Tijuana

San Diego Dialogue (1994) Who crosses the border? A view of the San Diego/Tijuana metropolitan region. San Diego Dialogue

[2] Rondinelli et al. 1998, argue that in metropolitan development promoting equity is compatible with entrepreneurial expansion and in the business community's enlightened self-interest; Pastor (2000) has expressed similar views with this region as an example in mind.

Schmaedick GL (1999) Compensation, inflation, and purchasing power in the Mexican maquiladora industry since the devaluation of 1994. Paper presented at the Western Economics Association International Conference.

Shirk DA (2000) Regional success stories: global engagement strategies for the San Diego/Tijuana region. Paper prepared for San Diego Dialogue's Forum Fronterizo series on The Global Engagement of San Diego/Tijuana

Shirk DA (1999) New federalism in Mexico: Implications for Baja California and the cross-border region. Paper prepared for San Diego Dialogue's Forum Fronterizo series on The Global Engagement of San Diego/Tijuana

Stern R (2001) Addressing cross-boundary air pollution: A comparative case study of the US-Mexico border and the Hong Kong-Guangdong border. Civic Exchange, Hong Kong

Sweedler AR (1999) Energy issues in the San Diego/Tijuana region. Paper prepared for the San Diego Dialogue Forum Fronterizo policy series on the Global Engagement of San Diego/Tijuana

Thompson G (2002) Mexico is attracting a better class of factory in its South. The New York Times, June 29:A3

Williams EJ (1995) The maquiladora industry and environmental degradation in the United States-Mexican borderlands. Latin American Studies Association, Washington, D.C.

Globalization and Los Angeles

Harry W. Richardson, Peter Gordon

School of Policy, Planning and Development, University of Southern California, Los Angeles, CA, 90089-0626, USA (e-mail: {hrichard, pgordon}@usc.edu)

Abstract. In some respects, Los Angeles is the most global city in the world. It does not have the highest foreign-born population share (although it is close), but it has the most varied. Hollywood, and everything that it means, probably has the most dominant global cultural penetration. The twin ports of Los Angeles and Long Beach vie for supremacy with Hong Kong and Singapore. On the other hand, not one Fortune 500 company is headquartered there; in terms of the "world city hypothesis" criteria, it fails miserably. How can we explain this paradox? According to Kevin Starr (the premier historian of California), Los Angeles is on the frontier of global urban life. Or, if we believe the views of Ed Soja, Allen Scott, Mike Davis and others, it is dysfunctional, with a bifurcated income distribution that is a direct result of globalization. The paper will explore some of these issues.

1. Introduction

Los Angeles is a paradox: one of the largest metropolitan areas in the world (16.23 million in 2000), yet it does not have the headquarters of a single, large (either national or international) bank and hardly any large firms (for example, the University of Southern California claims to be the largest private sector employer within the *City* of Los Angeles). In fact, it is an economy dominated by small and medium-sized companies. The local economy is highly diversified, with no major industry given its 9.9 million labor force. The defense-airspace sector has declined precipitiously since the 1980s, compensated in part by the rise of the entertainment sectors. Los Angeles remains an important manufacturing center, although some industries, such as its once thriving garments industry, are subject to increasing pressure from globalization trends.[1]

[1] In 1999 we wrote a long review article (Gordon and Richardson 1999) of a very large book (Scott and Soja 1996). That book's central argument was that globalization was responsible for a variety of ills in Los Angeles, and indeed the whole book is an indictment of Los Angeles. Although we were very critical of the book, we never addressed the globalization issues, except in passing. This paper returns to that book as a launching pad to discuss the impact of globalization on Los Angeles.

2. Census 2000 data

A starting point might be to look at some of the recently issued 2000 Census data. Table 1 presents selected data for the City and Counties of Los Angeles and for the State of California. Please note, however, that even Los Angeles County is not the metropolitan region. Our normal definition is the five-county region (Los Angeles, Orange, Riverside, San Bernardino and Ventura), and 41% of the region's population lives outside the core county of Los Angeles. Without discussing the data line by line, it is helpful to refer to some of the variables closely related to a globalization discussion.

Los Angeles has a very high proportion of foreign-born (more than two-fifths of the total population in the City of Los Angeles, somewhat less outside the city), and much higher than in California (more than one-quarter of the population), which is in turn much higher than the national foreign-born share (about 11%). Of the Los Angeles foreign-born, more than three-fifths are from Latin America and 30% from Asia.

More than one-quarter of the population has college degrees (despite the recent flood of modestly educated immigrants from Central America), and this helps to explain the more than one-third of the labor force working in professional and managerial jobs.

The City of Los Angeles has less wealth and more poverty than the surrounding region and California as a whole, with a median household income only 77% of the California average; also, 13.6% of households have an income

Table 1. Selected data from the Census of Population, 2000

	LA City	LA County	California
Total population	3,694,834	9,519,338	33,871,648
% of Foreign Born	40.9	36.2	26.2
Latin American Share (%)	65.9	62.1	55.6
Asian share (%)	24.9	29.6	32.9
% of Pop > 25 with college degrees	25.5	24.9	26.6
% in different house in 1995	44	42.7	45.4
% in labor force	60.2	60.5	62.4
% Professional and management	34.2	34.3	36
Mean commuting time	29.6	29.4	27.7
% Drive alone	65.7	70.4	71.8
% Public transit	10.2	6.6	5.1
% without cars	16.5	12.6	9.5
% with 2 or more cars	43.2	50.5	56.3
Median household income	36,687	42,189	47,493
% HH Income > $100 K	13.6	15.1	17.3
% HH Income < $15 K	20.8	17	14
% Families in poverty	18.3	14.4	10.6
% Female-headed families in poverty	32.7	28.5	25
% of owner-occupied households with costs > 35% of income	29.4	26.8	23.2
% of rental households with costs > 35% of income	37.1	35.8	34.1
Median house value	221,600	209,300	211,500
Median gross rent	672	704	747

Source: Census of Population 2000

greater than \$100,000 while 20.8% of households have an income less than \$15,000, and 18.3% of households live in poverty (compared to only 10.6% in California). Locally as well as nationally, the high poverty rate, in part, reflects the increase in increase in female-headed households. Not surprisingly, such high poverty rates creates a severe housing affordability problem (with almost 30% of owner-occupied households and 37% of rental households paying more than 35% of their income on housing), especially given the high house prices (a median price of \$221,600) and relatively high rents (a median monthly rent of \$672); conditions are not much better in the suburbs. As we will see, some analysts have attempted to draw a direct link between the economic forces of globalization and poverty. A key argument of this paper is that this argument is unconvincing, except in the trivial sense that globalization has facilitated low-income immigration into Los Angeles (but more compelling explanations are the United States' lax immigration policy, the porous border [with Mexico] and the wide cross-border income differential).

The remaining data in Table 1 refer to transportation, specifically about commuting. Commuting time in the region has increased between 1990 and 2000 by about three-plus minutes (by about 13%), but it is still less than 30 minutes (compared with 34 minutes in New York and 32 minutes in Chicago). Traffic congestion is frequently regarded as a major constraint on the growth of urban productivity, but despite its reputation (fostered by indices published by the Texas Transportation Institute) traffic congestion remains tolerable in Los Angeles. The city's bus transit use is double the State average and the number of zero automobile households (at 16.5%) is 74% higher than the State average (while the share of households with two or more cars is only 77% of the State average).

3. Advantages and problems in the Los Angeles Region

The region's advantages include:

1. A huge consumer market of 16.3 million;
2. a large number of vibrant small firms (about 400,000, averaging 12 employees), many of them involved in exports;
3. many universities, colleges and design studios, although most of the prestigious universities have not developed strong business connections;
4. the twin ports are, by far, the largest in the United States, with sufficient depth, rail access and amply facilities for the largest container ships; and
5. rail connections via the Burlington Northern Santa Fe and the Union Pacific railroads are superior to those from other cities.

On the other hand, the region suffers from several problems:

1. Land use constraints, especially in the more central counties of Los Angeles and Orange;
2. a severe TRI (toxic release inventory) problem in many parts of the core region (Sadd et al 1999); yet, air quality has improved dramatically (in secular terms) over the past quarter-century;
3. difficult to obtain agreement among business and political leaders, especially about trade infrastructure decisions (airports, ports, rail, highways, etc.);

4. vulnerability to natural disasters (e.g., earthquakes, brush fires, mudslides, tidal flooding, etc.; Davis 1998);
5. housing affordability (Southern California has experienced high and rising land prices in the upward phase of real estate cycles in recent decades, and the core county is almost fully built out, resulting in a very constrained housing supply);
6. the ranking of California among States in K-12 education has fallen dramatically in the past three decades, and some (but not all) of the Southern California school districts – most notably the mammoth Los Angeles Unified School District – are very poor performers;
7. traffic congestion (despite its repeated #1 ranking by the Texas Transportation Institute as the most congested metropolitan region in the United States, Los Angeles is ranked #8 among 50 metropolitan areas in terms of commuting times).

4. Some general issues

The twin ports of Los Angeles-Long Beach is the world's third largest container port (behind Hong Kong and Singapore), and is probably growing faster. The delivery of containers to markets has recently been made more efficient by the opening of the Alameda Corridor, a sub-grade rail line from the ports to the distribution yards near downtown Los Angeles (replacing a surface track that intersected city streets), a $2.4 billion project. A significant proportion of the traffic through these ports is through-traffic, neither destined for nor originating from Southern California. Both ports have very ambitious expansion plans.

Los Angeles has been more influenced by globalization than exerting an influence on globalization. The most obvious manifestation of this is the role that international immigration has played in the growth of Los Angeles in recent decades. Although the foreign-born share in Miami's population is a little higher, it is dominated by Cubans and lacks the extreme heterogeneity of Los Angeles. Los Angeles has a large Central American population (e.g., from Mexico, El Salvador and Guatemala) and a very diversified Asian population, plus several other national enclaves (e.g., Iranians in Beverly Hills).

LAX (the Los Angeles International Airport) faces both capacity and financial capital constraints. The LAX Master Plan is subject to frequent changes (such as the elimination of a proposed fifth commuter plane runway). Most of the recent emphasis has been on improving air cargo capacity and on expanding ground access. The consensus is that the best way to cope with the long-term increase in demand is to expand the role of other regional airports. Burbank Airport absorbs a significant amount of especially West Coast traffic, but it is located close to dense population, and there is strong NIMBY opposition to its expansion. John Wayne Airport in wealthy Orange County to the south plays a similar role but faces the same problems. Ontario International Airport, about 40 miles east of Los Angeles, is underused, and has substantial potential, especially for air freight. A new player is the 79-year old regional airport at Long Beach that has opened up to more commercial traffic, initially from Jet Blue with more recent competition for gates from American and Alaska Airlines. There has also been discussion over the years about making better use of Palmdale Regional Airport well to the north of Los Angeles, but the airlines have not been in favor. The proposal to turn the El Toro military base into a commercial airport ultimately failed. In the post-9/11 environment, airports other than LAX have become more attractive to passengers because they are faster to negotiate, and this may help to stimulate the long dormant regionalization plans.

Los Angeles remains an important manufacturing region, somewhat immune to the deindustrialization trends that have swept through the United States in the past two decades. It still retains about 1.030 million manufacturing jobs, more than 62% of them in the core county of Los Angeles. Of course, there have been many changes in industrial sectors: a sharp reduction in the aerospace-defense sector, defection of the furniture industry to Mexico under pressure from air quality regulations, increasing competition for the garments industry with its reliance on immigrant labor, and a general shift from large- to small-scale industry. With the partial exception of aerospace-defense (the decline of McDonnell-Douglas [a Boeing subsidiary] largely reflects increasing competition from Airbus), most of these trends reflect the impact of globalization.

There is some degree of interjurisdictional conflict in the Los Angeles metropolitan region that could potentially interfere with the opportunities offered by globalization. First, this is a five-county region that stretches over large geographical distances (about 130 miles from East to West, and 120 from North to South). The interests of the central city of Los Angeles and the peripheral areas of the peripheral counties are very different (for example, the core city is interested in job creation, whereas many of the cities in the peripheral areas of Ventura County have passed strict growth control ballot initiatives). Second, the City of Los Angeles itself is very bifurcated with the northern part (the San Fernando Valley on the north side of the Santa Monica Mountains) exhibiting strong suburban characteristics compared to the core city to the South). Third, there are strong, currently failing, secession movements: the San Fernando Valley wants to incorporate as a separate city, as does Hollywood, and the Wilmington-San Pedro area close to the Port of Los Angeles. Whether this would make much of a difference in a metropolitan region of almost 200 separate cities is unclear, but certainly it is a distraction. Some have argued that a regional governance system would be superior to a world of Tieboutian competition (Calthorpe and Fulton 2001; Pastor et al. 2000; Orfield 1997), but the argument is problematic and this "solution" is almost impossible to implement because of the fierce defense of local autonomy.

4.1. Immigration

Immigration has been a major force in Southern California in the past two decades. Between 1982 and 1997 the increase in the foreign-born population was 97.5% of the 1982 foreign-stock population (foreign stock means one or more parent born abroad) while 62.8% of the increase in population during that same period was because of international immigration (Bae 2002). The most remarkable part of the immigrant story is that most of them move up and assimilate (Myers 1999). Median income rises and home ownership increases with time spent in the U.S. for all immigrants, both citizens and non-citizens. Moreover, in recent years, the median incomes of naturalized foreign born citizens have exceeded those of natives (U.S. Department of Commerce 1997). Although Latinos can now be found throughout the region clustered into several distinct Latino communities, many of them linked by common overseas origin, "ethnographic research also revealed that the dispersion and residential mobility of Latinos throughout Los Angeles is so great that many of their social networks overlap in spatial terms ... Thus it is clear that the tendency to identify communities primarily or only in terms of physical space boundaries is of limited value" (Rocco in Scott and Soja 1996, p. 369). However, this is the result of critical mass. Latinos are such a large proportion of the total population, especially in the core counties, that the concept of the ethnic community increasingly makes little sense. Nevertheless, according to the 2000 Census, Santa Ana in Orange County was the most Latino city in the United States and East Los Angeles (an unincorporated area in Los Angeles County) was the most Latino neighborhood. On the other hand, the Asian population in Los Angeles is much more diverse, and has a much stronger tendency to cluster by national origin (e.g., Chinese in Monterey Park, Indians in Artesia, Koreans in Koreatown, Garden Grove and Cerritos, Vietnamese in Westminster, etc.).

4.2. Globalization and the Los Angeles economy

The UCLA geographer, Edward Soja, has been one of the most vocal supporters of the view that globalization has had severe negative impacts on Los Angeles. "Growth in the FIRE sector has fueled the emergence of Los Angeles as a major challenger to the triumvirate of Tokyo, London and New York atop the global hierarchy of 'capitals of capital'" (Soja in Scott and Soja (eds) 1996, p. 441). This may sound good, but it is wrong. The major banks have all left Los Angeles. Helping to sustain the oligarchs "is a teeming underground economy and an immigrant-fed pool of low-wage labor" (p. 441). "(D)owntown development in Los Angeles more directly reflected the effects of economic and cultural glocalization (*sic*). Its specific geography was split in two, with a half-city of First World skyscrapers and financial power standing starkly above a half-city of Third World cultures and street scenes." In fact, the decline of L.A.'s downtown is clear from the 1987, 1992 and 1997 Economic Census small-area employment data: the CBD incurred net losses of both retail and services jobs while CBD office vacancy rates are among the highest in the region. This occurred despite a 25-year $2.5 billion downtown renewal effort, a multi-billion dollar effort to build a rail transit system, and a major convention center expansion. Five years ago, *The Economist* (1997, p. 25) reported that "today not a single major bank, department-store chain or telecom company calls the nations' second largest city its home." The situation has deteriorated rather improved since then. The Los Angeles Community Redevelopment Agency (CRA) that subsidized many of the major office buildings in the 1980s has suffered from declining financial resources and mismanagement, and has been forced by political pressure to focus its dwindling funds more on deprived communities than on downtown.

Los Angeles is not Manhattan West. Although the city was once widely expected to become the new financial capital on the Pacific Rim, it is not. No major bank has its headquarters here. In fact, almost none of the Fortune-500 firms are headquartered here, compared with 46 in New York City. Moreover, several large corporations have left Los Angeles in the past decade. The face of global capitalism is not highly visible in Los Angeles. Instead, the city has become an incubator of small firms in fast-growing fields such as information technology, biomedicine and the multimedia. In Los Angeles and throughout the U.S. and most of the world, brains and skills matter more than ever; the returns to human capital keep growing (Murnane and Levy 1996). In the past two decades, there has been a significant relative increase in the wages of college-educated workers nationwide relative to others and a decline in the gender gap, the result of a combination of skilled-labor-biased technical change and changes in labor quality. But if schooling counts so heavily, the failure of the public schools monopoly hurts the poor the most. These two observations, the value added from a highly educated adult labor pool (primarily from elsewhere) combined with one of the largest but most ineffective school districts in the United States (the Los Angeles Unified School District), highlight what is probably the best and the worst of Los Angeles.

4.3. Globalization and income inequity

There is a body of thought that draws a link between globalization and a bifurcated distribution of income; the idea is that globalization creates a super-rich class employed in MNCs, finance and high-order services and this needs a supporting underclass in services (busboys, janitors, receptionists, etc.). At the same time, according to this view, manufacturing middle class labor has been "hollowed out." However, the 2000 Census data on income distribution (extrapolating from the data in Table 1) indicates that there is a substantial middle class.

Most of the contributors in the influential book by members of the self-proclaimed "Los Angeles School" (Scott and Soja 1996) view the city as a locale for class warfare and victimization, resulting largely from economic forces (such as globalization and the associated economic restructuring). They write that: "the social structure of Los Angeles is no longer characterizable in terms of a (numerically) dominant and relatively affluent blue-collar working class but is deeply divided into two distinctive segments, as represented on the one side by an upper tier of highly paid managers, professionals, and technicians and on the other side by a lower tier composed of low- skill, low-wage workers, the vast majority of whom are immigrants, many of them undocumented." Similarly, "The City of Angels, the city of sunshine, palm trees, suburban living, and movies with happy endings, has an underside – declining wages and rising poverty" (Ong and Blumenberg in Scott and Soja 1996, p. 311).

The argument is that increasing inequality since the early 1970s is the consequence of the emerging global economy. This differs from the views expressed in a symposium on "Income, Inequality and Trade" in the Summer 1995 issue of the *Journal of Economic Perspectives* who show that "trade matters, but it is neither all that matters nor the primary cause of observed changes" (Freeman 1995, p. 30). Galor and Tsiddon (1997) argued that a more compelling source of rising inequality was a high rate of innovation and technological progress resulting in a larger concentration of high-ability individuals in the more technologically advanced sectors.

To the extent that the globalization promotes income inequity argument has any truth, Los Angeles is a poor example, because it has been remarkably unaffected, at least negatively, by the economic structure aspects of globalization. The decline in aerospace-defense can be linked to globalization in only the most indirect manner, while the continued expansion of the entertainment sector has been a positive trend (at least in economic terms) closely related to the globalization of American culture. The increase in numbers at the low end of the income spectrum is closely associated with the high rates of international immigration; this is a different kind of globalization that is not closely tied to changes in economic structure. Also, the short-term diagnosis of a low-paid underclass ignores the strong upward mobility of immigrants, the increase in college education among second-generation immigrants, and an emerging class of small-scale immigrant entrepreneurs.

Moreover, in income distribution discussions, the dynamics should not be ignored. There is always a "below average," and there will always be a lower income strata. The most important insight to be sought from income distribution data is: What are the odds that any individual will remain at the bottom (or at the top or anywhere in between) and for how long? In fact, there is a high degree of social mobility. For example, citing national longitudinal data, Gottschalk (1997) reported that, of those in the lowest earnings quintile in 1974, 42% were still in that quintile in 1991, but 58 percent were not; 23% had moved up one quintile; 14% had moved up by two; 13% by three and 8% had gone all the way to the top. This comparison understates mobility because those found to be in the same stratum in the first and last years were not necessarily there in every year. The odds are even better if we chose another time period. For example, comparing 1979 to 1988, 86% of those starting in the lowest bracket had moved up.

Looking at region-wide measures of income inequality, e.g., Gini coefficients, from one decade to the next (Ong and Blumenberg in Soja and Scott (eds) 1996, p. 319), misses the point because of the failure to standardize for cohorts. Ong and Blumenberg are casual about their choice of measurement indicators (e.g., changes in the distribution of family incomes without controlling for changing family sizes and more female-headed households, especially among blacks), the adequacy of their variables (Census data on reported dollar incomes; the poor have substantial in-kind benefits, although less than a few years ago), and how to interpret their own results (see the social mobility discussion above). The most serious problem is in their comparison of cross-sections that they admit contain different people in different years. Nowhere do they qualify their Gini coefficients with the observation that were the 1989 low-income group (which they admit contains many recent arrivals) included in the Gini calculations of the previous decade with their then place-of-origin wages, we would find impressive gains.

Many of the Latin American immigrants of the 1980s and 1990s were not even in Los Angeles a decade before. Certainly, they contributed to the growth of the low-income population share, but almost all of them had significantly improved their living standards compared to their place of origin. For this group, often at the bottom of the income distribution, an increase in the Gini coefficient is irrelevant. What counts is whether they are better off than ten years before, and most of them are.

On a related issue, Jennifer Wolch wrote that "Los Angeles became the homeless capital of the United States in the 1980s" (Wolch in Scott and Soja

1996, p. 390). She takes it for granted that there are clear links between "globalization" and homelessness via the intermediate link of poverty creation. This is quite a stretch, an untested hypothesis. This argument does not surface in other empirical studies of the homeless (e.g., Jencks 1994; Fuller Torrey 1997) that emphasize: deinstitutionalization of the mentally ill, low-income housing supply constraints, substance abuse, destruction of skid rows, reductions (and now often the elimination) of cash welfare benefits, and the growth of female-headed households with children. There is no mention of globalization. To the extent that homelessness is the product of a housing problem, Quigley (1996) argues that the growth in the middle class demand for housing interrupted the filtering mechanism, and accounted for an extreme shortage of low-income housing.

Similarly, some (e.g., Davis 1990) view globalization and the accompanying "restructuring" of the economy as a capitalist plot linked to increased income dispersion, homelessness, the 1965 and 1992 riots, and other problems. Yet, the data are not supportive. Globalization is a minor factor in explanations of income inequality, particularly in Los Angeles. Rather, new technologies greatly increased productivity contrasts among workers (within as well as between occupations). Human capital investments and technological change are much more important than trade. In the modern economy job insecurity is almost a given. Increased trade and capital flows inevitably result in dislocations, but in net terms they tend to increase rather than decrease jobs. Moreover, on average, trade-related jobs pay better than others, while the lower prices that trade and increased competition benefit us all as consumers.

4.4. Transportation

Some have argued for an interventionist policy targeting the transportation sector, specifically electric cars and other advanced transportation technologies, often imported public transit vehicles and equipment. But the region's transit policy has been a disaster. Expensive rail transit proposals were sold on the basis of "doomsday" traffic forecasts for which there is little evidence. Rather, after a huge population increase and growth in vehicle miles traveled, the area's 1990 and 2000 mean average commuting times were lower than in some other large metropolitan regions. Also, to date, after billions of dollars worth of new rail capacity have been added, Los Angeles County's transit ridership fell; there was a minor uptick between 1990 and 2000 from 4.6% to 4.7% of all commutes (the comparative shares for New York were 24.9% and 26.6%; http://www.publicpurpose.com/ut-jtw2000metro.htm). Financial constraints have forced a scaling back of the rail plans (the subway system will remain a pitiful rump of the original design) and bus services have been cannibalized; bus riders have had to go to Federal court to force the Metropolitan Transit Authority (MTA) to improve service.

4.5. Cultural issues

Charles Jencks described Los Angeles as "a heteropolis, a new form of urban agglomeration that thrives on difference ... a global city of more than eight million with a high concentration of multinational corporations and having a variety of economic sectors, multiplying lifestyles, and a diversifying ethnic population heading toward full minoritization" (Jencks, p. 47). Oddly, he lists other places headed in the same direction, including Tokyo! Nevertheless, he suggests that the "Los Angeles school of architecture" is best explained by its enjoyment and exploitation of variety, difference, and plurality. Broad descriptions of this kind will accommodate almost everything including the Getty Museum (by Richard Meier), the Disney Concert Hall (by Frank Gehry) and the new Cathedral (by Rafael Moneo). A viewing of these (and other) architects' projects around the world certainly testifies to the globalization of architecture, a trend in which Los Angeles is beginning to participate.[2]

"Local art is a factor of production" (Molotch in Scott and Soja 1996, p. 225). Los Angeles is a great place for making this important point. This version of L.A. culture is found in all kinds of goods. Fashion and sports equipment are good examples. Not all of the goods are produced here (e.g., Japanese automobiles; interestingly, there has been no automobile production in Los Angeles for a couple of decades since the General Motors plant closed in Van Nuys), but their design often derives from local design shops.

In addition, there is a selective migration based on cultural choices and lifestyle preferences. Good weather, for example, breeds athleticism, attracts athletes, and creates job opportunities, such as personal trainers. Los Angeles is the home of individual as opposed to team sports, including, surfing, rollerblading, skateboarding, bicycling and swimming. These lifestyle choices have produced a whole range of somewhat esoteric consumer goods.

The movie-industrial complex includes many tie-ins and licensed products, with many indirect consumer products (few of which, however, are produced in Los Angeles). Union workers in the Hollywood business may work only 10% of the time, but make do by taking on other jobs while they wait for opportunities in their preferred professions. A two-hundred fold increase in real per capita consumption of video-audio products that occurred in the twentieth century (Lebergott 1993) is testimony to the growing importance of these occupations and helps to explain their expanding cultural influence.

Entertainment, food, tourism, furniture, and apparel are all part of this picture. When the goods and services are produced locally, they help to spawn large numbers of small businesses, many of them created by immigrant entrepreneurs.

5. Conclusions

When we adopt the criteria used in the standard methodologies for defining a "world city" or "global city" (Friedmann 1986; Sassen 1991; Taylor 2000), Los Angeles does not pass the test. It has no major transnational headquarters, it may exercise a degree of global influence but no global

[2] The other earlier famous architects of Los Angeles, such as Greene & Greene, Rudolf Schindler, Richard Neutra, Paul Williams and John Lautner tended to do most of their work locally and focused more on residential buildings.

control, and it is not a major financial center. It has not been as strongly impacted by globalization-related "deindustrialization" as other major U.S. cities, and it retains a strong manufacturing sector, a mix of very low-tech and high-tech industries, dominated by small and medium-sized firms. The distribution of income is somewhat more unequal in Los Angeles than in many other locations in the United States, and some have tried to relate this to economic restructuring as a result of globalization, but the argument is fuzzy at best. The presence of a large foreign-born population, with a significant proportion of them poorly educated with limited skills (largely from Central America), is a more satisfactory explanation of income inequities. Furthermore, this problem may be transient, dramatically transformed via second-generation assimilation.

Nevertheless, from some other perspectives Los Angeles certainly has a global impact, often more externally than internally directed. The increasing dominance of the twin ports is a case in point, as more and more facilities are relocating to Los Angeles-Long Beach from other Western seaports. Yet, despite the size of the Southern California economy (the sixth largest in the world if it were a country), the growth of the port is more related to national and international than to regional trends. Of course, there have been significant local impacts (direct and indirect jobs, a sharp increase in truck traffic on the freeways, and significant investments in trade infrastructure [especially the Alameda Corridor]).

Perhaps the most obvious impact of globalization on Los Angeles has been the increase in the immigrant population, largely from Latin America and Asia, but with non-negligible numbers from other parts of the world too. This has transformed Los Angeles in so many different ways that are most visible to people who live there. A few examples: a huge increase in relatively unskilled labor in the low-order service industries that keeps some living costs (e.g., restaurant bills) and some business costs low; the transformation of some ethnic neighborhoods into quasi-developing country city communities with street vendors and informal labor and housing markets (it is estimated that 60,000 households live in garages and another 200,000 live in illegally subdivided units in single-family homes); and an effervescent multiculturalism in the arts, culture, music, food and in many other dimensions.

A very important aspect of the globalization-Los Angeles linkage is the contribution of the region's very large and increasingly high-tech entertainment sector to cultural globalization (some might say, American cultural colonization). These cultural influences are far more important than the corporate influences (even the consumer-related ones, from Coca-Cola to McDonalds, Kentucky Fried Chicken, and now Starbucks and Kinko's). These influences are largely the result of Hollywood movies and TV productions. They can be interpreted either negatively or positively, depending upon the perceptions of the recipients. Decadence, homogenization of global culture, stimuli to crime and violence, the promotion of innovation and creativity, the diffusion of democratic ideals: the responses are varied from society to society and among groups and individuals (stratified by age, education and other variables) within each society. We are not experts in these areas, and they have not received much attention in this paper, but we suspect that they are the most important aspect of the interactions between globalization and Los Angeles.

References

Bae C-HC (2004) Immigration and densities: A contribution to the compact cities and sprawl debates. In: Richardson HW, Bae C-H C (eds) Urban sprawl in Western Europe and the United States. Ashgate, Aldershot, UK
Borjas GJ (1994) The economics of immigration. Journal of Economic Literature 32(4): 1667–1717
Boskin MJ, Ellen R, Dulberger RJ, Gordon ZG, Jorgenson, DW (1997) The CPI Commission: Findings and recommendations. Papers and Proceedings of the 109th Annual Meetings of the American Economic Association 87(2): 78–83
Bound J, Johnson G (1992) Changes in the structure of wages in the 1980s: An evaluation of alternative explanations. American Economic Review 82(3): 371–392
Calthorpe P, Fulton W (2001) The regional city. Island Press, Washington DC
Council of Economic Advisors (1996) Report to the President. US. Government Printing Office, Washington, DC
Davis M (1998) The ecology of fear. Metropolitan Books, New York
Davis M (1990) City of quartz. Verso Books, New York
Freeman RB (1995) Are your wages set in Beijing? Journal of Economic Perspectives 9(3): 15–32
Friedmann J (1986) The world city hypothesis. Development and Change 17: 69–84
Fuller TE (1997) Stop the madness. Wall Street Journal July 18, p. A14
Galor O, Tsiddon D (1997) Technological progress, mobility and economic growth American Economic Review 87(3): 363–382
Gordon P, Richardson HW (1995) Sustainable congestion, In: Brotchie J et al. (eds) Cities in competition: Productive and sustainable cities for the 21st century. Longman Melbourne, Australia
Gordon P, Richardson HW (1999) City of angels or city of angles? Urban Studies 36(3): 575–591
Gottschalk P (1997) Inequality, income growth, and mobility: The basic facts. Journal of Economic Perspectives 11(2): 21–40
Jencks C (1994) The homeless. Harvard University Press, Cambridge, MA, USA
Kanter L (1997) Corporate powers keep leaving: Is the changing economy to blame? Los Angeles Business Journal July 14–20
Knox P, Peter J, Taylor PJ (eds) (1995), World cities in a world-system. Cambridge University Press, Cambridge, UK
Lebergott S (1996) Consumer expenditures. Princeton University Press, Princeton, NJ
Lebergott S (1993) Pursuing happiness: American consumers in the twentieth century. Princeton University Press, Princeton
Mayer SE, Jencks C (1991) Recent trends in economic inequality in the U.S.: Income vs. material well-being. In: Papadimitriou DM, Wolff EN (eds) Poverty and prosperity in the United States in the late twentieth xentury. St Martin's Press, New York
Mills ES, Lubuele LS (1997) Inner cities. Journal of Economic Literature 35: 727–756
Myers D (1999) Upward mobility in space and time: Lessons from immigration. In: Hughes JJ, Seneca JJ (eds) America's demographic tapestry. Rutgers University Press, Brunswick, NJ, pp. 135–157
Myers D (1995) The changing immigrants of Southern California, University of Southern California, Lusk Center Research Institute, Research Report No. LCRI-95-04R
Morrison PA, Lowry IS (1993) A riot of color: The demographic setting of civil disturbance in Los Angeles. RAND (P-7819), Santa Monica, CA
Orfield M (1997) Metropolitics. Brookings Institution Press, Washington, DC
Pastor M, Dreier P, Grigsby III E, Lopez-Graza M (2000) Regions that work: How cities and suburbs can grow together. University of Minnesota Press, Minneapolis
Quigley JM (1996) The homeless. Journal of Economic Literature 34(4): 1935–1941
Rodriguez G (1996) The emerging Latino middle class. Pepperdine University Institute for Public Policy, Malibu, CA
Sadd JL (1999) Every breath you take: The demographics of toxic air releases in Southern California. Economic Development Quarterly 13: 107–123
Sassen S (1991) The global city: New York, London, Tokyo. Princeton University Press, Princeton, NJ

Scott AJ, Soja E eds. (1996) The city: Los Angeles and urban theory at the end of the twentieth century. University of California Press, Berkeley, CA
Slaughter M, Swagel P (1997) The effects of globalization on wages in the advanced economies. International Monetary Fund Working Paper. Washington, DC
Starr K (1993) Inventing the dream: California through the progressive era. Oxford University Press, New York
Taylor PJ (2000) World cities and territorial states under conditions of contemporary globalization. Political Geography 19(5): 5–32
The Economist (1997) How to remake a city. May 31, p. 25
U.S. Department of Commerce (1997) Census and you. June 1997, 32(6): 6

The impacts of globalization on St. Petersburg: A secondary world city in from the cold?

Nathaniel S. Trumbull

University of Washington, Box 353550, Seattle, WA 98195-3550 USA
(e-mail: trumbull@u.washington.edu)

Abstract. St. Petersburg has not been successful in overcoming a large number of social and economic obstacles inherited from its Soviet past. St. Petersburg is missing an important set of pre-conditions that are critical to attain a level of global interaction required to be considered for secondary city status in a semi-peripheral country. Only the city's cultural activities appear to qualify the city for world city status. As long as Russia itself remains "stuck in transition," world city status for St. Petersburg will remain elusive.

1. Introduction

It is a truism that the process of globalization is uneven. That process is uneven both across different cities and countries (Sassen 2001). The global reach of world cities brings opportunity and advantage to residents of those cities, but it also brings the threat of near abandonment of the role of other cities and their residents in the world economy. Those cities designated as world cities, or global cities, have been among both the leaders and beneficiaries of that uneven process. Access to those cities' financial and other networks has amassed some of the most unrivaled wealth in world history. But other cities' fates have been different. If anything, they would appear to be falling further and further behind in terms of relative importance in the global capital market. The transition economies provide a compelling laboratory for an evaluation of cities that by definition were outside of world-class status consideration. Are the capital cities of the former Soviet Union likely to recover and emerge as candidates for world class city status? Among them, St. Petersburg, the capital of the Russian Empire for more than two centuries

The author gratefully thanks the organizers of the Impacts of Globalization on Urban Development conference and the anonymous reviewers of this paper.

and the second largest city in Russia today, provides an obvious candidate for consideration of world city status.[1]

It is difficult to exaggerate the distance that cities of the transition economies have traveled in little more than a single decade. From drab city landscapes of little commercialism and entrepreneurs (with the exception of a longstanding black market), cities of the former Soviet bloc have made an astounding comeback. Billboard advertising and other external signs of commercialism are today readily on display throughout all of Russia's cities. The renewal of the capital cities of the former Soviet Union made them in particular the hotbed of business wheeling and dealing of the mid-1990s, in an atmosphere where everything seemed possible.[2] Many of the indicators of secondary world city status appeared to have emerged in St. Petersburg. Business leaders and government officials had begun to capitalize on the city's architecture and renewed vibrancy to attract an increasing number of international events and investors to the city. Based in large part on the city's cultural inheritance, the city appeared to be booming by the mid-1990s.

St. Petersburg has traditionally been perceived as the most Western of Russia's cities. Founded by the Peter the Great in 1703 as Russia's "Window on Europe," its architecture today reflects squarely its European roots. St. Petersburg developed in the 17th and 18th centuries as a representation of the internationalization of architectural expertise, an example of one of many precursors to today's globalization. The city's planning by Western European architects arguably had resulted in a higher percentage of architectural design by foreigners than any other city in the world. St. Petersburg was retired from its status as the capital of Russia in 1918 by the Bolsheviks in favor of Moscow. St. Petersburg's architecture survived the atheist Soviet period, and such monuments as St. Isaac's Church and the Church of Spilled Blood are among the best known of the city's sights today. Despite degradation of some of the buildings of Leningrad (as St. Petersburg was named between 1924 and 1991), St. Petersburg's historical center remains an architectural gem. St. Petersburg became the first city in Russia to adopt a Strategic Plan in the 1990s.

Cities of the former Soviet Union have traditionally been excluded from consideration of world city status. Friedmann, writing at the height of the Cold War, dismissed those cities in his hierarchical framework. In a footnote in his seminal article on world cities, Friedmann explained that "... eliminated from consideration were all centrally planned economies which are integrated into the Soviet block and are not part of the capitalist world city." (Friedmann 1986) Hall similarly ignored the cities of the Soviet bloc in his analysis due to the absence of a capital market in those cities (Hall 1998). Globalization has been viewed as more responsible for the collapse of the Soviet Union than any other single factor (Lockwood 2000). In an increasingly competitive world market of specialized goods and services, it became increasingly difficult for the Soviet Union to compete not only militarily but especially in providing its

---

1 For a discussion of Moscow as an emerging world city, see Kolossov et al. (2002).

2 The books Casino Moscow (Brzesinksi 2001), The Godfather of the Kremlin (Klebnikov 2000), The Oligarchs: Wealth and Power in the New Russia (Hoffman 2002), and Sale of the Century: Russia's Wild Ride from Communism to Capitalism (Freeland 2000) capture the somewhat unsavory story of the meteoric rise of Russian oligarchs, frequently with seeming consent by Western leaders and agency officials (Wedel 2000).

citizens with levels of consumer consumption resembling those available in the West. It also became increasingly difficult to hide that difference in lifestyle from the urban residents of the Soviet Union. Now that cities of the former Soviet Union have become battlegrounds of capital investment (and more usually pathways for capital flight), might they already have the potential infrastructure and amenities to qualify for world city status? This paper examines whether St. Petersburg can today be considered a "secondary" city in a "semi-peripheral country," as Friedman classified them.

2. St. Petersburg as a world city candidate

St. Petersburg faces a triple challenge if it is to pursue world city status. It must 1) integrate with the West, something so different as what evolved in Russia during the Soviet period, 2) not abandon its presence in Russia and all its ties with Russia, and then 3) catch up with a West that is changing so rapidly itself due to globalization. St. Petersburg's historical role as capital of the Russian Empire for almost two centuries, the second largest city of one of the world's superpowers during the Cold War, and Russia's official "cultural capital" today would appear to place it in good stead for consideration as a world city candidate in a larger historical context. On the surface St. Petersburg would appear to be functioning as any other European capital city. As one Western specialist on Russia notes, "There is peace, the buses run, the streets are lighted, people go about their business." (Gustafson 1999) International music and dance competitions, the Goodwill Games in 1994 and other regular international sport events, and a wide range of scientific and other conferences give the impression that St. Petersburg is indeed part of the world cultural and economic scene.[3] But at the same time a number of serious lacunae emerge on closer observation.

2.1. Impoverishment

One of the distinct challenges to many of the world's cities is an exorbitant number of resident poor. The burden of a disproportionately large impoverished portion of a city population severely limits a city's potential for vast improvement of its facilities and infrastructure. In addition to having to provide minimal social services, the city chronically fails to draw on an adequate tax base. City authorities cannot modernize city infrastructure adequately as a result of the loss of tax base and in the absence of other sources of capital. Firms flee as they find they cannot operate efficiently. Global capital continue to identify deeper and safer harbors elsewhere. The cities of the transition economies have not been able to avoid this vicious circle.

Under conditions of such major political and social upheaval, such as that of the transition period for the post-centrally planned economies, the challenges are daunting for urban residents. Many of the urban residents of those economies have found themselves unprepared to contribute to global

[3] As an example, several recent blockbuster Hollywood movies with scenes filmed in St. Petersburg, including Anna Karenina, K-19, and Goldeneye, have helped to integrate the city's landscape into the world cultural scene from the perspective of viewers outside of Russia.

Table 1. Population with income lower than the poverty line (%)

	1994	1995	1996	1997	1998	1999
St. Petersburg	23.0	20.0	22.4	22.9	24.3	33.2
Moscow	13.7	19.1	17.1	16.1	16.3	23.3
Overall in Russia	22.4	24.7	22.1	20.8	23.4	29.9

Goskomstat (2000) Rossiiskii statisticheskii ezhegodnik, p. 164.

Table 2. Real income in St. Petersburg and Moscow as a percentage of the previous year

	1994	1995	1996	1997	1998	1999
St. Petersburg	130.7	103.7	92.1	94.2	89.4	82.2
Moscow	172.1	77	106.2	106.9	83.2	81.6
Russia	111.9	83.9	100.4	105.9	83.6	86.4

Goskomstat (2000) Rossiiskii statisticheskii ezhegodnik, p. 143.

markets. Official poverty statistics hint at the extent of the economic disaster that has visited former urban citizens of the Soviet Union. For the vast majority of Russia's urban residents, the last decade of transition has also been a story of gross disappointment. St. Petersburg residents on average experienced a precipitous and sustained decline in real income from 1994 to 1999.[4]

Real income had yet to recover in absolute valuc in 1999 from its decline in the 1994, as Table 2 shows. While official reports of unemployment in Russia are generally considered to be underestimated at 8% to 10%, one observer has estimated that unemployment affects at least 13% of the workforce (Gustafson 1999). The real income levels in Table 2 reflect not only the overall decline of both St. Petersburg and Moscow residents, but also the relative average poverty of Petersburgers in comparison with Muscovites.

The abject poverty in which as much as a third of the residents of St. Petersburg has lived during the transition period has taken its toll on the city's urbanization process as a whole.

2.2. De-urbanization

A process of de-urbanization has occurred throughout the former Soviet Union during the transition period and has been particularly visible in St. Petersburg. A city that under Soviet times grew at a steadily upward rate, St. Petersburg's equally steadily declining population reflects a number of social ills of the transition period of the 1990s. Some of that decline has come from a health crisis and increased morbidity and mortality rates, but a significant source of that decline has also been the widespread departure of residents from the city. There is no indication yet that the trend has been reversed. The numbers are dramatic and not representative of cities of world city stature.

[4] Comparisons of income levels with the Soviet period are problematic, due to the high number of subsidies that Soviet urban residents received. Nonetheless, the high level of discontent of Russians with current conditions would also appear to reflect a serious deterioration in living standards for a large portion of the population.

Table 3. Urban population in Russia's capital cities (in thousands)

	1991	1992	1993	1994	1995	1996	1997	1998	1999	2000
St. Petersburg	5035	5004	4952	4883	4838	4801	4779	4749	4728	4694
Moscow	9003	8957	8881	8793	8717	8664	8639	8629	8630	8631

Goskomstat (2000) Rossiiskii statisticheskii ezhegodnik, p. 54.

Table 4. Investment from Russia's federal budget in the city of St. Petersburg (%)

	1994	1995	1996	1997	1998	1999
Percentage	24.5	12.8	12.2	10.7	4.0	2.5

Goskomstat (2000) Regiony Rossii, p. 62.

Such a sustained de-population of an urban area, seemingly unprecedented in Western cities outside of periods of war, is only slightly counterbalanced by the modest growth of exurbia and suburbia in the region (Ioffe 1999). St. Petersburg today has a long way to go in terms of supplying large amounts of reasonably comfortable housing.

The legacy of the Soviet period of inferior housing is alive and well. Leningrad had one of the highest percentages of communal apartments in Russia. At the end of the 1990s, one-third of the city continued to live in communal apartments, sharing kitchen and bathroom (Strategic Plan of St. Petersburg 1998). A large number of social ills have been traced to the communal apartments, including higher levels of child and spousal abuse. St. Petersburg's city government has sought to reduce the number of communal apartments by encouraging the move of communal residents to new apartments on the outskirts and the consolidation of the previously communal apartments into single-owner apartments in the center.[5] City legislation governing the privatization of apartments and the institution of the condominium has been critical in assisting this development. As the federal budget's contribution to the city has fallen in the 1990s, as Table 4 shows, so has the city's ability to help finance housing construction, renovation, and the liquidation of the communal apartments. Threats and murders, especially of elderly, for the express purpose of transferring apartments became common occurrences in the 1990s.

2.3. Cultural, education, and IT renewal: an only partially realized opportunity

St. Petersburg would appear to have achieved at least a modest success in terms of its export of its cultural riches to the world market. A number of cultural alliances have developed during the transition period of the 1990s. A number of joint exhibitions have been held at the Hermitage and then

[5] Communal-apartment families are offered smaller apartments outside the city center and the centrally located apartments are renovated for new owners. In this way, the number of communal apartments in the city has been reduced.

Table 5. Number of organizations and institutions conducting research

	1992	1993	1994	1995	1996	1997	1998	1999
St. Petersburg	401	392	419	471	485	472	464	483
Moscow	841	836	783	881	901	903	892	899
Russia overall	4555	4269	3968	4059	4122	4217	4019	4089

Goskomstat (2000) Regiony Rossii, p. 718.

traveled in Western Europe. St. Petersburg's Marinsky Theater (formerly the Kirov Theater) is considered to be more innovational than the Bolshoi Theater in Moscow. Such visible figures as the chess champion Gary Gasparov, the champion skating pairs 2002 Winter Olympics (contested), and the 2002 winner (again, later discrowned) of the Miss Universe competition are all St. Petersburg natives. Cultural icons such as the St. Petersburg Philharmonic are well-recognized abroad. Similarly, the Hermitage has benefited from a new relationship with the Museum of Modern Art in New York and a joint exhibit in Las Vegas. Many of the city's other theaters and galleries are also of worldwide renown. Foreign consulates in the city, numbering 30 in 2002, also enrich the city through on-going cultural and educational sponsorships. Several of the consulates have dedicated libraries and information offices for the use of public. President Vladimir Putin has made a showcase of the city by regularly inviting high-level delegations to visit St. Petersburg in addition to Moscow.

The number of academic and research institutions in St. Petersburg is extraordinary by any city's standards. During the 1990s, the total number of the former declined only slightly, whereas the number of the latter grew. Their numbers remain high. The city boasts a very high literacy rate of 99.5% in 1989 (Goskomstat 2000). The 1999 Nobel Prize winner in Physics, Zhores Alferov, conducted his work in St. Petersburg.[6]

Yet other statistics may be more revealing in terms of the future potential of Petersburg's contribution to science and scholarship at the global level. The number of researchers working in the city has been on the decline since the early 1990s, to an extent that far surpasses the overall decline in population in the city. The decline is explained in large part by the necessity of researchers to switch to more gainful employment. Some exceptions to the rule do exist (Soros 2002).[7]

[6] Russia's total number of Nobel Prize winners remains miniscule in comparison with other Western European nations and the United States.

[7] Funding for fundamental research remains a critical issue, and a hedge market specialist no less visible than George Soros has played a palpable role in providing ongoing support for such research in St. Petersburg. "I proposed that a $10 billion IMF program for Russia be earmarked for the payment of pensions and unemployment benefits and that its disbursement be organized and supervised by the IMF.... Since the scheme was not even considered, I set out to demonstrate that it was feasible.... I established the International Science Foundation with $100 million and distributed less than $20 million to some 35,000 leading scientists in the former Soviet Union according to very transparent criteria of excellence." (Soros 2002) Indeed, an Internet education center was established by Soros in St. Petersburg in the mid-1990s and assisted in the creation of several public access computer laboratories for academic and student use.

Table 6. Number of academic institutions preparing graduates

	1993	1994	1995	1996	1997	1998	1999
St. Petersburg	159	161	155	154	154	150	155
Moscow	495	477	473	448	444	439	447
Russia overall	1338	1332	1334	1323	1332	1338	1357

Goskomstat (2000) Regiony Rossii, p. 720.

Table 7. Number of city residents who work as researchers

	1992	1993	1994	1995	1996	1997	1998	1999
St. Petersburg	204667	173478	159679	141399	128454	113352	101154	97748
Moscow	480917	407853	324354	337357	318365	290384	253393	275446
Russia overall	1532618	1314008	1106250	1061044	990743	934637	855190	872363

Goskomstat (2000) Regiony Rossii, p. 730.

Table 8. Comparison of economic indicators for Russia, Netherlands, United Kingdom, and United States

	GDP ($US billion, market exchange rate)	Export of goods and services ($US billion)	Import of goods and services ($US billion)	Population (thousand)
Russia	7,063 billion rubles or 224 billion US dollars at 31.5 RUR/USD exchange rate (in 2001)	115.2 (in 2001)	62.2 (in 2001)	145,925 (in 2000)
Netherlands (in 1997)	363.3	198.123	184.082	15,277
United Kingdom	1282.9	267.422	308.709	58,105
United States (in 1997)	7824	682.977	944.586	266,792

Adopted from OECD (March 2000 and February 2002) economic surveys: Russian federation.

Obstacles remain in other sectors of the city's development. They are perhaps no more visible than in the realm of tourism, a direction in which St. Petersburg by any measure should be flourishing. The city only in the spring of 2000 opened a Tourist City Office. Mid-range hotels are all but absent. During the city's annual "White Nights" festival, the small number of the city's luxury and mid-range hotels is booked months in advance. Similarly, air transportation remains a bottleneck and Russian and foreign airlines continue to have an adversarial relationship in terms of receiving flight permission.[8] A recent observation of St. Petersburg's only international airport

[8] Western European airports have blocked some Soviet-made aircraft due to high sound levels, and as a result, landing permission frequency for some foreign air carriers into St. Petersburg has been restricted.

Table 9. Volume of investment by leading foreign countries in the Russian economy

	1995 (mill. $U.S.)	1995 (% of total)	1996 (mill. $U.S.)	1996 (% of total)	1997 (mill. $U.S.)	1997 (% of total)	1998 (mill. $U.S.)	1998 (% of total)	1999 (mill. $U.S.)	1999 (% of total)
Overall	2983	100	6970	100	12295	100	11773	100	9560	100
U.S.A.	832	27.9	1767	25.4	2966	24.1	2238	19.0	2921	30.6
Germany	308	10.3	332	4.8	1647	13.4	2848	24.2	1695	17.7
Cyprus	41	1.4	825	11.8	992	8.1	917	7.8	923	9.7
U.K.	183	6.1	507	7.3	2411	19.6	1591	13.5	733	7.7
Netherlands	85	2.9	981	14	540	4.4	877	7.4	541	5.7
Switzerland	436	14.6	1348	19.3	1756	14.3	411	3.5	405	4.2
France	108	3.6	43	0.6	209	1.7	1546	13.1	312	3.3
Sweden	63	2.1	157	2.3	72	0.6	146	1.2	70	0.7
Austria	81	2.7	200	2.9	378	3.1	83	0.7	43	0.4
Japan	75	2.5	22	0.3	139	1.1	60	0.5	42	0.4
Other	771	25.9	788	11.3	1185	9.6	1056	9	1875	19.6

Goskomstat (2000) Rossiiskii statisticheskii ezhegodnik, p. 555.

on a summer weekend revealed not a single foreign airliner at the airport.[9] Frequent reports of widespread corruption have accompanied federal efforts to fund renovation of major tourist sites for St. Petersburg's 300-year anniversary in 2003.

As concerns another crucial obstacle, a significant digital divide has emerged in Russia's capital cities as it has in so many of the world's aspiring world cities. Kiselvyova and Castells have identified a "dualization" in their analysis of Russia. They distinguish between "a public telecommunications infrastructure still lagging behind the rest of Europe's, and specialized telecommunications links catering to business and global connections ... between the largest urban centers, and the rest of the country." (Castells 2001) One of the Internet's most important contributions has been its use in education. George Soros' Open Society Institute has been influential in Petersburg in opening free-of-charge computer rooms for Internet access for students and in some cases for the public at large.

Yet there has been another negative side to St. Petersburg's entry into the IT sector. The role of Petersburg programmers in world finance break-ins, including a highly publicized break-in into Citibank's computerized accounts in 1998, resulted in some deserved notoriety for Petersburg computer specialists. Dmitry Sklyar's arrest in California is further indicative of problems in this sector as concerns abiding by international copyright regulations. Other complications have emerged over the development of the IT sector in Russia's largest cities. The question of software piracy is serious, and has likely slowed the development of local software. The cellular phone industry is booming, though the overall percentage of cell phone owners is significantly less than in Western cities. Communication costs generally exceed those in the West, despite significantly lower wages in Russia. The absence of the wide use of credit cards make the emergence of a growing e-commerce sector problematic in future. Nonetheless, the foundation for IT development would appear to be promising for Russia's capital cities. As one Western

[9] Author's observation in August 2002 at the height of the tourist season in Western Europe.

commentator observes, ".... there is no intrinsic reason why Russia should not be a worldwide software leader." (Lynch 2002)

2.4. Prevalence and pervasiveness of Russian-style capitalism

Official Russian government economic statistics are widely viewed as capturing only about one-half of the activity of the Russian economy, due to the prevalence of barter and unreported transactions. Those statistics' failure to capture the "gray market" belies some signs of growing consumer strength in Russia. It is widely accepted that Russia's cities and their underfinanced budgets suffer at the hand of corruption and organized crime. Russia's cities have been left with increasingly large financial responsibilities while suffering from low tax revenue. As Castells has observed, "the oligarchs and illicit money deals in deals in the new Russia appear to have far surpassed that of the U.S. period of robber barons (Castells 1999)."

The level of corruption of the Russian bureaucracy, from the lowest to the highest positions, is legendary. *The New York Times* in the late 1990s brought to international attention a sophisticated scheme for the illegal transfer of capital from Russia through the Bank of New York. The Italian newspaper *Corriere della Sera* has repeatedly exposed corruption by a Swiss firm contracted to refurbish buildings in the Kremlin. Shadow companies, based in Britain, Switzerland, the U.S., and several offshore locations made this arrangement possible. Estimates of the amounts involved in this and other illegal schemes have been in the billions of dollars (Castells 2000).[10] A significant share of IMF loans to Russia was diverted abroad. IMF officials quipped that they could save work for everyone if they would simply transfer IMF funds to Swiss bank accounts for Russian officials (Stiglitz 2002).

The concentration of violence in Russia's urban environment is endemic. Such visible city murders as that of Mikhail Manevich, vice-governor of St. Petersburg, in broad daylight and Galina Starovoitova, a member of the Duma, in her apartment building stairwell, have given the city the dubious distinction as the "criminal capital" of Russia in the Russian press. Foreign businessmen have not been insulated from the killing, and a number of highly visible cases have surfaced in St. Petersburg. Contract killings became a way of life. While less violent, the regular payment of a *krysha* (roof) for protection is a common business requirement. Globalization has arguably aggravated the level of illicit activity that occurs in Russia. International communication and influence have facilitated the growth of illicit economic activity in Russia through the ease of improved communication with operatives abroad (Castells 2000).[11] Russia continues to rank very low in

---

[10] Castells notes that the new criminal networks were formed in the 1987–1993 period for the sake of proceeding with a pillage of Russia, and they consolidated their intertwining with the business world and the political system throughout the 1990s.

[11] Post-Soviet criminal networks operating abroad, particularly in the United States and Germany, use the latest technological solutions for untraceable money laundering. Castells writes: "These criminal networks in America operated at a high level of financial and technological sophistical, usually organized by highly educated, young professionals, who did not hesitate in backing up their operations with extreme, but calculated, violence, often performed by ex-KGB officers, who found themselves a post-Cold War professional career," p. 183.

transparency ratings. The consequences for a major city like St. Petersburg are highly detrimental to its image abroad. Russia continues to be viewed among the lowest tier of countries in terms of corruption. In 2001, it ranked 79 out of 91, tied with Ecuador and Pakistan.[12]

One of the more indisputable indicators of the perception of a negative business environment is the extremely modest level of foreign direct investment in St. Petersburg. Indeed, Leningrad Oblast has been more successful in increasing its investment level than Petersburg. Western firm representatives commonly complain of the bureaucratic constraints they face in doing business in Petersburg. Ford, Wrigley, Gillette have all chosen to develop factories in Leningrad Oblast. They report that it was easier to organize production in Leningrad Oblast than doing business than in St. Petersburg, as there are fewer bureaucratic problems. As a result, they have chosen to invest in production outside of St. Petersburg, and then sell their goods on the St. Petersburg market. An overall policy of extraction of taxes and "rents" from local businesses pervades the policies of local officials (Stiglitz 2002).[13]

An arrangement of a "virtual economy" based on barter and non-payments is widely accepted as having characterized the economic underpinnings of much of the Russian economy in the 1990s (Gaddy and Ickes 1998). The engine of that "virtual economy" was the discounted sale of Russia's natural resources. The sale of oil and gas abroad dominate Russia's export earnings today. (OECD 2000 and 2002). The Russian economy continues to undergo a process of "primitivisation" where lower levels of processing such as raw material extraction and energy production provide the basis for this type of economic growth (Oldfield 2000).

Does St. Petersburg show any sign of shedding its negative image among business people of the global economy? St. Petersburg had become a leader among Russian cities in the mid-1990s. It followed a liberal approach in terms of issuing international bonds. But after the Russian default of August 1998, St. Petersburg was effectively penalized for its economically liberal approach. Repayment schedules in hard currency became much more difficult for the city to make with the devalued value of the ruble. International loans to the city came to a near halt. By the end of 1999, Standard & Poors had increased St Petersburg's credit rating only to CCC for long-term, foreign currency-issued debts.[14] Despite a reduction in the federal income tax rates, which indeed raised overall tax revenue amounts for the Russian federal budget in 2000 and 2001, city taxes for firms have remained prohibitively high. City budgets have increasingly been left responsible to care for some of the most acute social problems in the absence of federal funding. Corruption of mid and lower-level city officials continues to be prevalent.

---

[12] See http://www.transparency.org/cpi/2001/cpi2001.html

[13] As Stiglitz observes, "a city like, say, St. Petersburg, or an oblast (regional government like Novgorod), could use a host of regulatory and tax measures to extort 'rents' from firms that operated in their jurisdiction.... But in a world in which high interest rates and an overall depression make such investments unlikely in any case, local governments spent little time creating attractive 'environments for investments' and focused instead on seeing how much they could extract from existing enterprises....

[14] See http://www.bisnis.doc.gov/Bisnis/Country/9908nwnews.Htm

3. The challenge of scale – Russia's participation in the global market

As the above indicators of the effects of globalization on St. Petersburg during the last decade suggest, certain inroads have been made that might be termed achievements in terms of St. Petersburg's potential emergence as a secondary world city. But much more often, St. Petersburg has been the target and recipient, if not victim, of globalization, rather than a key player herself. This brings us to perhaps the most critical issue, one of scale, in terms of the size of Russia's role in the world economy. Comparisons of statistical aggregates only reinforce the picture that Russia itself cannot yet qualify as more than a peripheral country. With a dollar gross domestic product ($224 billion in 2001) equal to one-half that of the Netherlands and a foreign trade equal to one-half that of the United Kingdom's, the Russian Federation as a whole represents a decidedly minor player in the world economy. According to World Bank data, Russia in 2000 had a GDP that was less than two-thirds of what it was in 1989 (Stiglitz 2002). According to the OECD, real GDP declined by about 45% between 1990 and 1998 (OECD 2001). Russia's GDP decline is likely not as dramatic as the OECD reports because of widespread gray market activity, but such official statistics still place Russia and its cities far outside the scope of nations with gross national products that are perceived as significant contributors to the world economy.

The Russian Federation had attracted its share of global capital in the mid-1990s. The Russian economy appeared to benefit handsomely from the flow of global capital into emerging Russian stock markets (Cohen 1998).[15] But that period of solid optimism over the Russian equities market was to be the last before the August 1998 default. Despite growth, the Russian equities market remains minor by international standards. On a daily basis in the late 1990s, only about 100 USD million in stocks changed hands over the RTS [Russian Trading System] system, and another 30 USD million passed through direct trades among Russian-based brokers (Gustafson 1999). The offshore market accounted for another $40 million in daily trades of Russian ownership in New York and London. In sum, trade in Russian stocks totaled no more than 170 to 200 million USD a day in the late 1990s. The New York Stock Exchange traded at volumes approximately 300 times this level.

On balance, foreign direct investment in Russia was insignificant throughout the 1990s. It amounted to an average of about two billion dollars anually between 1995 and 1998 (Gustafson 1999 and Cohen 2000). As one Western specialist concludes: "Uncertainties about political stability and legal and administrative reliability have scared off investors from a risky Russian market and caused them to look elsewhere." (Lynch 2002) At the same time, capital flight has been estimated at 18–24 billion US dollars a year (Cohen 2000). In sum, from 80 to 150 billion dollars is estimated to have left Russia during the 1990s in the form of capital flight, a number that far surpasses FDI levels. The estimated world stock of foreign direct investment was 4.1 trillion in 1998 (Sassen 2001). At two billion US dollars a year of FDI, Russia attracted only one tenth of a percentage point of world FDI in 1998.

[15] According to Cohen (1998), after Russia's Eurobond offer of $1 billion in 1996, the Moscow stock market increased in value by 127% in 1996, and then by an additional 65% in the first three months of 1997.

Investment in Russia would appear to be barely large enough qualify Russia as a semi-peripheral country.

4. Conclusions

Pessimists and optimists on Russia will likely co-exist for a long time. Significant progress has been made in the last decade. Russia returned in the late spring of 2002 to have the world's fastest rising stock market. The port of St. Petersburg is Russia's largest commercial seaport by volume, and handles over a third of Russia's imports.[16] In May 1998, a new container terminal was launched. New large oil export terminals continue to be constructed at a rapid pace in the vicinity of St. Petersburg. The new port in Primorsk may soon surpass Novorossissk as Russia's largest oil export port. Optimists of Russia's potential point to Russia's geographic size and location as a relevant factor. They assert that "a world without Russia would be like globalization without a large part of the globe." (Benn 2002) World transportation routes continue to make inroads in Russia. Improvements in terms of facilitating the transportation of natural resources from Russia, and improvements in air, truck, rail, and ship delivery for Russia's cities all suggest that the impacts of globalization on a city such as St. Petersburg will grow in future.

Others appear resigned to Russia's overall decline. After evaluating the IMF's attempts to improve Russia's plight in the 1990s, Stiglitz offers the most pessimistic of prognoses: "Russia has gotten the worst of all possible worlds – an enormous decline in output and an enormous increase in inequality." (Stiglitz 2002) The poor enforcement of laws and regulations, including a judicial system that is widely perceived as corrupt, remain substantial obstacles to Russia's participation in the world economy on a highly competitive basis. Indeed, secure property rights will likely continue to be one of the most insurmountable obstacles for an economic *chudo* (miracle) to occur in Russia in the coming decade (Yergin and Gustafson 1993).

Yet a dose of humility is also warranted on the part of Western commentators. Russia will continue to have its Western detractors as long as Russian cities operate so differently from how Western observers understand they should operate. The transition economies' major cities face a unique challenge among other aspiring world cities. One of the best long-term hopes may be the prospect, admittedly still distant, of a reversal of the continuing "brain drain" to the West. The repatriation of some of Russia's best minds and talents, many of whom have presumably acquired first-hand practical knowledge in the West, could serve Russia well in future. They have the potential of bringing back not only knowledge but also resources for investment in Russia's capital cities. As St. Petersburg celebrates its 300th year anniversary in 2003, the obstacles to the city's candidacy as a secondary city in a semi-peripheral country are daunting but not insurmountable.

In conclusion, St. Petersburg has not yet been successful in overcoming a large number of obstacles it has inherited from its Soviet past. Whether it be

[16] See http://www.tradeport.org/ts/countries/russia/trends.html

the poverty of a large portion of the city's residents, its inferior infrastructure in terms of transportation and of related services, deterioration in its research and educational base, only fledging use of information technology, or a perceived corrupt business environment, St. Petersburg is missing an important set of pre-conditions that are critical for the level of interaction required to be considered even a secondary city in a semi-peripheral country. The city's overall connectedness to the outside world continues to be much too minimal to qualify the city for world city status. St. Petersburg might in future become a good candidate for a secondary city of a semi-peripheral country, but it is not yet there. Only the city's cultural activities appear to qualify the city for secondary world city status today. Indeed, as long as Russia itself remains "stuck in transition," world city status for St. Petersburg will remain elusive.

References

Benn DW (2002) The West's role in post-communist Russia: A review article. Europe-Asia Studies 54:2

Brzesinksi M (2001) Casino Moscow: A tale of greed and adventure on capitalism's wildest frontier. Free Press, New York

Castells EK (2001) Russia in the information age. In: Bonnell VE (ed) Russia in the new century: Stability or disorder? Westview Press, Boulder, Colorado, pp 126–157

Castells M (2000) End of millennium. Blackwell Publishers, Malden, MA

Cohen SF (1998) Russia: Tragedy or transition? Rethinking the Soviet collapse: Sovietology, the death of communism and the New Russia. Pinter, New York

Freeland C (2000) Sale of the century: Russia's wild ride from communism to capitalism. Crown Business, New York

Friedmann J (1986) The world city hypothesis. Development and Change 17:69–84

Gaddy C, Ickes B (1998) Russia's virtual economy. Foreign Affairs 77(5)

Goskomstat (2000) Rossiiskii statisticheskii ezhegodnik. Goskomstat, Moscow

Goskomstat (2000) Regiony Rossii. Goskomstat, Moscow

Gustafson T (1999) Capitalism Russian-style. Cambridge University Press, New York

Hall P (1998) Globalization and the world cities. In: FCL, YM Yeung (eds), Globalization and the world of large cities. United Nations University Press, New York

Hoffman DE (2002) The Oligarchs: Wealth and power in the New Russia. Public Affairs, New York

Ioffe G (1999) The environs of Russian cities. Edwin Mellen Press, Lewiston, N.Y

Klebnikov P (2000) Godfather of the Kremlin: Boris Berezovsky and the looting of Russia. Harcourt, New York

Kolossov V, Vendina O, O'Loughlin J (2002) Moscow as an emergent world city: International links, business developments, and the entrepreneurial city. Eurasian Geography and Economics 43(3):170–196

Lockwood D (2000) The destruction of the Soviet Union: a study in globalization. St. Martin's Press, New York

Lynch AC (2002) Roots of Russia's economic dilemmas: Liberal economics and illiberal geography. Europe-Asia Studies 54(1):44

Oldfield JD (2000) Structural economic change and the natural environment in the Russian federation. Post-Communist Economies 21(1):82

Organisation for Economic Co-operation and Development (2000, 2002) OECD economic surveys: Russian federation. OECD, Paris

Organisation for Economic Co-operation and Development (2001) The social crisis in the Russian federation. OECD, Paris

Sassen S (2001) The global city: New York, London, Tokyo. Princeton University Press, Princeton, NJ

Soros G (2002) George Soros on globalization. Public Affairs, New York

Stiglitz J (2002) Globalization and its discontents. WW Norton, New York
Strategic Plan of St. Petersburg (1998) Leontiev Center, St. Petersburg
Wedel J (1998) Collision and collusion: the strange case of Western aid to Eastern europe, 1989–1998. St. Martin's Press, New York
Yergin D, Gustafson T (1993) Russia 2010–and what it means for the world: the CERA Report. Random House, New York

Building world city Tokyo: Globalization and conflict over urban space

André Sorensen

Centre for Urban and Community Studies, Department of Social Science, University of Toronto at Scarborough and Department of Geography and Programme in Planning, University of Toronto
(e-mail: sorensen@utsc.utoronto.ca)

Abstract. Japanese policy makers have, since their contact with the colonial powers in the mid 19th century, been acutely aware of the pressures and challenges of national survival in a globalizing world. In this sense, the Japanese experience of modernity has been deeply intertwined with, and is in important ways inseparable from the ongoing processes of globalization during the last century and a half. While their main response was to foster the growth of Japanese industrial, military and diplomatic power, one consistent theme has been the development of the capital city Tokyo as emblem of Japan as a civilized nation, location of national institutions, and center of economic power. This project, however, has long been an arena of considerable conflict between city builders and the residents of central Tokyo. The most recent conflict over the control of urban space in Japan's premier world city emerged in the last few years when major developers lobbied successfully for massive increases in allowable building volumes and heights in special regeneration areas, arguing that without further deregulation Tokyo would lose its competitive position in relation to Shanghai, Hong Kong and Singapore. This paper argues that in Japan an important feature of globalization and international competitive pressures has been their use by urban actors in disputes over the control of urban space, and examines this use of globalization debates in the competition between economic space and life space in Tokyo.

1. Introduction

> "*Competition between cities is international – to revitalize Tokyo is to revitalize Japan ... if Japan is to prosper in an age of globalization, its cities must attract residents, goods, finance and information from around the world.*"
>
> Mori Building Website, July 2002

One of the key contributions of urban studies to the globalization debate has been the concept of 'world cities'. The research agenda about world cities as first proposed by Friedmann and Wolf (1982), Friedmann's more developed hypothesis (1986) and the monograph by Sassen (1991) which proposed a triumvirate of leading 'global cities' (London, New York, and Tokyo) have informed a vast literature on globalization and world cities. The core idea was that a number of global processes including increased integration of world commodities, finished goods and financial markets, and growing interconnection through communications networks were likely to result in a convergence of economic structures, and that this would in turn have similar spatial and social impacts in diverse world cities. Looking at the leading 'global cities,' Sassen (1991: 4) found that indeed such parallel changes in economic base, spatial organization and social structure were occurring, and strongly asserted the primary role of global processes in those changes.

Subsequent research put more emphasis on the role of national and local actors and institutions in mediating, contesting, and shaping the particular products of economic changes in particular cities (Goetz and Clarke 1993; Knox and Taylor 1995; Eade 1997). The prevailing interpretation today is that while global forces are generally the more powerful, and affect all major cities depending on their degree of interconnectedness with the world economy, local histories and institutions do influence outcomes in particular places, which are diverse (e.g., Pacione 2001: 8).

Tokyo has played a lead role in globalization debates from the beginning. Sassen (1991) stressed the importance of Tokyo as a key node in the world economic system alongside London and New York, and a large body of work discerned a range of globalization induced changes to the Tokyo space-economy (Rimmer 1986; Douglass 1988; Fujita 1991; Douglass 1993). In particular, Tokyo's emergence as a key global command and control center, the increasing importance of financial, insurance and real estate industries in its economy and their consequent demand for central city office space were seen as having major impacts on the space economy of central city areas (Sassen 1991). Fujita (1991) argues that Tokyo's development into a world city is primarily a result of its flexible manufacturing prowess, which captured a major share of world markets, allowed the creation of vast trade surpluses, and encouraged the growth of financial services industries. That in turn increased the capital's dominance over the Japanese economy as well as intensified competition for space in central areas, exacerbating housing problems and other social tensions. Others described the adverse social impacts of urban restructuring including upward spiraling land prices and rents resulting from buoyant markets for office space, the displacement of population from central city areas, the uprooting of long-standing communities, and lengthening commutes (Douglass 1993: 88). He suggests that while economic growth had certainly brought Japanese people higher incomes and greater consumption, urban quality of life had not improved, and may even have worsened (Douglass 1993: 88). Machimura (1992, 1998) stresses the political conflicts arising from urban restructuring, and argues that the concept of world city has been used symbolically as a political level in domestic political conflicts over urban space.

Recent work has contributed case studies of specific globalization-related changes, such as the development of the waterfront subcenter on reclaimed land in Tokyo Bay, which was developed explicitly to advance Tokyo's world city ambitions (Saito 2003). Saito examines the political dynamics behind the subcenter project, and finds that the main player was the Tokyo Metropolitan Government, which saw its role as fostering Tokyo's emergence as a premier world city by creating an advantageous location for high tech office towers and high amenity living space. Saito's fascinating play-by-play description of the evolving political dynamics behind the project provides a useful glimpse into Japanese policymaking. In contrast to much of the Anglo-American literature on globalization and world cities, which sees market forces as the overwhelmingly dominant force behind spatial restructuring in world cities, in Saito's examination of the waterfront subcenter it was the State that dominated the process, not private enterprise. Following Hill and Kim (2000) he explains this strong role of the state as a product of Japan's history of "developmental state" policies.

In the present context his stress on the importance of the developmental state is significant. While there has been an extended debate among students of Japanese political economy of the relative importance of the state bureaucracy, political parties, and big business (see, e.g., Johnson 1982; Deyo 1987; Gao 1997), no one would argue that Japan is a liberal market economy in the pattern of the United States. Here it is not necessary to take sides in the debate over the precise degree of credit for Japanese economic success to assign the Japanese bureaucracy. It is important, however, to understand that Japan had a much different experience of modernization, industrialization and urbanization than any of the other developed countries, and that this contributed to the development of a highly distinctive planning culture. The Japanese leadership always saw the building of a strong State as the primary national project – a project to which the people should subordinate themselves – and which was commonly cast in a framework of fierce international competition in which Japan played the role of outsider catching up. While there were dramatic changes over the course of the 20th century, the focus of resources on developmental goals rather than public welfare has proven highly enduring, as shown below.

Far from the competitive pressures of globalization being a phenomenon new to the 1980s, therefore, in Japan they have been a driving force behind national policymaking for at least a century. In this competitive world environment, the Japanese leadership consistently put national development and international stature ahead of private welfare or even collective quality of life. This makes it somewhat difficult to distinguish a particular period during which globalization pressures begin to impact Japanese public policy. While it is often suggested that deregulation and the hollowing out of the welfare state are prominent manifestations of globalization, in Japan the welfare state was always thin, the state sector small, and as shown below, regulation of urban development weak. The priority was economic development, and urban planning was carried out primarily to foster that growth, not to help create or maintain amenities or improve the quality of life in urban areas (see Sorensen 2002). In Friedmann's (1988) terms, the priority was always "economic space" not "life space."

Friedmann's concept of the conflict between "life space" and "economic space" is particularly helpful for understanding Tokyo's restructuring conflicts. Tokyo was already a giant city of over a million during the feudal era two centuries ago, and the current structure of land uses is still strongly influenced by its long urban history (see Cybriwsky 1998; Sorensen 2002). Urban restructuring and redevelopment in the early postwar period was carried out primarily along major new arterial roads and at nodes in the public transport system. This bypassed many older traditional neighborhoods that are characterized by extremely fragmented land ownership patterns and narrow roads inherited from earlier periods. Apart from the real difficulty of land assembly for redevelopment in such areas, a building code regulation first passed in 1919 ties allowable building height to a slant plane drawn from the opposite side of the road on which a property fronts (Sorensen 2002: 116). Throughout Tokyo, but particularly in areas of narrow roads and small lots, this regulation severely limits the height of buildings and development capacity (Onishi 1994). It also helped to protect from redevelopment many inner city districts, which commonly maintained many of the characteristic features of traditional Japanese cities; narrow roads, small neighborhood commercial centers (*shotengai*) of family run shop-houses with the shop at ground level and residence above, strong neighborhood organizations which managed the local shrine and festival, recycling collection, park maintenance and fire patrol among other functions (Bestor 1989). The central area of Tokyo thus retained many close-knit residential communities, which were geographically distinct and separated from the main areas of modern high-rise development. As shown below, however, such areas of "life space" have come under repeated pressure for profitable redevelopment to "economic space" since the 1960s.

While this has been a long-term struggle between the forces of economic change and community stability, however, it is only in the 1980s and 1990s that the language of globalization and world cities began to be used to legitimize and explain these conflicts, as shown below. Section 2 outlines the weak planning system of the rapid growth period in the 1950s and 1960s, and describes several key planning protections won by progressive political forces and social movements in the 1960s and 1970s. Section 3 outlines the swings from deregulation in the 1980s to re-regulation after the bubble to the most recent period of deregulation from the late 1990s. Section 4 summarizes the main findings.

2. Shifting the balance between developers and communities, 1960s–1970s

During the rapid economic growth period of the 1950s and 1960s Japan had an extremely weak system of urban land planning and development control. This assertion seems to contradict the widely held perception of a "Japan Inc." that was a highly efficient, technocratic, well-planned developmental state which effectively mobilized national resources in pursuit of economic growth (Johnson 1982). In fact, while the latter description is certainly an oversimplification of the case (for other interpretations see, e.g., Muramatsu and Krauss 1987; Calder 1988), it is widely agreed that during the rapid growth period an "iron triangle" of Liberal Democratic Party (LDP), central government bureaucracy, and big business worked effectively to mobilize available national resources, and produced spectacular economic growth. At the same time, this focus of the nation's resources on industrial development and capital formation resulted in ongoing shortages of investment in social overhead capital. As Honjo put it: "The conditions under which Japan developed were so severe that it was impossible to do more than the bare minimum. The accumulated capital was always mobilized for investment in productive sectors, and an urban development policy focused on infrastructure was promoted ... The housing supply was left to the private sector, and only during emergencies such as natural disasters were public measures initiated or expanded" (Honjo 1984: 28). The role of city planning was seen as the supply of infrastructure for economic growth: highways, ports and airports, industrial water supply, serviced industrial sites, and low-cost public housing for the workers who migrated in their millions to the cities (Morimura 1994). Little money was spent on residential areas and low priority was put on investment in the more discretionary public goods such as parks, local roads or sidewalks. Instead of creating a system to regulate private urban development, the state provided a range of basic infrastructure such as water supply and arterial roads, while encouraging private investors to provide other needed urban investment such as in electrical generation, commuter railways, and housing development.

The weak planning system was thus a result not of a lack of state capacity, as in many developing countries today, but of a narrowly focused urban policy which prioritized economic development. The main planning tool was a weak zoning system, with only four zones, residential commercial, industrial and quasi-industrial. Housing could still be built within industrial and commercial zones, and small-scale industry within residential and commercial zones. Within zoned areas land development was as-of-right, with no requirements for basic urban infrastructure before land development, no subdivision control, nor any minimum housing standards. The result was extremely rapid growth of haphazard un-serviced sprawl combining housing, commercial and industrial uses at high densities. In primarily residential areas much housing was built along narrow, unpaved private roads, and large areas were built up without municipal sewers, parks, piped gas supply or even sidewalks (Sorensen 2001a).

This weak planning system was very much the product of strong central control. This is partly because local governments are highly dependent on grants from the central government, and that funding was tightly focused on the developmental priorities noted above. It is even more a result, however, of the fact that planning law was written and interpreted by central government ministries, and local governments had no legal authority to go beyond the parameters set by national legislation. For example, because the national government had set no minimum housing standards, minimum plot sizes, or minimum infrastructure requirements for land development, municipal ordinances that attempted to introduce such measures could not be legally enforced, and local governments frequently lost court challenges to them (Jain 1991). In this way central government effectively limited the planning tools available to local governments.

While in the early post-war period there was a broad agreement that economic growth was a top priority, the success of that project created other pressing problems that effectively shattered the consensus around growth during the 1960s. Large-scale development of heavy and chemical industries intermixed with or in close proximity to residential and commercial areas, combined with almost non-existent pollution controls, resulted in a severe environmental crisis. Pollution of air, water and food supplies was directly related to the spread of environmental diseases, and hundreds died, thousands suffered debilitating and painful diseases or were born deformed, and hundreds of thousands suffered from asthma and other chronic pollution-related ailments (see Huddle, et al. 1975; McKean 1981; Ui 1992; George 2001). Eventually, large numbers of local environmental protest movements developed to lobby for better pollution control regulations and against industrial development (McKean 1981; Upham 1987).

This conflict extended also to urban planning policy. Krauss and Simcock (1980: 196) suggest that there was an "explosion of protest in urban and suburban areas" against industrial plants and highway interchanges, and demanding that local governments provide essential services such as sewers, parks and sidewalks. As Samuels (1983: 190) described it, "The left came to power by convincing enough of the electorate that the conservative central government and their allies in the localities were responsible for the pollution, the lack of social programs, and the support of business interests at the expense of residents." The growing political strength of progressives in both local and central government elections scared the ruling LDP into passing new city planning legislation in 1968 (Calder 1988: 405). The New City Planning Law of 1968 was the first major post-war swing of the pendulum towards greater emphasis of urban planning on urban quality of life and tighter regulation of development, and it generated high hopes that local governments would finally have the tools to be able to control land development and improve urban environments.

Although the new planning system encountered serious difficulties in managing urban growth on the fringe (see Nakai 1988; Hebbert 1994; Sorensen 1999; Sorensen 2001a), the new zoning system did have a significant impact on development in existing built-up areas. The key factor was the introduction of the Exclusive Residential Zone #1, which was the first land use zone meaningfully restricting land uses. In the new zone not only was land use restricted to residential uses and related compatible land uses (e.g., churches, small-scale retail), but a strictly enforced absolute height limit of 10 meters was also imposed. The height limit was important. The Japanese building code had since the prewar period maintained a strictly enforced absolute height limit of 30 meters on all buildings because of concerns about earthquakes. However, the limit was abolished by the 1970 revision to the Building Standards Law because of dramatic improvements in engineering technology using steel reinforced concrete. As a result, extensive low- and medium-rise areas were suddenly ripe for redevelopment into higher-rise buildings, and the 1970s saw a rush to inner-city condominium building, the so-called "manshon boom."

The condominium boom created severe conflicts in many areas, in part because the high-rise buildings brought with them increased local congestion and noise, but even more because they almost always blocked direct sunlight to neighboring houses for part of the day. In Japan direct sunlight is an essential aspect of residential quality of life, houses have long been routinely oriented towards the sun, and an important part of housewives' daily routine – even today – is to hang bedding out in the sun to air it out. Where buildings block the sun, residential amenity is permanently impaired. In residential areas throughout Tokyo local citizens' groups organized to oppose the building of high-rise apartment buildings which blocked the sunlight from surrounding houses (Ishizuka and Ishida 1988: 30).

As the only land use zone that retained any height control function was the Exclusive Residential Zone #1, designation of such zones became a highly contested process, as it effectively barred redevelopment to high rises. In the early 1970s, the Tokyo Prefecture and most Tokyo wards were controlled by progressive administrations, and in many cases the rezoning to the new zoning system gave priority to the protection of existing traditional residential communities. In 1972, again responding to electoral pressure and increasingly vocal citizen movements, the government passed an amendment to the

Building Standards Law that allowed the creation of Height Control Zones with a maximum building height of 10 meters that could be designated over other land use zones. Such height control zones were widely designated by sympathetic ward governments to protect residential areas throughout central Tokyo and became an increasing source of conflict later, as discussed below.

A third factor that served to protect low-rise residential areas from high-rise redevelopment was directly the result of the activities of the citizen movements of the early 1970s. A Tokyo-wide organization of sunshine rights groups won a series of court cases against developers of high-rise buildings, forcing them to compensate the neighbors they had deprived of light. In 1972, the Supreme Court determined that Article 25 of the constitution, which guarantees "minimum standards of wholesome and cultural living," protected the right to sunshine, and that infringements of sunshine rights were liable for damages (McKean 1981: 113). Then in 1973 the citizens' movement drafted and presented their own proposal for a sunlight protection ordinance (*Hiatari Jôrei*) to the Tokyo Metropolitan Government. As Ishida and Ishizuka suggest: "This was an epochal development in the citizens' movement in that it progressed from simply opposing things to actively proposing policies" (Ishizuka and Ishida 1988: 30). Through the 1970s a large number of sunshine rights cases were won against offending builders and even against the government in the case of an elevated expressway.

In this context the government worked quickly to revise the building regulations. The level of uncertainty about what was permissible and what would incur liability to pay damages was high enough that builders ran an unacceptably high risk of losing court battles with neighbors, even where they had complied with existing regulations. The Ministry of Construction (MoC) drafted a revision to the building standards law that included many of the proposals of the citizens' movement, and those revisions came into effect in 1976. The revision required all local governments to draft their own sunshine standards that specified the minimum hours of unimpeded sunlight cast to the north of new buildings on the winter solstice when the sun is at its lowest.

These three changes, the creation of Exclusive Residential #1 zones, the ad hoc height control zones, and the sunlight preservation regulations, significantly changed the balance of power between urban residents and the development industry, and permitted local governments to increase their controls over development in existing built up areas. For the first time residential neighborhoods had some leverage to protect themselves from redevelopment initiatives. That this new regime really did represent a significant shift in the power balance is suggested by the fact that from the early 1980s the central government, urged on by the development industry, started to work hard to weaken these regulations to permit more redevelopment in central Tokyo.

3. From deregulation in the 1980s to re-regulation in the 1990s and incentives in 2000

In the early 1980s the urban policy climate shifted abruptly. The new Prime Minister Nakasone, inspired by the neoliberal policies of Thatcher and Reagan, promoted policies of deregulation, privatization and fiscal retrenchment. A key rationale for deregulation was to enhance Japan's international economic competitiveness, and urban planning deregulation efforts were increasingly cast in terms of the economic importance of World City Tokyo in a globalizing world. At the Tokyo Metropolitan Government level the conservative administration of governor Suzuki strongly supported a "world city" strategy for Tokyo's glorious future as an international city (Tokyo Metropolitan Government 1987), although Machimura (1998) argues that this use of the term was primarily symbolic, designed to impress and gain support for the deregulation program.

Deregulation of city planning regulations was carried out throughout the 1980s. While Nakasone's neoliberal agenda closely followed those of Thatcher and Reagan, urban policies were explicitly oriented towards the remodeling of Tokyo into a competitive World City. Hence, a central and early part of Nakasone's deregulation campaign focused on encouraging redevelopment in central Tokyo. For example, one of the first actions of the Nakasone government upon taking office in 1982 was to direct the MoC to review the zoning of all the areas in central Tokyo that were zoned Exclusive Residential #1. The idea was to rezone them to Exclusive Residential #2 in which high-rise buildings can be built, so that Tokyo could begin to look more like New York (Hebbert and Nakai 1988: 386; Miyao 1991: 132). Then in March of 1983 the Ministry of Construction ordered all local governments to encourage development by relaxing regulations. Specifically, they were to increase the ratio of building volume to lot size, rezone residential zones to commercial, and weaken various restrictions on urban fringe land development (Hayakawa and Hirayama 1991: 153). The central government also strongly pressured local governments to weaken or abolish their non-statutory "Development Manuals" which specified required levels of contribution to public infrastructure to get a development permit.

The relatively low intensity of land use in central Tokyo compared to other developed country major cities was seen as a problem. For example, the Tsukuba National University economist Takahiro Miyao argued that planning restrictions limiting the height of buildings in much of central Tokyo were a key urban problem because they made it difficult to redevelop central city areas to more intensive uses such as high-rise condominiums. He argued for further deregulation, suggesting that the vigor of the private sector needed to be freed from excessive planning regulations in order to "take full advantage of the vitality in the metropolitan regions" (Miyao 1987: 58–9). Specifically, deregulation should ensure that "excessive restrictions of the residential area development guidelines by local municipalities would be corrected" (Miyao 1987: 59).

Even though most ward governments successfully resisted pressure to abolish the Exclusive Residential #1 Zones in central Tokyo, the list of national planning deregulations was long, and these had powerful impacts on urban redevelopment patterns (Hayakawa and Hirayama 1991; Otake 1993; Inamoto 1998). One particularly important new planning measure for central area redevelopment was an incentive to provide more inner city public space. Modeled after New York's Plaza Bonus system, it rewarded developers with extra height and floor space allowances in return for the provision of public open space or plazas at ground level. This was a logical measure in a city as crowded as Tokyo, with a shortage of public open space, particularly in core areas. Developers were eager to use it. Even though there were no absolute height restrictions in much of central Tokyo, floor area ratios, slant plane restrictions and sunlight ordinances still put serious limits on building heights and volumes. The plaza bonus measure allowed them to negotiate significant increases in height and bulk over and above those limits.

At the Tokyo Metropolitan Government level the conservative administration of governor Suzuki actively supported its own vision of polycentric development within the greater Tokyo area (Sorensen 2001b). Of the various subcenters, the most closely related to the world city project was the waterfront subcenter to be built on reclaimed land in Tokyo Bay (Saito 2001). Promoted initially as Tokyo Teleport Town, which was planned to function as Japan's main international communications gateway, the concept was to provide a major new supply of high quality office space in a high tech cluster. Other major infrastructure projects pursued by the Suzuki administration such as new subway lines, water supply projects, wastewater treatment plants, and garbage incinerators were also designed to facilitate central area redevelopment and intensification.

Planning deregulation, fiscal stimuli, and infrastructure spending were successful beyond expectations. In the second half of the 1980s the Japanese economy boomed and redevelopment of central Tokyo proceeded apace. While at the time the boom seemed very impressive, and "triumphalist" predictions abounded that Japanese economic output would soon surpass that of the US, in retrospect the boom was an unmitigated disaster. Land prices soared, first in central Tokyo and then in the rest of the country, resulting in sharp increases in inequality as those with land assets gained and those without found themselves ever farther away from owning their own home (Tachibanaki 1992; Noguchi and Poterba 1994). The frenzy of real estate investment amid continuously rising land prices created powerful incentives for the high-rise redevelopment of existing low-rise inner city residential areas.

While there is no doubt that in many cases small inner city landowners were happy to sell their property at very high prices and move out to the suburbs, in many other cases owners wished to stay in communities where they had long ties. Even more reluctant to move were tenants who often had low rents and legal protection against eviction. In cases where owners were reluctant to sell, or tenants preferred not to move, land assembly became the work of "land sharks" (*jiageya*), or real estate gangsters who used intimidation, threats and violence to encourage people to leave (Hayakawa and Hirayama 1991: 156; Cybriwsky 1993: 140). Another tactic that was particularly harmful to inner city communities was the buying up and closure of privately operated public baths that functioned both as an essential public facility (in areas where many houses had no baths of their own) and as a key neighborhood meeting place. The number of public baths declined from 22,650 in 1964 to 39 by the end of 1986 (Douglass 1993: 98). There is no doubt that the real estate investment explosion of the 1980s greatly heightened conflict over space in central Tokyo, and that deregulation weakened the ability of communities to maintain life space against the encroachment of economic space. In order to increase profits to real estate developers, inner city communities were destroyed. Housing problems increased sharply, particularly for the very poor (Kodama 1990; Watanabe 1992; Oizumi 1994). Unfortunately, the boom also seriously damaged the Japanese economy. When the bubble burst, the nation's financial system almost collapsed under the weight of bad real estate loans, and the country has suffered economic stagnation since 1991 up to the present.

By the late 1980s there was increasing public pressure to address the land inflation crisis. The ongoing process of deregulation and government downsizing was, at least temporarily, derailed, and the committee in charge of planning and land deregulation in particular was forced to do an about face and start promoting strengthened land development and speculation controls as detailed by Otake (1993). In the late 1980s and early 1990s there were several moves in the direction of re-regulation of land development, especially the Basic Land Law of 1989. The Law declared that: "First, public welfare should be given priority over private profit in the ownership and use of land. Second, land should be used in a proper and orderly fashion. Third, land should not be an object of speculation. Fourth, landowners should return a part of their profits to the public through imposition" (Oizumi 1994: 210).

Another step was a significant strengthening of the City Planning Law, including provisions for Master Planning and improved zoning regulations among others (Watanabe 1992; Oizumi 1994: 211; Sorensen 2002: 302). While there has been considerable debate about the effectiveness of many of these measures, it is clear that the excess of the bubble economy period had effectively undermined the political viability of the deregulation argument. As a result, the pendulum swung again in the early 1990s in favor of greater public and governmental support for stronger planning and the tighter regulation of land development.

More recently, the extended recession of the 1990s has again tipped the political advantage in favor of the property development industry. In particular, the financial system has been on the brink of collapse because of massive bad loans resulting from real estate deals during the bubble, the crash of equities values, and the continuing decline in Japanese land prices since 1991. Hence, government policy has given priority to stabilizing the financial system. This has included major bailouts to the banks and huge spending on infrastructure projects to inject funds into the construction and development industries.

Perhaps most important in the present context have been moves to deregulate the property development industry to make land development profitable once again to compensate for bubble-related losses. During the 1990s a series of changes by the central government to the Building Standards Law have allowed significant increases in allowable building heights and volumes in order to make urban redevelopment more profitable. The most recent change results from the passage in April of 2002 of the Special Urban Regeneration Act by the Koizumi government. This act established an urban regeneration office within the national cabinet. This office has the authority to designate Urban Regeneration Areas in which greatly weakened development regulations will apply and FAR bonus systems such as for Plazas can be permitted directly by central government instead of requiring local government consultation. This avoids the head-on confrontation with local governments over rezoning that proved so problematic in the 1980s. The main advocates of these measures have been the largest property development companies that stand to profit considerably from floor area bonuses and deregulation. These companies have argued strongly that competition from Singapore, Shanghai and Hong Kong requires urgent measures if Tokyo is to remain competitive in the global property market. The main opponents have been local governments and local communities that have seen a significant erosion of local legal powers to regulate inner city redevelopment.

By giving cabinet authority to designate regeneration areas, the central government has made it much easier and faster to grant approval for huge

FAR bonuses for redevelopment of inner city sites into high-rise global space. This sidesteps the protests of local residents and the sometimes extended processes of public consultation demanded by local governments. The government hopes this will contribute to the high-rise redevelopment of the low-rise areas of inner Tokyo, provide more housing and office space to allow Tokyo to compete better with other world cities, and restore land development companies to profitability.

4. Conclusions

There are different ways of interpreting this history. It could be argued that Tokyo provides a classic case of globalization impacts on urban change. The last two decades have seen the unremitting encroachment of life space by economic space, repeatedly sponsored and encouraged by the central government in the name of building a competitive global city. While Japan's developmental state history makes it distinctive in many aspects of its relationships between State, society and market, it is possible to argue that in Japan one important impact of global economic integration and increased international competition has been increased pressure for the redevelopment of traditional residential areas to high-rise office space. A significant consequence has been the weakening of the planning protections inner-city communities had gained during the struggles of the 1970s.

On the other hand, it can also be argued that the concept of globalization in Japanese political discourse is primarily used a strategic tool to gain political advantage. In this sense, the stress on the need to compete with Shanghai and Hong Kong in the lobbying by property developers for weaker development regulations, more ad hoc FAR bonuses and greater public subsidy of infrastructure improvements can be interpreted as mere opportunism. The fact that the development industry has gained significant benefits from their use of the globalization threats does, however, indicate the continuing political usefulness of globalization/world city discourses. In the Japanese case, therefore, globalization does not seem to influence urban change primarily through foreign direct investment in urban (re)development, but by providing a convincing political argument for the weakening of local planning controls and participation processes.

What is clear is that since the high point of citizen mobilization over environmental issues and progressive control of local governments in the mid 1970s, communities in inner city areas have, on the whole, been fighting a losing battle against a resurgent property development industry that seeks to redevelop inner city neighborhoods into high-rise towers. Issues of quality of life and urban livability continue to be given short shrift, communities in inner city Tokyo continue to feel pressure, and life space continues to be redeveloped as economic space.

References

Bestor TC (1989) Neighborhood Tokyo. Stanford University Press, Stanford

Calder KE (1988) Crisis and compensation: public policy and political stability in Japan, 1949–1986. Princeton University Press, Princeton

Cybriwsky R (1993) Tokyo. Cities 10(1):2–11
Cybriwsky R (1998) Tokyo: The changing profile of an urban giant. Wiley, Chichester
Deyo FC (ed) (1987) The political economy of the new asian industrialism. Cornell University Press, Ithaca
Douglass M (1988) The transnationalization of urbanization in Japan. International Journal of Urban and Regional Research 12(3):425–454
Douglass M (1993) The 'New' Tokyo story: Restructuring space and the struggle for place in a world city. In: Fujita K, Hill RC (eds) Japanese cities in the world economy. Temple University Press, Philadelphia, pp 83–119
Eade J (1997) Living in the global city: Globalization as local process. Routledge, London
Friedmann J (1986) The world city hypothesis. Development and Change 17:69–84
Friedmann J (1988) Life space and economic space: Contradictions in regional planning, in life space and economic space: Essays in third world planning. Transaction Books, New Brunswick, N.J, pp 93–108
Friedmann J, Wolff G (1982) World city formation: An agenda for research and action. International Journal of Urban and Regional Research 6(3):309–344
Fujita K (1991) A world city and flexible specialization: Restructuring of the Tokyo metropolis. International Journal of Urban and Regional Research 15(1):269–284
Gao B (1997) Economic ideology and Japanese industrial policy: Developmentalism from 1931 to 1965. Cambridge University Press, New York
George TS (2001) Minamata: Pollution and the struggle for democracy. Harvard University Press, Cambridge
Goetz EG, Clarke SE (eds) (1993) The new localism: Comparative urban politics in a global era. Sage, Newbury Park
Hayakawa K, Hirayama Y (1991) The impact of the minkatsu policy on Japanese housing and land use. Environment and Planning D: Society and Space 9:151–164
Hebbert M (1994) Sen-biki amidst Desakota: Urban sprawl and urban planning in Japan. In: Shapira P, Masser I, Edgington DW (eds) Planning for cities and regions in Japan. Liverpool University Press, Liverpool, pp 70–91
Hebbert M, Nakai N (1988) Deregulation of Japanese planning. Town Planning Review 59(4):383–395
Hill RC, Kim JW (2000) Global cities and developmental states: New York, Tokyo and Seoul. Urban Studies 37(12):2167–2195
Honjo M (1984) Key issues of urban development and land management policies in Asian developing countries. In: Honjo M, Inoue T (eds) Urban development policies and land management: Japan and Asia. City of Nagoya, Nagoya, pp 15–35
Huddle N, Reich M, Stiskin N (1975) Island of dreams. Autumn Press, New York
Inamoto Y (1998) The problem of land use and land prices. In: Banno J (ed) The political economy of Japanese society, vol. 2, Internationalization and domestic issues. Oxford University Press, Oxford, pp 229–264
Ishizuka H, Ishida Y (1988) Tokyo, the metropolis of Japan and its urban development. In: Ishizuka H, Ishida Y (eds) Tokyo: Urban growth and planning 1868–1988. Center for Urban Studies 3–35, Tokyo
Jain PC (1991) Green politics and citizens power in Japan. The Zushi Movement. Asian Survey 31(5):559–575
Johnson C (1982) MITI and the Japanese miracle, the growth of industrial policy, 1925–1975. Stanford University Press, Stanford
Knox P, Taylor PJ (eds) (1995) World cities in a world system. Cambridge University Press, New York
Kodama T (1990) The new aspects of housing problems in Tokyo. Osaka City University Economic Review 25(1):1–12
Machimura T (1992) The urban restructuring process in Tokyo in the 1980s: Transforming Tokyo into a world city. International Journal of Urban and Regional Research 16:114–128
Machimura T (1998) Symbolic use of globalization in urban politics in Tokyo. International Journal of Urban and Regional Research 22(2):183–194
McKean M (1981) Environmental protest and citizen politics in Japan. University of California Press, Berkeley
Miyao T (1987) Japan's urban policy. Japanese Economic Studies 15(4):52–66

Miyao T (1991) Japan's urban economy and land policy. Annals of the American Academy of Political and Social Science (513 January):130–138
Morimura M (1994) Change in the Japanese urban planning priorities and the response of urban planners 1960–90. In: University of Tokyo Dept. of Urban Engineering (ed) Contemporary studies in urban environmental management in Japan. Kajima Institute Publishing 8–24, Tokyo
Muramatsu M, Krauss E (1987) The conservative policy line and the development of patterned pluralism. In: Yamamura K, Yasukichi Y (eds) The political economy of Japan, vol. I. The domestic transformation. Stanford University Press, Stanford, pp 516–554
Nakai N (1988) Urbanization promotion and control in metropolitan Japan. Planning Perspectives 3:197–216
Noguchi Y, Poterba JM (eds) (1994) Housing markets in the United States and Japan. University of Chicago Press, Chicago and London
Oizumi E (1994) Property finance in Japan: expansion and collapse of the bubble economy. Environment and Planning A 26(2):199–213
Onishi T (1994) A capacity approach for sustainable urban development: An empirical study. Regional Studies 28(1):39–51
Otake H (1993) The rise and retreat of a neoliberal reform: Controversies over land use policy. In: Allinson G, Sone Y (eds) Political dynamics in contemporary Japan. Cornell University Press, Ithaca, pp 242–263
Pacione M (2001) Urban geography: A global perspective. Routledge, London
Rimmer P (1986) Japan's world cities: Tokyo, Osaka, Nagoya or Tokaido Megalopolis. Development and Change 17:121–158
Saito A (2003) World city formation in capitalist developmental state: Tokyo and the waterfront sub-centre project. Urban Studies 40(2):283–308
Samuels RJ (1983) The politics of regional policy in Japan: Localities incorporated? Princeton University Press, Princeton, New Jersey
Sassen S (1991) The global city: New York, London, Tokyo. Princeton University Press, Princeton, New Jersey
Sorensen A (1999) Land readjustment, urban planning and urban sprawl in the Tokyo metropolitan area. Urban Studies 36(13):2333–2360
Sorensen A (2001a) Building suburbs in Japan: Continuous unplanned change on the urban fringe. Town Planning Review 72(3):247–273
Sorensen A (2001b) Subcentres and satellite cities: Tokyo's 20th century experience of planned polycentrism. International Journal of Planning Studies 6(1):9–32
Sorensen A (2002) The making of urban Japan: Cities and planning from edo to the 21st century. Routledge, London
Tachibanaki T (1992) Higher land prices as a cause of increasing inequality: Changes in wealth distribution and socio-economic effects. In: Haley JO, Yamamura K (eds) Land issues in Japan: A policy failure? Society for Japanese Studies, Seattle, pp 175–194
Ui J (ed) (1992) Industrial pollution in Japan. United Nations University Press, Tokyo
Upham FK (1987) Law and social change in postwar Japan. Harvard University Press, Cambridge
Watanabe Y (1992) The new phase of Japan's land, housing, and pollution problems. Japanese Economic Studies 20(4):30–68

Measuring world city formation – The case of Shanghai

Jianming Cai[1], **Victor F.S. Sit**[2]

[1] Department of Urban and Rural Studies, Institute of Geographical Sciences and Natural Resources Research, Chinese Academy of Sciences, Beijing 100101, China People's Republic (e-mail: caijm@igsnrr.ac.cn)
[2] Department of Geography, University of Hong Kong, Pokfulam Road, Hong Kong, China People's Republic

Abstract. One of the important issues related to world cities studies is the lack of systematic measurement of the formation of world cities. Such a measurement technique would be a useful tool for cities aspiring to attain world city status, especially those cities in Pacific Asia, such as Hong Kong, Singapore, Seoul, and Shanghai. This paper approaches this task by devising a measurement methodology based on quantifiable indicators to generate a World City Index and then uses Shanghai as a case study to test how the city stands compared to 32 current and potential world cities.

JEL Classification: R0, R00, R1, R12

1. Introduction

The existing literature on world cities has focused mainly on the relationship between the world city and globalization, and on qualitative description of city characteristics. Only limited attention has been given to quantitative indices of the formation of the world city. The latter is very important for governments and planners who want to promote their cities to world city status. The post-WWII economic success of the Asian NIEs in the Asian Pacific region has raised hopes that many cities in the region, such as Hong Kong, Singapore, Taipei, Seoul, Bangkok, Kuala Lumpur and even Manila, are on the path to becoming a world city (Chua 1998, Shin and Timberlake 2000; Hill and Kim 2000; Yeoh and Chang 2001). In 1994, the Shanghai Municipal Government supported an international research project on "Shanghai towards the 21st Century". The study recommended becoming a future world city as a strategic goal (Research Team 1998). This has provided the initiative and data for our attempt to device a measurement method to chart the extent to which the city has reached its development towards

---

This paper is a part of the result of the research projects sponsored by the Chinese Academy of Sciences and the National Science Foundation of China with project numbers KZCX2-307 and 40171036.

becoming a world city. In this paper we first propose a descriptive model for measuring the formation of the world city, and then we apply the methodology to the case of Shanghai.

2. Existing measurements of world city formation

Some scholars have attempted to apply quantifiable measurements in their world city studies based on general qualitative descriptions. Such a tendency is increasingly noticeable in recent years, partly due to recognition of the importance of world city studies for planning purposes and partly to the increasing number of scholars of diverse background in this field of research. However, most existing measurements are uni-dimensional and focus either on the economy or infrastructure of relevant cities. Let us briefly review them as follow.

A common economic measure is the number of MNC (multinational corporations) headquarters (Sassen 1991; Holloway and Wheeler 1991; Lyon and Salmon 1995). More emphasis might be given to higher order financial services (Cai 2000). Knox (1995) adds international involvement (e.g., the number of international organizations) and cultural centrality. Others emphasize infrastructure, especially transport capacity (air freight and container shipping (Dick and Rimmer 1993, 1997; Rimmer 1986) or airline linkages (Keeling 1993, 1995).

3. Six Dimensions for measuring world city formation

The quantification of world city formation has relied on a few economic variables (see also Keil 1998; Beaverstock and Taylor 1999; Godfrey and Zhou 1999; Taylor and Catalano 2001; Hill and Kim 2000; Skin and Timberlake 2000). The purpose of this paper is to develop a multidimensional approach that includes more than economic variables, and to apply the methodology to Shanghai in comparison with other leading world cities. The dimensions that we selected are: Politico-economic circumstances; population and skills, economic vitality, enabling infrastructure and overall urban image (for more details, see Cai 2000). These are considered attraction amenities for MNCs and other global firms. These dimensions interact multiplicatively and are not independent. The research problem is to identify the best variables that represent each of these dimensions, a choice that will certainly be restricted by limited data availability.

4. Shanghai as the leading Chinese city

For more than one and half centuries since about 1850 Shanghai had been China's biggest economic center (excluding Hong Kong). This pre-eminence reached its peak in the 1920s–30s when Shanghai became an important international city in East Asia with thriving global and local trade. Under Maoism (1949–1978) in the People's Republic of China, it became more an industrial production center. In 1990 when the Chinese central government decided to open Pudong (former eastern suburb of the city) as the biggest special economic area in the country, the city started rapid overall development under an open door policy (Sit 1995).

For the recent 10 years, it has recorded two-digit overall annual economic growth. As a result, its economic strength and economic controlling power in China have increased (People's Daily 1999; Research Team 1998). More importantly, its role in the country has been changed too. In the eyes of most MNCs, the city is at present the most attractive place for setting up their local control office as well as production facilities in China, though not as a place for their regional headquarters in Asia Pacific. In the eyes of the central and municipal governments, it is not enough for Shanghai to be just China's biggest economic center but it should also regain its previous role in the world and be a world city. For realizing such a goal, they want to fully tap the overall potential of the city. Instead of just developing its industrial economy as it had been done under central planning, other economic sectors, particularly finance and foreign trade, have been actively promoted. Under the new orientation, Shanghai is targeted to be the new flagship leading China into an increasingly more integrated world economy.

To illustrate Shanghai's recent pre-eminent position among the Chinese cities, we have selected 11 key Chinese cities for comparison. The selection is mainly based on their urban population[1] size and their economic strength in 1999.

Table 1 shows that in overall economic power Shanghai is far stronger than any other key cities in China. Its GDP value was larger than the combined values of the other three centrally-administrated municipalities, Beijing, Tianjin and Chongqing. It was also much larger than the combined values of Guangzhou and Shenzhen, the most important cities in the Pearl River Delta of the southern province of Guangdong.

Table 1. Comparison of overall economic strength among Chinese key cities (1999)

Cities	Population (million)	Area of city proper (sq.km.)	Built-up area (sq.km.)	GDP (billion RMB)	GDP per capita (RMB)	GDP per city proper area (RMB/sq.km.)
Shanghai	11.1	3924	550	361.6	32577	9215
Beijing	10.5	6496	488	182.5	17381	2809
Tianjin	6.0	4335	378	114.5	19083	2641
Chongqing	8.4	12449	243	57.2	6810	459
Guangzhou	4.1	1444	284	145.1	35390	10048
Shenzhen	1.2	1949	132	143.7	119750	7488
Nanjing	2.8	1026	194	67.5	24107	6579
Hangzhou	1.8	683	171	60.5	33611	8858
Shenyang	4.8	3495	202	84.3	17563	2412
Dalian	2.6	2415	234	58.6	22538	2427
Wuhan	7.4	8467	208	108.6	14676	1283

Source: Urban Statistical Yearbook of China 2000, China Statistics Press, 2000, Beijing.

[1]Urban population here refers to the permanent household registered population without including the city's rural population and temporary migrants within its administrative boundary. Therefore, the population size in cities of Shanghai, Beijing, Guangzhou and Shenzhen, which have relatively larger numbers of such in-migrants, have been underestimated. Their in-migrants are all over 2 millions at present.

In terms of "GDP per city proper area", Shanghai's lead among China's key cities is also obvious. As a spatially compact city, the urban proper of the city is still relatively small comparing with other key cities, considering its large population and economic achievement. Shanghai is not only outstanding in its overall economic strength, but also relatively high in land economic efficiency because of high residential and employment densities.

Shanghai also leads urban China in many other economic indicators (Table 2). With the largest total volume of wholesale and retail sales and high values in "residents' savings" and "total premium income", it is undoubtedly the biggest trading center and market in China, moderately challenged by Beijing and Guangzhou. This is one of the reasons for the city's attraction for foreign direct investment (FDI). Since 1990, the city has accounted for up to 15% of the country's total FDI and has dwarfed other Chinese cities.

As the biggest industrial center, Shanghai used to be the most important revenue generator in Maoist China when its contribution accounted for one sixth of the country's total. Since 1978, the revenue share of the city in the country has declined, but is still the highest in the country. The local revenue contribution is important, as the municipal government has become more important than the central government in financing infrastructure.

Considering its larger stock market (comparing with Shenzhen) and possession of China's only foreign exchange center, Shanghai's economic control of the country is even more distinctive. However, Beijing may pose some challenge to Shanghai in the near future because of the high concentration of headquarters of China's banks and pronounced information resources there. Yet as the new market-oriented economic system expands, Shanghai's advantage in financial services should be consolidated even more. China's accession to the World Trade Organization should enable the city to continue its leading role in the more open and globalized economy of China.

To measure the pre-eminence of Shanghai in urban China in these economic aspects more precisely, we adopt Shanghai's index as 100 and compare the results with cities ranking second and third highest in the country. Table 3

Table 2. Comparison by selected economic aspects in 1999 (billion RMB)

Cities	Total volume of wholesale and retail sales	Total retail sales	Utilized FDI (bil. $US)	Fiscal revenue	Fiscal expenses	Residents' savings	Premium income
Shanghai	367.6	151.3	3.05	43.2	54.6	259.7	10.3
Beijing	229.1	128.6	1.15	10.7	14.7	242.9	8.6
Tianjin	69.3	49.9	2.53*	10.3	14.5	102.5	2.9
Chongqing	57.6	30.4	0.29	6.4	11.0	41.9	2.5
Guangzhou	232.5	83.9	2.26	15.6	19.5	160.2	5.8
Shenzhen	68.5	46.7	1.78	18.5	21.2	95.2	3.5
Nanjing	98.3	31.0	0.56	5.8	6.1	48.2	2.6
Hangzhou	129.4	21.1	0.30	2.9	3.4	43.4	2.2
Shenyang	126.1	48.8	1.02	5.5	7.4	84.3	2.1
Dalian	57.2	35.4	1.09	6.3	7.2	57.8	1.2
Wuhan	45.1	54.0	0.48	6.0	7.4	57.5	2.4

Source: Same as Table 1.
*Contracted FDI in billion $US.

demonstrates that Shanghai clearly stands out. Beijing, Guangzhou and Shenzhen are the other potential competitors.

As the two biggest air transport hubs in China, Shanghai and Beijing have given priority on the construction of their international linkages. In terms of international air transport and telecommunications, they have left other cities far behind (Table 4). The completion of the Pudong New International Airport, construction of the new seaport and rapid increase of telecommunications capacity will further consolidate and strengthen Shanghai's

Table 3. Shanghai's pre-eminence in the economic dimension in urban China

Indicators	Shanghai's value	2nd rank city	As % of Shanghai	3rd rank city	As % of Shanghai
Population	11.1	Beijing	94.6	Chongqing	75.7
Total GDP	361.6	Beijing	50.5	Guangzhou	40.1
Total volume of wholesale & retail sales	367.6	Guangzhou	63.2	Beijing	62.3
Total retail sales of merchandise	151.3	Beijing	85.0	Guangzhou	55.5
Actual utilized FDI	3.05	Guangzhou	74.1	Shenzhen	58.4
Fiscal revenue	43.2	Shenzhen	42.8	Guangzhou	36.1
Fiscal expense	54.6	Shenzhen	38.8	Guangzhou	35.7
Residents savings	259.7	Beijing	93.5	Guangzhou	61.7
Total volume of insurance	10.3	Beijing	83.5	Guangzhou	56.3

Source: Calculated from Table 1 and Table 2.

Table 4. Comparisons of selected aspects

Cities	Urban infrastructure in 1997				Other aspects in 1999			
	No. of airports	No. of international flights per week	Total freight volume (mil. Tonnes)	No. of telephones per 100 persons	% of tertiary industry in employment	% of tertiary industry in GDP	No. of theaters and cinemas	SO_2 ton per sq. km.
Shanghai	2	290	406.4	50	46.5	49.8	43	79.2
Beijing	1	361	341.3	20	62.9	59.0	209	24.9
Tianjin	1	23	244.6	27	46.0	49.2	28	29.5
Chongqing	1		239.8	13	45.4	42.1	25	NA
Wuhan	1		126.9	28	60.8	57.5	14	59.8
Shenyang	1	28	145.5	22	44.3	48.3	118	13.8
Guangzhou	1	73	234.0	48	50.0	51.2	96	112.9
Nanjing	1		117.1	43	55.2	51.3	14	53.4
Dalian	1	40	186.3	31	47.6	52.8	26	36.0
Hangzhou	1		16.7	38	52.4	51.6	7	34.0
Shenzhen	1		38.6	131*	52.7	48.7	69	13.7

Source: Compiled by authors from various sources.

*The number could be much overestimated considering its underestimated actual urban population (about 3.5 million, acording to the estimation of author based on some investigations).

advantage over Beijing. However, Beijing's successful bid for the Olympics 2008 will give it infrastructure investment advantages over the next five years.

Because of its long-held prominence as an industrial node, Shanghai remains somewhat underdeveloped in services and cultural amenities (Table 4). It also is the second-worst city for pollution, where Guangzhou leads.

5. Testing the six-dimensional model on Shanghai

For the case of Shanghai and for most existing and potential world cities, data are available only for selected variables. The ones chosen are listed in Table 5. The final data set covers 32 potential world cities plus Shanghai (Table 6). The purpose is to explore whether our measurement methodology generates a ranking close to standard existing rankings and to illustrate where Shanghai stands in such a world city scale.

Table 5. Selected attributes and their weights

Dimensions (weights)	Attributes (weights)*	Original data scale
D1, politico-economic system (1/6, 0.1, 0.1)	1. D11, Urban primacy classification (0.3)	Ordinal
	2. D12, State Economic power (GDP) (0.5)	Ratio
	3. D13, Urbanization degree (0.2)	Ratio
D2, population and skills (1/6, 0.1, 0.1)	1. D21, Total urban population (0.3)	Ratio
	2. D22, % of population at age 60+ (0.1)	Ratio
	3. D23, College students per 10000 (0.4)	Ratio
	4. D24, Ratio of middle school student enrollment (middleschool student/population at age 12–19) (0.2)	Ratio
D3, economic vitality (1/6, 0.3, 0.35)	1. D31, GDP per capita (0.1)	Ratio
	2. D32, Stock value (0.3)	Ratio
	3. D33, Number of MNCs' headquarters (Fortune Global 500) (0.3)	Ratio
	4. D34, % of tertiary employment (0.1)	Ratio
	5. D35, Advertising value (0.2)	Ratio
D4, enabling infrastructure (1/6, 0.15, 0.2)	1. D41, Air passengers (0.3)	Ratio
	2. D42, Air cargo (0.2)	Ratio
	3. D43, Water-borne cargo (0.15)	Ratio
	4. D44, Telephone number per 100 persons (0.25)	Ratio
	5. D45, Electric power consumption per capita (0.1)	Ratio
D5, living environment (1/6, 0.15, 0.1)	1. D51, Average rooms per household (0.15)	Ratio
	2. D52, Doctors per 1000 persons (0.15)	Ratio
	3. D53, Living cost index (0.3)	Ordinal
	4. D54, Life quality index (0.4)	Ordinal
D6, overall image (1/6, 0.2, 0.15)	1. D61, General impression classification	Ordinal

* An explanation of the weights of attributes is presented in the text.
Source: Cai (2000).

Table 6. World city index for 33 Cities

World cities	Indices of six dimensions						Aggregate index
	D1	D2	D3	D4	D5	D6	
New York	9	8	9	9	5	9	93.8
Tokyo	9	8	8	9	2	8	83.8
London	8	8	7	8	2	8	75.6
Paris	7	9	7	7	3	7	72.5
Chicago	9	7	5	8	6	6	68.1
Los Angeles	9	6	5	9	3	6	65.6
Sa Francisco	9	6	3	7	7	6	56.9
Frankfurt	7	4	5	6	3	6	53.1
Osaka	9	8	4	5	3	5	51.9
Toronto	6	6	4	4	7	6	50.0
Montreal	6	7	3	4	8	5	46.3
Washington	9	5	3	3	6	5	42.5
Amsterdam	4	4	4	5	4	5	41.9
Hong Kong	8	3	2	8	1	5	40.6
Boston	9	6	3	2	5	5	40.0
Sydney	5	4	3	2	9	5	37.5
Seoul	6	8	3	4	1	4	36.9
Seattle	9	3	2	3	8	4	36.3
Miami	9	4	1	5	6	4	35.6
Vancouver	6	5	1	4	8	5	35.0
Zurich	4	3	4	3	5	4	35.0
Milan	5	4	4	2	2	5	33.1
Munich	7	4	3	2	3	4	30.6
Houston	9	4	1	3	7	3	30.0
Madrid	5	5	2	3	5	4	30.0
Singapore	6	3	1	5	3	5	28.8
Berlin	7	4	1	2	3	5	23.8
Moscow	5	5	1	1	7	2	19.4
Shanghai	**4**	**6**	**1***	**3**	**1**	**4**	**19.4**
Rome	5	4	1	2	2	4	18.1
Bonn	7	3	1	2	3	2	16.9
Sao Paulo	6	4	1	1	2	1	11.3
Mexico City	5	5	1	1	1	1	10.0

Source: Compiled from (Cai 2000).
* The international economic controlling power of Shanghai here is much exaggerated due to the limited choice of the scaling classification. In fact, the international economic controlling power of Shanghai is only one tenth of Singapore in the original data but both are assigned 1 here, the minimum scaling number we have.

If we had a complete data set with all the desired attributes, we could identify impartial weights via factor analysis. In the absence of this approach, our weights are arbitrary, both for the attributes and the dimensions. They were based on commonsense, references to other studies and peer discussions. However, at the dimensional level, we compared three alternative weighting systems: Equal weights, unequal weights reflecting discussions in the literature, and unequal weights giving even higher priority to economic vitality and enabling infrastructure. We chose the last of these in terms of presentation of results.

For measuring cities by a specific dimension i, we used the following equation:

$$C_{id} = (\sum_{j=1}^{m} W_j C_{ij} - V_{\min}) \times 100/(V_{\max} - V_{\min}) \qquad (1)$$

where, C_{id} is the evaluation of city i for dimension d, falling between 0–100;
W_j is the assigned weight for attribute j;
C_{ij} is the value of city i for attribute j (1,2,3,...);
$V_{\max}$ is the maximum assigned value for the attribute, usually 9;
$V_{\min}$ is the minimum assigned value for the attribute, usually 1;
m is the number of attributes for dimension d.

For a comprehensive assessment of city i, we need to re-scale each specific dimension by assigning it a nominal value according to its previous evaluation. We then apply Eq. 1 again to conduct the six-dimensional assessment. Of course, the arbitrarily assigned weights, to some extent based on subjective judgment, may result in some distortion. Nevertheless, it is similar to approaches adopted elsewhere, e.g., in the Global Competitiveness Report series by the Institute of International Management Development of Switzerland.

6. Shanghai at an early stage of world city formation?

Our calculations have generated indices for the individual dimensions and an aggregate index in each of the 33 cities (Table 6). This aggregate index might be labeled as a "World City Index" (WCI), and these are presented in rank order.

We then applied a cluster analysis to assign the cities into four levels: Comprehensive world cities (Level 1:New York, Tokyo, London and Paris with a WCI > 70); other world cities (Level 2: WCI > 50, < 70, of which there are six members); A. sub-world cities (Level 3: WCI > 30, < 50 with 15 members); and B. sub-world cities (Level: WCI < 30, with 8 members, including Shanghai, ranked 29 in the overall list). Cities at Level 1 and Level 2 are genuine world cities, pre-eminent in almost all the six dimensions. Cities at Level 3 are close to genuine world cities, with regional if not global influence. Level 4 cities are in the early stages of world city formation, with international aspects but largely influential in their home countries.

As for Shanghai, it is clearly at an early stage. It ranks low in terms of the politico-economic system, despite the increasing market orientation of China. Its best score was in terms of population and skills (largely because of its population size), while economic vitality remains modest despite relatively rapid economic growth. Its stock of infrasture compares reasonably well with other emerging cities, but it ranks very low internationally in terms of the quality of its living environment (despite comparing well with other large Chinese cities). Its overall urban image is reasonably good, at least in a regional context.

7. A five-city comparison with Shanghai

Next, we compare Shanghai with five world cities, i.e. New York, London, Tokyo (Level 1 cities) and Hong Kong and Singapore (direct competitors with Shanghai in Pacific Asia. Table 7 shows the results in terms of attributes, while Table 8 shows ratio indices for Shanghai relative to the average for the two sub-groups for most of these attributes. Comparing across attributes,

Shanghai appears to have reached levels in the 30–40% range of the Hong Kong-Singapore average and 10–15% of the major world city average. It stands well in terms of population size and port capacity. Its high score in terms of doctors per capita is, in part, an artifact of the Chinese medical (and, incidentally, higher educational) system, where large cities provide services over a large region, not merely locally. In terms of its aspirations to be a world city, it continues to lag the others severely in terms of the key economic

Table 7. Comparisons between Shanghai and selected world cities

Attributes	SH	NY	LD	TK	HK	SG
D13: Urbanization degree (%)	72*	76	89	77	95	100
D21: Total population (mil. 1996)	13.7	16.4	7.6	27.2	5.9	3.4
D22: % of population at age 60+	14.2	17.4	19.7	17.1	13.4	9.4
D23: College student per 10,000 persons	118*	516	n/a	582	116	173
D24: Ratio of high middle school attendance	75.9**	95	90	97	86	92
D31: GDP per capita (US$, 1994)	3400*	25468	16853	37211	21650	23532
D32: Stockvalue (bil. Pounds 1997.12.31)	65	5463.4	1251.4	1287.5	250.5	64.6
D33: Number of MNCs headquarters (Fortune Global 500)	0	38	27	78	0	0
D34: % of tertiary employment	40.5	88.7	86.2	76.2	78.5	65.8
D41: Air passenger in mil. in 1997	6.7	57.6	58.0	49.3	15.8	15.8
D42: Air cargo in 1997 (10,000 short tonnes)	48	298.7	139.8	191.6	199.8	149.7
D431: Port handling volume in 10,000 tonnes in 1995	16400*	n/a	5136	7369	12718	30548
D432: Port container handling volume in 10,000 TEUs in 1996	253*	227	n/a	230	1341	1295
D433: Container transport rank in 1996	17	12	n/a	11	1	2
D44: Telephone per 100 persons	23	56.1	91.0	77.2	68.3	41.2
D45: Electricity consumption per Capita (kwh)	290.2	1152	1576	2901	1184	744
D51: Average rooms per household in 1994	<2***	5.2	4.0	4.2	2.3	3.0
D53: Doctors per 1,000 persons	3.9*	4	1.9	3.9	1.5	1.7

Note: SH = Shanghai; NY = New York; LD = London; TK = Tokyo; HK = Hong Kong; SG = Singapore

D(i) here refers to the Dimensions we have proposed in our descriptive model. (i) stands for the dimension no.

* Refers to data in 1997.

** The ratio of junior middle school attendance in Shanghai was 98.5% in 1990.

*** In 1997, the average living room area per person in Shanghai was around 10 sq.m. and the average per persons per household was 2.8 persons. Accordingly, the total household area in average is around 28 sq. m.. Thus we may assume that in average, the rooms per household in Shanghai is <2.

Source: Cai (2000).

Table 8. Shanghai's position compared to the selected world cities %

Attributes	SH/(HK-SG)	SH/(NY-LD-TK)
D21: Total population (mil. 1996)	295	80
D22: % of population at age 60+	119	76
D23: College student per 10,000 persons	86	21
D24: Ratio of high middle school attendance	86	80
D31: GDP per capita (US$, 1994)	15	11
D32: Stock value (bil. Ponds 1997.12.31)	41	2
D34: % of tertiary employment	55	50
D41: Air passenger in mil. in 1997	42	12
D42: Air cargo in 1997 (10,000 short tonnes)	28	23
D431: Port handling volume in 10,000 tonnes in 1995	76	262
D432: Port container handling volume in 10,000 TEUs in 1996	19	111
D44: Telephone per 100 persons	41	33
D45: Electricity consumption per capita (kwh)	33	12
D51: Average rooms per household in 1994	76	43
D53: Doctors per 1,000 persons	239	99

variables. Continuing the last decade's investment in large-scale infrastructure may be a prerequisite for propelling Shanghai up the rank order of world cities.

8. Discussions and conclusion

8.1. Appraising the six-dimensional model

Most measurements of world city status have focused on economic dimensions and infrastructure aspects, in which the number of MNC headquarters, financial concentration and air transportation are the most popular and widely applied indices. However, world cities possess many other important aspects not reflected in the more common indices. Hence, we developed a six-dimensional model to fill the gap in this research field.

As indicated before, there are various classifications of world cities provided by different scholars and institutions, such as Friedmann, Thrift, Gottmann and LPAC and lately the works of Taylor, Beaverstock and Taylor, and Godfrey and Zhou. Among them, the list of world cities provided by Friedmann (1995) is most comprehensive and generally accepted. Accordingly, we have compared our classification with that of Friedmann's results to test our six-dimension methodology in a four-level hierarchy. We found that out of 26 identical selected world cities, there are only 9 cities falling into the same categories in both lists. The t-test on the paired samples shown a correlation coefficient of only 0.45 with a significance of 0.19. In Friedmann's classification, cities like Paris, Chicago, San Francisco, Hong Kong, Toronto and Osaka are ranked less important in the world urban hierarchy, while cities like Singapore, Mexico City, Sao Paulo and Miami occupied higher ranks in the list compared with our list. His ranking appears to deviate more than ours from general perceptions of these world cities. This may suggest that a quantitative multidimensional approach is more satisfactory than Friedmann's more subjective classification.

With respect to our six dimensions, we would argue that a compatible politico-economic system is a prerequisite; population and skills are basic requirements; economic vitality is the engine of growth; enabling infrastructure is a facilitator and boost; the living environment is a symbol of maturity; and the overall image is the indicator of the city's eminence.

Of course, there remain some qualifications to our research. The selected variables on each dimension are limited by available databases, especially internationally. Also, the weights we chose are arbitrary. Even our study may give too much attention to economic factors; for example, Osaka and Toronto are ranked above Washington, D.C. There is a need for more research, a prerequisite of which may be building a stronger comparable world urban database.

8.2. Shanghai's position in world city formation

Economic globalization is speeding up and the focus of world economic growth is shifting towards the Asia-Pacific region. As the leading economic center in China, Shanghai enjoys the most favorable location within the country for international trade, and it is likely regain its position as one of the leading cities in the world urban system as it was in the late 19th and early 20th century. Encouraged by both the Chinese central government and Shanghai municipal government, Shanghai aims to catch up with Hong Kong and Singapore by the year 2010, and New York by the year 2040–2050 as a world class city.

Shanghai is pre-eminent compared to other key Chinese cities, especially in the dimensions of economic vitality and enabling infrastructure. However, comparing it to other world cities suggests it has a long way to go. Judged by key indicators, Shanghai has reached about 30–40% of the level of the newly emerged world cities i.e., Hong Kong and Singapore, and only 10–15% of the level of the mature world cities, i.e., New York, London and Tokyo. Nevertheless, with its large economic size, rapid economic growth and relatively sophisticated infrastructure, Shanghai has attained the early stage in world city formation, despite a potential challenge from Beijing. If economic vitality and enabling infrastructure are the most critical dimensions for world city formation, the entry of China into WTO and its increasing exposure to globalization influences, there are good prospects for a world city in China, and Shanghai remains the most promising candidate.

References

Beaverstock JV, Taylor PJ (1999) A roster of world cities. Cities 12(6):445–458

Cai J (2000) Measuring the formation of world cities: Case of Shanghai. Ph.D. thesis, The University of Hong Kong

Chua B-H (1998) World cities, globalization and the spread of consumerism: A view from Singapore. Urban Studies 35(5–6):981–1000

Cybriwsky RA (1998) Tokyo: The Shogun's city at the twenty first century. J Wiley, Chichester

Dick H, Rimmer PJ (1993) The tans-pacific economy: An approach to spatial structure. Asian Geographer 12(1 & 2):5–9

Godfrey BJ, Zhou Y (1999) Ranking world cities: Multinational corporations and the global urban hierarchy. Urban Geography 30(3):268–281

Hill RC, Kim JW (2000) Global cities and developmental status: New York, Tokyo and Seoul. Urban Studies 37(12):2167–2195

Holloway SR, Wheeler JO (1991) Corporate headquarters relocation and changes in metropolitan corporate dominance, 1980–1987. Economic Geography 67:1, Clark University

Keeling DJ (1993) Transport and regional development in Argentina: Structural deficiencies and patterns of network evolution. Yearbook of the Conference of Latin Americanist Geographers 19:25–34

Keeling DJ (1995) Transport and the world city paradigm. In: Knox PL, Taylor PL (eds) World cities in a world system. Cambridge University Press, cambridge, pp 115–131

Keil R (1998) Globalization makes states: Perspectives of local governance in the age of the world city. Review of International Political Economy 5(4):616–646

Knox PL (1995) World cities in a world-system. In: Knox PL, Taylor PL (eds) world cities in a world system. Cambridge University Press, Cambridge, pp 3–20

Lyons D, Salmon S (1995) World cities, multinational corporations, and urban hierarchy: The case of the United States. In: Knox PL, Taylor PL (eds) world cities in a world system. Cambridge University Press, Cambridge, pp 98–114

People's Daily (Beijing)(1999.04.30) Shanghai will be constructed as China's largest financial center from five aspects (in Chinese: shang hai jiang cong wu fang mian jian she wo guo zui da ji rong zhong xin) http://www.peopledaily.com.cn/lbw/199904/30/ 99043019013.html

Ren M-e Guobao Y (1998) Factors affecting port development in China, with special reference to Shanghai international shipping center. Acta Geographica Sinica 53(3)

Research Team (1998) Shanghai economy: Long-term trend and 1998 forecast (in Chinese: shang hai jing ji: chang qi zeng zhang de qu shi yu 1998 nian yu ce). Shanghai Financial and Economic University Press, Shanghai

Rimmer PJ (1997) The trans-pacific oceanic economy revisted. Tijdschrift voor economische en sociale geografie (TESG) (Journal of Economic and Social Geography). Special Issue: The dynamics of The Asian Pacific Rim, Koninklijk Nederlands Aardrijkskundig Genootschap 88(5)

Sassen S (1991) The global city: New York, London, Tokyo. Princeton University Press, Princeton

Shin K-H, Timberlake M (2000) Urban studies 37(12):2257–2285

Short JR, Kim Y-H (1999) Globalization and the city. Addison Wesley Longman Limited, New York

Sit VFS (1995) Shanghai's role in China's modernization: An historical review. Asian Geographer 14(1):14–27

Sit VFS, Cai J (1998) Economic globalization, MNCs and the relevant theories (in Chinese). Economic Geography 18(1):1–7

Taylor PJ (2000) World cities and territorial states under conditions of economic globalization. Political Geography 19:5–32

Widmayer P, Greenburg G (1998) Putting our minds together: The digital network infrastructure and metropolitan Chicago. Information Technology, Northwestern University, Illinois, http:/ www.nwu.edu/it/metrochicago/

Yeoh BSA, Chang TC (2001) Globalizing Singapore: Debating transnational flows in the city. Urban Studies 38(7):1025–1044

Karachi – a case of asymmetric inclusion in the current globalization?

Syed Ayub Qutub

Pakistan Institute for Environment-Development Action Research (PIEDAR) 1st Floor, 64-E, Masco Plaza, Blue Area, Islamabad, Pakistan (e-mail: saqutub@yahoo.com)

Abstract. Karachi is a mega-city and the only seaport of a populous country. It contains a concentration of Pakistan's financial and industrial sectors. However, it does not have any of the advanced productive service functions associated with a world city; neither does it show any evidence of developing them. Several scholars have suggested that the various forms of globalization – trade liberalization, development assistance, global communications, economic migration, and international terror/organized crime – have had negative impacts on the economics and livability of Karachi. By critiquing the writings of the city's intellectuals, polling the intentions of investors, and observing the actual practices of its traditional and non-traditional administrators, this paper seeks to triangulate perceptions of what has thwarted development. Flawed governance and national policies emerge as the root causes. The lack of mechanisms for business disputes resolution, low levels of education and awareness, and unstable energy supplies are the main operational obstacles to investment in Karachi. The uncertain law and order is a pervasive background factor. Should these issues be addressed simultaneously or would a strategic intervention suffice for progressive change?

1. Scope of inquiry, some definitions and sources

> *"The city acts to draw surrounding areas into the net of urban influence through the pervasive actions of her intellectual, administrative, and enterprising classes" (Friedmann 1961).*

Karachi has a 275 years old history and 11 million living stories waiting to be heard [1]. A leading team of scholar-activists has recently attempted to present its understanding of Karachi (Hasan 2000). Building a little upon existing

---

[1]Karachi was founded in 1729 (by Hindu merchants) when Karak Bunder on the Hub River silted up; the population of the four districts comprising Karachi was 9.86 million in the census of March 1998, which is estimated to have grown to 10.64 million in 2001 (National Institute of Population Studies).

research, this paper is limited in its scope to appraising the impact of globalization on the development of Karachi, to assessing the obstacles to investment in the city and to some speculations about the pathways to sound and equitable urban development.[2]

What is globalization? Peter Taylor states that at the core of the idea of globalization is the notion of the enhanced importance of trans-state processes (Taylor 2000). Saskia Sassen says that while there have long been cross-border economic processes – flows of capital, labor, goods, raw materials, travelers – in the last hundred years, it was the inter-state system which was the dominant organizational form for cross-border flows (Sassen 2002). In the last decade, this condition has changed dramatically as a result of privatization, deregulation, the opening up of national economies to foreign firms and the growing participation of national economic actors in global markets.

Yet, Schuurman warns that despite all the forms of glob-talk, globalization is essentially the uneven global spread of capitalism and modernity (Schuurman 2001). It is not a new phenomenon[3]. There has been a marked downturn in the share of developing countries in the world economy since the beginning of the 1980s. Despite the impoverishment, there have been many other ways that developing countries are included in global processes: through structural adjustment programs, global communications, development cooperation, and so on. Nederveen Pieterse calls these "asymmetrical inclusions" (Pieterse 1996).

For the operational purposes of this paper, I define globalization as consisting of foreign direct investment, trade liberalization, structural adjustment programs and development assistance, global communications, economic migration and international terror along with organized crime. While the other aspects are reviewed in Sect. 2, foreign direct investment is the subject of a major hypothesis of this paper and is addressed separately in Sect. 3. Urban development and governance are dealt with in Sect. 4.

What are advanced productive services? Sassen writes that the emergence of global markets for finance and specialized services and the growth of investment as a major type of international transaction have contributed to the expansion in command functions and in the demand for specialized services for firms. By central functions, she means not only the top-level headquarters but rather all the top-level financial, legal, accounting, managerial, executive and planning functions necessary to run a corporate organization operating in more than one country, and increasingly in several countries. This "corporate services complex that is network of financial, legal, accounting and advertising firms" are the core of advanced productive services.

---

[2]In preference to 'sustainable development.' See, for example, Peter Marcuse in Environment and Urbanization, 1999, for why sustainable development may be less appropriate in an urban context with gross inequities.

[3]The previous peaks of globalization (measured as ratio of transnational investment to trade) occurred during 1870 – 1914, associated with imperialism and UK's economic hegemony; and during the 1950–60s, with the USA as the dominant economic power (Oman, Nayyar quoted in Schuurman).

What is the world city hypothesis? According to Taylor, world cities are concentrations of monopoly power based on advanced producer services. In such services as finance, accountancy, and corporate law, practitioners are not just servicing 'global' cities; they are creating new products based on their unique collective knowledge. Production is geared to quality rather than quantity so that instead of the usual market economies of scale, a monopoly 'economy of variety' is created. In this way, assets are created which cannot be easily imitated elsewhere. Thus world cities have prospered despite potential economic decentralization through distance-shrinking technologies.

Taylor lists 55 world cities and the nation-states with which they are associated. In the array of nation-states by size of economy, Pakistan is the largest national economy not to have a city with any minimal evidence of emerging advanced productive services. On the contrary, there are 14 nation-states with smaller GDPs that have a city providing some degree of global service functions.

Equipped with these definitions and information, Sect. 2 reviews some recent perceptions of the problems of Karachi under the conditions of contemporary globalization. The review is restricted to selected books and articles about the impact of globalization on the development of Karachi. This is a twice-filtered approach to reality in a traditionally oral, and now increasingly, TV and cable oriented culture. However, some of the scholar-activists whose works I have reviewed believe in participatory action learning. Their books and reports are based on observing and talking to people. This mitigates to a degree the narrowness of sources for this section. Section 3 is based on the responses of 48 entrepreneurs (22 abroad, 26 living in Karachi) to a survey undertaken for this paper. The respondents have an average of 12 years experience in running businesses and together claim to employ more than 6,000 professionals. Section 4 draws largely on a narration by a retired Army colonel involved in Operation Clean-up, and on the writings of Dr. Akhtar Hameed Khan on the Orangi Pilot Project. Finally, I draw some conclusions with reference to the question posed in the title of this paper.

2. Impacts of globalization on Karachi

> *"Every city is to some degree a center of high culture and intellectual life, and it is principally the intellectuals who are involved in keeping active and if necessary in transforming, the cultural traditions they inherit"(Friedmann 1961)*

2.1. The changing informal sector under trade liberalization

Arif Hasan describes how much Karachi's population relies on the informal sector for housing, water and sanitation, healthcare, education and employment (Hasan 2002). He argues that the changes brought about by trade liberalization include the decline of light engineering (unable to compete with imports), and of carpet and textiles production (owing to increased electricity charges). He asserts that while the informal organizations and the middlemen that manage them will no longer be able to bridge the gap between the needs and aspirations of most of the population, there is no sign of new private investment. As such, he forecasts growing unemployment and widening inequalities.

Hasan admits his paper is not the result of scientific research, more a result of observation and dialogue with informal sector operators and residents of informal settlements. Yet, it is an appealing thesis. The arguments should be tested for internal validity and matched with external facts at several levels. Has textile production in the power loom sector in Karachi really declined? Has the decline of lathe machine operations owing to imported intermediate goods not been compensated for by more production of final goods in the light engineering sector based on the cheaper but better quality components? What is the net impact on small enterprises of higher tariffs but more stable electric supply?

2.2. International development assistance

David Sattherwaite has carefully explicated the inherent limitations on the effectiveness of aid agencies in reducing urban poverty (Satterthwaite 2001). He argues that the official aid agencies and development banks do not implement projects, they fund others to do so. They are only as effective as the institutions they fund, generally government ministries and agencies. The World Bank and regional development banks are banks. They make capital available to member governments, whether or not the member governments are effective with regard to poverty reduction. The need to lend money often conflicts with the best development course, which is for recipient governments to keep down capital expenditures. Yet, governments are tempted to take project loans for their macro-economic and budgetary support implications. He describes how a $ 70 million loan from the Asian Development Bank (ABD) for a part of the Greater Karachi Sewerage Plan was not actually needed but pushed by the federal and provincial bureaucracy. The need for capacity building of partner agencies is increasingly recognized. However, development agencies are constrained by their limited knowledge of local conditions and by the need for a lengthy and consistent process of institutional transformation.

On the other hand, the Asian Coalition for Housing Rights (ACHR) has detailed the constituent elements of "urban infrastructure boondoggles" and the "international tender scam" perpetuated by the World Bank and the ADB in Karachi and other Asian cities (ACHR 2001). ACHR points out that 52% of Pakistan's budget goes into servicing foreign loans. Over the past 18 years, the Karachi Water and Sewerage Board (KWSB) has accumulated a debt of 46 billion rupees to finance a series of large sewerage projects, which treat less than 12% of the city's sewage. ACHR reports that the ADB funded projects of KWSB superimpose entirely new sewage systems ignoring existing sewers and natural drains. They entail use of expensive and inappropriate technology. The designs by foreign consultants call for pumping sewage uphill over long distances to centralized treatment plants. They are to be built by foreign contractors at five to 15 times the local rates. Because the KWSB has not yet begun paying back past loans, provincial revenues badly needed for education and health are being increasingly diverted to servicing the debt.

The limitations of international agencies pointed out by Satterthwaite require precise and well thought out responses, such as creating platforms for institutional reform rather than projects for capacity building. On the other hand, the critique by ACHR provides its own solution; get local experts to design alternative better plans and mobilize collective action by many local groups so that government says no thanks to more loans, and implements the projects through local resources and technology.

2.3. Global communications

According to the 1998 census, 79% of Karachi households said that television was their main source of information, and Arif Hasan reports that more than 50% of them have access to some form of cable television. Informal enterprise has made varieties of entertainment and news available to homes in the low-income settlements of Karachi. It has undoubtedly brought about a clash of values and cultural confusion. It has also brought about a generation gap, which seems presently unbridgeable. Liberalization and the communications revolution have also brought the "corporate culture to Karachi". While scornful of the corporate golf clubs and recreational facilities, Hasan also appears unhappy with the emerging shallow consumerism of the lower- and middle- income classes. He is worried both by the large aspiration-means gap and by the fact that the informal sector appears to be successfully filling up that gap through pirated videos and audiocassettes, for example.

Of particular significance among the messages coming through the enhanced global mediums are value-loaded buzzwords. Words like 'modern', and catchy phrases such as 'sustainable development' have huge connotations, particularly for the self-image of an individual or community. One such concept ('social capital' popularized by Robert Putnam of Harvard) has recently been deconstructed in the context of local government in Karachi. Farhan Anwar finds Karachi breeding 'negative' social capital (Anwar 2002). There is not much commonality of interest among the dominating forms of social capital in the city. Exclusive groups are engaged in turf battles over the acquisition of public services, land, trade, or quite simply street power. A vast majority of the powerful forms of social mobilization is based on *biradari* (clan) linkages or ethnic, linguistic and religious bonding and, in many cases, are criminally oriented. Do powerful political parties serving communal interests, he asks, qualify as social capital? What about the private transporters association that provides jobs and housing but is in the control of a particular ethnic group? These difficult questions cannot be answered by wallet dropping experiments to quantify the 'trust' level of a society. But the results can validate and spur the urge of city youth to emigrate.

Pregnant ideas have not only come from the West. Pakistani migrants returning from work in the Middle East have brought back with them reinforced concepts of personal piety and charity but also of pan-Islamic society and governance that resonate strongly, especially among the lower-middle class of society. Political struggles among the Islamic countries have also been extended into Pakistan in the form of sectarian strife. Arabian and Iranian sponsors have liberally financed the political organizations and militant wings of affiliated sects. Thus traditions of sectarian harmony and tolerance that held long sway in this land have been cast aside. Karachi as home to various religious groups is one of the centers of sectarian trouble in Pakistan.

2.4. Economic migration

In their paper on promoting sustainable livelihoods for coastal fisher-folk, Aly Ercelawn et al quote the following from women of a marginalized fishing community of a coastal village within the Karachi metropolitan area (Ercelawn 2001):

> *"There are too many outsiders. Bengalis and Burmese fish all year round. Wherever we step, there are Bengalis. They should all be sent back to their own country. Ibrahim Hyderi has been rid of Bengalis. But this is of little use, since they are now sitting in nearby Rehri and go fishing in the same water as us. On our boats, if there are two locals as crew, there are 40 Bengalis. Incomes from the sea go to Bangladesh".*

The women go on to register major complaints against the introduction of nylon nets, which have destroyed their livelihoods making twine nets, against international trawling vessels which intrude into the 35 nautical miles zone reserved for local fishers, and against capitalists and smugglers who have barged into the fishing trade. They do not yet understand how they have lost potential income from shrimp exports to the USA as a result of the appeals level decision in WTO on the turtle excluder device. These are good reasons to empathize with the women of Ibrahim Hyderi. It is still a shock to learn afresh how strongly the poor practice social exclusion of the even poorer. Prejudice against economic migrants is not limited to the wealthy enclaves of the world.

It is doubly ironic in that Karachi is home largely to migrants, primarily the children and grandchildren of those that migrated from India at Partition and who still call themselves *Muhajirs*. It is also home to first and second-generation economic migrants from upcountry. The tension caused by the influx of Afghanis, Bangladeshi and others is just the tip of ethnic troubles associated with the mix of national populations.

2.5. International terror and organized crime

Governments in Pakistan have always been too willing to discern a foreign hand in the country's law and order situation. Yet, it is a nightmare that has been true for some time. International terror groups have achieved global salience after September 11, 2001. But Karachi has been suffering from the activities of terrorists with an international agenda for over two decades, (verifiably since 1986 when Palestinian hijackers seized a Pan Am plane at Karachi airport).

Similarly, organized crime has acquired international dimensions. Advances in communications technology are such that national boundaries have ceased to provide any impediment to unlawful activities. Criminology expert, Professor Ernesto Savona, in a report prepared for the UN Conference on Crimes (Cairo, May 1995) has asserted that criminal syndicates with many decades of sophisticated money laundering experience behind them are recycling money all over the world (Savona, 1995). The small arms and drugs culture in Pakistan is correlated with the influx of refugees from Afghanistan in the early 1980s. Sohrab Goth in Karachi became a center for cross-border criminals.

Pakistan is seen as a soft target with porous borders and without an adequate system of national identification. Its own ethnic and sectarian terrorist groups and criminal gangs make the situation murkier. According to Azher Hassan Nadeem, the situation became so extreme in the 1990s that Pakistan faced an inter-twined crisis of collapsing economy and deteriorating law and order situation (Nadeem, 2002). The anonymity of flats and squatter settlements has made Karachi a favored arena. The events of 2002 with the Daniel Pearl murder, the bombing of the French submarine builders and the fertilizer bomb near the American consulate reveal an ongoing assault on the city.

3. Obstacles to investment in Karachi

> *"It is the city as a center of economic affairs that breeds that restless type, the entrepreneur, venturesome, ambitious, and always ready to strike out in new direction" (Friedmann 1961).*

Karachi is the financial and industrial capital of Pakistan. The city generates a third of the national value-added in manufacturing, 62% of that in banking and insurance, and 37 percent of that arising in services. Overall, it contributes a quarter of national GDP and a quarter of Federal revenues. More than half the country's deposits lie in banks in Karachi and almost three-quarters of all capital loans are raised in the city. Karachi has a GDP per capita estimated at almost two-and-a-half times higher than the average for Pakistan. Less than eight percent of Pakistanis live in Karachi, but they own 35% of all television sets in the country. Almost half the cars in Pakistan are registered in Karachi (Zaidi 1999).

Nevertheless, Karachi needs more investment: in jobs, in housing and services, and in trunk infrastructure. Acute shortages of electricity and water are pervasive in Karachi, and sanitation services are often non-existent. The Karachi Electric Supply Corporation (KESC) generates more megawatts than the peak demand, yet the city faces constant outages owing to a decaying distribution system, inadequate maintenance and theft. Around 75% of houses have piped water connections but only 40% actually receive piped water, mostly for a few hours a day. The majority gets water from standpipes or purchases it from tankers. It is estimated only 15–20% of the sewage is treated while the rest flows directly into the sea. Industrial effluents result in concentrations of metals, salts, bacteria, acids and oils in water bodies and surrounding land. Similarly, only a third of the city's solid waste is transported to dump sites; the remaining refuse is picked over by scavengers and animals in the streets (Gizewski 1996).

Karachi has the human resources to absorb the investment. Three quarters of the males are literate compared to a 55% average for the country. Perhaps more important for a country seeking to take advantage of the phasing out of the Multi-fiber Agreement and textile quotas, two-thirds of the women are literate compared to an average of one-third across the country[4] (NIPS 2001). Karachi (except Malir) is also better placed for the future, with only 29 to 36 percent of 5–9 years old out of school compared to 60 to 86 percent for the rest of Sindh province (MSU, 2002). Orangi, a township of 1.2 million people within greater Karachi, has achieved 90% literacy among men and women (SPDC 2002).

Yet there are few prospects in the short to medium term for significant investment by multinationals in Karachi. It is not just a matter of what Harvey has called the central paradox of time-space compression: " the less important the spatial barriers, the greater the sensitivity of capital to the variations of place within space"(Harvey 1991). Karachi has a badly blotted copybook. The killings of several thousand citizens over the past decade, the murder of the US Consulate staff (1995), Union Texas auditors (1999), and French submarine builders (2002) stand out in a backdrop of pervasive disorder, in which around ten thousand vehicles are stolen every year in the city.

Pakistan as a whole has an equally botched record. After nuclear testing in 1998, anticipating sanctions and capital flight, Government froze the foreign currency accounts of residents and non-resident Pakistanis. Earlier during the 1990s, one Government entered into contracts with Independent Power Producers; a subsequent regime re-negotiated the agreements to obtain more favorable terms after the plants had been installed. After the recent tension with India, the governments of many industrialized countries advised their citizens against travel to the region. Few multinationals and emerging market investors retain Pakistan on their prospectuses.

There remains the possibility of investment by émigré entrepreneurs of Pakistani origin. Several score have done rather well, while a dozen have achieved spectacular success, especially in the information technologies sector. Fashion is another field in which a few Pakistani designers are starting to make a name. It is a high value-adding specialty with links to the garments sector. As a legacy of British colonial rule, in particular an educational system for an English speaking elite that has maintained links to universities in the West, Pakistan has a number of qualified lawyers, accountants, and professionals in banking and finance. Some of them along with doctors, engineers, and other professionals have done quite well for themselves abroad. There are also Pakistani-origin entrepreneurs in retailing, indenting, Hilal meatpacking, real estate and so on. Many are tied to their places of establishment and local markets in the industrialized West by fixed capital, and human and institutional networks. Others are increasingly footloose. Some are seeking again the cultural moorings of the home country.

[4]Literacy is defined as any person above 10 years of age who can read a newspaper and write a simple letter in any language.

By definition, these are bright people. By definition, they have learnt what it takes to succeed in sophisticated world markets. Can Pakistani-origin entrepreneurs in the advanced productive services sectors be induced to invest in their home country, especially now that global networks are being put in place? What reforms are needed to enable them to invest (more) in Pakistan, and in particular, in Karachi? It is true, almost as an axiom that they or their parents left the country because they were stagnating or felt frustrated here. Even if they cannot be induced to personally re-locate, what lessons do their experiences hold for resident entrepreneurs and for Pakistani policy makers?

3.1. Perceptions of non-resident and resident entrepreneurs

Several categories of audiences, including national and provincial policy makers in Pakistan, are likely to be interested in the perceptions of émigré entrepreneurs about Karachi. Particularly illuminating could be two sets of perceptions. First, what do the entrepreneurs recall as critical to their own success, for example, is place and timing more important than knowledge and skills or less? Second, what do they feel about past and present policies and projects, what do they perceive as current obstacles, future opportunities and threats to business in Karachi? It could be revealing to compare these perceptions with those of businesspersons resident in Karachi.

A survey of non-resident and resident Pakistani entrepreneurs was designed and accomplished specially for this paper[5]. The objective was to seek responses relevant both to short and longer-term issues – such as institutional change. More than a survey of the current business climate was intended. Therefore the design elicited recall of past and present events, policies and issues[6]. The methodology comprised seeking largely structured responses from self-selecting and quota samples of the two groups[7]. However, the section on recent government decisions and events with a significant impact on Karachi was deliberately left open-ended to capture individual expressions.

The survey targeted émigré entrepreneurs in accountancy, advertising, banking and finance, fashion, information technology, and law. These pre-designated sectors are those that over time can hopefully become the core of advanced producer services. An opportunity was also provided for entre-

---

[5]The questionnaire is available upon request from the author. I am grateful to Mr. Mazhar Hussain Tawawalla and his team at HT Consultants, Karachi who re-formatted the questionnaire for web application, uploaded the survey, distributed the forms, collected the returns, and tabulated the raw data.

[6]The design is quasi-experimental, because truly random assignment was not possible. The form is post-test only non-equivalent control group design (RXO/RO), where the fact of emigration is taken as the experimental variable X, to which the control group has not been exposed.

[7]It is possible that some of the self-selecting expatriate respondents are 'aspiring' rather than actual entrepreneurs, given the basic option to reply anonymously. However, it should be noted that 82% made a declaration of their payrolls, and half gave their names and e-mail addresses in response to an optional clause, seeking identification only if the respondent was interested in feedback.

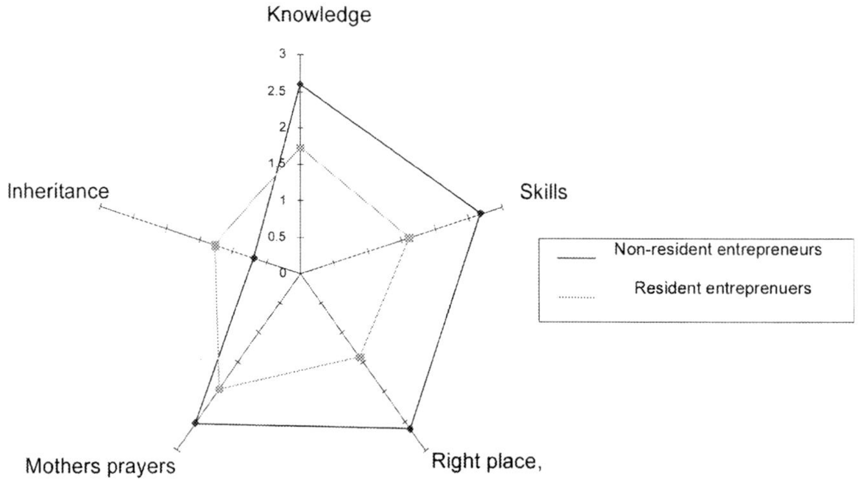

Fig. 1. Factors contributing to success as entrepreneurs

preneurs in other sectors to respond. A small number of responses from self-selecting non-resident entrepreneurs in other 'knowledge-intensive' sectors has been entertained. The interest of Pakistani-origin businesspersons in such fields as civil engineering, medicine and medical supplies, biotechnology, real estate and emerging technologies, is by itself a positive indicator for Karachi. To maintain the internal validity of the experiment, the quota sample of resident entrepreneurs was extended to cover the equivalent sub-categories[8], for example, a local architect to balance the form submitted by a civil engineer in the USA[9].

The questionnaire was designed to elicit answers to the following precise questions that were developed from the basic questions:

- Do the groups ascribe similar or different weights to the 'elements' of their success as entrepreneurs?

[8]The quantitative target for the survey was 50 Pakistani-origin entrepreneurs (25 non-resident, 25 resident in Karachi) in accountancy, advertising, banking/finance, fashion, information technology and law sectors, or a sector specified by the respondent. For the expatriates, an advertisement was placed in the electronic version of Dawn newspaper during the period June 11 to 19, 2002 and thereafter at an electronic survey site (Brinkster/htc). Till closing date, it elicited 22 responses from persons that met the qualifying criteria. This included four respondents in the category 'Other'. The same questionnaire was administered to a quota sample of 26 Karachi-based business leaders, of which 17 persons were in the pre-designated professions, while nine were selected to correspond to the sectors specified in the category 'Other' by the non-resident entrepreneurs. This part of the survey was accomplished by drawing names from a short list made from the telephone directory, calling the person, delivering the questionnaire and subsequently collecting it back. A total of 48 completed questionnaires (22 non-resident and 26 resident entrepreneurs) have been tabulated and analysed. There are only four female respondents, but as a proportion that is probably representative. The responses from four accountants were late and have not been included in the analysis.

[9]The distribution of expatriate respondents was 15 from USA, 3 from Canada, 2 from UK, and one each from Australia and Sri Lanka.

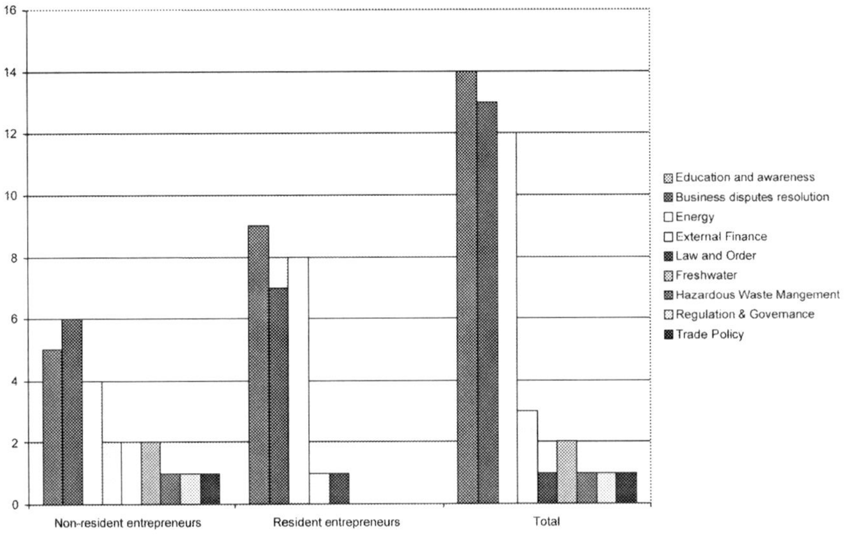

Fig. 2. First priorities of entreprenuers

- Which issues facing Karachi are of greater concern to émigré entrepreneurs than to resident businesspersons, and which ones less?
- Are the non-resident entrepreneurs more concerned about the culturally conservative (staid, hypocritical) nature of Pakistani society than the locals are?
- Which actors in the city are perceived as relatively more effective in the city, and how are their roles seen as changing over time? And
- With reference to the prospects for the development of Karachi, do the two groups ascribe similar or different weights to the opportunities and threats exemplified by recent events and processes?

A comparison of the two sets of results reinforces some traditional conclusions and provides some fresh insights:

- Non-resident entrepreneurs ascribe greater significance than do locals to education and knowledge, to particular skills, and to being in the right place at the right time (Fig. 1). This is particularly true for émigré entrepreneurs in information technology. For a majority in both groups, inheritance has played an insignificant or marginal role in their success, but 'fresh starters' dominate (68%) among the émigré entrepreneurs. The strongly bi-modal responses of both groups display their ambivalence with regard to the efficacy of 'mother's prayers'.
- The questionnaire provided a list of 19 issues from which to select the five most important for the sustainable development of Karachi. The respondents also had the option to add other issues to the list. Both groups included 'law and order' more frequently than any other issue among their choice of the five major problems facing Karachi. Energy supplies and regulations/governance were the second and third most common entries by the locals. The second and third most common entries by the émigré entrepreneurs were education/awareness and business disputes resolution. However, the questionnaire was designed to further probe this selection.

- The respondents were asked to rank the five selected issues from most important to next in importance, and so on. Education/awareness (29%), business disputes resolution (27%), and energy (25%) rank as the first priority issues in the combined responses. Business disputes resolution is the most important single issue for 27% of the émigré entrepreneurs. Education/awareness and energy follow it as first choices. For the resident entrepreneurs, education/awareness, energy and business disputes resolution vie for the most important issue (Fig. 2). The modal rank for Law and Order is third. Mass transit emerges as a fourth ranked issue along with regulations and governance, tax administration, and technology development.
- Among past policies, local and émigré entrepreneurs ascribed a high impact to the nationalization of industry and banks in the 1970s more than to any other Government decision. Sindh urban and rural quota for admissions to colleges was the second decision with a high impact for local entrepreneurs, whereas more émigré entrepreneurs thought that job quotas (giving preference to rural *Sindhis* over urban *Mohajirs*) had a high impact. Both local and non-resident entrepreneurs agree that the decision with the least impact was the ban on liquor and gambling.
- Both sets of respondents have listed events or government decisions that have had a high or significant impact on Karachi during the 1990s. The list of 70 items can be collapsed into fewer categories, the number depending on level of the generalization sought (Table 1). What is important to note is that only five of the original 70 – better telephony (VoIP) information technology, Internet, mobile communications, investment by independent power producers – relate to globalization. This may be compared to the 31 entries bearing on the failures of governance and another 23 that point out flawed and inconsistent national and provincial policies. In response, there have been ethnic riots and strikes of all kinds, and business migration (4 entries).
- The sharpest differences of perception are with respect to international financial institutions (IFIs). Local entrepreneurs see IFIs as very highly, highly or moderately influential (69 %). Undoubtedly, they have read in the newspapers about the macro-economic conditions or reforms imposed upon Pakistan or a state agency by the IMF. Some may have provided goods and services to a large project funded by a multilateral bank. On the other hand, 59% of the émigré entrepreneurs, who have largely made their mark in the private sector in the industrialized world, rate the IFIs as having very low or low influence.

In sum, entrepreneurs are willing to risk capital in Karachi once assured of secure business transactions, a workforce getting more educated, and stable energy supplies.

4. Urban planning and management in a turbulent time

> "*As progress continues to be made*...behind these efforts will be discovered the spirit and social patterns of the administrative class, resident in cities, and acting as surveyors of the creative organizing powers of the city" (Friedmann 1961)

Table 1. Government decisions or events with significant or high impact on Karachi during 1990s (Combined responses of local and non-resident entrepreneurs)

Category	Entries	Frequency
Government policies	• Army action against MQM, Operation Clean-Up [2] • Army monitoring cells • Ban on liquor and gambling [2] • Break up of One Unit (1970) • Defense spending, increased • Devolution Plan (2001) • General Sales Tax [2] • Incentives, lack of ("no lucrative offers") • India, relations with • Nationalization of industry and banks [2] • Taxation, high rate of, maximum [2] • Shifting Federal Capital to Islamabad (1955) [2] • Sindh urban and rural quotas [3] • Sindhi in schools, on electoral rolls, ID cards • Water distribution among province	23
Governance	• Biased implementation of law for Karachi-ites, step brotherly treatment [2] • Blind eye to problems of multi-ethnic city • Changes in governments • Corrupt police • Corruption, institutionalized [2] • In provincial government agencies • Feudal system, failure to abolish • Islamic laws (blasphemy, etc), implemented • Inability to take swift action, (govt.) • Inconsistent policies, (govt.) • Intelligence agencies, failure to re-organize • Judiciary, subservient • Law and Order, failure of, experiments to control [7] • Mob rule, support of • Ousting of Chief Justice Sajjad Ali Shah • Power breakdowns [2] • Quota system, failure to abolish • Recruitment, undereducated/untrained persons • Radical groups, set up to counter past mistakes • Wastage in name of technology – no solution • Water problem, shortage [2]	31
People's response	• Business migration • Ethnic riots • Strikes of all kinds [2]	4
Development	• Dry ports • Infrastructure projects • Micro-finance • Monetary and credit sector, development of • Port Qasim, move to • Press, freedom of • Road structure, new	7
Trans-state related processes	• Independent power plants • Information technology • Internet • Mobile communications, better telephony [2]	5

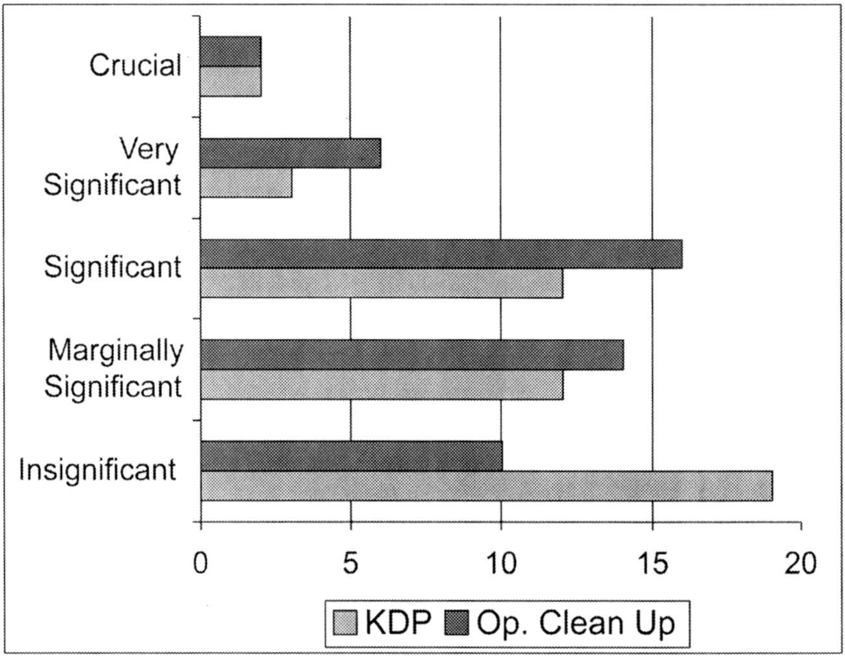

Fig. 3. Comparative significance of KDP 1990–2000 and army action 1992–1994

What sense can an urban planner make of the conversations between and among globalization theorists and businesspersons? There has been some mention thus far about inappropriate and top-down sewage systems planning, fleeting references to corporate golf courses and to the need for mass transit, but little else of direct interest to the city planner. The planner may note the low significance ascribed by our respondents to the Karachi Development Plan (Fig. 3). Among the entries on significant decisions and events impacting on the city during the 1990s (Table 1), she may also notice that rather few bear on the physical development of Karachi. In fact, three in all: the move to Port Qasim, the new road structure, and a generic entry on infrastructure projects[10].

Yet, the separation between governance, economic processes, and physical processes forming and re-forming the cityscape is formal, for administrative and academic convenience, not real. There may be no capacity left in the designated government agencies to implement Master Plans or Development Packages owing political preemption. On the other hand, the military operations to restore law and order did have a huge impact on the physical features of Karachi. A novel self-help program for upgrading communal infrastructure and for provision of credit, a health and education service through the non-formal sector has immense ramifications, extending beyond Pakistan to other cities of the South.

[10]The entry on dry ports in Table 1 refers to the creation of dry ports upcountry, which have reduced jobs in the city.

4.1. Master plans and development packages: No capacities to implement (honestly)

The plan document for the Karachi Development Plan 2000 was accomplished by the (now defunct) Karachi Development Authority with the help of the UNDP in 1990. A sum of US$ 21 million was spent on the preparation of the plan and the hardware (computers, digital mapping equipment) that accompanied it. Essentially the plan consisted of a computer model that would monitor developments in Karachi so that investments could be directed appropriately. It contained institutional recommendations for an independent Karachi Division Physical Planning Agency (KDPPA). Building control under this arrangement was to be subservient to the KDPPA.

However, as Arif Hasan notes, the monitoring and related planning could not be carried out without a constant supply of data for which no system was proposed (Hasan 2000). The powerful interest groups that control land allotment and building development in the city were never seriously consulted nor were their possible roles analyzed. It is not surprising that the plan was never given legal cover. Many of its important provisions (such as not developing any more land till the over 200,000 vacant plots are build upon) are being violated. Fragmented development continues to occur, with inadequate coordination among the many agencies making and implementing plans.

When 73% of our sample of entrepreneurs says there has been no progress or insignificant progress on the KDP 2000, they cannot be faulted. It is a commentary on the plan process that a number of our respondents in Karachi called back first to find out what KDP was.

Political governments during the 1990s began the practice of pooling together diverse infrastructure projects as a development package for the city. This gave the appearance of coherent development. A more common outcome was physical and institutional confusion, such as arterial traffic routed through a residential district without consulting the owners of the homes fronting the road. There were distinct physical consequences also of the way that area development contracts were packaged. Chief Minister Abdullah Shah gave a construction company the authorization to commence 12 residential projects simultaneously in Gulistan e Johar, instead of the usual four. He deprived clients, who have to book flats in advance, their limited voice in the design by observing the development and voting with their feet. The result is a slum with no parking spaces.

4.2. Operation clean-up: Imposing order from above

On May 28, 1992, the Federal Government under Article 147 of the Constitution entrusted to the army the functions of public security and maintenance of law and order in the province of Sindh, including Karachi. The program for elimination of gangs of dacoits and terrorists was named Operation Clean-Up. The impact of the operation on the crime situation in Karachi has been reviewed by a number of reputed scholars and agencies, including the Human Rights Commission of Pakistan. This sub-section is limited to discussing the impact of Operation Clean-Up on the built environment of Karachi and on the agencies providing public utilities.

How did the army perceive the conditions in the city at the start of Clean-Up? A few examples are provided[11]:

- Gated communities had emerged in Karachi in response to the deteriorating public security situation. The army perceived that many of these 1,082 gates had been put in place, not by the residents for their collective security, but by the Mohajir Quami Movement[12] (MQM), in order to regulate the movement and livelihoods of residents. Furthermore, sanctuary was given in the cordoned-off areas to dacoits and terrorists, provided they had made a contribution to the MQM. The Karachi administration was denied entry to whole areas of the city ("no-go areas").
- Illegal construction had occurred over the route of a high-pressure oil pipeline in Korangi[13]. The army suspected that the huts were being used as a cover for illicit tapping into the pipeline. In a few minutes, a whole tanker load could be drawn off.
- Goths (villages) on the beachfront had replaced Sohrab Goth as centers for smuggling and drugs. They were now adjacent to the posh Clifton area, where adolescents had the money to buy drugs.
- A water *mafia* had invested in a large number of tankers. In league with groups in the Karachi Water and Sewerage Board (KWSB), they had disconnected the water supply to a number of areas, making them dependent on the tankers for their daily water requirements.
- By virtue of a growing list of defaulters, mainly other government agencies, the KESC had an excuse for not keeping up with the maintenance needs of its power distribution network. During the early 1990s, power outages lasting for days became common, especially in the sticky summer heat. Thieves and bandits had easy pickings, and the citizens of Karachi responded with demonstrations and strikes.
- The old Sabzi Mandi (the fruit and vegetables wholesale market) on Jail Road was causing traffic congestion and problems of waste management. It needed to be shifted to the outskirts of the city, to the Super Highway where land had been allocated for this purpose since 1965-1966.

What did Clean-Up achieve or not achieve?

- Within six months all the gates had been removed. The Army achieved this using bulldozers and its own troops. It took two years to open up the no-go areas to the extent that the para-military and police could enter them. In the subsequent decade, gated communities have not been allowed to re-emerge in Karachi.

[11]Much of this sub-section is based on a narration by Lt. Col. (retired) Mohsin Haider, then General Staff Officer–1, Internal Security Operations, Corps Reserve Headquarter, Malir, Karachi.

[12]A political party of Urdu speaking people who migrated to Pakistan in 1947 or their descendants.

[13]Korangi is an industrial and low-middle income coastal township of Karachi.

- The army managed to clear up the illegal structures on the high-pressure trunk oil pipeline, and to stop the presumed illicit tapping.
- The drug dens near the seafront are still there. There was effort through the police to get hold of the drug addicts. It turned out that they are like water, leaving areas where there is pressure and turning up elsewhere. One of the areas where pressure was applied has seen impressive change. The tract of *acacia* scrub forest from Jinnah terminal to Shahrah e Faisal that was infested with drug addicts has been cleared and beautified as a park for evening outings by families.
- When the army investigated the KWSB and the water *mafia*, it discovered that the senior management was hostage to an extended kinship network controlling the middle management. The empty pipes had rusted and a restored water supply could not meet potable quality standards. The annoyed consumers thought they were better off with the tankers. The bottom line is that tankers are still in booming business in Karachi.
- The KESC did manage to enhance its recovery, but the army could not address the core issue of huge line losses owing to illegal connections. A decade later, efforts are continuing to make enough recovery to enable privatization of KESC. However, the problems are so deep rooted that government has still not been able to find a buyer.
- In the aftermath of Clean-Up, the government did manage to enforce the shifting out from the old Sabzi Mandi in 1995. However, it is reported the process of establishing the new Sabzi Mandi was badly flawed (URC, 1996). Space was allotted to favored parties rather than real traders. No provision was made for basic services, such as water, electricity, gas and telephones, and for cold storage. The new Mandi remained largely unoccupied till as recently as 2001.

Some hugely important matters, such as the revival of the circular railway as mass transit remained outside the field of perception of the army. Others such as the Gulistan e Johar scandal happened under their noses, but the military had no concept of what was happening and could not deal with it. In yet others, such as the vandalizing upon recovery of stolen vehicles by a *mafia* of police and spare parts dealers, the army surrendered to administrative complexity. When the General Officer Commanding Karachi was being dined out two years into the operation, he admitted to his officers that he had never been clear about the mission of Operation Clean-Up.

Among the areas where the army faced resistance was Orangi, where the MQM dug deep trenches and threw live wires on moistened approach paths. In that same area, before, during and after that time, a determined old man promoted grass roots development[14]. I turn next to the story of Akhtar Hameed Khan in the last two decades of his life at the Orangi Pilot Project.

[14]He was in fact arrested for a short while by the Army, but let go because of uproar by his influential supporters.

4.3. Orangi pilot project: promoting development from below

Akhtar Hameed Khan started working in Orangi, Karachi's largest *katchi abadi* (informal settlement) in 1980, after several decades of a distinguished career as a rural development theorist and practitioner. He brought to the township a development approach based on the mobilization techniques that he had fine-tuned in his rural fieldwork. He sought an entry into the community through common property that he knew a priori to be the most neglected aspect of life in a squatter settlement. He found it in the overflowing open drains in each lane of the area. He branded them the cause of most disease in Orangi.

Akhtar Hameed Khan then assembled a team of architects, engineers and social organizers. They provided low-cost designs for shallow, small bore sewers and mobilized lane residents to lay their own sewers on an entirely self-help basis, with only technical assistance from the project, now formally called the Orangi Pilot Project (OPP)[15]. Having established the procedures for a technically appropriate, economically affordable, and socially acceptable approach to sanitation, Khan went on to launch interventions in education, health and micro-credit in Orangi.

The internal infrastructure project in Orangi has been virtually accomplished with toilets upgraded in 100,000 houses and underground sewers laid in 7,000 out of the 7,256 lanes of the settlement. People have invested US$ 1.5 million in this effort. By technical research, modifying engineering standards and making the work procedure compatible with community-managed construction and self-finance, OPP has brought down the cost of these services to US$16.5 per household.

Khan was careful to secure external validation for the impact of OPP's interventions. As verified by third party surveys, the infant mortality rate in Orangi fell from 130 in 1982 to 37 per thousand by 1991, which has been mainly attributed to the sanitation program (Khan 1994). Over the same period, immunization coverage rose to 98 % and family planning practice among women to 54 %, at least partially the results of the OPP health program. OPP helped set up and sponsored the training of the staff of a number of private schools in Orangi. By 1994, 60% of Orangi children in primary classes and 71% in secondary classes were in private schools. Orangi has now among the highest rate of male and female literacy in Pakistan, though it remains a low-income informal settlement.

Akhtar Hameed Khan died in 1999. Several teams of committed professionals are carrying on his work through the four institutions set up by him, dedicated to research and training, and for provision of micro-credit, health, and rural development services.

OPP's sanitation model is being replicated in other low-income settlements of Karachi, in other Pakistani cities and rural areas. The principles of the project are being applied to projects in Nepal, Central Asia, South Africa, and Sri Lanka. In this way, Karachi has made a contribution to globalization and urban development!

---

[15]Especially noteworthy from our globalization perspective, OPP fought off an early rival to funding and fame in the form of an UNCHS project based on a subsidized approach.

5. Conclusions

The case for "asymmetric inclusion," that is of across-the-board adverse impacts of globalization upon Karachi, has not been proved. Where trans-state processes have been shown to operate negatively, it has been argued that they do so as extensions of national processes. In particular, many of the adverse outcomes for the people of Karachi are the consequences of weak governance and flawed national policies. Loan-loaded projects of IFIs that have been too readily accepted by governments can be countered and stopped through the informed and organized will of good men and women. This has been demonstrated in a specific case.

Pakistan needs to develop institutions for the effective and transparent application of modern company, contract and banking laws; and mechanisms to protect intellectual property rights in the information technology sector and in fashion wear designs. Declarations of pro-investment policies by government are necessary but not sufficient. The autonomy of key economic management agents and institutions, such as the Governor of the State Bank and the Securities and Exchange Commission, must be assured. With these changes, Karachi can attract some of the leading Pakistani-origin entrepreneurs working abroad. What is good it seems is that they can bring in capital from international markets, beyond the bureaucracy of the international financial institutions. Equally sensibly, they are not asking for wholesale change in the cultural codes prevailing in the country at present, at least in its public spaces.

Retaining the investors will be a much more difficult task because crime will not cease, not till the youth of the city and country are truly educated. The two-tier system of elitist and vernacular education has to change. Widespread education and world awareness among citizens as now discernible in Orangi is one element of a longer-term strategy. The norms of governance need to change – not least because this is the core demand of the most innovative and creative elements of Pakistani society, its entrepreneurs at home and abroad. Order imposed from above does not last. Urban management must become more local, inclusive and participatory. In fact, trunk infrastructure development can wait till robust community-empowering institutions are in place and good governance is assured.

> *"Hope in the future is largely related to the creation of a national self-image. It is again the urban intellectual who will eventually provide an image of this kind" (Friedmann 1961).*

References

ACHR (2001) Housing by people in Asia. Newsletter of the Asian Coalition for Housing Rights 13: 22–23

Anwar F (2002) Weaving social capital in local government. NGORC Journal, March 2002, pp 6–9

Ercelawn A, Shah B (2001) Promoting sustainable livelihoods for coastal fisher folk. Law and Policy, Shirkatgah, Karachi

Friedmann J (1961) Cities in social transformation. In: Friedmann J, Alonso W (eds) Regional development and planning. A Reader. The MIT Press, Cambridge, Mass

Gizewski P, Homer-Dixon T (1996) Environmental scarcity and violent conflict: The case of Pakistan. Occasional paper: Project on environment, population and security. American Association for the Advancement of Science and the University of Toronto, Washington, D.C. April 1996
Harvey D (1991) The condition of postmodernity. Blackwell, Oxford
Hasan A, Yunus M, Zaidi A (2000) Understanding Karachi, planning and reform for the future. City Press, Karachi
Hasan A (2002) The changing nature of the informal sector in Karachi as a result of global restructuring and liberalization. Environment and Urbanization, Globalization and Cities 14(1): 69–78
Khan A (1994) Orangi pilot project programs. Mimeo, Karachi
Multi-donor Support Unit (2002) Profile for education and literacy planning. Sindh districts, MSU for the Social Action Program, Islamabad
Nadeem A (2001) Pakistan: The political economy of lawlessness. Oxford University Press, Oxford
National Institute of Population Studies (2001) Pakistan population data sheet
Pieterse J (1996) Globalisation and emancipation. From local empowerment to global reform. Paper for the CERES-Workshop on Globalisation. Wageningen, The Netherlands
Sassen S (2002) Locating cities on global circuits, Environment and Urbanization, Globalization and Cities 14(1): 13–30
Satterthwaite D (2001) Reducing urban poverty: constraints on the effectiveness of aid agencies and development banks and some suggestions for change. Environment and Urbanization 13(1):137–157
Savona E (1995) Criminal Syndicates. The UN Conference on Crime 9 May, Cairo
Schuurman F (2001) Globalization and development studies. Challenges for the 21st century, Vistaar Publications, New Delhi
SPDC (2002) Social development in Pakistan. Annual review. Social Policy and Development Centre, Karachi
Taylor P (2000) World cities and territorial states under conditions of contemporary globalization. Political Geography 19(1): 5–32
Urban Resource Center (1996) Proceedings of the Sabzi Mandi Forum, Karachi
Zaidi S (1999) The new development paradigm: Papers on institutions, NGOs, gender and local government, Oxford University Press.

IV. Issues

Information technology and urban spatial structure: A comparative analysis of the Chicago and Seoul regions

Jungyul Sohn[1], **Tschangho John Kim**[2], **Geoffrey J.D. Hewings**[3]

[1] Regional Economics Applications Laboratory, University of Illinois and National Center for Smart Growth, University of Maryland (e-mail: jsohn@umd.edu)
[2] Department of Urban and Regional Planning, University of Illinois, Champaigu, IL 61820, USA (e-mail: tjohnkim@uiuc.edu)
[3] Regional Economics Applications Laboratory, University of Illinois, Urbana, IL 61801-3671, USA (e-mail: hewings@uiuc.edu)

Abstract. This paper examines comparatively the impact of information technology on urban spatial structure in the Chicago and Seoul metropolitan regions in an attempt to measure the potential influence of IT on urban form and structure. We analyzed the metropolitan areas to understand ways in which the information technology has influenced the distribution of urban economic activities: concentration or dispersion by examining two aspects of impacts: an attraction effect on a zone (level of activity) and a spillover effect on surrounding areas (distributional effects).

1. Introduction

The spatial distribution of urban activities often results from various economic location decisions of an individual or a group of firms. In this sense, location and distribution are just two sides of the same coin. Many possible factors can affect the locational decision-making process of those agents in an urban area. Traditionally, the most popular factor or explanatory variable for urban economic activities is the economic imperative. Since most private firms consider increasing profits in the decision making process, it is not so unusual to consider this as a primary moderating factor.

In recent decades, one of the major breakthrough achievements in the world is the development of information technology (IT). Along with the rapid development of computer technology, IT has had a great influence on society in general as well as on the personal lifestyles of individuals. Without doubt, there seems to be a certain relationship between IT and the changing urban spatial structure in that geography is somehow the spatial reflection of society. There has been a significant volume of research on this topic, especially since the late 1980s. Most of the research has been conducted using qualitative and descriptive methods, while there are relatively few studies that have adopted quantitative models. One major reason for this trend is the lack of adequate data to measure or depict the level of IT and the lack of adequate methodologies to measure the spatial impact of IT on distribution patterns. In addition, if such data are needed at a more disaggregated geographic scale, then the difficulty increases. For this reason, some of the empirically driven analysis related to this topic has focused on the intermetropolitan context. Some examples include telecommunication and the transition of regional (Alles et al. 1994; Wheeler and Mitchelson 1989) or the global urban hierarchy and urban systems (Warf 1989) and the Internet network and the accessibilities of cities (Wheeler and O'Kelly 1999).

The purpose of this analysis is to measure the potential influence of IT on urban spatial structure in an intrametropolitan context and to compare the significance of IT-related and non IT-related variables. Combined with IT-related variables, formal models are developed, and a spatial econometric version of the models are also derived.

2. Information technology and urban spatial structure

To some extent, the question whether IT has been important or not in explaining urban forms has been narrowed down to whether IT has an influence on the spatial distribution pattern of urban activities. Yen and Mahmassani (1997) noted that the development of telecommunication technologies might affect land use patterns and play a role in the growth of economic activities and the spatial distribution of industry. Specifically, these authors suggested two aspects of office-location decisions by organizations in assessing the impact from the new technology: i. the need for certain organizations to locate where they can access telecommunication networks; and ii. an increased opportunity for the organizations to locate their offices in the areas where infrastructure costs are generally lower than traditional office locations such as downtown areas.

Gaspar and Glaeser (1998) tried to uncover the relationship between IT and face-to-face interactions and/or the cities that facilitate these interactions. In an empirical analysis using telephone call data, the authors concluded that these are complements rather than substitutes. As a result, the centralizing forces in cities did not seem to vanish. However, as the authors noted, it is very hard to separate the exclusive effect of IT in their regression models.

Gordon and Richardson (1997, p.95) conjectured that IT technology may lead to a dispersion of economic activities and population, possibly up to the stage where "geography is irrelevant." They noted that high-rise or concentrated settlement has been dominant when transport or communication costs were high but that such costs are likely to continue to fall in the future. It might be possible to summarize that "office work, rather than office workers, will do the traveling" (Drucker 1989, p.38). The critical issue here is whether transportation and communication are complementary or competitive. If the former is the case, geography still might matter even with the advent of the new communications technology.

Arguing against the optimistic view of technology, Salomon (1996) mentioned that there have been excessive expectations of the information age, for instance, that telecommunications can eliminate the effects of distance and as a result can have profound effects on the spatial organization of society. He also identified four assumptions underlying the proposition that cities will disperse due to an improved IT: i. the substitutive relationship between transportation and telecommunications; ii. the substitution of information for material goods; iii. the ubiquity of telecommunications; and iv. the recognition that dispersal has been constrained by congestion and travel costs. Even though he claimed that a complete change of urban form could not be expected in the information age, he agreed that there are some changes that may result from these technological changes.

One example of the telecommunications dispersal effect is an emergence of the back office activities located remotely from the core organization (Richardson and Gillespie 1996; Salomon 1996). Further, there exists a gap between introductions f the new IT and the changes in the spatial pattern of firms (Capello 1994). This is ascribed to an overestimation of technological potential and to an optimistic and superficial analysis on the relationship between the new technology and spatial restructuring. She also noted that in the long run, those technologies lead to a new production strategy such as the "just-in-time" (JIT) system and it will require a physical proximity (either in an interurban or intraurban context) between firms and eventually a spatial clustering of economic activities are expected. However, as Fujita and Hamaguchi (2001) noted, firms (specifically the buyers of intermediate goods in the research) can be more dispersed if they have a better-developed transportation/communication infrastructure as in the examples of many developed countries.

Conceptually, the geography and/or distribution of economic activities can be redefined on the basis of information flows. Echeverri-Carroll (1996) noted that an effect of the geographical relationships between organizations cannot be conceptualized without understanding the intra-organizational and inter-organizational computer networks that bind particular locations together. Even though spatial decentralization continues to be relevant, the process is characterized by a much higher functional integration using the information network (Echeverri-Carroll 1996). It is implied that network connectivity can be a more important factor in deciding the geographical relationships than physical distance especially in the information age. Echeverri-Carroll does not agree that such technology leads to the demise of the concept of distance. Echeverri-Carroll concluded that since "these technologies also impose higher investments on inter-firm linkages and more stringent restrictions on labor's skills and flexibility, both ... restrain the location of industry in space (1996, p. 148)."

Mokhtarian (1998) focused more on the spatial residential pattern of commuting. She noted that the effect of the new technology is not to reduce travel but to increase the flexibility of travel and, as a result, the total number of trips may be higher with a substantial portion of travel shifted to off-peak periods. The ability to commute because of telecommuting often leads to a relocation of residences further away from work enough for total VMT (vehicle miles traveled) on a smaller number of commuting days to exceed the previous levels (Mokhtarian 1998). On a system-wide level, this trend may result in a decentralizing effect on urban form (for a more detailed discussion on the theoretical model of residential relocation due to telecommuting, see Stough and Paelinck 1996 or Lund and Mokhtarian 1994).

3. Analysis

Urban spatial structure is defined as the distribution pattern of urban economic activities. Urban spatial structure is examined separately in three economic sectors (manufacturing, retail and service) as well as a whole. Different sectors are expected to show different patterns and explanations. There are also two types of activity patterns considered in the analysis. The first one is density measured simply as the number of establishments (in 1995 in Chicago and in 1996 in Seoul) divided by area: 306 ZIP code zones in the Chicago Consolidated Metropolitan Statistical Area (CMSA) and 61 administrative districts in the Seoul Metropolitan Area (SMR) in which they are located. By examining these variables, the analysis is able to determine whether IT-related or other variables are significant in explaining the levels of such activities. In this context, it is more related to an "attraction" effect. The attraction effect in this analysis is defined as the effect of a variable in a zone on the level of urban economic activities in the same zone.

The second is the distribution pattern of economic activities around a zone of interest. This characteristic is measured by a local indicator of spatial association (LISA). LISA is the statistic that provides an indication of the extent of significant spatial clustering of similar values around that observation (Anselin 1995a, p.94; 1995b, p.42). One of the frequently used LISAs is the local Moran index that is defined as:

$$I_i = \left(z_i / \sum_i z_i^2 \right) \sum_j w_{ij} z_j \tag{1}$$

where

z_i = observation in i in the form of deviation from the mean
w_{ij} = spatial weight matrix composed of the inverse values of distance between i and j.

The local Moran index is used for a simple exploratory spatial data analysis (ESDA) as shown in Figs. 1 to 8. The interpretation of this statistic is conceptually the same as in Moran's I. For example, higher values reflect positive spatial autocorrelation, or the concentration of similar values of observation. Lower values reflect negative spatial autocorrelation, or the dispersion or repulsion of similar values of observation over space. It should not, however, be considered that a higher local Moran always reflects the spatial concentration of higher values, since the exact opposite (the spatial concentration of lower values) also provides the same result. This type of

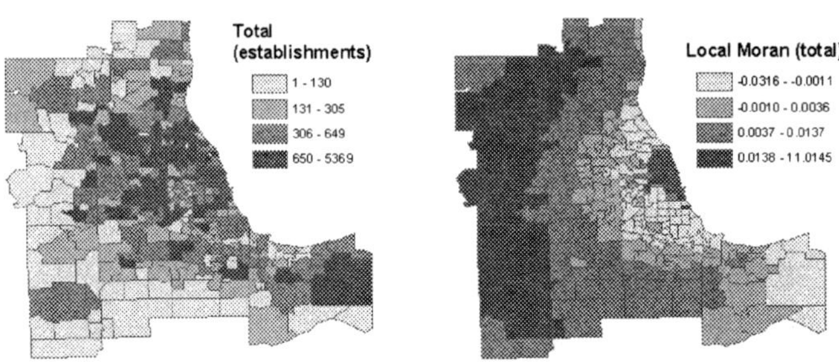

(a) spatial distribution (b) spatial association

Fig. 1. Total establishments in Chicago

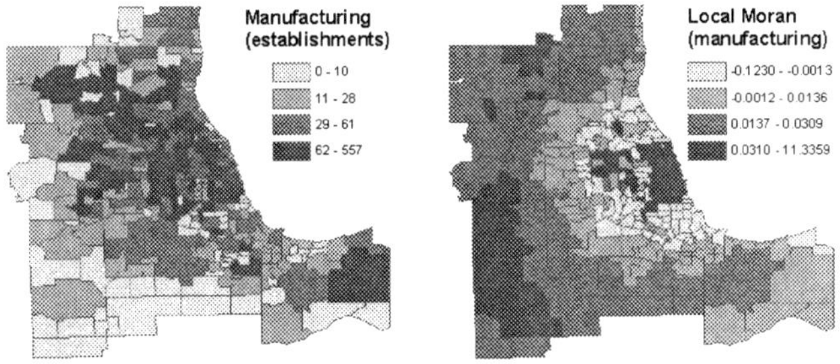

(a) spatial distribution (b) spatial association

Fig. 2. Manufacturing establishments in Chicago

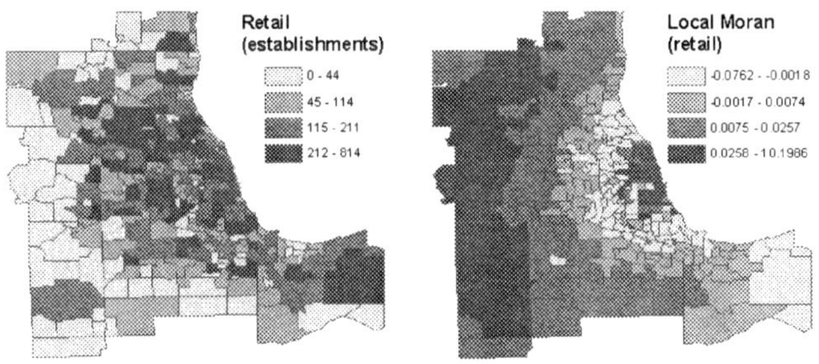

(a) spatial distribution (b) spatial association

Fig. 3. Retail establishments in Chicago

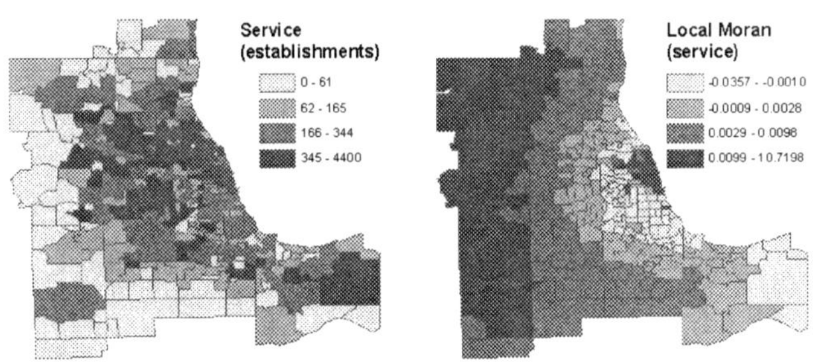

(a) spatial distribution (b) spatial association

Fig. 4. Service establishments in Chicago

confusion can be avoided if the G_i* statistic in Eq. (2) is used to measure the distribution pattern.

$$G_i^* = \frac{\sum_j w_{ij}x_j - W_i^*\bar{x}}{s\{[(nS_{1i}^*) - W_i^{*2}]/(n-1)\}^{1/2}}, \quad \text{all } j \tag{2}$$

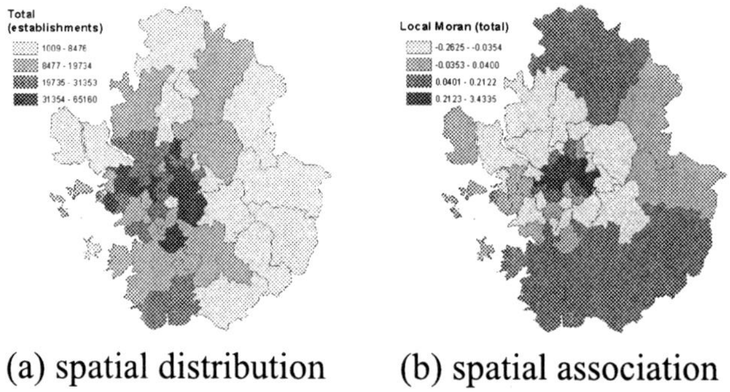

Fig. 5. Total establishments in Seoul

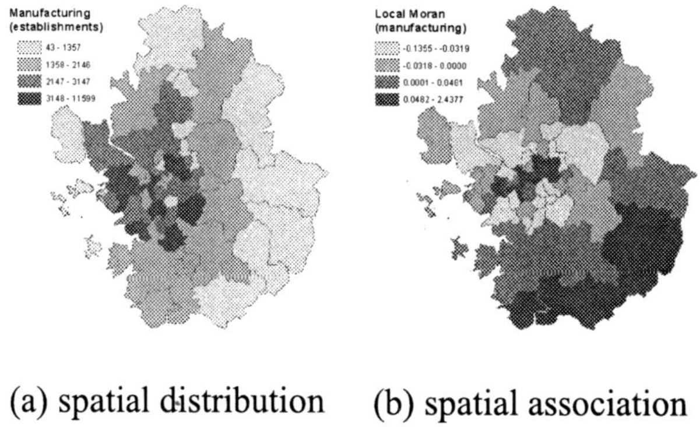

Fig. 6. Manufacturing establishments in Seoul

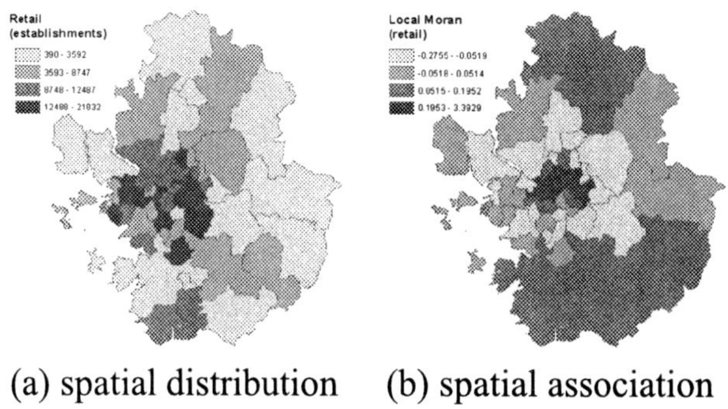

Fig. 7. Retail establishments in Seoul

where

x_j = observation in j
$W_i^* = \sum_j w_{ij}$
$\bar{x} = \frac{\sum_j x_j}{n}$

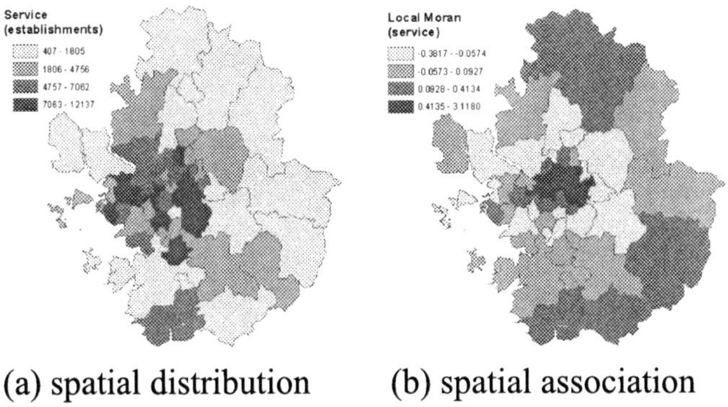

Fig. 8. Service establishments in Seoul

$$s = \sqrt{\frac{\sum_j (x_j - \bar{x})^2}{(n-1)}}$$

n = number of region
$S_{1i}^* = \sum_j w_{ij}^2$.

It was first developed by Getis and Ord (1992) and later revised by Ord and Getis (1995). The uniqueness of this statistic is that a positive G_i* statistic indicates spatial clustering of high values, whereas a negative value indicates spatial clustering of low values (Anselin 1995b, p. 23-2). By investigating these variables, the analysis is able to reveal whether the IT-related variables and others are significant in explaining the spatial distribution pattern of urban activities. In this sense, it is related to the "spillover" effect. The spillover effect in this analysis is defined as the effect of a variable in a zone on the distribution pattern of urban economic activities in surrounding zones. It is also noted that G_i* follows a standard normal distribution (Ord and Getis 1995).

A set of regression models are established and these two variables are used as the dependent variable in the model. Combining these dependent variables (attraction and spillover) enables the analysis to provide a comprehensive picture of the spatial distribution of urban activity patterns and the impact of information technology.

In sum, there are eight dependent variables (attraction and spillover for three economic sectors and for the total) to be explained. As a result, eight regression models are built with a series of independent variables for Chicago and Seoul respectively. The sets of independent variables are grouped in Table 1. The first group is about IT-related variables. Because there are few available data sources at the level of this function by disaggregated zones within an urban area, alternative indices will be used to represent the level of IT intensity. These indices are: i. the number of information intensive firms; ii. the number of usual telecommuters; and iii. the number of potential telecommuters.

The first one is related to the level of information infrastructure that seems to be more closely linked to firm activities rather than individuals or households. Sinden (1995) used SIC 7902 (telecommunications) to examine the British economic restructuring process in the telecommunication services. More often than not, secondary data do not allow this level

Table 1. Classification of independent variables

Group	Variable	Description
IT	ITFIRM	Number of firms in the information -intensive sector in 1995 (Chicago) and 1996 (Seoul)
	UTEL	Estimated number of usual telecommuters in 1990
	PTEL	Potential number of telecommuters in 1990
Center orientedness	CBD	Distance from the CBD
	JHR	Job-housing ratio for 92/90 (Chicago) and 91/90 (Seoul)
People	POP	Total population in 1990
	POPM	Employed residents in manufacturing in 1990
	POPR	Employed residents in retail in 1990
	POPS	Employed residents in services in 1990

of detailed information to be adapted, especially when the research is conducted at a more disaggregated geographical level. As a result, several authors have tried to use surrogates. Moulaert and Djellal (1995) used NAE (nomenclature des activités économiques or nomenclature of economic activities) 7703 (information technology and organization consulting sector) and 7704 (computer services) as alternatives in research in France. Another study by Tofflemire (1992) focused on SIC 6000 (F.I.R.E.), 73 (business services), 81 (legal services), and 87 (engineering, accounting and management services) in the U.S. Both studies share common features in that they considered the level of producer services in a region as reflecting the level of IT. ITFIRM in the present analysis is composed of those firms in SIC 73, 81 and 87 in Chicago and KSIC 642 (telecommunication), K (financial institutions and insurance), L (real estate, renting and leasing) and M (business activities) in Seoul.

The "usual" telecommuters (UTEL in this analysis) are defined as those who reported "work at home" to the Census, excluding self-employed workers and workers in particular occupations (Handy and Mokhtarian 1996, p.168). The latter include private household workers, protective services, farming, forestry and fishing, precision production, craft and repair, operators, assemblers, inspectors, transportation and material moving and handlers, helpers, laborers. At the more disaggregated geographical level of the analysis, this number is estimated using the relative employment share of UTEL in each area. While usual telecommuters are substantial participants in telecommuting, the number of potential telecommuters (PTEL) has to be estimated indirectly. Adopting Nilles' proposition (1988) that 50 percent of workers are "information workers" and 80 percent of them are potential telecommuters, Handy and Mokhtarian (1996) defined potential telecommuters as those in occupations classified as conducive to telecommuting: executive, administrative, managerial; professional specialty; technicians and related; sales; and administrative support. These two telecommuter variables are included in the model to measure their significance in explaining urban spatial structure. They are used as a proxy for the level of IT infrastructure in a zone. In other words, a zone with a higher proportion of these information-related workers are assumed to have higher levels of information network infrastructure than others.

The second group of variables is to examine the impact of centrality on the level of activity and distribution patterns. It is clear that the variable CBD focuses on the influence of the urban center. JHR is defined as the ratio between the number of employment opportunities and the number of residents in a zone. Usually, a center is characterized as having a higher number of economic activities and a relatively lower number of residents. As a result, a higher rate of JHR is expected to represent stronger centrality trends; this feature is used for measuring the influence of urban sub-centers as well as the CBD.

The third group of variables includes population and employed residents. The number of employed residents is the number of employees by residence. Population is used as a general measure for the product market (demand) while the employed residents in an individual sector are used as a measure of the labor market (supply).

There are four possible outcomes for the relationship between the IT variables and the two dependent variables: activity level (attraction) and distribution patterns (spillover). Table 2 summarizes those outcomes. By examining the sign of the coefficient of the IT- related variables, the analysis is able to determine whether the hypotheses about the impact of IT are valid or not: Whether the IT factor is crucial in explaining the location and/or distribution of economic activities and whether it leads to a concentration/dispersion of activities or not.

The impact of the center-oriented variables is also interpreted based on the sign of the coefficients. A positive sign for the CBD implies that economic activities are more intense as distance increases from the CBD and a negative value indicates the opposite. In the case of positive relationship, it does not support the traditional monocentric shape of a city. On the other hand, a positive JHR reflects a higher level of economic activity in and around more generally defined city centers (whether the CBD or subcenters).

To remove the influence resulting from different area size, some variables (i.e. the number of establishments, residents, employment etc.) are divided by the area to be transformed into standardized numbers – similar to a density measure. Other variables such as ratios and distance are not transformed because they do not depend on the size of an area. All the variables except LISA (the dependent variable for the "spillover" equation) take the form of $(I+W)$*_Variable*, where I is the identity matrix and W is a spatial weight matrix. When data are based on administratively determined units, there is no reason to believe that economic behavior conforms to these units (Anselin and Bera 1998). As a result, it is appropriate to incorporate adjacent economic values into a value of interest weighted by distance. However, the LISA index in itself already combines such information and does not take the same form $(I+W)$ as the others in the model.

Table 2. Possible outcomes of the model for IT impact

		Distribution pattern (spillover)	
		+	–
Activity level (attraction)	+	Higher activity level with concentrated pattern	Higher activity level with dispersed pattern
	–	Lower activity level with concentrated pattern	Lower activity level with dispersed pattern

4. Results: IT and urban activities

The empirical analysis considers 306 ZIP code zones in the Chicago CMSA. Relevant variables are derived from the 1990 U.S. Population Census, the 1992 U.S. Economic Census and the 1995 ZIP Code Business Pattern. The analysis on Seoul is based on 61 administrative zones in the Seoul Metropolitan Region. Variables are obtained from the 1990 Korean Population Census and the Korean Report on Establishments Census for 1991 and 1996.

4.1. Chicago

Figures 1 to 4 show the overall distribution of economic activities as well as the spatial association patterns represented by the local Moran index in Chicago. Overall, the spatial distribution pattern of establishments is not very different among sectors. The suburbanization of economic activities has been extended to the outer area of the city of Chicago, but not to the edge of the CMSA. Economic activities are still concentrated in he city of Chicago. The distribution of the local Moran index shows an interesting pattern. The higher values, reflecting a positive spatial autocorrelation and a cluster of similar values, are found both in the city of Chicago where economic activities are concentrated as well as at the edge of the Chicago CMSA where there are relatively few establishments. The former is more related to a cluster of higher values (more economic activity) whereas the latter is more related to a cluster of lower values (less economic activity). Intermediate values are found in suburban areas, implying less clustering and more heterogeneity in the distribution of economic activity.

The second and third columns in Table 3 show the estimated results for total economic activity in Chicago. In the equation for activity levels (attraction effect), ITFIRM shows a significant positive relation with the dependent variable among the IT-related variables. It suggests that more firms will be attracted to areas with more IT infrastructure. This is plausible. For the distribution pattern (spillover effect), ITFIRM revealed a positive sign, but it was not very significant.

Two other IT related variables in the analysis, UTEL and PTEL displayed conflicting signs. Combining both estimation results (for the activity level and the distribution pattern), UTEL was negatively associated with the level of activity and positively associated with the distribution pattern. On the other hand, PTEL was positively associated with the level of activity and negatively associated with the distribution pattern. In a sense, the fact that no common pattern is identified between the two telecommuter variables in explaining the establishment location pattern implies that the information network infrastructure designated for households (i.e., telecommuters) does not attract firms.

The two variables measuring center -orientation reveal a strong preference for firms to locate centrally. A negative coefficient for the CBD means less economic activity with increasing distance from the CBD, while a positive coefficient of JHR implies more economic activity in centers, both the CBD and subcenters. As for the distribution pattern, a negative coefficient for the CBD suggests that more concentration near the CBD. The coefficient for JHR is positive, but insignificant. However, POP, as the labor supply and the

Table 3. Estimation results for Chicago

	Total		Manufacturing		Retail		Service	
	A	D	A	D	A	D	A	D
Constant	1.8608	0.9496	0.3288	1.7078	0.5214	1.7556	0.1970	1.5952
	(0.002)**	(0.000)**	(0.000)**	(0.000)**	(0.004)**	(0.000)**	(0.459)	(0.000)**
ITFIRM	1.3195	0.0079	0.0300	0.0075	0.1710	0.0039	0.6929	0.0217
	(0.000)**	(0.628)	(0.000)**	(0.720)	(0.000)**	(0.836)	(0.000)**	(0.191)
UTEL	−0.1387	0.0486	0.0050	0.0415	−0.0016	0.0351	−0.0724	0.0465
	(0.000)**	(0.000)**	(0.084)	(0.000)**	(0.811)	(0.001)**	(0.000)**	(0.000)**
PTEL	0.0229	−0.0042	−0.0021	−0.0032	0.0093	0.0002	−0.0037	−0.0207
	(0.000)**	(0.018)*	(0.000)**	(0.150)	(0.000)**	(0.941)	(0.536)	(0.000)**
CBD	−2.258	−3.872	−0.401	−5.734	−0.3642	−5.720	−0.3237	−4.029
	(0.005)**	(0.000)**	(0.000)**	(0.000)**	(0.127)	(0.000)**	(0.363)	(0.000)**
JHR	14.774	4.089	1.357	4.843	−5.816	5.088	3.947	0.826
	(0.022) *	(0.145)	(0.125)	(0.180)	(0.004)**	(0.122)	(0.215)	(0.770)
POP	0.0042	0.0031	0.0143	0.0507	0.0077	0.0362	0.0308	0.0379
	(0.000)**	(0.000)**	(0.000)**	(0.000)**	(0.289)	(0.003)**	(0.002)**	(0.000)**
Adj-R^2	0.9896	0.8096	0.8321	0.7975	0.9491	0.8089	0.9906	0.7838

Note: Values in parentheses indicate the significance level.
* i at 95%; ** Significant at 99%.
A: Activity level; D: Distribution pattern.

market (demand) variable, was significant in both equations as a determinant of firm location.

The IT factor (especially ITFIRM) stimulates more intense economic activity and a relatively concentrated distribution pattern over space. Despite the suggestion of dispersion influences because of IT factors, its limited spatial availability and accessibility has resulted in concentration tendencies.

The fourth and fifth columns of Table 3 show the estimated results for the manufacturing equations. The pattern for the ITFIRM variable in both equations is the same as for all establishments: a positive and significant attraction effect and a positive but insignificant spillover effect. The effect of the two-telecommuter variables is mixed. The CBD has both attraction and spillover effects while JHR is insignificant. The implication is that more manufacturing firms prefer to stay near the CBD. The labor force attracts firms in this sector, given that POPM is positive and significant in both equations.

The estimation results for the retail sector are summarized in the sixth and seventh columns of Table 3. Again, ITFIRM is positively significant in the activity equation, but insignificant in the spillover equation. The influence of two telecommuter variables conflicted is contradictory in the attraction equation. The center-orientation variables show a slightly different pattern. The CBD is not significant in the model, reflecting the fact that retail activity does not depend on the distance from the CBD. The negative and significant coefficient of JHR implies that more retail activities are observed outside centers. The obvious explanation is the market orientation of retail trade, i.e., proximity to customers. However, the combination of the negative and significant coefficient for the CBD and the insignificant coefficient for JHR in the spillover equation implies a more concentrated pattern close to the CBD (higher density population in the core city). Also, the labor force factor is insignificant in the attraction equation, but positive and significant in the spillover equation.

Finally, the estimation results for the service sector are summarized in the eighth and ninth columns of Table 3. As before, ITFIRM show a similar pattern in both equations while the two telecommuter variables have a mixed impact. The center-orientation variables are not significant in this sector except for the CBD in the spillover equation; the diversity of services may blur trends in this case. Higher order services (e.g., business or producer services) may prefer to locate centrally while personal services are more market-oriented. Proximity to the labor force is also significant in both of the equations.

In terms of the attraction effect of IT, the service sector is the most sensitive sector while manufacturing is the least sensitive. Hence, some service firms rely more on IT infrastructure. There is more interaction within and between companies in the business component of the service sector, thus locations equipped with IT infrastructure offer efficiency advantages. In contrast, manufacturing focuses more on handling tangibles, for example, transporting, processing and shipping products. Hence, the benefits derived from using IT are less dramatic. However, the spillover effect is similar in all sectors. As for the IT measure, it was insignificant in all sectors. All of them showed an insignificant spillover effect for the IT measure even if the sign is positive.

4.2. Seoul

Figures 5 to 8 show the overall distribution of economic activities and the spatial association pattern represented by the local Moran index in Seoul. Seoul has a similar spatial distribution of economic activity to Chicago across sectors. Decentralization of economic activities has taken place to the outer areas of the Metropolitan Seoul but has not to the edge of the SMR. Economic activities are still heavily concentrated in Metropolitan Seoul. A high local Moran index is found both in Metropolitan Seoul where economic activities are concentrated as well as at the edge of the SMR where establishments are sparse. Again, an intermediate value is observed in suburban areas, reflecting less clustering and heterogeneous levels of economic activity.

Table 4 summarizes the estimation results for the distribution of total employment in Seoul. In the equation for total activity, ITFIRM is positively significant, implying that a high level of IT infrastructure attracts more firms. However, the implicit IT indices (UTEL and PTEL) show conflicting signs. The results are similar to those for Chicago. The CBD variable is not significant, suggesting that urban form is not very monocentric (there has been significant decentralization to Kangnam south of the Han River). The JHR variable is positively significant. Combining these two results, the inference is that despite the limited concentration in the CBD, relocation of firms was limited to major subcenters. The population variable is positively significant, indicating that market orientation and/or labor supply are important considerations, although the coefficient is less significant than in Chicago.

In the equation for the distribution pattern, ITFIRM is negatively significant. A higher IT level leads to a less concentrated pattern than in Chicago. UTEL and PTEL again reveal the mixed results observed in Chicago. The negative coefficient for the CBD variable means a much more

Table 4. Estimation results for Seoul

	Total		Manufacturing		Retail		Service	
	A	D	A	D	A	D	A	D
Constant	−751.9	0.1559	−183.3	−0.4115	1.1153	1.5912	22.01	1.4413
	(0.000)**	(0.821)	(0.000)**	(0.531)	(0.985)	(0.045)*	(0.350)	(0.026)*
ITFIRM	7.7584	−0.0130	1.2032	−0.0147	2.7760	−0.0093	1.0396	−0.0073
	(0.000)**	(0.022)*	(0.000)**	(0.007)**	(0.000)**	(0.079)	(0.000)**	(0.153)
UTEL	0.7146	−0.0023	0.2111	−0.0020	0.2600	−0.0041	0.2318	−0.0011
	(0.051)	(0.280)	(0.038)*	(0.287)	(0.086)	(0.032)*	(0.000)**	(0.515)
PTEL	−0.2495	0.0009	−0.0299	0.0007	−0.0916	−0.0001	0.0386	−0.0002
	(0.000)**	(0.014)*	(0.001)**	(0.000)**	(0.000)**	(0.716)	(0.081)	(0.734)
CBD	0.0017	−0.0001	0.0005	−0.00004	−0.0001	−0.0001	−0.0000	−0.0001
	(0.363)	(0.000)**	(0.368)	(0.000)**	(0.895)	(0.000)**	(0.947)	(0.000)**
JHR	6540.8	19.159	1460.4	20.107	515.13	10.4119	−0.8505	9.5869
	(0.000)**	(0.003)**	(0.000)**	(0.001)**	(0.303)	(0.106)	(0.997)	(0.108)
POP	0.0688	−0.0001	0.0529	−0.0002	0.4518	0.0023	−0.0324	0.0016
	(0.000)**	(0.390)	(0.000)**	(0.367)	(0.000)**	(0.006)**	(0.554)	(0.264)
Adj-R^2	0.9850	0.7638	0.9473	0.7122	0.9810	0.8028	0.9777	0.8289

Note: Values in parenthesis indicate the significance level.
* At 95%; ** Significant at 99%.
A: Activity level; D: Distribution pattern.

concentrated pattern close to the CBD. The JHR variable is positively significant, implying more concentration around the CBD and subcenters rather than more dispersion. The population variable did not suggest a spillover effect.

The results for the manufacturing sector are displayed in the fourth and fifth columns of Table 4. In the attraction equation, all the IT-related variables suggest a similar pattern to that for total establishments. A higher level of IT-related facilities attracts manufacturing activities. In the distribution equation, ITFIRM is negatively significant and UTEL and PTEL had conflicting signs. Combining these two results, IT-related variables appear to attract more manufacturing activities but in a less concentrated pattern, similar to the results for total employment. However, the spillover equation shows a different result from that in Chicago where the ITFIRM variable is insignificant but positive. The center-oriented variables exhibit a similar pattern as before (the CBD is less important, while the subcenters role is significant), although there is a difference with the Chicago result where the CBD was more important.

Government-driven decentralization policies for the manufacturing sector in Seoul explain this result. As for the spillover effect, the CBD variable is negatively significant (as in Chicago) and the JHR variable is positively significant. More concentration is observed near the CBD as well as in the subcenters. Compared to Chicago where there is a spillover effect only with proximity to the CBD, the manufacturing sector in Seoul capitalizes on the benefits of localization and urbanization economies (e.g. the availability of infrastructure and/or industrial linkages) by locating close to subcenters as well as to the CBD. POPM is positively significant, suggesting the importance of labor supply accessibility. However, there was no spillover effect.

The sixth and seventh columns of Table 4 summarize the results for the retail sector. In the activity equation, the IT-related variables show a similar pattern as in the above two cases: a positively significant ITFIRM and conflicting results for UTEL and PTEL. In the distribution equation, the ITFIRM variable is negative and insignificant. UTEL has a negative coefficient while PTEL is insignificant. Both the CBD and JHR variables are insignificant, implying that centrality is not very important.. In terms of the spillover effect, the CBD variable is negatively significant, but the other center-oriented variable, JHR, the other center-oriented variable, is insignificant, as in Chicago. The POPR is positively significant, relecting the importance of market demand and/or labor supply. The POPR variable is also positively significant in the distribution pattern, confirming spillover effects into surrounding areas.

The results for the service sector are summarized in the eighth and ninth columns of Table 4. In the attraction equation, as in the other sectors, ITFIRM is positively significant as is UTEL, while PTEL is insignificant. In the distribution equation, all three IT-related variables show negative but insignificant signs. Neither of the center-oriented variables is significant. Nothing supports centrality. It is similar to the Chicago result. While the CBD variable in the distribution pattern is negatively significant, the JHR variable is insignificant; as a result, no clear pattern around subcenters can be found. As before, the heterogeneity of the service sector may be the source of the problem. POP was not important in both equations. The location of the service sector is not strongly influenced by market orientation or labor supply.

In terms of the attraction forces of IT, retail shows the highest dependence while service shows the lowest, and manufacturing is in-between. The higher coefficients for retail result from i. the dominance of large department stores in the city taking advantage of IT facilities; and ii. the transition from manufacturing to retail in the core city area with its higher level of IT infrastructure. The lower coefficients for services are probably related to the heterogeneity of the sector and the continued dominance of traditional services in Seoul. As for the spillover effect (distribution pattern), the rank order is manufacturing, retail and services.

5. Conclusion

The purpose of the paper was to develop formal models of urban spatial structure combined with IT-related variables and to derive a spatial econometric version of these models. This analysis attempted to explore the impact of information technology on the distribution pattern of urban economic activities (manufacturing, retail and services) in both the Chicago CMSA and the Seoul Metropolitan Region. We used regression models with IT-related variables to measure two types of impact: a zonal attraction effect (level of activity) and a spillover effect on surrounding areas (distribution pattern). The results can be summarized as follows.

First, information technology has a very influential and positive effect on the agglomeration of firms in the sectors examined in both Chicago and Seoul (Table 5). Despite the dispersion-inducing factors of information technology, the limited availability of and accessibility to a well-equipped information network in many areas restrict the locational choices of firms, and as a result the distribution pattern is more concentrated.

Table 5. Sectoral classification for IT impacts

		Distribution pattern (spillover)	
		+	–
Activity level (attraction)	+	Manufacturing (Chicago) Retail (Chicago) Service (Chicago)	Manufacturing (Seoul) Retail (Seoul) Service (Seoul)
	–		

While this might change in the future as IT facilities disperse, for now the uneven distribution of IT infrastructure is a centripetal force. This tendency also occurs in an interurban context. Fujita and Hamaguchi (2001) noted that customers of intermediate goods are more dispersed with a well-developed transportation/communication infrastructure (found in most developed countries) than with limited infrastructure (found in many developing countries).

The signs on the coefficients of ITFIRM in the spillover equations show that the spillover effect of IT is different in the two cities: concentration in Chicago and dispersion in Seoul. A probable explanation of this difference is that establishments in Seoul are more sensitive to distance from IT infrastructure. In other words, the benefits provided from the adjacent IT infrastructure quickly vanish as establishments move further away from this infrastructure. It may depend on how easy (or difficult) it is to extend IT infrastructure spatially. The results also provide insights into how the urban economic spatial structure might change as the IT infrastructure network expands. Because of the observed spillover effects of IT infrastructure, Chicago will have more large clusters of economic activities around areas with IT infrastructure, as the network is expanded to different locations, whereas Seoul might have more very small clusters as its IT infrastructure network is extended. Because the spillover effect has a greater spatial extension in Chicago, if the de-concentration with more IT infrastructure hypothesis is true, Chicago could be the first of the two cities to show a more even spatial distribution of economic activity. Seoul might have to wait because IT infrastructure lags and the spillover effect remains weak.

References

Alles P, Esparza A, Lucas S (1994) Telecommunications and the large city-small city divide: Evidence from Indiana cities. Professional Geographer 46(3):307–316

AnselinL (1995a) Local indicators of spatial association-LISA. Geographical Analysis 27:93–115

Anselin L (1995b) SpaceStat version 1.80 user's guide. Regional Research Institute, West Virginia University, Morgantown, WV

Anselin L, Bera AK (1998) Spatial dependence in linear regression models with an introduction to spatial econometrics. In: Ullah A, Giles DEA (eds) Handbook of applied economic statistics. Marcel Dekker, New York, NY., pp 237–289

Capello R (1994) Towards new industrial and spatial systems: The role of new technologies. The Journal of the Regional Science Association International 73:189–208

Drucker PF (1989) Information and the future of the city. Urban Land 48:38–39

Echeverri-Carroll EL (1996) Flexible production, electronic linkages, and large firms: Evidence from the automobile industry. The Annals of Regional Science 30(1):135–152

Fujita M, Hamaguchi N (2001) Intermediate goods and the spatial structure of an economy. Regional Science and Urban Economics 31:79–109
Gaspar J, Glaeser EL (1998) Information technology and the future of cities. Journal of Urban Economics 43(1):136–156
Getis A, Ord K (1992) The analysis of spatial association by use of distance statistics. Geographical Analysis 24:189–206
Gordon P, Richardson HW (1996) Beyond polycentricity: The dispersed metropolis, Los Angeles, 1970–1990. Journal of the American Planning Association 62(3):289–295
Handy SL, Mokhtarian PL (1996) Forecasting telecommuting: An exploration of methodologies and research needs. Transportation 23:163–190
Lund JR, Mokhtarian PL (1994) Telecommuting and residential location: Theory and implications for commute travel in the monocentric metropolis. Transportation Research Record 1463:10–14
Mokhtarian PL (1998) A synthetic approach to estimating the impact of telecommuting on travel. Urban Studies 35(2):215–241
Moulaert F, Djellal F (1995) Information technology consultancy firms: Economies of agglomeration from a wide-area perspective. Urban Studies 32(1):105–122
Nilles JM (1988) Traffic reduction by telecommuting: A status review and selected bibliography. Transportation Research A 22(4):301–317
Ord JK, Getis A (1995) Local spatial autocorrelation statistics: Distributional issues and an application. Geographical Analysis 27(4):286–306
Richardson R, Gillespie A (1996) Advanced communications and employment creation in rural and peripheral regions: A case study of the Highlands and Islands of Scotland. The Annals of Regional Science 30(1):91–110
Salomon I (1996) Telecommunications, cities and technological opportunism. The Annals of Regional Science 30(1):75–90
Sinden A (1995) Telecommunications services: Job loss and spatial restructuring in Britain, 1989–1993. Area 27(1):34–45
Stough RR, Paelinck J (1996) Substitution and complementary effects of information on regional travel and location behavior. In: Proceedings, New International Perspectives on Telework Workshop, Brunel University, London, UK, pp 380–397
Tofflemire JM (1992) Telecommunication external economies, city size and optimal pricing for telecommunications. Journal of Regional Science 32(1):77–90
Warf B (1989) Telecommunications and the globalization of financial services. Professional Geographer 41(3):257–271
Wheeler DC, O'Kelly ME (1999) Network topology and city accessibility of the commercial internet. Professional Geographer 51(3):327–339
Wheeler JO, Mitchelson RL (1989) Atlanta's role as an information center: Intermetropolitan spatial links. Professional Geographer 41(2):162–172
Yen J, Mahmassani HS (1997) Telecommuting adoption: Conceptual framework and model estimation. Transportation Research Record 1606:95–102

Globalization and urban environmental transitions: Comparison of New York's and Tokyo's experiences

Peter J. Marcotullio[1], **Sarah Rothenberg**[2], **Miri Nakahara**[3]

[1] United Nations University, Institute of Advanced Studies, 53-67, Jingumae 5-chrome, Shibuyaku, Tokyo 150-8303, Japan (e-mail: pjmarco@ias.unu.edu)
[2] University of California, Environmental Science and Engineering Program, Los Angeles, USA (e-mail: srothenb@ucla.edu)
[3] National Institute for Environmental Studies, Onogawa 16-2, Isukuba, Ibaraki, 305-0053, Japan (e-mail: m_nakahara@ias.unu.edu)

Abstract. This article argues that urban environmental transitions (McGranahan et al. 2001) are experienced differently by cities, such as New York and Tokyo. While New York has experienced shifts in its environmental burdens over long periods of time and in sequential order, Tokyo, which developed rapidly under the forces of globalization, has experienced shifts in environmental burdens over shorter periods and simultaneously. Starting from the viewpoint that associates long waves of development with the Western experience, the paper demonstrates that there were different transitions among sets of environmental conditions within the United States in general and New York City in particular. Then, the focus turns to the contemporary urban development of Japan and Tokyo. David Harvey's (1989) notion of "time-space compression," helps to explain the compressed and telescoped transitions.

JEL classification: R00, N9, F01

1. Introduction

Recent work on the relationship between development and the environment suggests that there are sets of environmental transitions associated with wealth. As nations and their cities grow in income the environmental burdens they experience change. These transformations have been conceptualized under the rubric of urban environmental transitions; a powerful conceptual tool for understanding these complex relationships (McGranahan et al. 2001). Empirical work on shifts in environmental conditions in cities of the United States (Melosi 2000) and Asia (Bai and Imura 2000; Webster 1995) as well as those in different developing regions (McGranahan and Songsore 1994) suggests that cities have undergone urban environmental transitions. There

The authors would like to thank the United Nations University Institute of Advanced Studies, the Summer Program in Japan, sponsored by the National Science Foundation and the Japanese Ministry of Education for their financial support.

has been a lack, however, of comparative research between different development experiences.

East and Southeast Asian countries have undergone rapid development since 1950. Their high economic growth experiences differ from those of the West (see for example, Crafts 2000). It is hypothesized, therefore, that globalization-driven growth has created significantly different development contexts in these nations than previously encountered in the West, thus altering their experiences of environmental burdens. Specifically, a comparison of their urban environmental transitions demonstrates that while New York City underwent a series of environmental problems in sequential order and over a long period of time, Tokyo's experiences were more compressed in time and telescoped (experienced with increasing overlaps of sets of burdens).

The article is divided into five sections. After the introduction, the second section presents a brief discussion of the urban environmental transition theory (McGranahan et al. 2001) and previous drivers of change defined by factors underpinning shifts in long waves of development. It also explains how the current context of development has altered these patterns as globalization driven growth has accompanied what Harvey (1989) has called "time-space compression." These differences provide an understanding of Japan's experiences.

The third and fourth sections elaborate on the environmental histories of New York City and Tokyo. The analytical goal of the New York City discussion is to associate specific environmental problems to specific techno-economic paradigms (Berry 1997). Among a variety of other factors, besides shifts in economic activities and technologies, that influence environmental transitions, the section highlights the roles of increased knowledge of environmental problems and local catastrophic events. Japanese development is also viewed through the lens of long wave development (Mosk 2001), but its period of rapid development came later than that of New York as did attention to environmental problems. While Tokyo exhibits the pattern described by urban environmental transition theory, the shifts from "brown" to "gray" to "green" environmental burdens came largely after World War II. The fifth section provides a discussion and conclusion by summarizing the results of the comparison.

2. Conceptualizing the underlying reasons for difference experiences

The task of understanding how the urban environmental experiences in Tokyo differ from those of New York City requires a perspective that associates trends in development with those of the environment and also demonstrates how and why patterns might differ. In this article, the relationship between the environment and development is viewed through the lens of urban environmental transition theory (McGranahan et al. 2001). Drivers of environmental transitions in the nineteenth and early twentieth centuries, when western cities underwent their rapid development, are associated with factors underpinning long waves of development. During the post-World War II era, however, the context of development has changed profoundly. Contemporary globalization has brought about "time-space compression" (Harvey 1989), altering the way environmental transitions are experienced. These three concepts, urban environmental transitions, long-wave development and globalization-driven "time-space compression," are the keys to understanding the differences in the urban environmental experiences faced by cities that industrialized beginning in the early nineteenth century and those that industrialized later.

2.1. *The urban environmental transition theory and the notion of shifting environmental challenges*

As a result of the unsatisfying fit described by the simple environmental Kuznets curve (EKC) model, scholars from a variety of fields interested in the environmental issues of developing countries have developed a more elaborate model of the relationship between environment and development. In a recent text that sums up 10 years of research in this field, Gordon McGranahan and his collaborators (2001) present a persuasive argument entitled urban environmental transition theory, which demonstrates a shift in type and geographical scale of impact of environmental burdens that accompany growing affluence.

The transition is defined by a shift from "brown" agenda issues to those of rapidly industrializing cities, the "gray" agenda, to "green" agenda challenges. "Brown" agenda issues include lack of safe water, inadequate waste management and pollution control, accidents linked to congestion and crowding, occupation and degradation of sensitive lands, and the interrelationships between these problems (Bartone et al. 1994). These burdens are typically local in scale impacting homes and neighborhoods. The "gray" agenda issues include increases in air pollutants (SO_2, total suspended particles – TSP) and chemical water pollutants (as measured, for example, by chemical oxygen demand – COD, and levels of phosphorus), which impact regional air and watersheds. Finally, "green" agenda issues include non-point source pollution, consumption related burdens (such as CO_2 emissions and waste production) and persistent chemicals, among others, which have regional if not global impact. That is, as cities grow in wealth, environmental burdens shift from localized, immediate and health threatening to global, delayed and ecosystem threatening (McGranahan et al. 2001).

2.2. *Long waves of development, shifts in understanding environmental problems and catastrophic events*

Associated with the long-term trends in price cycles (Kondratieff waves; Kondratieff 1979) are shifts in technologies. Brian Berry (1997), for example, suggests that US history is marked by a rise and fall of a succession of techno-economic systems, defined by interrelated sets of technologies and economic activities. The first set of techno-economic systems involved the use of wind, water and wood for mercantile activities. This was followed by the coal, steam and steel system for early industrial activity. Thereafter petroleum, internal combustion engines and electricity drove the mature industrial capitalist system.

Borchert (1967) and Yates (1998), among others, have suggested that these long waves are inherently associated with US urban development patterns. Four periods of urban development can be discerned including the frontier mercantilist (to 1845), early industrial capitalist (1845–1895), national industrial capitalist (1895–1945), and mature capitalist (1945-present) eras.

Moreover, urban environmental historians have identified a shifting set of environmental burdens in American urban history. Melosi (2000), for example, has added two more explanatory factors for the shifting patterns of urban environmental solutions; evolution of theoretical understanding of the problem and the decisions to implement new technologies. In recent work on the history of urban water supply, sanitation and solid waste he suggests that there were shifts in the understanding of environmental problems from the early nineteenth century to the turn of the twentieth century and then again during the middle of the twentieth century (miasma theory to germ theory to ecological theory). At the same time, decisions to implement new systems were often related to catastrophic events (fires, plagues, accidents, etc). These two factors played an important role in how and when city managers provided solutions to urban environmental problems. Throughout history "solutions," often meant the export, both geographically and temporally (i.e., into the future), of the particular set of environmental problems. His work is complementary to urban environmental transition theory.

2.3. Globalization and "time-space compression"

One unique characteristic of the current era of development has been the emergence of globalization processes or the deepening, thickening and speeding up of cross-border economic, social and political interdependencies (Dicken 1998; Held et al. 1999; Knox and Agnew 1998; Johnston et al. 1995). Through the fixed and immobile transport, communications and regulatory-institutional infrastructures, physical movements of commodities through space are accelerated (Brenner 1999). Cities, through the "world city formation process" (Friedmann and Wolff 1982), have become nodes in the global economic system (Knox and Taylor 1995; Sassen 1991).

While processes of global integration have been at work for centuries, they have reached "hyperactive" status in recent times (Thrift 1995). The result, David Harvey (1989) describes as "time-space compression," associated with revolutionary shifts in the objective qualities of space and time. While Harvey has treated his idea of "time-space compression" primarily as a way to express the sped-up pace of urban life and intended it as a description of individual and societal experiences (i.e., it explains underlying social and individual disturbances and even terror that has accompanied globalization),[1] it has been used here in the sense of overlapping or "telescoping" of material conditions that impact daily life. The concept provides notions missing from the notion of time-space convergence (Janelle 1968), specifically the aspect of "telescoping."

During the current era, both the processes of time-space compression and "world city formation" have combined. For those cities that are competing successfully within the world market and have opened their doors to

[1] According to Thrift N (1995) A hyperactive world. In Johnston RJ, Taylor PJ, Watts MJ (eds) Geographies of Global Change. Blackwell, Oxford, pp 18–35 (p 21), Harvey uses this idea in two main ways. He uses it to express the increasing the pace of life brought about by innovations like modern telecommunications. Second, it signals the upheaval in our daily experiences of life, as we are increasingly unable to map the representations of space and time.

economic integration, previously unheard of development scenarios have accompanied rapid development. As global processes focus on cities, the associated environmental transitions not only shorten in some cases, but also increasingly overlap (Fig. 1).

Figure 2 demonstrates the current state of overlapping environmental agendas. An analysis of data for three different types of environmental burdens supports the main points of this argument. As the figure demonstrates, there are relationships among the following variables, all calculated for 1995: GDP per capita with percent non-access to safe water, SO_2 emissions per capita and CO_2 emission per capita. Each function represents a significant relationship between wealth (in this case income) and the three sets of environmental issues.

The first interesting aspect of the graph is that it demonstrates the environmental transition. The severity of environmental problems experienced by low-income cities, such as access to safe water, has an inverse relationship to wealth. While "brown" agenda issues are "solved" another set of challenges associated with rapid industrialization, such as SO_2 emissions, emerge. This group of environmental challenges makes up the "gray" agenda, which includes environmental challenges associated with industrialization and motorization. In terms of these largely chemical inputs, Kates (2000) suggested that in the US, between 1970 and 1996 the levels of some air and water pollutants decreased (with the exception of nitrogen oxides, which remained constant). He noted the drop in particulate matter and lead from the air and phosphorus from water. The curve for SO_2 per capita by GDP per capita demonstrates this trend by forming the "inverted U-shape" of the EKC. The turning point when pollution intensity de-links from economic growth is believed to be a function of increased environmental regulations (Sawa 1997). CO_2 is used as a measure of "green" agenda issues. Increased CO_2 emissions within cities are the partial result of an increase in automobile use. The trend in the relationship between these variables and GDP per capita increases exponentially (see also World Bank 1992).

The second interesting aspect of the chart is the extent to which these sets of challenges overlap. From these estimations it is further possible to approximate the share of the global urban population experiencing different types of environmental risks. That is, the points where the curves meet mark shifts in the types of environmental challenges and when related to GDP per capita provide a very rough estimate of the number of people living under different situations (Table 1). These educated guesses demonstrate that the majority of the world's urban population (over 50%) is living under conditions of at least two sets of burdens and that over 20% is living under conditions of all three types of burdens. These figures also demonstrate that less than a quarter of the world's urban population is living under conditions largely related to the "green" agenda. This agenda, however, is increasingly the basis of the sustainable development mandate while a significant percentage of the world's urban population (18%) is living in conditions dominated largely by the "brown" agenda.

While this is a static representation of the development process, it demonstrates what could be happening to cities in the current age. Tokyo and New York have already passed through many phases in their environmental transitions. To explore the differences in the way that globalization has impacted these cities we need to turn to their transition histories.

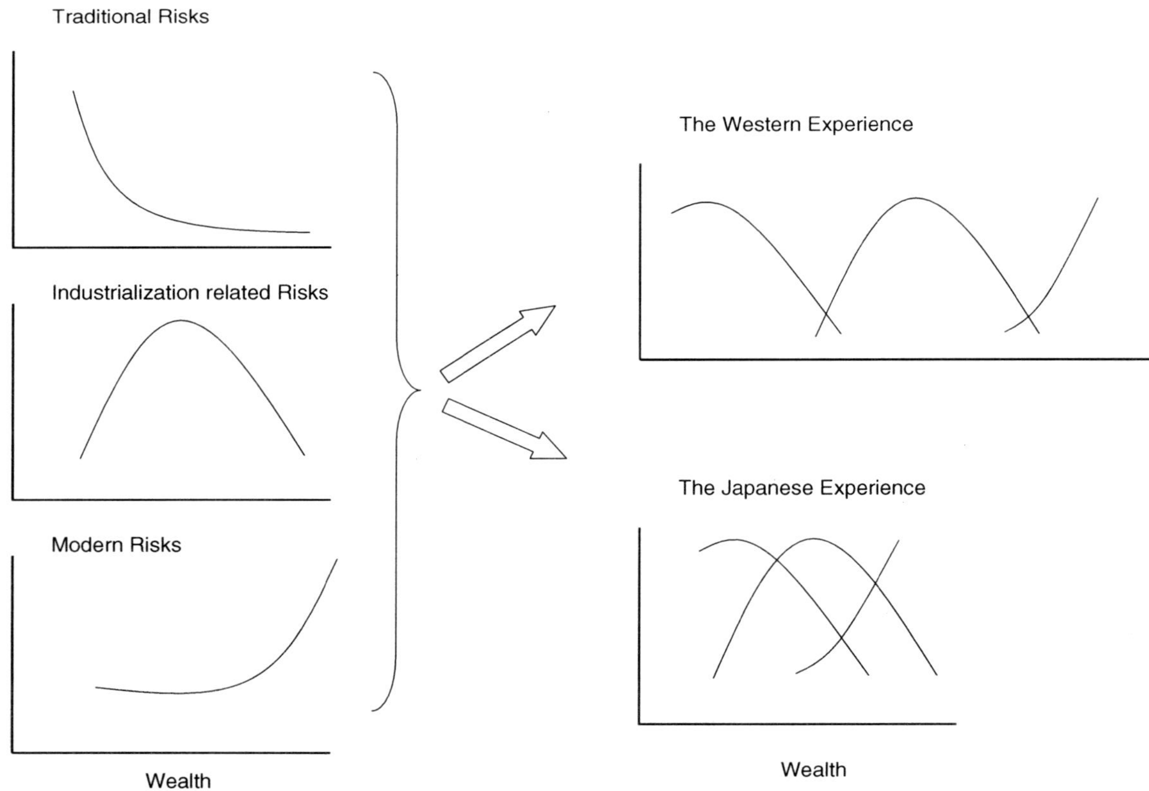

Fig. 1. Schematically different urban environmental transition experiences

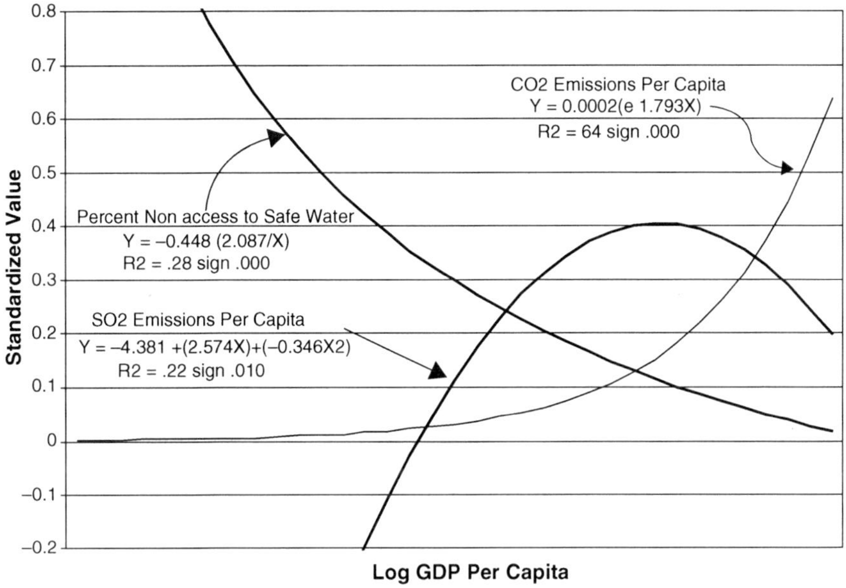

Fig. 2. The environmental transition (1995 data)

Table 1. Estimated urban population living under various environmental conditions 1995

1995 GDP Category (US$)	Environmental challenges	Total urban population (thousands) (N)	Share of total (%)
< 467.74	Lack of water and sanitation ("brown" issues)	456,985	17.8
> 467.75 < 1,071.52	Rising industrial pollution ("gray" issues), and significant "brown" issues	518,812	20.3
> 1,071.53 < 3,981.07	High "gray" issues, increasing modern risks ("green" issues) and "brown" issues	526,315	20.6
> 3,981.08 < 14,125.3	High but decreasing "gray" issues, rising "green" issues	296,993	11.6
> 14,125.3	Largely "green" issues	613,480	24.0
Missing		147,610	5.8
Total global urban population		2,560,195	

3. The New York City experience

New York City's history provides examples of shifts in extreme environmental conditions. While not the nation's political capital (except for a short period after the War of Independence), it has been the commercial emporium of the country since independence. It experienced the greatest immigration flows of any city in the country and was often the center of urban technological innovation. While never a typical US city the study of New York's experience provides powerful insights into how western cities experienced and solved their most difficult environmental challenges.

Certain environmental issues appeared with specific epochs, technologies, scientific understanding and catastrophic events. It is evident that different periods were plagued by different sets of environmental problems and that solutions came about slowly as challenges were met sequentially; and very often these solutions led to new problems in later periods.

Before 1845, both economic development and urban growth were slow, although New York did reach 120,000 by 1820. Transportation technologies limited outward growth, and land uses were mixed. In this period, the city's urban environmental problems were local and "brown" in nature. Early challenges were largely related to water supply and waste removal and management. Mud and stagnant water, overflowing outhouses, open sewers, farm animals, manure, refuse (including fat, bones and other wastes discarded by butchers, fishmongers and tradesmen) tossed into streets gave the city's air a pungent odor (Grava 1995). One of the first urban solutions to these challenges was street grading and side gutter systems (first implemented in Boston in 1713). The initial reason for this new technology was to facilitate the removal of horse waste and provide safe and healthy gathering spaces (McShane 1979). Under the circumstances these challenges were largely insoluble and adaptation meant adjustment or leaving.

Toward the end of this period, improvements in transportation allowed for the decentralization of the population and the creation of the first suburbs and commercial districts. In New York City, the first commuter suburb was established in Brooklyn Heights with regular steam ferry service after 1814, affording improved environments for wealthy Manhattan workers (Jackson 1985).

Aaron Burr's privately run Manhattan Water Supply Company provided water to affluent neighborhoods and central business districts received most of the water, while working-class districts often relied on polluted wells and other potentially unhealthy local sources. There were several health epidemics (e.g., yellow fever and cholera) that led to public sector control over water (the construction of an aqueduct, 1835–1842, to bring water from the Croton River) and improvements in environmental sanitation.

The period 1845–1895 witnessed a period of intense industrialization (usually relatively small-scale firms), the growth of immigration, and major changes in transport technology (steam engines and the horse-drawn streetcar).

With rapid growth and the beginnings of industrialization the first set of urban environmental problems that emerged during the previous period grew to critical levels, increasingly impacting urban life. Water supply and wastewater removal, or "brown" issues, remained the main focus of urban environmental specialists. For New York, the first and foremost problem was access to drinkable water. Providing water became an increasingly important part of urban public services, particularly after diseases such as cholera and yellow fever impacted elites (Miller 2000). By the end of the century, a bigger and much more sophisticated water supply system would be in the planning.

In contrast to the growth of water supply systems, underground waste-water systems were meager and only began to appear later. Privy vaults and cesspools were relatively widespread. As water supplies continued to provide only the necessary levels for hygienic life, these technologies and open ditches, as storm drains, were common. From 1800 to approximately 1880, sewerage treatment in most American cities was based upon the use of these technologies to rid the city of wastes (Tarr 1999).

This situation changed, however, with increased water consumption through the installation of water closets and the advent of combined sewerage technologies. The health principles behind the practice of environmental sanitation clearly pointed to the need to evacuate liquid wastes as quickly and as conveniently as possible from homes and businesses, but what to do with those wastes once they reached the end of the pipe was not always clear. The solution was simply displacing the fluid into the nearest water body.

These forces, when taken together, increasingly promoted centralized organizational structures and capital-intensive technical innovations for water supply and later waste water removal and treatment. In New York, changes in the city's charter in 1870, crafted by William M. Tweed, centralized management of the city in the Department of Public Works. Thereafter, professional engineers directed infrastructure development pursuant to sanitary reform ideas. The centralized Department of Public Works introduced comprehensive sanitary reform to the city (Goldman 1997). Part of the reform was to implement combined sewerage systems, which simplified the problems of transporting household wastes and storm water, but further complicated the pollution of the receiving water body.

The complex relationship between the implementation of water supply and wastewater remedies demonstrates the interaction between the scale impacts of shifting environmental problems, the "first things first" attitude in solving these challenges and the understanding of these problems. As the solutions to water supply demand were successful, wastewater problems grew, spilling over to larger geographically areas, but improving conditions inside the city. At the time, however, river pollution, in most urban areas, was almost completely ignored unless impacting powerful political forces downstream.

In the next phase (1895–1945), New York became increasingly global, the busiest port in the world, and was already by 1910 twice the size of Chicago, with more than two-fifths of its population foreign-born (Hammock 1987; Rosenwaike 1972). Nationally during this period four important environmental consequences of urban growth and development emerged. First, advances in water supply and sewerage created larger-scale problems, particularly for locations downstream of large cities. Concerns over sanitation forced new solutions in wastewater treatment, including treatment for biological contaminants. Second, the first major shift in urban environmental challenges occurred. As "brown" challenges were increasingly "solved," chemical industrial-related problems began to emerge. During this period the emphasis in urban environmental management shifted from biological aspects of pollution to chemical issues. Third, increasing energy consumption in cities, which demanded large amounts of coal fuel created smoke filled cities. Fourth, with general increasing consumption, municipal solid waste emerged as new challenge.

Nationally, the number of sewered communities increased from approximately 100 in 1870 to 3,000 in 1920, serving 87% of the urban population. By the end of World War II, sewerage provision was almost universal (Melosi 2000). New York City had built its sewerage system during the previous era, but the original 112 kilometers of sewers were lengthened to 747 kilometers in the 1890s.[2] By 1902, the city had built more than 1,400 miles (2240 kilometers) of sewers and most newly constructed tenements had private flush toilets (Opdycke 1995).

But other problems were emerging. Approximately 90 percent of the nation's sewage was dumped into water bodies without treatment, resulting in high typhoid death rates in downstream cities (Tarr 1999). The newly created New York City Metropolitan Sewerage Commission (1910–1914) turned its attention to sewerage disposal, but it was not until the 1930s that seven sewerage treatment plants were built with New Deal funds. The first of which opened on Coney Island in 1937 (Opdycke 1995).

The emergence of bacteriology brought a sea change in the way the world would view health and disease. While the old view of public health was concerned with the environment; the new public health paradigm was concerned with the individual (Melosi 2000). Advances in biochemistry during this period then helped sever the association of density and disease. The use of bleaching powder, chlorine gas and chloride of lime as water treatment enhanced its purity. With these techniques a dramatic decline in typhoid fever rates followed; a decline from 33.8 per thousand in 1920 to 3.7 by 1945 (Melosi 2000).

The third emerging environmental burden was air pollution. New York City's air, which during most of the nineteenth century, was known to be clean, changed when industrialists took advantage of a national coal strike in 1902 to turn from the more expensive, but less polluting anthracite coal to bituminous coal (Stradling 1999).

Fourth, it was also during this period that the collection, disposal and treatment of refuse began. In pervious periods, the "garbage problem" was site-specific and largely the individual's responsibility. With the rise of the consumer society, increasing amounts of waste had to be removed from city streets and treated. Organized incineration and the sanitary landfill solutions emerged to handle these concerns (Melosi 2000).

Also, in the latter half of this period the automobile entered the urban scene. National car registration reached 20 million in 1925 and 30 million by 1937 (Schneider 1972). The automobile facilitated further urban decentralization but was also an important public health solution to the ubiquitous horse manure problem. Toward the end of the period air travel developed. New York City opened LaGuardia Airport in 1939. By 1949, over 160,000 planes carrying over 3.2 million passengers, 36,000 tons of cargo and 14,500 tons of mail, were moving over its two runways annually. This new modern city had conquered the "brown" agenda, but had mounting industrial and motorization related challenges ahead.

New York City's environmental experiences during the most recent period (1945-present) can be characterized by two distinct phases. During the first phase of the period the focus of urban environmental managers changed as chemical pollution levels reached record-high levels and increasing suburbanization strained infrastructure capacity. In New York City in November 1953 a temperature inversion trapped sulfur dioxides, particulates and other contaminates over the city, resulting in approximately 200 deaths

[2] This was more than any other American or European city, expect Chicago.

and the hospitalization of many more. These levels of pollutants were attributed to industrial plants, the 17,000 incinerators in apartment building and municipal garbage burning plants that added soot and toxins to the environment.

In addition, New York City's surrounding water bodies were subjected to toxic pollution attacks from a number of sources. From the 1940s to the 1970s two manufacturing plants operated by General Electric located north of Albany flushed more than 500,000 pounds (227,000 kilograms) of polychlorinated biphenyls into the Hudson River. Oil spills in the Arthur Kill along Staten Island, not only fouled the water, but hurt both river and sea life and birds. Hundreds of businesses drained chemical wastes into the city's sewers, which ultimately ended up in New York Bay. For example, as much as 7,000 pounds (3,178 kilograms) of heavy metals such has zinc, copper, lead, chromium and nickel exited the city's plants every day (Goldstein and Izeman 1995).

In addition to air and water pollution problems, other "gray" issues were also placed on the political agenda as the need for infrastructure to accommodate new demands in the suburbs and to replace aging infrastructure in the core increased. Infrastructure demands within cities, however, were difficult to meet, not so much because of technical issues but rather for political and fiscal reasons. An increasing number of suburban communities turned themselves into incorporated bodies to fight off city annexation and resist responsibility for further urban investments. The flight of the well-off resulted in severely diminished resources in the urban core.

During the second phase, an attack on point source pollution successfully brought down levels of toxins in the air and water. New York City was among many localities to reduce air pollution levels, for example. The city was making moves to control environmental pollution in the late 1960s and early 1970s. First, they lowered the sulfur context allowed in coal and heating oil in 1966 and 1971. This yielded significant reductions in sulfur dioxide and soot. The City Council also prohibited new incinerators in apartment buildings as of 1970 and those that remained were phased out by 1993.

By 1970, the Federal Environmental Protection Agency's requirement for a reduction of lead in gasoline precipitated a drop in lead levels in the city by 95%. By the mid-1990s federally required pollution controls on automobiles and annual automobile inspections helped to lower official carbon monoxide readings from the harmful levels of the preceding decades. Moreover, attempts to clean up the Hudson have had some success in increasing the dissolved oxygen levels in the river and suggest the ability of the river to support and sustain marine life once again.

At the same time, however, authorities did not deal with more long-term issues such as persistent pollutants, non-point source pollution (i.e., urban runoff) and increasing consumption. Hence, as industrial-related pollution conditions were improving, the second shift in environmental issues occurred; "green" agenda issues gradually emerged.

In New York City alone, for example, 18 Federal Superfund sites were identified and New York State lists 33 inactive hazardous waste disposal sites. Further, brownfields (i.e., abandoned, idle or underused industrial and commercial properties) are concentrated along the waterfront and are still waiting for environmental cleanup (New York Conservation Education Fund 2001). The Hudson River's PCB problem remains: it is unsafe to eat fish from the River and there is a ban on fishing in the upper Hudson Bay (New York Conservation Education Fund 2001).

The production of these and other wastes were seen as "consumption" problems. Another consumption-related problem concerns lack of space for solid waste. This is an important challenge for New York City, because the Fishkill landfill site will close sometime soon, and over 7 million people will need to export all their trash somewhere else. This gave rise to the call for reusing, reducing and recycling, integrated management and community-oriented operations, but because of marketing problems the city has disbanded many of its recycling efforts.

One of the most important "green" issues is the increase in greenhouse gas emission levels and their impact on the planet's temperature (i.e., global warming). Warming can be observed in New York, although this may be due more to the "heat island"[3] effect than to increased emissions of gases. Whatever the reason, the city has experienced an average temperature increase of 0.5 degrees Celsius since the 1940s.

In summary, New York City has experienced a series of environmental challenges largely in sequential order and increasing in scale of impact and changing in terms of timing and character. These challenges are related to a set of factors including both structural changes in the techno-economic paradigm of development as well as to increasing scientific knowledge and catastrophic events. The shifts in environmental challenges occurred over a long period in a serial manner with minimal overlap facilitated by a "first things first" approach to problem solving.

4. The Tokyo experience

The systematic interaction of domestic infrastructure investment and industrial expansion and Japan's involvement with global economic and geopolitical circumstances facilitated both Kondratieff long wave shifts and innovation shifts simultaneously. As a result, Japanese industrial history has undergone four long swings since 1887 including the period 1887–1904, 1904–1930, 1930–1952 and 1952 – present. These intervals are similar, but not exactly the same as those of the western experience (Mosk 2001).

As attention was on military and industrial development (before World War II) left many environmental challenges unresolved, industrial development and income generation (after the war) had to be accomplished while "solving" sets of environmental challenges simultaneously. This makes the history of Tokyo one of compressed and telescoped urban environmental transitions.

---

[3] The "heat island effect" is warming due to urbanization. When streets and buildings replace open fields and other vegetation, outdoor temperatures tend to be higher than they naturally would be for two reasons. First, trees and other vegetation provide shade and evapotranspiration, which have a cooling effect. Second, sidewalk pavements and building exteriors do not reflect sunlight, which causes more warming near the Earth's surface. See Intergovernmental Panel on Climate Change, and Working Group II (1996). Climate Change 1995: Impacts, Adaptations and Mitigation of Climate Change. Cambridge University Press, Cambridge.

The "early modern" era of Japanese history starts around 1600 and ends in 1868 (the Meiji Revolution). During this period, rural demilitarization and almost total isolation from the West conditioned the economic growth of the country. However, a nationwide and domestically derived system of infrastructure and economy developed (e.g., castle towns, road networks, canals and irrigation districts).

Environmental problems in Edo, i.e., feudal Tokyo, were tempered by the need to conserve resources and minimize waste. At the same time, fires, unpaved streets and water supply were significant problems. The dense population, wooden architecture and idiosyncratic mix of lanes and alleys were susceptible to large fires, which occurred periodically. Unfortunately, preventive building codes were not enforced (Sorensen 2001).

Within the city, service provision was based on status. Consequently, geographically distinct neighborhoods developed with their own facilities. Water supplies were first provided to the high-income areas (Hatano 1995). As the city developed, however, complex waterworks were built, but maintenance was turned over to users; many dug their own wells and disconnected themselves from the system because of deteriorating water quality (Sorensen 2001). Sewage disposal, on the other hand, was part of the closed-loop system developed between the city and its hinterland. Night soil was collected and sold to farmers. There were several major cholera epidemics in the mid-nineteenth century (e.g., an epidemic in Edo in 1858 claimed 286,000 lives; Yamamura 1983). As the city expanded in size and density, "brown" agenda burdens became life-threatening.

The first period of modernization began with the Meiji (1868–1914), meaning "enlightened rule." The Meiji era is marked by an opening up of the Japanese society after centuries of isolation and the adaptation of western technology. This period formed the basis of the country's future industrial growth. Western models and technologies were adapted for steamships, educational and postal services architecture and shipbuilding. Growth was financed by a proliferation of credit-creating institutions, particularly banks, as stock and bond markets were weak. Giant combinations, *zaibatsu*, emerged as engines of capital accumulation. The model *zaibatsu* included a financial cluster (banks, trust and insurance *companies*), a general trading company (*sōgō shōsha*), raw materials suppliers and industrial enterprises. Most included a powerful bank at its core.

Transportation and related facilities also changed in a number of ways The *jinrikisha*, a hybrid of the Chinese rickshaw with rubber wheels from western bicycles was also introduced to Japan in the 1870s to transport people. Railroads did not play a major role until the next phase of development. International trade was helped by improvements in port facilities so that larger sea-going vessels could be accommodated.

Tokyo's rise was a result from the profound impact of the Meiji era. First, the city was made into the imperial capital as the Emperor was moved from Kyoto to the Shogun's castle in Edo. Second, the name Edo was dropped in favor of "eastern capital," Tokyo. Third, the new government modernized the city physically according to western influences.

The city needed re-building at the time. First, it lost over 25% of its population as the *diamyō* (warlords) returned to their home provinces, leaving large tracts of vacant land. Second, a series of earthquakes in 1854 and 1855 followed by flooding and then by a cholera epidemic ravaged the city. Third, a fire in 1872 in the *shitamachi* burnt down part of the commercial quarter, called Ginza. These events called for a series of changes to the city and its administration. The *Ginza* was re-built as the "Ginza Brick Quarter," designed by Thomas Waters, English architect, who also helped to fireproof the district. The *diamyō* tracts immediately to the south of the castle were claimed by the military and then by various government agencies as office sites. Eventually, all the areas of *Nagatachō* and *Kasumigaseki* were given over to government functions.

In 1889, the city code was enacted as a hybrid European concept of municipal government. At that time the city included 81.2 square kilometers and began as a municipality with thirteen wards. The Tokyo City Improvement Ordinance planned for the construction and widening of roads, 49 parks, the new excavation of 8 rivers and improvement to 22 rivers and canals as well as other public works, including water supply and sewerage (Ishizuka and Ishida 1988; Sorensen 2001). By the time the Ordinance was implemented the city had regained its former size of one million (Cybriwksy 1991). Most of the industrialization in Tokyo was small-scale, although heavy industries developed in the Tokyo Bay between Tokyo and Yokohama.

The main goal of Japanese modernization was increased military and industrial strength (Sorensen 2001). Basic public infrastructure was neglected. Pollution problems were largely ignored. For example in 1887, when local residents suffered from poor drinking water contaminated by the Ashio Copper Mine the case went before the Diet (Parliament), but no action was taken (Okada and Peterson 2000). The government was aware of the problems, but was unwilling to appropriate funds or enforce codes. At the same time, untreated sewerage was still a commodity and individuals removed the night soil from sewerage tanks for farmers. Hence, both government apathy and private opposition to sewerage systems militated against changing the system. As a result, epidemics spread. In 1882, a cholera epidemic in Tokyo's *Kanda* area killed over 33,000 people (3.5% of the Tokyo population). This followed a national epidemic in 1879 when 105,000 people died and preceded another in 1886 when 108,000 died. Despite these catastrophes the Home Ministry, which controlled the development of housing and building, still did not support sewerage measures. However, in 1890 the Water Supply Law and in 1900 the Sewerage Law were enacted. Both laws gave municipalities the responsibility for managing these public works projects, but did not provide the funding (that came much later; after WWII).

During the next period (1904–1952) Japan was still playing "catch-up" and coping with "brown" agenda challenges. Industrialization proceeded apace, and Tokyo's population trebled between 1890 and 1920, to 3 million, largely because of rural-urban migration. With increasing densities and environmental burdens left unresolved, the city's environment degradation continued. Severe overcrowding and environmental degradation were common features and urgent problems regarding waste disposal arose. The old system of homes selling their night soil deteriorated because of increasing distances between the urban center and farms. Homeowners had to pay for it to be hauled away. Sometimes, these contractors dumped en route, and consequently Tokyo developed a pervasive bad smell (Cybriwksy 1991).

One of the most sweeping attempts to correct urban environmental problems in the country was the 1919 City Planning Plans and Building Code. This code was based upon the previous Tokyo City Improvement Ordinance of 1888. The 1919 Code, however, provided the first planning system designed for entire urban areas (rather than the previous view of working within individual neighborhoods). The ideas for this system were largely borrowed from western examples and the goal was to control urban growth. The highly centralized urban planning apparatus of the Japan government was located in the Home Ministry. The implementation of the law was largely the work of a small elite group of bureaucrats.

The initial version of the 1919 law included provisions in the Tokyo City Improvement Ordinance, such as the building of roads and a zoning system and ways to pay for more improvements through land taxes. The Urban Building Law detailed the building regulations including permissible building uses, heights and lot coverage for the use zones of the zoning system (Sorensen 2001). These laws were opposed, however, by other agencies within the government, which insisted that city planning was not their responsibility and in an attempt to weaken them, the powerful Finance Ministry removed key provisions, including sections relating to the financial support by the government. As local governments were unable to implement planning policies that differed from those of the central government and passed laws in 1919 further strengthened the central government, central government's hold on localities increased. So, for example, while sewerage plans were created, they were not implemented.

In 1931, government reorganization in Tokyo substantially expanded its size (by 400 km^2) and the number of wards (to 35). The city government appropriated various waterworks that had previously served individual areas. Ten different waterworks systems were added to city's system and three privately managed systems were acquired. These components, connected sometime during the 1930s, formed the basis of a modern water supply system for the city (Tokyo Metropolitan Government 1999d).[4]

During World War II, two-fifths of the city was destroyed, as was most of its water supply system. Reconstruction was undertaken rapidly, but once again "brown" issues were neglected, in part because of political centralization and lack of community participation (Sorensen 2001). The pressure to become an economic and military giant resulted in delayed attention to environmental problems.

The period since the early 1950s has seen Tokyo's emergence as a world city (it was already 9.8 million by 1965). The remaining "brown" agenda challenges have been addressed, there has been some success with "gray" agenda issues, and "green" agenda problems have become part of the national consciousness.

As part of the industrial development strategy for the country, Japan promoted the development of New Industrial Cities (NIC) and Special Industrial Districts (SID). These were included in the First NDP (National Development Plan) in early 1960s and involved the decentralization of "smokestack" industries from large cities. The First and Second NCRDPs (National Capital Region Development Plans, in 1958 and 1965 respectively) were also aimed at decentralizing factories. This effort was promoted through

[4] While these individual components provide the backbone of the system, Tokyo still needed more water. The government had plans to build the Ogouchi Dam on the Tama River in the 1930s, but did not. The dam was finally finished in 1957.

the designation of New Urban Development Areas on the fringes of the National Capital Region (NCR). In these locations new factories were encouraged to locate and at the same time, restrictions on the establishment and expansion of factories within the built-up areas, such as Tokyo's 23 Wards, were promulgated. These policies aimed at decentralizing the main industries of the period including energy, steel, automobiles and ships, petrochemicals and chemicals and transportation infrastructure. Industries quickly took advantage of the government incentives and infrastructure and relocated to the 20 coastal areas that the government promoted, where they provided the basis of the country's rapid economic development.

As a result of rapid industrialization during the 1950s and 1960s, Japan experienced high levels of pollution and urban sprawl. Japan's chemical pollution problems were more significant than those of the US (Sorensen 2001). Further, earlier attempts at applying building codes and zoning were inadequate. Urban sprawl occurred before roads, sewerage systems, parks and schools were planned, creating problems in the suburbs. Living space was limited, there were few parks and open spaces, and exposure to pollution was significant. Tokyo had poor air and water quality, housing problems, traffic congestion, inadequate land-use planning, and deficient social services and urban infrastructure (Cybriwsky 1991).

One of the main environmental challenges was the city's battle with "brown" issues, in particular water supply and sewerage. In 1960, 10,000 people experienced dysentery. Just before the 1964 Tokyo Olympics, water rationing was in effect[5] and 60% of Tokyo's population was without sewerage. The city employed special trucks to vacuum the sewerage from septic tanks, while night soil, was still carted out to farms for use as fertilizer (Seidensticker 1990). Nationally, even by 1965, only 14% of the country's population was provided with sewage systems (Okada and Peterson 2000).

Around the same time, another set of problems arose. "Gray" issues from rapid industrialization were developing. As industrial development advanced, localities became more aware of its negative externalities, especially from the heavy chemical industries. For example, fish from Tokyo's Sumida River disappeared by 1955, largely due to chemical wastes.

By the late 1960s, these problems had become a major national issue. Among the most important environmental concerns were air pollution, water pollution, waste disposal, noise and vibration, and ground subsidence. Victims of pollution began to take their cases to court, as they suffered both physical and financial losses without compensation. The grass roots outcry peaked with the "Big Four" court cases in the early 1970s. One was the infamous Minamata Bay, Nippon Chisso, shellfish mercury pollution case; another case concerned the "Itai-itai" (ouch-ouch) disease, caused by heavy metals including cadmium, which contaminated rice paddies. After a special "pollution session" held by the Diet, the government finally recognized the problem and moved to reverse these trends.

---

[5] In 1963 and 1964, precipitation the upper basin of the Tama River fell precariously driving the level of water behind the Ogouchi Dam down from 180 million cubic meters to 2 million cubic meters. For a time, in August prior to the Olympics event, seventeen of the twenty-three wards had water supply for only nine hours a day. Parts of the city were completely dependent on water trucks for their supplies (Seidensticker 1990).

The 1968 New Planning Law was a reaction to the problems associated with rapid urban development. Before that time, developers were able to expand without adding infrastructure and other improvements, such as roads, sewer systems, schools and parks. At the same time, 14 other laws relating to pollution control were either revised or passed. In addition, the Environment Agency was created to oversee the new pollution laws (Sorensen 1999).

While the Japanese public was becoming more aware of the despoliation of the environment, global economic forces and new technologies were at work shaping its future. Specifically, 1973 was a crucial turning point marked by the worldwide energy crisis. As a result of the tripling in the price of oil, the rate of national economic growth dropped from 5.1% in 1973 to –0.5% in 1974. The oil shocks of 1973/1974 and later in 1978/1979 led to a decline in the Japanese manufacturing sector. Heavy industries, such as steel and ship making, were hit hard. The oil and environmental crises enhanced the perception that the income-generating industries of the time could no longer support Japan's future economic growth. The crises accelerated the replacement of these industries by newly emerging high-tech industries such as microelectronics (semi-conductors, computers, and communication equipment) and other related manufacturing industries, such as automobile and consumer durable goods.

During the transformation to a high-tech society after the world energy crisis of 1973–1974, the "gray" and "brown" environmental problems were addressed simultaneously. For example, in Tokyo SO_2, TSP, O_3 and other air pollutant levels dropped significantly. At the same time, the city systematically improved its sewerage and improved its water supply systems (Tokyo Metropolitan Government 1999).

Planners welcomed these changes, although the battles were hard won. Despite these improvements, by 1980 26% of the 23 central wards area and 53% of Tama were still without sewers. Also, Tokyo continued to grow as policies to relieve concentration had failed. For example, the daily flow of commuters into Tokyo's 23-Ward area from outside the city increased from 2,640,000 in 1980 to 3,690,000 persons in 1995. The situation was somewhat relieved by the expansion of the public transport system, especially rail.

Tokyo's current environmental challenges can be categorized into four types, similar to those currently experienced by New York City. Specifically, Tokyo is struggling with: i. both point and non-point source related pollution; ii. increased waste production and emissions generated from increased consumption and quality of life issues such as green space, noise, etc; iii. toxic substances; and iv. persistent and bio-accumulative toxics related to water quality.

Air pollution challenges have been a constant struggle for city managers. Tokyo has been able to control air pollution from point sources and have seen some reductions in SO_2 emissions per capita and TSP levels, but with less success in controlling the pollutants associated the increase in automobile use (Sawa 1997; Tokyo Metropolitan Government 1999c). Two remaining important issues for citizens are air pollution emissions from waste treatment facilities and the increasing amounts of CO_2. Also, dioxin levels from waste incineration are high in Japan.

Further, global warming has become more important; the average temperature in Tokyo is increasing twice as fast as in most other countries. One view is that global warming is expected to increase the sea level 10–50 cm by

2050 (Intergovernmental Panel on Climate Change and Working Group II 1998). If this is correct eastern Tokyo would be threatened with severe flooding (this area includes 3% of Japan's population and 17% of national commercial activity, but only 0.06% of the total land area; Center for Global Environmental Research in Japan 1993). For Tokyo, Nagoya, and Osaka, three of Japan's largest coastal cities, the estimated cost of these changes to industries is US$92 billion (Center for Global Environmental Research in Japan 1993).

Water pollution in Tokyo Bay from household waste effluents is a concern for Tokyo's citizens and the city is therefore promoting the use of rainwater and the recycling of wastewater (Tokyo Metropolitan Government 1999b).

In general, however, Japan is responding much more to its challenges via several legal and regulatory actions. In Tokyo, several new laws including the Tokyo Metropolitan Basic Environment Plan (1997) and the new Environmental Impact Assessment (1998) are attempts to improve the city's environmental quality. Of the five major current strategies put forward by the city, four deal with social and environmental issues. High on the list is the creation of an appealing and livable city (see Tokyo Metropolitan Government 1999). Demand management and recycling strategies have been implemented. Recent attempts to combat pollution from incinerator plants have been successful.

In summary Tokyo's environmental experiences are based upon: i. its rapid globalization-driven development; ii. the governmental system and policy priorities at various stages of its growth; iii. the cultural and community focus on recycle and waste reduction; and iv. a continued positive attitude toward technology and engineering.

During the Meiji era, Japan and Tokyo placed industrialization at the forefront of their development practices, making the country a "polluters' paradise" (Matsui 1993). Rapid development accompanied diffusion of technologies from other countries. Japan's arm's length approach to globalization (adapting selective technologies for Japanese needs and tastes) was accomplished through a highly centralized and managed governmental system. Top-level bureaucrats often made policy based upon the decisions of a few, without feedback in the other direction. Government officials gave priority to economic performance and growth and ignored the associated environmental problems. This prolonged the overlap between environmental agendas as unresolved issues remained and new ones arose.

The government, however, was not the only actor within the Japanese society responsible for its different urban environmental transition. Another aspect that helped to shape Japan's and Tokyo's transition was cultural attitudes towards recycling and resource efficiency. Specifically, the importance of night soil as a marketable commodity, and the resource conservation efforts embedded in Japanese traditions, discouraged modern sewerage systems. This helped to keep sewerage off the policy agenda and made it more difficult to enforce "brown" agenda laws.

One last issue that is important in explaining the Japanese experience is their continued positive attitude toward technology. Incineration and recycling technologies are looked upon more favorably than in the United States. In New York City it has been impossible to build a waste volume-reducing incinerator in decades. In Tokyo, there are 17, and the newer incinerators have relatively clean emissions.

5. Conclusions

A comparison of New York City's and Tokyo's urban environmental experiences demonstrates that each city followed the broad outlines of the urban environmental transition. At the same time, however, Tokyo's experiences differed from those of New York City. Tokyo's experiences were compressed, creating overlapping agendas, while the New York experienced sets of environmental burdens sequentially. That is, increasing wealth, advances in technology, catastrophic events and scientific understanding can help to provide the broad outlines of the process, but they do not fully explain the contours of the urban environmental transition. We must also understand how globalization has impacted urban growth.

There are two major conclusions that can be drawn from the changing shape of the urban environmental transition, as suggested by the Tokyo experience. First, in terms of practice, with globalization as a driving force, developing world cities growing via export-orientation and open foreign direct investment policies will find their environmental experiences different from those in the West. Cities need to deal simultaneously with several environmental problems, such as water supply, traffic, and carbon dioxide emissions. This will require new, creative ways of handling these problems, because western (and, specifically, U.S.) solutions were specific to their development context. Policies will have to be integrated both within and across sectors, hence requiring a large role for planning and government.

Second, at a conceptual level, we need to further explore how the processes of globalization are impacting urban environments. Much attention has been paid to the "trade and environment" debate in the search for "pollution havens" and "races to the bottom." The findings of this study suggest, however, that in defining urban environmental conditions, the intensity and speed of development is as important as individual decisions made by firms to locate in areas of cheap labor. "Time-space compression" provides a conceptual tool for approaching this phenomenon, but more work must be done to flesh out its structure and dynamics.

Finally, we would like to provide a note of caution in interpretation of the empirical evidence and the somewhat speculative arguments offered. Much more work is needed to provide a representative picture of the complexities associated with rapidly growing cities and the environmental implications of this growth.

References

American Lung Association (2001) Trends in air quality. Best Practices and Program Services

Bai X, Imura H (2000) A comparative study of urban environment in East Asia: stage model of urban environmental evolution. International Review for Environmental Strategies 1(1):135–158

Bartone C, Bernstein J, Leitmann J, Eigen J (1994) Toward environmental strategies for cities: Policy consideration for urban environmental management in developing countries. World Bank, Washington, DC

Berry BJL (1997) Long waves and geography in the 21st century. Futures 29(4/5):301–310

Borchert JA (1967) American metropolitan evolution. Geographical Review 57:301–332

Brenner N (1999) Globalization as reterritorialisation: the re-scaling of urban governance in the European Union. Urban Studies 36(3):431–451

Bruchey S (1992) The sources of the economic development of the United States. International Social Science Journal 134:531–548
Burns R, Sanders J, Ades L (1999) New York: An Illustrated History. Alfred A. Knopf, New York
Center for Global Environmental Research, and Japan, E. A. O. (1993) The potential effects of climate change in Japan. Center for Global Environmental Research, Tokyo
Crafts N (2000) Globalization and growth in the twentieth century. In: IMF (ed) World economic outlook, supporting studies. International Monetary Fund, Washington, DC
Cybriwksy R (1991) Tokyo: The changing profile of an urban giant. G.K. Hall & Co., Boston
Dicken P (1998) Global shift: Transforming the world economy, 3rd ed. Paul Chapman, London
Edington DW (1994) Planning for technology development and information systems in Japanese cities and regions. In: Shapria P, Masser I, Edington DW (eds) Planning for cities and regions in Japan. Liverpool University Press, Liverpool, pp 126–154
Friedmann J, Wolff G (1982) World city formation: an agenda for research and action. International Journal of Urban and Regional Research 6(3):309–343
Goldman JA (1997) Building New York's sewers, developing mechanisms of urban management. Purdue University Press, West Lafayette, Indiana
Goldstein EA, Izeman MA (1995) Pollution. In: Jackson KT (ed) The encyclopedia of New York City. Yale University Press, New Haven, pp 914–916
Grava S (1995) Streets. In: Jackson KT (ed) The encyclopedia of New York City. Yale University Press, New Haven, pp 1130–1132
Haines MR (2001) The urban mortality transition in the United States, 1800–1940. NBER Working Paper Series on Historical Factors in Long Run Growth. Cambridge
Hammack DC (1987) Power and society, greater New York at the turn of the century. Columbia University Press, New York
Harvey D (1989) The condition of postmodernity: An enquiry into the origins of cultural change. Blackwell, Oxford
Hatano J (1995) Edo's water supply. In: McClain JL, Merriman JM, Kaoru U (eds) Edo and Paris, urban life & the state in the early modern era. Cornell University Press, Ithaca, pp 234–250
Held D, McGrew A, Goldblatt D, Perraton J (1999) Global transformations, politics, economics and culture. Polity Press, Cambridge
Hobsbawn E (1996) The age of extremes: A history of the world, 1914–1991. Vintage Books, New York
Intergovernmental Panel on Climate Change, and Working Group II (1996) Climate change 1995: Impacts, adaptations and mitigation of climate change. Cambridge University Press, Cambridge
Intergovernmental Panel on Climate Change, and Working Group II (1998) The regional impacts of climate change: An assessment of vulnerability. Cambridge University Press, Cambridge
Ishizuka H, Ishida Y (1988) Tokyo, metropolis of Japan and its urban development. In: Ishizuka H, Ishida Y (eds) Tokyo: urban growth and planning 1868–1988. Tokyo. Metroplitan University, Center for Urban Studies, Tokyo, pp 3–68
Jackson KR (1985) Crabgrass frontier, the suburbanization of the United States. Oxford University Press, Oxford
Janelle DG (1968) Central place development in a time-space framework. Professional Geographer 20: 5–10
Johnston RJ, Taylor PJ, Watts MJ (1995) Geographies of global change: Remapping the world in the late twentieth century. Blackwell, Oxford
Kates RW (2000) Has the environment improved? Environment, vol. 42, pp Editorial
Kelly WW (1995) Incendiary actions: fires and firefighting in the Shogun's capital and the people's city. In: McClain JL, Merriman JM, Kaoru U (eds) Edo and Paris, urban life & the State in the early modern era. Cornell University Press, Ithaca, pp 310–331
Knox P, Agnew J (1998) The geography of the world economy, 3rd ed. Arnold, London
Knox P, Taylor PJ (eds) (1995) World cities in a world-system. Cambridge University Press, Cambridge
Kondratieff ND (1979) The long waves of economic life. Review II(4): 519–562
Kubo T (no date) Historical factors/overviews and recent development in wastewater treatment/management in Japan and the way directing toward 21st Century, 6th JADE's Conference

Maddison A (1991) Dynamic forces in capitalist development: A long-run comparative view. Oxford University Press, Oxford
Matsui S (1993) Industrial pollution control in Japan: a historical perspective. In: University UN (ed) Environmental pollution control, the Japanese experience. UNU, Tokyo, pp 1–54
McGranahan G, Jacobi P, Songsore J, Surjadi C, Kjellen M (2001) The citizens at risk, from urban sanitation to sustainable cities. Earthscan, London
McGranahan G, Songsore J (1994) Wealth, health, and the urban household: weighing environmental burden in Jakarta, Accra, Sao Paulo. Environment 36(6): 4–11, 40–45
McShane C (1979) Transforming the use of urban space: a look at the revolution in street pavements, 1880–1924. Journal of Urban History 5(3): 279–307
Melosi MV (2000) The sanitary city: Urban infrastructure in America from colonial times to the present. Johns Hopkins Press, Baltimore
Miller B (2000) Fat of the land: Garbage of New York: The last two hundred years. Four Walls Eight Windows, New York
Mosk C (2001) Japanese industrial history, technology, urbanization and economic growth. M. E. Sharpe, Armonk
New York Conservation Education Fund (2001) New York City citizen's guide to government and the urban environment. NY Conservation Fund and NY League of Conservation Voters, New York
Okada M, Peterson SA (2000) Water pollution control policy and management: The Japanese experience. Gyosei, Tokyo
Opdycke S (1995) Sewers. In: Jackson KT (ed) The encyclopedia of New York City. Yale University Press, New Haven, pp 1062
Riis JA (1972) How the other half lives; Studies among the tenements of New York. Corner House, Williamstown
Rosenwaike I (1972) Population history of New York City. Syracuse University Press, Syracuse
Sassen S (1991) The global city: New York, London, Tokyo. Princeton University Press, Princeton
Sawa T (1997) Japan's experience in the battle against air pollution. Committee on Japan's Experience in the Battle against Air Pollution, Tokyo
Schneider KR (1972) Autokind vs mankind. Schocken Books, New York
Sorenson A (1999) Land readjustment, urban planning and urban sprawl in the Tokyo Metropolitan Area. Urban Studies 36(1):2333–2360
Sorenson A (2001) The making of urban Japan: Japanese urbanization and planning from edo to the 21st century (Draft for comments). Routledge, London
Stradling D (1999) Smokestacks and progressives. The Johns Hopkins University Press, Baltimore
Takahashi J, Sugiura N (1996) The Japanese urban system and the growing centrality of Tokyo in the global economy. In: Lo F-c , Yeung Y-M (eds) In emerging world cities in Pacific Asia. UNU Press, Tokyo, pp 101–143
Tarr J (1999) Decisions about wastewater technology, 1850–1932. In: Roberts GR (ed) The American Cities & technology reader. Routledge and the Open University, London, pp 154–162
Thrift N (1995) A hyperactive world. In: Johnston RJ, Taylor PJ, Watts MJ (eds) Geographies of global change. Blackwell, Oxford, pp 18–35
Tokyo Metropolitan Government (1999a) Suginami incineration plant wins ISO environmental certification. Tokyo Metropolitan News, A Quarterly Journal of the Tokyo Metropolitan Government 49:5
Tokyo Metropolitan Government (1999b) Tokyo announces water environment master plan. Tokyo Metropolitan News, A Quarterly Journal of the Tokyo Metropolitan Government 49: 5
Tokyo Metropolitan Government (1999c) Tokyo Current Issues. TMG, Tokyo
Tokyo Metropolitan Government (1999d) Water Supply in Tokyo. TMG, Tokyo
Warner SB (1968) The private city: Philadelphia in three periods of its growth. University of Pennsylvania Press, Philadelphia
Webster D (1995) The urban environment in Southeast Asia: challenges and opportunities. In: Institute of Southeast Asian Studies (ed) Southeast Asian affairs. ISAS, Singapore, pp 89–107
World Bank (1992) World development report. World Bank and Oxford University Press, New York

Yamamura T (1983) A comparison of the development of public water supplies in England and Wales and in Japan. A dissertation submitted in partial fulfilment of the requirements of the diploma of Imperial College, London
Yeates M (1998) The North American City, 5th ed. Longman, New York

Above and below the line: Globalization and urban form in Bangkok

Mike Jenks

Department of Architecture, School of the Built Environment, Oxford Brookes University, Oxford, UK (e-mail: mjenks@brookes.ac.uk)

Abstract. This paper uses the introduction of a mass rapid transit system into the existing urban form of the city of Bangkok as a metaphor to explore issues of globalization and urban form. The aspirations of Bangkok to become one of the world cities in the global economy were clear prior to the economic crisis of the 1990s. The Bangkok mass transit system – the Skytrain – was initiated in 1992 and opened in 1999 in response to major problems of traffic congestion and pollution, and the expansion of central business districts. The Skytrain is promoted as a symbol of modernity, comparable to the best in the world. It was built over existing streets some 3–4 stories above ground level. At this level there are direct pedestrian links from the stations into some of Bangkok's prestigious shopping malls and hotels, and links to commercial areas. On the streets beneath this massive structure, the vibrant chaos of Thailand exists, seemingly untouched by the world above. The streets are jammed with traffic, the footways with street traders and food stalls, and the night markets teem with people. Those, the majority, who find the Skytrain too expensive, ride in cheap buses, and on motorcycles, polluting the streets with fumes and noise. Two separate patterns of use, almost different "worlds" exist, one above and the other below the transit lines. The paper argues that both the local and global co-exist, and that globalization may not always be the winner.

1. Introduction

In April 2002 McDonald's launched a new product in Bangkok – the Sticky Rice Roast Pork Burger (Fig. 1, Bangkok Post 2002). The local franchisee, the McThai Co. was proud of the fact that all the ingredients were locally sourced, and it was the first time that the fast food chain had used Thai rice. Adapting food to local tastes has been McDonald's policy for a number of years, but such direct local sourcing of a product bearing only a passing resemblance to the "normal" Big Mac is unusual. So unusual, it raises some interesting questions. What has happened to the claims of many commentators that globalization is a form of cultural imperialism? How real is the

Fig. 1. Thai actress Pornchita na Songkhla launching the Sticky Rice Roast Pork Burger, a global compromise? (*Source*: Bangkok Post)

Fig. 2. Globalization and cultural imperialism? (*Source*: Ellwood 1998: 11)

boast of the Chief Executive Officer of the Disney Corporation that it "doesn't matter whether it comes in by cable, telephone lines, computer or satellite. Everyone's going to have to deal with Disney" (cited in Ellwood 1998: 11; see Fig. 2). And if a global product changes to match local tastes, is it because the culture (particularly urban culture) has forced it to do so, or is it just a cynical attempt to exploit local markets? Or is such a phenomenon just indicative of one business, competing in a melee of other global and local business, in the cultural melting pot of a large city?

Globalization is a complex field where many different positions are taken, with those at the extremes believing on the one hand that it is a "takeover" by western values and corporations, and on the other hand that it is a beneficial creator of wealth (e.g., Held 2000). Much has been written about the way cities compete for foreign direct investment and for global corporations and their headquarters (winner takes all), about world or global cities, about the death of distance in a telecommunications age, and the homogenization of culture and lifestyle (e.g., Hall and Pfeiffer 2000; Sassen 2001). The debate about globalization is significant and reified, attempting to understand the forces at work, but it often neglects the smaller scale impacts and meanings that may affect the quality of peoples' lives.

This paper addresses the local level and speculates about some of the symbols of globalization, and what it may mean to urban populations when faced with the reality of a city and its streets. A critique by the UNDP (1999:33) suggests that the "rise of culture as an economic good has added to the identification of culture with commodities that can be sold and traded... Although the spread of ideas and images enriches the world, there is a risk of reducing cultural concerns to what can be bought and sold, neglecting custom, community and tradition." However, the suggestion here is that globalization, whether characterized as economic or cultural, may not be as black and white as painted, but that the reality may be infinitely more colorful. This is one reason why, with its energy and vitality Bangkok is taken as a symbolic example. Its recently introduced mass transit system, the Skytrain, provides a metaphor through which to explore some issues of globalization and urban from.

2. Bangkok

Bangkok is a large city by any standards, primate in Thailand and important in the South East Asia Region. Its population is estimated to be 5.7 million with a further 3.6 million in the greater Bangkok area (Alpha Research 2001). But these are registered citizens and the Governor of Bangkok estimates that there are as many as a further 4 million unregistered people within the city, making it a city of around 10 million people (Sundaravej 2001). But it is not classified as a world or global city. It may have had aspirations in the 1990s when Thailand was one of the key Asian tiger economies, and it is not without global significance as in 1998 it was one of the top 25 cities in the transnational banking sector (Sassen 2000, p. 53). The economic boom of the early 1990s saw a quadrupling of capital flows of foreign investment into the South East Asia Region to around $110 billion in 1996. Thailand liberalized its foreign exchange regime, relinquishing exchange controls in 1990, and opening up a banking facility for foreign financial institutions in 1993. Much of the foreign investment went into Thailand's property market, and the explosion of high-rise development in Bangkok gave all the appearances of a 'globalized' city. But this market was over-extended and by 1997 there was $20 billion of unsold property in Bangkok. By July 1997 $105 billion of foreign money had left South East Asia (Ellwood 2001). Thailand allowed its currency to float, and as a result loan repayments on property could not be met. The evidence was visible in 'the empty shells of abandoned high-rise construction sites in Bangkok's central areas' (Laird 2000: 404).

Yet in many respects Bangkok has changed little. Of course the global consequences of the 1997 Asian crash were serious, and in Bangkok bankruptcies amongst developers were endemic, construction workers (largely from rural areas) lost work and many returned to the countryside, and unemployment rose. But the property boom had not changed the form of the city in its streets and layout, only in some places buildings were higher. The life of the city remained vibrant, its notorious traffic congestion was little affected, and during it all a 100% privately financed mass rapid transit system, the Skytrain, was constructed and opened in December 1999.

3. Congested spaces

Bangkok has had a long history of attempts to accommodate traffic, from the filling in of canals post-war, large-scale infrastructure investment from the late 1950s, through, more recently, to the construction of major raised expressways, toll roads and flyovers (Bae and Suthinarnat 2003). The impact on congestion has been minimal. An urban form that is characterized by relatively low road capacity, combined with poor traffic management, leads to virtual gridlock in some streets and average speeds for buses in the core area of 9 kph (Barter 2000; Bae and Suthinarnat 2003). While some politicians think that the raised expressways are a 'good thing' (e.g., Sundaravej 2001), the latent demand encouraged by new roads, and seemingly inexorable rise in car ownership leave the streets of Bangkok as crowded as ever (Table 1).

Not surprisingly, mass transit edged onto the agenda, and in 1992 a concession was let for an elevated rail, preceding the Bangkok Public Transport Master Plan of 1995, advocating 200 km of transit lines (Moor and Rees 2000). The hope was to reduce commuting times, relieve congestion and leave behind the congested world of Bangkok's busy streets.

4. The world of the Skytrain

The opening in December 1999 was rushed to coincide with the King of Thailand's 72nd birthday celebrations. Its building had been fraught with difficulties as the costs rose from some 30 billion to 50 billion baht[1] caused by the economic crash and the Thai currency devaluation (Sundaravej 2001). The Bangkok Mass Transit System Public Company Ltd. (BTS) raised 100% of the money privately and it has a 30-year concession, retains 100% of the revenue and has the first refusal on the building and operating of any extensions to the lines. The numbers of passengers required to break even were three times more than actually used the service at the start, although by 2001 numbers were rapidly increasing and the Skytrain now carries 250,000 passengers per working day (BTS 2002). With daily operating costs of 5 million baht against revenue of 4 million, and an additional 8 million a day to service the loans (Sundaravej 2001), the necessity to attract more passengers and to serve greater areas of the population was clearly an imperative. The

[1] At the beginning of November 2002, 100 Thai baht = US$2.3, and US$1 = 43 Thai baht.

Table 1. Vehicle registrations in Bangkok by type

	1997 (000s)	1998 (000s)	1999 (000s)	% change
Cars	1,156	1,232	1,217	+14
Vans	553	595	664	+20
Motorcycles	1,617	1,647	1,666	+3
Taxis	51	56	61	+20
'Tuk-Tuks'	7	7	7	0
Buses	135	130	124	-8
Trucks	110	104	99	-10
Other	242	244	229	-6
Total	3,871	4,015	4,161	+7

Source: Alpha Research 2001.

tension between the needs of a private company to cover its costs and achieve profitability and the government with its control over consent is apparent in the planned extensions to the service, The Thai government's Cabinet approved three extensions (totaling 19.6km) on 29 February 2000 – one serving a new business district – but none giving access to significant areas of Bangkok's population. A further 94 km are planned to suburbs in the north, east and west of the city and this may serve the critical mass of population needed to make the system viable. At the same time a ring route (of 127 km) linking these three extensions is being studied. However, another mass transit project (Hopewell) was placed on hold, and the future of extensions to the Skytrain remain uncertain.

The Skytrain has a strong physical presence in the city (Fig. 3). The two lines (23.5 km in total) and its 23 stations, are all built over existing streets. Whether consciously or not it represents a highly globalized 'world'. The transit system itself uses the latest technology from Europe, overseas designers were employed and maintenance inspections are carried out in collaboration with experts from the USA. The result is a safe, efficient, clean

Fig. 3. The massive structure of the Skytrain's line and stations over Bangkok's streets (*Source:* Mike Jenks)

Fig. 4. A Sky bridge being constructed to link Chit Lom Station with an international hotel and shopping mall (*Source*: Mike Jenks)

and cool air-conditioned service, speeding passengers over the congested streets below. Trains run every 3.2 minutes at peak times and the maximum journey time is 30 minutes – three to four times faster than traveling on the roads.

Its separation into what is to all appearances another world is reinforced not only by its physical elevation, but also by the connections to many of Bangkok's international facilities. Eight of the elevated stations have high level direct connections (Sky Bridges) to international hotels or major shopping malls (Fig. 4). The Skytrain thus gives direct connections either at the same level, or in close proximity to stations, to 32 International Hotels, 17 International Shopping Malls, and to two night markets (aimed at tourists) and one weekend market.

As a mass transit system, it can be questioned as to who the 'masses' might be, as it is a relatively expensive mode of transport. The average annual GNP per capita in Thailand is 76,269 baht, and in Bangkok the average monthly wage is 9,750 baht (Alpha Research 2001). Of this, around 14% of household expenditure will be spent on transport. However, a single journey on the Skytrain will cost between 10–40 baht (from a trip to one station, a trip to 10 or more stations away), and multi journey tickets lasting approximately one month would cost 900 baht for one member of a household, representing nearly 10% of their monthly income. Clearly the benefits of this system do not extend to all, but favor those with money. The main beneficiaries are the middle classes and businessmen, school children (who have subsidized fares), and in addition, tourists and international visitors. Indeed, the advice given to visitors now is to stay in a hotel that is accessible to the Skytrain.

The stated objectives for the Skytrain are to help '...alleviate the chronic traffic problem in Bangkok and to provide a more efficient means of transportation...' (BTS 2002). Pragmatically the system is clearly highly efficient, and with its quarter of a million passengers each day, it takes some people off the roads. However, symbolically it is a different story. The relatively high cost of travel, numerous direct links to international facilities, its cleanliness and efficiency, reinforced by its elevation, all make the Skytrain into a different environment. It exists as an almost unreal and separate world, occupying the same spatial location as the streets below, yet operating serenely above them.

5. The world below the line

Four stories beneath the Skytrain stations a different reality exists. The efficient, ordered environment is replaced by the vibrancy, noise and dirt of the streets. There is no single use, but a rich and chaotic mixture of pedestrians, street traders and stalls, shops and eating-places (Fig. 5). So crowded are the pavements that pedestrians spill out onto busy streets to face a vast array of traffic, sometimes moving, sometimes in gridlock, and always polluting. The streets all interconnect to a variety of places, most of which are local businesses, but also with the usual mix of international franchises such as McDonald's and Haagen Daz.

The options for getting around are many and varied, but all are affected by traffic delays because of congestion. Buses provide transport for most and they are affordable by all but the very poor. The publicly funded services (by the Bangkok Metropolitan Authority (BMA)) charge 3.5 baht for each journey regardless of distance, and the equivalent private company charges 5 baht. These buses are not air-conditioned, but those that are charge a minimum of 12 baht, a price that increases with distance traveled. Like the Skytrain, buses are frequent, but by contrast are unpredictable and at peak hours often full. Journeys of two hours are common. For those wishing to avoid the traffic, and willing to risk their lives, motorcycle taxis wait at most busy junctions – the prices are cheap and negotiable. The Tuk-Tuks[2] are little used by locals because they are expensive and tend to serve tourists. Taxis too are relatively expensive, with a starting price of 35 baht, and tend to serve the same sector of the population as the Skytrain (school children excepted).

Fig. 5. The vitality of Bangkok's street life (*Source:* Mike Jenks)

[2] Three-wheeler taxis powered by highly polluting motorcycle engines (one can be seen in Fig. 5).

Fig. 6. The Skytrain and crossroads at the Erewan Shrine with street traders below (*Source:* Asian Images CD)

But the streets are not just a route to travel through or a means to access one of the many shopping malls, but are places that are inhabited, and used for trade and social life (e.g., Levitas 1986). The streets below the Skytrain are no exception. For example, in what can be classified as a business district, at the junction of two major roads (Rama 1 and Ratchadamri) the two Skytrain lines cross overhead, and there is a station close by. This has Sky Bridges linking major international facilities – the Grand Hyatt Erewan Hotel and the Gaysorn Plaza Shopping Mall. Below is the ancient Buddhist Erewan Shrine, with numerous street stalls making floral offerings and selling incense (Fig. 6). Gathered around the steps up to the station are motorcycle taxi riders and beggars. Further up the street, close to a McDonald's are street traders selling silk ties, household goods, and trinkets. The place is teeming with life and always changing.

Within a short distance, under the Skytrain's Sukhumvit line, a rich mix of Bangkok life can be experienced, including a number of shopping malls and offices, numerous food shops, restaurants, bars, markets, and, of course apartments for the many who live there. While the Skytrain operates from six in the morning to twelve at night, the streets are alive for 24 hours a day. If, as Czarnowski (1986: 211) suggests, streets are places 'to be read, interpreted and given meaning', then on the transit line above and the streets below, any reading of them suggests that two different worlds appear to co-exist.

6. Two worlds?

Perhaps the metaphor, contrasting a mass transit system with city streets, is a tenuous one. However, it has some strength in the fact that the physical configuration is effectively one and the same. Both occupy the same geographic location, but at different levels. Bangkok is a complex network of streets and open spaces, of different districts and centers of population. The choices are infinite and the connections with the city as a whole are open and varied. The Skytrain makes particular connections, linking together a large

Table 2. Comparisons of above and below

Above	Below
International, global chain stores and hotels	Local and diverse shops and markets, and apartments for locals
Air-conditioned, cool	Hot, and polluted air
Designer goods, international products	Fake designer goods, local products
McDonald's, KFC, Haagen Daz	Local food and street stalls
Sanitized, protected, safe	Messy, some potential dangers
Closed to the poor	Open to everyone
Operates 06.00 – 24.00	Operates 24 hours a day

number of the 'globalized' spaces and facilities in Bangkok. It is overlaid on the existing street pattern, maintaining the same configuration, but creating an entirely different symbolic space of its own. Above the streets, if one had sufficient money, it is possible to live without any real connection to the city or to Thailand. It is possible to experience globalization to the full, traveling in a foreign-built train, eating at international restaurants, staying in global hotel chains and buying international designer goods. Below, Thailand is impossible to avoid. Table 2 characterizes some key differences.

Does the metaphor of the separate worlds of transit lines and streets lead to any insights beyond the particular? It is perhaps the fact that such differences can exist together in exactly the same place that has some meaning. The impact of globalization on the form or configuration of Bangkok in this example is negligible. The impact on development is more noticeable, as development has absorbed some smaller buildings and tower blocks have emerged. The link to modern transit systems and the stations is also noticeable, and the business opportunities are gaining ground – for example, the Governor of Bangkok advocating an international convention center attached to one of the Skytrain extensions (Sundaravej 2001). Yet, where the 'global' development has taken place, the street life still inhabits the same areas, with stalls outside selling fakes of the designer goods sold inside the shopping malls.

The view that globalization is some form of cultural imperialism does not seem to ring true, and neither is it true that it has no impact. Many different worlds seem to coexist, and it is this that needs to be further considered. The form and development of cities is vastly complex. However much foreign direct investment is attracted, and high-rise property developed, the configuration of the streets usually remains. Here life goes on, and extends well beyond the business districts to areas that will evolve in response to local needs.

The identification of any links between globalization and urban development and its form is complex. Using a metaphor to illustrate the issue may seem trivial. However, not only in Bangkok, but also throughout the world it is obvious that the symbols of globalization exist. Yet, even the most superficial of observations tell us that the form, feel and look of different cities around the world are not the same, or homogenized by globalization. Neither do the international headquarters or franchised stores and restaurants appear identical, even if the products are often recognizably the same. Certainly, the streets and life inhabiting them maintain a high degree of local identity.

Fig. 7. A dominating sign, but not dominating Thai culture or tastes (*Source:* Mike Jenks)

It seems worthwhile to focus the debate and our understanding of the impacts of globalization on cities at the smaller scale. At this level the richness and vitality of local people and environments, interact and co-exist in a variety of ways. It is not always the seemingly rich, powerful and corporations that prevail. Interestingly, the Erewan Shrine and its street traders make no concessions to globalization or international mores – rather, it intensely reflects Thai culture and religion. Yet about 50 meters along the road, it is the McDonald's that has made the compromise with its Sticky Rice Roast Pork Burger (Fig. 7).

References

Alpha Research Co., Ltd. (2001) Thailand in figures. Alpha Research, Bangkok

Bae C, Suthiranart Y (2003) Policy options towards a sustainable urban transportation strategy for Bangkok. International Development Planning Review 25: 31–51

Bangkok Post (2002) Rice-based burger breaks new ground. April 5, p 12

Barter P (2000) Transport dilemmas in dense urban areas. In: Jenks M, Burgess R (eds) Compact cities: Sustainable urban forms for developing countries. Spon Press, London, pp 271–284

Bangkok Mass Transit System Public Company Ltd. (BTS) (2002) Company Profile, http://www.bts.co.th/

Czarnowski T (1986) The street as a communications artifact. In: Anderson S (ed) On streets. MIT Press, Cambridge, MA, pp 207–211

Ellwood W (2001) The No-nonsense Guide to Globalization. Verso, London

Ellwood W (1998) Inside the Disney dream machine. New Internationalist 308:11

Hall P, Pfeiffer U (2000) Urban future 21: A global agenda for twenty-first Century Cities. E & FN Spon, London

Held D (ed) (2000) A globalizing world? Culture, economics, politics. Routledge, London

Laird J (2000) Money, politics, globalization, and crisis: The case of Thailand. Graham Brash, Singapore

Levitas G (1986) Anthropology and sociology of streets. In: Anderson S (ed) On streets. MIT Press, Cambridge, MA pp 225–239

Moor M, Rees C (2000) Bangkok mass transit development zones. In: Compact cities: Sustainable urban forms for developing countries. Spon Press, London, pp 285–294

Sassen S (2000) Cities in a world economy. Pine Forge Press, Thousand Oaks, CA

Sassen S (2001) The global city. Princeton University Press, Princeton and Oxford
Sundaravej S (2001) Keynote speech at the international conference achieving sustainable cities in the SE Asia Region. Bangkok
UNDP (1999) Human development report, UNDP. Oxford University Press, Oxford

Printed in the United States
205636BV00002B/34/A

9 783540 223627